Sisters or Citizens?

Sisters or Citizens?

Women and socialism in France since 1876

CHARLES SOWERWINE
University of Melbourne

CAMBRIDGE UNIVERSITY PRESS
CAMBRIDGE
LONDON   NEW YORK   NEW ROCHELLE
MELBOURNE   SYDNEY

Published by the Press Syndicate of the University of Cambridge
The Pitt Building, Trumpington Street, Cambridge CB2 1RP
32 East 57th Street, New York, NY 10022, USA
296 Beaconsfield Parade, Middle Park, Melbourne 3206, Australia

First published 1982

Printed in Great Britain at the
University Press, Cambridge

Library of Congress catalogue card number: 81-7692

British Library cataloguing in publication data

Sowerwine, Charles
Sisters or citizens?
1. Women and socialism — France — History
I. Title II. Les femmes et le socialisme.
English
335'.00944   HX546

ISBN 0 521 23484 0

FOR VANESSA AND SAMANTHA

Contents

Contents

Contents

Preface

Ever since I began working on the problem of women and socialism in France, I have been confronted by people who wished me to confirm one or another of the big generalisations which spring to everyone's mind when women in southern European countries are mentioned and to which even historians are prone in their cups: Frenchmen are more sexist than men of other countries, because of 'Latin' or 'southern' conditions, climate, race, or whatever; Frenchwomen are more 'womanly' or subordinate to men because of the Catholic church, Mediterranean traditions, or again something 'Latin'. To be sure, such arguments are rarely made so baldly as this. I put them forth in this manner not to raise straw men or women but to demonstrate the kinds of problems which arise when we move to large-scale ideas to answer specific questions. The point I wish to make is that Occam's razor is needed here: we should not posit more entities than are needed to explain a phenomenon.

In this case, the phenomenon under discussion is the fact that French feminism never got off the ground compared to English, American, and Australian feminism, and that French socialism never reached masses of women compared to the German socialist women's movement. Because these comparisons are generally only implicit, the usual assumption is that the English or German case is somehow normative and thus needs no explanation, while the French case is abnormal and has to be explained. In fact, of course, both types of case require explanation. In 1976, in *Historical Reflections* (III, 2), I made the following suggestions about these comparisons:

Large, militant women's movements are not a necessary component of late nineteenth-century development. Their occurrence in England and America is more unusual than their failure to occur on the continent. There is no need to explain this failure on the continent by peculiar characteristics of individual countries. Rather we should turn our attention to close study of specific organizations in terms of variations on continental themes.

This book is such a study. Occam's razor applies in that a study of organisations, leaders, and ideas can to a great extent explain the phenomenon we are considering. We do not need to posit larger-scale questions and answers until we have exhausted such study and still have unexplained phenomena.

That does not mean that such work need be of narrow import. On the contrary, I believe that this book, as a case study, bears out in the French context the general line of reasoning I put forth tentatively in the same article:

The fact that social strife was greater, or at least more obvious than in England or America, is the most important of these continental themes. The recent revolutionary past (or in some cases the recentness of national unification) and the existence of mass parties committed in theory to the abolition of capitalism gave European social strife at least the appearance of endangering the existing order. Perhaps this appearance made class loyalties seem more important than those of sex to continental women. The militant, radical stance of English and American women's movements might then be explained by the peculiar stability of these countries, or rather the illusion of stability shared by so many. Perhaps this sense of stability enabled these movements to use radical tactics without fearing they would endanger the structure of society. In any case, it seems clear that continental women chose to orient themselves by class in the last analysis . . .

The connection of women's movements with the recent revolutionary past (or with mass socialist parties whose reformist tendencies were not yet counted upon) would explain not only the subsequent retreat of bourgeois feminists toward class loyalties, but also a certain initial confusion between feminism and socialism which tended to sort itself out once stable parliamentary government was established and the basic objectives and class loyalties of all parties clarified. This closed options on both sides. The feminists were unable to attract a mass following and the socialist women shrank from feminist positions. The feminists came more and more to pose their demands on narrow, legal grounds and to exclude mass agitation even for the suffrage. The socialist women saw themselves more and more in class terms. Any tendency they had to see issues in sex terms was discouraged by their own hostility to the feminists and their fear of appearing to be similar to these 'enemy sisters'. This was the general situation of European women's movements, not the particular property of one country.

The class basis of nineteenth-century feminism in France and the nature of the French socialists' answer to 'the woman question' closed off the possibility of an alliance between feminism and socialism, leaving open only the possibility of a women's organisation within the socialist movement. This is the conclusion of part I of this book. It lays the basis for part II, in which it is argued that the impact of the split between feminism and socialism determined the nature of the French socialist women's movement, which was created between 1899 and 1914. Part III argues that this heritage has weighed ever since upon the socialists' attempts to recruit women into the party and that the nature of the women's organisations of the party as determined by this heritage in itself tended to prevent the party from recruiting women effectively.

This book is the English edition of *Les Femmes et le socialisme: Un siècle d'histoire* (Paris, 1978), but it is not a simple translation of the French edition. Rather it is a revised version which is in some respects a new book. I have sought to clarify the argument made above and to reduce slightly some of the detailed evidence, particularly concerning women in the anti-war struggle during the First World War. This version is aimed at least as much at the reader interested in socialism or women's movements as at the specialist

Preface

in French history. The scholarly annexes of the French edition have been omitted and a bibliographical essay on printed sources has taken the place of the detailed bibliography. French terms are translated whenever possible, with the exception of such words as *syndicat* (roughly equivalent to trade-union) and arrondissement (the electoral and administrative divisions of French cities).

I would like to renew my thanks to all those who helped me in preparing the French edition of this study, who are named therein. For the preparation of this version, I must first thank my Melbourne colleagues in general, and in particular my chairman, Alison Patrick, for support and forbearance and for generously providing help to reduce my teaching burden during the 1979 academic year. I have had the pleasure of friendly and supportive co-operation from Marilyn Boxer, who has written about many of the same problems and to whose research I owe several particular points as acknowledged in the relevant text or notes. Special thanks go to Joan Scott and to David Jordan, for encouraging this project in countless ways for what seem like countless years and for generally brightening up the dreary decade of the 1970s. Similarly, I owe a special debt, both personal and academic, to my Melbourne colleagues Pat Grimshaw and David Philips, who have listened to me, supported me, and read virtually the whole of the manuscript, often in several successive drafts and at short notice. I am deeply grateful to all those who have read sections of the manuscript and who have so generously given me suggestions from which I have profited in many ways. In addition to the foregoing, they are John Foster, Steven Hause, Jolyon Howorth, Peter McPhee, and Ed Rice-Maximin. In the instances where I have obstinately refused the salvation they proffered, I have only myself to blame. Finally, I express thanks to Mary Comodromos, for patient help from the office, and to Bev Goldsworthy, for typing the manuscript impeccably with patience and unfailing cheerfulness.

Charles Sowerwine
Melbourne, 14 December 1979

William Davies has given kind and patient editorial support and Maureen Leach has made a valiant effort to take the kinks out of the text; I offer warm thanks to both of them.

Tourgéville, 20 July 1981

Abbreviations of organisations

CAFSPC   Comité d'Action Féminine Socialiste pour la Paix contre le
           Chauvinisme ('Feminine Socialist Action Committee for Peace
           against Chauvinism'). Formed by Louise Saumoneau in 1915,
           in order to provide a basis for her delegation to the inter-
           national socialist women's conference at Berne, after the
           GDFS had refused to support her anti-war activities. It dis-
           appeared in 1917.

CAP   Commission Administrative Permanente ('Permanent Adminis-
           trative Commission'). The executive body of the SFIO from
           1905 until the Second World War.

CE   Commission Exécutive ('Executive Commission'). The govern-
           ing body of an organisation. The term usually appears in trans-
           lation, as 'executive'.

CGT   Confédération Générale du Travail ('General Confederation of
           Labour'). The syndicalist central organisation, founded in
           1895, roughly the equivalent of the AFL-CIO or the TUC.

CIFPP   Comité International des Femmes pour une Paix Permanente
           ('International Women's Committee for Permanent Peace').
           The French title of the women's anti-war organisation founded
           in Amsterdam by Dr Aletta Jacobs and Jane Addams in 1915
           which became in 1919 the Women's International League for
           Peace and Freedom. The French section was founded by
           Mme G. Duchêne and Jeanne Halbwachs.

CN   Conseil National ('National Council'). The decision-making
           body of the SFIO, consisting of delegates from all federations.
           It met every three months. The term usually appears in trans-
           lation, as 'national council'.

CNDFS   Comité National des Femmes Socialistes ('National Committee
           of Socialist Women'). The national women's organisation of
           the SFIO, founded in 1931.

CRC   Comité Révolutionnaire Central ('Central Revolutionary Com-
           mittee'). Founded in 1881 by followers and admirers of

Auguste Blanqui, the best-known revolutionary leader of the nineteenth century. In 1889 it came under the control of Edouard Vaillant and began to take a frankly political orientation, though it retained a commitment to profound social change and scepticism toward ideology. It became the PSR in 1898 (q.v.).

CRRI   Comité pour la Reprise des Relations Internationales ('Committee for the Resumption of International Relations'). Formed in January 1916, it was a reconstructed version of the Comité d'Action Internationale, the first group founded to propagate the anti-war ideas of the Zimmerwald conference of September 1915. Its new title referred to its aim of forcing the resumption of fraternal relations between the socialist parties of the warring nations. In 1919 it became the Comité de la Troisième Internationale, and led the struggle for the SFIO to join the Third International.

FFU   Fédération Féministe Universitaire ('University [Women's] Feminist Federation'). Founded in 1903 by Marie Guérin, the FFU sought to defend women's interests within the Amicales ('Friendly Circles') of primary-school teachers (government employees were forbidden to join unions). Although their main preoccupation was with issues like equal wages for women teachers, the FFU promoted many general feminist causes in the years just before the First World War, including Elisabeth Renaud's campaign in the 1910 legislative elections and Emma Couriau's struggle for membership in the printers' union in 1913–14.

FTSF   Fédération des Travailleurs Socialistes de France ('Federation of Socialist Workers of France'). 1. Name of the socialist party from 1879, although the official title was actually Fédération *du Parti* des Travailleurs Socialistes de France and although PO (q.v.) remained the term in general use. 2. Name of the reformist socialist party from 1883 on. The FTSF, led by Brousse and Malon, worked for municipal reform and was willing to ally with republicans. Its members were derided as 'Possibilists' by their opponents because they only sought what was immediately possible. The name stuck. *Note:* the first worker party, founded in 1880 following a resolution of the congress of Marseilles (1879), was called a federation to emphasise the decentralised vision of Brousse and Malon, who dominated the collectivists at Marseilles. When the party split between the Broussists and the Guesdists, in 1882, the Guesdists formed the POF (q.v.) and the Broussists adopted a new title, POSR (q.v.), whilst maintaining the old name (without 'du Parti') as a sub-title. The full title of the party was thus POSR: FTSF. The party published the accounts of the 1881 and 1882 congresses under the names POSF and POSRF (q.v.), respectively, but the new title never caught on and in 1883 it was dropped. The party remained the FTSF throughout its existence (it disintegrated during the 1890s, following the formation of Allemane's POSR, q.v.).

GDFS   Groupe des Femmes Socialistes ('Socialist Women's Group'). Founded in January 1913, by Marianne Rauze, Elisabeth Renaud, Louise Saumoneau, and others, to provide a women's group within the SFIO. Torn apart during the war, it was not reconstituted until 1922. In 1931, upon the founding of the CNDFS, it disappeared.

GFM   Groupe Féministe Mixte ('Mixed [i.e. male and female] Feminist Group'). Founded in 1900 by Elisabeth Renaud and Louise Saumoneau as a branch of the GFS (q.v.), it took on a life of its own under its first secretary, Adèle Kassky, and ultimately became a section of the PSDF.

GFS   Groupe Féministe Socialiste ('Socialist Feminist Group'). Founded in 1899 by Elisabeth Renaud and Louise Saumoneau, it declined after their split in 1902 and disappeared when the SFIO refused to accept it as a constituent organisation, at the time of unification in 1905.

PCF   Parti Communiste Français ('French Communist Party'). The name taken by the SFIO (q.v.) in 1920, when it joined the Third (Moscow) International.

PO   Parti Ouvrier ('Worker Party'). 1. Name commonly given to the political arm of the labour movement during the period of formation (1876–80). Although the resulting political party was officially named the Fédération du Parti des Travailleurs Socialistes de France (see FTSF), the term PO persisted in common use. 2. Name of the Guesdist party founded in 1882 (see POF). 3. Name of the ephemeral splinter party founded in 1914 by Jean Allemane, Elisabeth Renaud, and others.

POF   Parti Ouvrier Français ('French Worker Party'). Upon the split of the socialist party in 1882 (see FTSF), the followers of Jules Guesde took the name Parti Ouvrier (see PO). Although it was only in 1893 that they added the word 'Français' to the title of the party, POF is used throughout this book for the Guesdist party founded in 1882 in order to avoid confusion. The POF had a more centralised conception of the party than the reformist wing of the collectivists (led by Brousse and

Malon) and they opposed alliances with republicans. They considered themselves to be distinguished from other socialists by their attachment to German, 'scientific' socialism, or Marxism, although they had in fact little access to Marx's work.

POSF   Parti Ouvrier Socialiste Français ('French Socialist Worker Party'). See POSR, 1.

POSR   Parti Ouvrier Socialiste Révolutionnaire ('Socialist Revolutionary Worker Party'). 1. Name taken by the reformist collectivists under Brousse and Malon after the expulsion of the Guesdists in 1882, occasionally given as POSR Français (POSRF) and sometimes as POSF. In 1883 the party reverted to the title FTSF (q.v.), which is used throughout in this book to refer to the Broussist party. 2. Name taken by the followers of Jean Allemane for the party they founded in 1890 after their break with the FTSF. They emphasised the party's working-class base and opposed the Broussists' alliances with republicans, as well as the Marxists' centralised conception of the party.

POSRF   Parti Ouvrier Socialiste Révolutionnaire Français ('French Socialist Revolutionary Worker Party'). See POSR, 1.

PS   Parti Socialiste ('Socialist Party'). The socialist party formed in 1971 out of the old SFIO, Mitterrand's Convention des Institutions Républicaines, and other small groups. Although the SFIO was officially called PS (SFIO), it is referred to in this book as the SFIO, not the PS. PS will be reserved for the post-1971 Socialist Party led by François Mitterrand.

PSDF   Parti Socialiste de France ('Socialist Party of France'). The party founded by the fusion of the Guesdist POF and the Vaillantist PSR in 1901 after the failure of efforts to unify these parties with the reformists under Jaurès (who in turn founded the PSF). The PSDF rejected socialist participation in a non-socialist ministry, while the PSF refused to expel Millerand for having joined the Waldeck—Rousseau ministry called in 1899 to resolve the Dreyfus affair. Both parties, however, joined to form the SFIO in 1905.

PSF   Parti Socialiste Français ('French Socialist Party'). The party founded in 1902 by the followers of Jaurès and the remnants of the Broussist FTSF after the failure of unity and the formation of the PSDF (q.v.). The PSF (like the PSDF) was absorbed into the SFIO in 1905.

PSR   Parti Socialiste Révolutionnaire ('Socialist Revolutionary Party'). The name taken by the CRC under Vaillant in 1898, reflecting the fact that it was really functioning much more as a party than as a revolutionary central committee.

SFIO   Section Française de l'Internationale Ouvrière ('French Section of the Workers' International'). The unified socialist party founded in 1905 in response to a decision of the International at its Amsterdam congress (1904). It lasted in this form until December 1920, when at the congress of Tours a majority voted for the party to join the Third (Moscow) International and take the name Parti Communiste Français (PCF, q.v.). The minority walked out and reconstructed the old SFIO, which survived until it was merged into the new PS in 1971.

SPD   Sozialistiche Partei Deutschlands ('German Socialist Party').

UFC   Union Fédérative du Centre ('Federal Union of the Centre [of France]'). The Paris region federation of the FTSF, founded in 1880. It sided with the Broussists (FTSF) against the Guesdists (POF) in 1882, but became the mainspring of the POSR when the latter was founded in 1890 and soon merged into the POSR, disappearing as a separate organisation.

Bibliographical abbreviations

Am IAV	International Archief voor de Vrouwenbewegung ('International Archives of Women's Movements'), Amsterdam.
Am IISG	International Instituut voor Sociale Geschiedenis ('International Institute of Social History'), Amsterdam.
AN	Archives Nationales, Paris.
APP	Archives de la Préfecture de Police, Paris.
AR	Bibliothèque de l'Arsenal, Paris.
BDIC	Bibliothèque de Documentation Internationale et Contemporaine, Nanterre.
BHVP	Bibliothèque Historique de la Ville de Paris.
BMD	Bibliothèque Marguerite Durand, Paris.
BN	Bibliothèque Nationale, Paris.
CHS	Centre d'Histoire du Syndicalisme, Paris.
DMO	*Dictionnaire biographique du Mouvement Ouvrier français*, Jean Maitron (ed.) 15 vols. to date. Paris, 1962– .
FS	*Le Femme socialiste*, newspaper published by Elisabeth Renaud and Louise Saumoneau from 1901 to 1902, and by Louise Saumoneau alone from 1912 to 1940 and from 1947 to 1949.
HR/RH	*Historical Reflections/Réflexions Historiques*, Waterloo, Ontario.
IFHS	Institut Français d'Histoire Sociale, Paris.
MS	Musée Social, Paris.
TR/TR	*Third Republic/Troisième République*, De Kalb, Illinois.
WSFH	*Proceedings of the Annual Meeting of the Western Society for French History*, Santa Barbara, California.

Introduction

Sisters or citizens? The title of this book refers to the basic choice confronting working-class women and those who chose to identify themselves with them: would they fight for the rights of women or the rights of workers? Would they join together with other women, of whatever class, in the feminist movement, or with other workers, men as well as women, in the socialist movement? For the feminists, in theory, all women were sisters, whether rich or poor. In the words of a prominent French feminist at the turn of the century, they called upon 'working women' to join with their 'bourgeois sisters'. For the socialists, also in theory, all those who joined the party were equal, whether women or men. They were all 'citizens', determined to work for the fulfilment in society of the promises of the great revolution. Indeed, 'citizen' was the term of address in the unified French socialist party, like 'comrade' in labour and communist parties today.

The question was which oppression was deemed in theory to be primary: sex or class. The answer to the question, however, was determined in practice, by the relations between feminists and socialists. Many women believed that they were oppressed both as women and as workers and that to emphasise one oppression over the other would distort the reality of their dual oppression. This proved to be the case. But all efforts to ally feminism and socialism failed.

Until the end of the nineteenth century, feminism and socialism were embryonic movements sheltering together under the broad umbrella of republicanism as inherited from the 1848 revolution. Thus the efforts to forge an alliance between the two seemed promising for a while. Feminists proclaimed sentiments of social justice in the name of sisterhood and the nascent socialist party expressed firm support for women's rights on the grounds that all human beings were entitled to the status of citizenship.

By the 1900 feminist congress, however, the would-be alliance had given way to hostility between the two movements. Feminists shrank back from the social and economic reforms demanded by the socialists and the socialist women in turn recoiled before what they saw as the determination of the feminists to maintain their privileged position in society. Class differences outweighed those of sex in the practical, human world in which the women of both movements operated. The feminists were bourgeois, as they them-

1

selves said. (They saw nothing pejorative in the term.) Most were either
beneficiaries of independent incomes or at least well-to-do. Virtually all of
them had servants, usually more than one. The socialists, on the other hand,
if they were not all of the working classes, tended to be of the lower strata
of the middle classes and close enough to the working classes to identify
with them through the socialist movement. Socialist women did not regard
bourgeois women as their sisters and they would not ally with the feminists,
whom they regarded as bourgeois women unwilling to give up their class
privileges. Instead they would create their own movement, which would be
socialist and for women but in the end not feminist: after some hesitation,
they preferred to call their group not 'socialist feminist' but 'the socialist
women's group'.

The experience of the socialist women was that class oppression seemed
more fundamental than sex oppression. Finding the feminists bourgeois,
they turned away from them and opted instead for organisation within the
party. But in the party they did not find a positive counterpart to their
negative experience with the feminists. It was not class oppression which
operated to weld the socialists together (as may have been the case in trade
unions). If we look for a bond among socialists, it is rather their commitment to political action. Comradeship in the party stemmed from common
participation in political activity, the more so as socialism became more and
more enmeshed in the political processes of the republic. Women, however,
were not citizens and could not participate in political life at the point where
it really counted: the ballot box. To be sure, they were free to discuss
politics, to join political groups, and to participate in the lower levels of
political activity, such as leafleting. But these activities had less meaning for
them than for men. Not only did their exclusion from the ballot (and hence
from political office) deprive them of the fruits of political activity, but also,
and more importantly, their exclusion from political life was reinforced by
the effect of traditional roles, which kept them uninterested in politics. Thus
their condition was different from that of their fellow men socialists.

In founding a group of their own within the socialist party, socialist
women recognised this instinctively. But in rejecting the feminists so totally
as they did, they prevented themselves from articulating clearly their situation as women vis-à-vis their fellow socialists in the party. In rejecting sisterhood with the feminists, which was never a reality in any case, they also
rejected the sisterhood they shared with each other and which they could
have emphasised within the limits of their class background and their commitment to socialism. Their situation in the party would exclude all reference to their common experience as women, treating them only as citizens.
But citizenship was as unreal for them as sisterhood.

Reacting against the feminists, the socialist women created not an independent movement, but a women's auxiliary to the socialist party, an

'internal commission', as one of its leaders would call it, aimed more at pro-tecting socialist women from subversion by the feminists than at creating a mass movement of women, still less at obtaining women's rights. When women obtained the vote after the Second World War, even this organisation would be disbanded, without having attracted substantial numbers of women to socialism. Since then the socialist party has not been more effective in recruiting women.

Yet women suffer more than men under the present society. To the extent that the socialist party purports to offer a solution to the problems of this society, it must regard women as potential supporters whom it ought logically to attract in greater numbers than men, rather than less, as is the case. In 1977, in France, women were suffering much more than their share of unemployment. They represented 54 per cent of the unemployed and 82 per cent of the unemployed under twenty-five years of age, as against only 38 per cent of the workforce. Moreover, those women who did work were losing ground in relation to men. The total number of skilled workers had increased 17.3 per cent while the women among them had decreased 6.1 per cent since 1968. This movement toward unskilled jobs probably masked a continuation of the old policy of lower wages for women. To be sure, all this does not represent the same misery which working women endured a century earlier. But whatever the nature and extent of working-class misery, women suffered more than men, in 1977 as in 1877. Why then do they represent less than 20 per cent of the membership of the socialist party today? The answer lies in the history of the socialist party, its relations with women and feminists, and its approaches to the 'woman question'.[1]

These problems, which are the substance of this study, can be put most clearly as questions. The question posed in the nineteenth century, sisters or citizens?, gives way in the twentieth century to the question, why did a strong socialist women's movement not emerge in France? Historically, each of these questions calls up a corollary, leaving a series of four questions for us to answer: (1) why did the alliance between feminism and socialism fail, after promising beginnings? (2) what ideals and ideologies governed the socialists' conduct toward feminism and toward women in general? (3) why did the French socialist party never develop a strong women's movement, while the socialist parties of neighbouring countries did? and (4) would separate separate women's groups and a more autonomous women's organis-ation have helped the French party to recruit women? The aim of this book is to answer these questions by examining the movements and militants who, as women, as feminists, and as socialists, sought to attract the masses of women to their cause.

This book is focused primarily on the Third Republic (1870—1940), because it was during this period that both feminism and socialism developed in their definitive forms, that the alliance between them was sought and then rejected, and that the socialist women's movement began and ended. The development of feminism and socialism before the Third Republic and their emergence as major movements during the Third Republic are not in themselves subjects of this book, but they are essential to our story. It is therefore necessary to give here a short account of the early development of both movements, together with a brief description of the relevant social and economic factors. Furthermore, since many of the problems of French socialist women were discussed in relation to German theory and practice, these too are described in the remainder of this introduction.

French feminism

The Second Empire (1852–70) fell after the Prussians defeated the imperial armies at Sedan in 1870. A republic, the Third, was founded immediately thereafter. In 1871 the republic faced a brief patriotic revolt from the left known as the Paris Commune. To put it down, some 25,000 Parisians were massacred in one week and thousands more were imprisoned, deported, and exiled. But the Third Republic flourished despite the brutality of the repression of the traditional Parisian working-class and republican movements, or perhaps because of it, since it reassured conservatives that a republic could protect order and property. The Third Republic lasted until 1940 and provided the framework for the growth of democratic movements such as feminism and socialism.[2]

During the Second Empire, the repression of political activity had maintained republicans in a confused amalgam, running from moderate republicans to anarchists and adherents of the International Workingman's Association, the 'First International', founded in 1864. So long as the Empire existed, they saw only their common antipathy to the Empire and ignored their different ideals and conflicting interests. The ideal of 1848, the 'social and democratic republic', continued to weld together a wide range of movements and ideas which would only be sorted out through open political activity in the last quarter of the nineteenth century. Only then would feminism, like socialism, emerge as a movement distinct from the various strands of republican and utopian thought inherited from 1848.

Feminism had already begun to emerge during the Second Empire's 'liberal' phase, in the late 1860s. This was also the period when feminism appeared throughout the western world. John Stuart Mill's essay, 'The subjection of women', was published in both England and France in 1869 and this date is often cited as a convenient marker for the beginning of feminism. To be sure, there are myriad examples of women who struggled for their rights long before 1869, in France and elsewhere, but these struggles were largely individualistic and intertwined with other causes. Only in the last third of the nineteenth century did there appear a feminist movement as we understand it today: the movement which culminated in women's obtaining the suffrage.[3]

The immense success which Mill's essay enjoyed suggests that it articulated grievances which were already deeply felt. Richard J. Evans suggests that these grievances were those of middle-class women and argues that 'the most fundamental social development underlying the rise of feminism was the emergence of the middle classes'. Middle-class values of professional and civic activity, legal equality, and the career open to talent contrasted sharply with the situation of middle-class women. Mill's essay was addressed precisely to those women who suffered from this discrepancy.[4]

In France, new possibilities for middle-class women were symbolised by the rise of a handful of women into the professions and their successes in turn inspired other women. The first woman received a medical degree in France in 1870. She was not French, but the first Frenchwoman followed in 1875. The first Frenchwoman took, and passed, the examination to practise in hospitals in 1882: she was Blanche Edwards-Pilliet, later a feminist militant. The first Frenchwoman passed the bar examination in 1900. Public perception of women's new roles was increased by their entry into more arcane areas. In 1900, for instance, there appeared the first women students at the Ecole des Beaux-Arts (they had to use separate studios from the men) and the first women cab-drivers (horse-drawn cabs, of course).[5]

Further down on the social scale from the professionals, but still in a position to share some middle-class aspirations and to provide what there was of a rank and file for feminism, were the women who moved into what we would now call white-collar positions. The censuses suggest that there were many of them in the years before the end of the century. In the sector called 'commerce, banks', for example, women trebled their participation between 1866 and 1901, from 238,000 to 690,000, going from 25.56 per cent to 37.85 per cent of the total labour force in the sector. Over the same period, the census developed a new category, non-existent in 1866: 'liberal professions'. By 1896 women constituted 40.96 per cent of this category and during the next five years they took 35,500 of 61,500 new positions. It is not clear what was included in this category. At the turn of the century there was certainly nothing like this number of Frenchwomen in the professions we now call liberal. Nevertheless, it does indicate a significant rise in women's participation in the economy in visible positions outside the home and above the status of the working classes.[6]

These women provided not only an inspiration but also a contrast for women of the bourgeoisie who were still at home. All these women, from mistresses of wealthy households to professionals and white-collar workers, were in a position to perceive the sharp contrast between their position of wealth or security or their newly achieved professional status and the legal humiliation, indeed oppression, which they continued to undergo.

French law of the Third Republic was still the Napoleonic Code, with few modifications. Women had no standing in law, no citizenship in the republic. Upon its constitution in 1882, the Ligue Française pour le Droit des Femmes ('French League for Women's Rights') drew up a programme which outlined women's complaints against the laws: paternity suits were forbidden; illegitimate children were the sole responsibility of the mother; promises of marriage were of no legal value; and women could not even act as witnesses for baptisms, marriages, or deaths. Within the family, all authority was in the husband's hands. He could arrange marriages for his children against his wife's wishes. He could make use of his wife's fortune as if it were his own. He could even sell his wife's possessions to pay his mistress! The double standard was enshrined in law. The husband could commit adultery not only with impunity but in all legality, except in the conjugal home, while the wife exposed herself to the full rigours of the law if she committed adultery anywhere. The husband was even 'excused' if he murdered his wife and her lover in the act at the conjugal home, while the inverse circumstance did not mitigate the same crime when the wife committed it.[7]

The humiliating legal situation of Frenchwomen during the Third Republic can also be judged from the limited nature and scarcity of the reforms actually accomplished. Divorce was re-established in 1884. Women were granted the right to sign as witnesses at baptisms and marriages (but not for deaths) in 1897. Married women who earned a living were granted the right to dispose of their earnings without their husband's written authorisation and 'even' to bring suits at law when required for their business by a law of 1907. Women were granted the right to vote for members of Conseils de Prud'hommes in 1907 and the right to be elected to them in 1908. (The Conseils were special courts handling work-related disputes between employers and workers.) Paternity suits were authorised in 1912, but only with written proof and there were stiff penalties for those who lost their cases. The suffrage, which was the key to all other aspects of formal equality, was voted by the Chamber in 1919, but the bill was rejected by the Senate in 1922. Until after the Second World War women remained non-citizens in the republic as well as non-persons before the law. Feminism was the response of bourgeois and professional women to the disparity between their professional, social, and economic status and their legal and political status.[8]

French feminism can be traced back to many pioneers, but as a movement it begins with Maria Deraismes and Léon Richer. Patrick Bidelman has told their story. Deraismes (1828—94) was the daughter of a wealthy, republican father. An unusually extensive education and a very substantial independent income enabled her to begin a successful writing and speaking career in the mid 1860s. Deraismes was a republican above all. Even her feminism was circumscribed by her concern for the republic. Until the 1880s, she steadfastly opposed seeking women's suffrage for fear that women, still too subject to the clerical influence, might overturn the fragile republic by their votes. A perfect liberal, she even joined a Freemasons' lodge in 1882, but was thrown out when the hierarchy discovered that a woman had been admitted. In 1893 she helped found a dissident lodge open to both men and women. On social matters she remained a steadfast supporter of liberal capitalist society. She had no sympathy whatsoever with the Communards. Collectivist or communist ideas inspired her with loathing.[9]

In 1866, Deraismes joined in the founding of the first feminist group in France, the Société pour la Revendication des Droits de la Femme ('Society for the Demand of Women's Rights'). This group also included militant social republicans like André Léo, Paule Mink, and Louise Michel, who joined on the side of the Communards and after exile became leaders of the working-class movement. Deraismes took another path. In 1870, she founded the Association pour le Droit des Femmes ('Women's Rights Association'). After several changes in name, it became in 1881 the Société pour l'Amélioration du Sort de la Femme et la Revendication de ses Droits ('Society for the Improvement of Women's Lot and the Demand of their Rights'). In this form, it lasted well into the twentieth century and became one of the two main pillars of French feminism.[10]

The other pillar of French feminism was the group created by Deraismes's sometime collaborator, Léon Richer (1824–1911), an anti-clerical and republican journalist. He had been co-founder with Deraismes of the Association pour le Droit des Femmes in 1870. But Richer was even more reluctant than Deraismes to support the vote for women and in the early 1880s they quarrelled. Richer believed that 'the feminine mind was still too crushed by the yoke of the Church' to consider giving the vote to women. The republic would not last six months if women voted. In 1888 he explained that 'millions of female votes would be subject to the occult domination of the priest, the confessor', an understandable fear in an era when women seemed visibly attached to the church and when the church still condemned the republic as unacceptable to Christians. Richer founded his own group in 1882, the Ligue Française pour le Droit des Femmes ('French League for Women's Rights'), whose grievances were outlined above. Under his leadership, the League avoided the question of the suffrage altogether. Subsequently, under less conservative leaders, it became one of the most active feminist groups of the Third Republic.[11]

French feminism in the twentieth century continued to bear the conservative imprint of Richer and Deraismes. The efforts of some leaders to enlarge its perspective and its audience met with resistance both from their own followers and from the women they attempted to reach. The bulk of French feminists were concerned above all to maintain the republic and the social stability it represented. They feared the overthrow of the republic and the disturbance of social order more than they desired equal rights with men.

Richer and Deraismes shared with republican men a deep-seated fear of giving women the vote lest they use it against the republic. They and their followers feared still more to stir up the lower orders by examples of public action.

Most nineteenth-century feminists could well remember the revolution of 1848, which was touched off by demonstrations for a widening of the franchise. During Deraismes and Richer's lifetimes France had been governed by five different regimes: the restored Bourbon monarchy (1814–30), the Orléans monarchy (1830–48), the Second Republic (1848–52), the Second Empire (1852–70), and the Third Republic (1870–1940). Most observers assumed that the era of revolution was only beginning. The Third Republic, born amidst the anguish of the Paris Commune of 1871, was shaky throughout the 1870s as monarchists controlled the government and appeared intent on restoring the monarchy. At the end of the century a series of 'affairs' seemed once again to menace the survival of the republic: Boulanger, Panama, and most of all Dreyfus. Now that France enjoyed a republic which maintained order, most feminists preferred not to risk overthrowing it by getting people out on the streets. Feminists had both ideological and material stakes in the continued existence of the republic. They instinctively avoided public demonstrations and any attempt at creating a mass movement, seeking instead to influence their fellow republican men in positions of power. Like the socialist women, they chose class over sex allegiance. This choice helps explain their inability or reluctance to mobilise women in public demonstrations and to use the forceful methods of the English and American suffragist women.[12]

Working women

During the Second Empire, and particularly during the 1850s, the French economy surged forward. The basis of the French rail network was constructed — railway mileage increased sixfold during the Empire — and large-scale credit institutions developed to finance the creation of a major industrial sector: between 1852 and 1870, industrial production doubled, foreign trade tripled, and the use of steam power increased fivefold. The growth of the economy and the spread of wage labour called up worker discontent which expressed itself in strike activity, to such an extent that the government finally legalised it in 1864, and in the formation of trade unions, known as *syndicats* or *chambres syndicales*, which were 'tolerated' after 1867.[13]

It is the effect of these developments on the household which is of interest to us. From the Second Empire on, the industrial mode of production gradually replaced the domestic mode, to use the terms suggested by Louise Tilly and Joan Scott in their *Women, Work, and Family*. The most common patterns of domestic production were the craftsman and peasant households. The key aspect of this mode was that the family was the production unit. What it produced was sold in order to maintain the members of the household. The husband was both head of the family and head of the production unit, for the two were one and the same thing. The role of women and children was to contribute labour to the household. They were not paid a wage.[14]

Capitalist economic development subjected the household economy to what became intolerable strains. Between 1850 and 1920, the domestic mode of production was generally supplanted by the industrial mode. The factory became the place of production and members of the household left the home to earn a wage in a factory. This wage they contributed to the family budget, constituting what Scott and Tilly call the family wage economy. While in the domestic mode all members of the family were doubly dependent upon the husband/father, who was both head of the family and of the business, in the industrial mode all members of the family became wage earners, equally independent of the family and dependent upon their employers.

To speak in these terms abstracts the concrete pressures felt by individual families. Capitalism did not mean a sudden transition from home to factory so often as it meant a gradually increasing tendency for the members of the family to earn wages in order to make their contribution to the family budget. This was the result both of the decreasing viability of the household production unit in the face of larger-scale competition and of the increasing possibility for earning wages. These wages did not have to be earned in factories. Indeed, in the early days of industrial capitalism, particularly in France, wages were more often earned in the home than in the factory.

The result was that, in France more than elsewhere, an intermediate form of production tended to persist, in which the household remained the place of work while the economic source of the work moved from the householder to the entrepreneur and members of the family became wage earners dependent upon the entrepreneur although they continued to work at home, usually doing piecework. Often in this situation the husband went to work outside the home while the wife and children remained there to earn their wages, although single daughters in early adolescence were increasingly sent off to urban centres to undertake domestic work, garment-making, and textile manufacturing, again earning wages part of which they tried to send home.[15]

One measure of the shift of women from the domestic mode of production to wage earning is provided by the census counts of the labour force ('population active'), which lump together those working outside the home and those working at home for a wage. They show a remarkable increase in the number of women earning wages. Between 1866 and 1901, the total labour force increased some four and a half million, from 15,143,000 to

19,715,000. The number of women in the labour force increased over two million, from 4,643,000 to 6,805,000. Thus women accounted for almost half (47 per cent) of the increase in the labour force. There was an increasing likelihood that a woman would work to earn a wage, independent of her husband, as the Third Republic wore on.[16]

These figures, however, indicate not necessarily the entry of women into the factory, although they do include this, but rather their switch from the domestic mode of production to wage-earning either in the home or in the factory. The very persistence of the household as a place of work probably accounts for the greater increase in women's participation in the economy as wage earners in France than in Britain, since for women to undertake piece-work in the home did not involve so great a break with customary life as to enter the factory.

The key phenomenon of the economic development of the Third Republic is thus the proletarianisation of workers and especially of women, 'of which factory labour was but one example', as Scott and Tilly point out.[17] What this proletarianisation meant to the French working class of the nineteenth century is described in a vast mass of statistics and model budgets proliferated by bureaucrats and reformers. Using figures for 1891–3, the Office du Travail (the state 'Labour Bureau') set up a model budget for a working-class family of six. They allotted the family a total each day of twelve pounds of bread, seven pounds of potatoes, thirteen ounces of meat, and one quart of wine. That was all. For our purposes, the point is not the quality of this diet. Two pounds of bread, a pound of potatoes flavoured with two ounces of meat and washed down with a glass of wine for each person – this is hardly enticing for a whole day's diet, but it is not starvation. The point is not even the extent to which this budget corresponded to reality, but rather the fact that, to achieve it, the Labour Bureau had to count on every member of the family's being regularly employed.[18]

Proletarianisation led to the establishment of the family wage economy. In the emerging working-class family, everyone was forced to bring in a wage to contribute to the family budget in order for the family simply to survive. While professional and white-collar women sought formal equality with their male counterparts, and well-to-do women sought to escape from the banality of their existence as mistresses of the home, working-class women, forced from an accepted role in the home into wage labour and often the misery and drudgery of the nineteenth-century factory, tended to idealise home and hearth.

The household mode of production at least integrated the different aspects of women's lives. They could arrange their work to suit their needs as bearers and rearers of children. As control of the production unit resided in the household, work patterns could be adjusted to facilitate women's changing situation as children were born and reared. Once women ceased to

be part of an integrated domestic production unit and worked for a wage
paid by an outside entrepreneur, even if they worked at home, their freedom
to accommodate family needs was severely restricted. If they left the home
to work in a factory, it was completely destroyed.

The twelve-hour day and the six-day week were universal until the 1890s
and then gradually reduced in law if not in fact to ten hours and six days on
the eve of the First World War. Even after the forty-hour week was introduced in 1936, only to be largely repealed in 1938, French workers still
faced a six-day week and were often required to do overtime. (This author,
working in the Peugeot warehouse near Paris in 1963, discovered that the
'eight-hour day' was in fact nine hours of work with an hour for lunch, from
8 a.m. to 6 p.m. and that it did not exclude five hours of work on Saturday
morning.) Even for piecework at home very long hours were required to
bring in the wage required for the family's needs. Moreover, the entrepreneur
would demand that those to whom he put work out keep up with heavy
demand during peak seasons. Dressmakers were commonly involved in
fifteen to eighteen-hour days during the height of the fashion season. A
Senate investigation in 1891 found cases of women who had worked twenty-
four-hour days.[19]

A woman worked whether married or single, but if married she at least
had company and the hope that her wages, together with those of the rest of
the family, would enable the family to survive. For a single woman, life
was even harder. There was a proliferation of books on the condition of
single working women, all written by reformers whose fear of social revolt
was not foreign to their concern. As one of these put it, 'Let us be on our
guard: she [the seamstress] almost always has someone to whom she can say
in the evening: "I earn 3 francs 50 a day sewing this 500 franc dress." And
of this is born not only misery, but all sorts of anger as well!'[20] The most
famous of these books was *L'Ouvrière*, written by the moderate republican
politician, Jules Simon. It was first published in 1861 and ran through eight
editions by 1876.

In the 1871 edition of his book, Simon set up his model budget for a
single woman worker with optimistic assumptions: she would earn 2 francs a
day and earn steadily, with no interruption due to illness or unemployment.
On this basis, Simon concluded, she could rent a mansard room three feet by
five and buy (or take time off from work to make) four thin cotton dresses
and one set of underclothing. After paying for soap to wash her clothes and
minimal heating and lighting to work by, she would have 59 centimes left
over each day. This was just enough to eat one warm meal at a canteen and
save some bread and cheese for supper. But what about the many who
earned less or were sick or unemployed at times? For them, Simon concluded, there was no way out but prostitution.[21]

Simon's figures tallied with official statistics, which indicated an average salary for working women of 1 franc 70 to 2 francs 10 per day in 1860—5 (for Paris, base for all these figures). By 1891—3, the average wage had risen to 3 francs a day, but prices had risen in similar fashion. Women's wages were generally less than half those of men, partly because of a pay differential even for the same work and partly because women's trades were underpaid. No wonder women as well as men looked back with nostalgia on the domestic mode of production, perhaps still more if they had never known it themselves.[22]

French socialism

French socialism shared a common heritage with the republican movement of the 1840s of which it was originally a part. Bernard H. Moss has argued convincingly that most 1848 republicans shared a vision of what he calls co-operative socialism, which was an integral part of their republicanism. The heart of this vision was an ideal of producer co-operatives federated together in trade-based mutual aid or mutual credit associations, whence the term 'mutualism'. Mutualism predominated in the emerging working-class movement of the half century between 1830 and 1880. During the early 1860s, Proudhonism came to be the dominant 'theoretical idiom' in which this ideal was expressed. At the core of Proudhon's vision, as of mutualism in general, lay the small, independent craftsman and peasant whose home was his workshop and whose family was his workforce. Mutualism was a romanticised version of the household mode of production.[23]

Courbet's famous portrait of Proudhon showed him seated on the steps of his cottage, deep in thought and surrounded by books, his children playing discreetly in the background, his wife nowhere to be seen. In Proudhon's view, this was as it should be. Women had two roles open to them: 'Prostitute or housewife, no other choice.'[24] He meant this barb seriously. In Proudhon's utopia, the husband was both head of the family and head of the workshop, directing the labour of his wife and children. Women's role was to work under the supervision of their men. In the absence of opportunities for employment as wage labourers, there was no alternative to this role except prostitution. Such a view did not result uniquely from Proudhon's personal misogyny, although his misogyny may have facilitated the expression of this view. The subordinate role of women was a necessary consequence of mutualism, because the traditional family was essential to the household production unit, which was at the root of the mutualist vision. Proudhon simply gave this vision its sharpest expression.

As an articulation of the mutualist utopia, Proudhon remained the key thinker of the working-class movement through the mid 1870s. Proudhon's popularity was due above all to his last book, *On the Political Capacity of the Working Classes*. He was inspired to write this work by the mutualist labour movement of the 1860s and the book provided the best expression of their ideal. In Bernard Moss's words, Proudhon in this book 'recognised the working class as the leading reformist class with its own mutualist idea for the transformation of capitalism'. Published shortly after Proudhon's death in 1865, the book enjoyed a great success. Proudhonians were the most important group in the Paris Commune. Paris was, to be sure, a centre of small-scale industry, in which Proudhon's ideas did not seem so out of place. Large-scale capitalist industry was growing mainly in provincial centres, particularly in the north. But since Paris dominated the working-class movement in France, Proudhonian ideas dominated the French section of the First International, much to Marx's chagrin.[25]

Yet Proudhon's ideas were of limited relevance to wage-earning labourers. The workers he had in mind were small peasant proprietors and artisans. His socialism consisted mainly of remedies for their ills, such as mutual associations and credit banks. He opposed strikes and political action and in their place offered only nostalgia for the old household economy. Even before the Commune, during the last years of the Second Empire, a number of leaders of the French section of the International were beginning to turn away from Proudhonian ideas simply because they were not useful in the face of the new realities of industrial strife. The failure of the Commune discredited both 1848 republicanism and mutualism. The repression of the Commune eliminated the traditional Parisian leaders of the working class and ended Paris leadership of the movement. Finally, the repressive activity of the nominally republican governments during the 1870s demonstrated the need for a political orientation to the working-class movement. Between the late 1860s and the 1880s, the French working-class movement discarded mutualism and adopted new ideas.

These ideas were called 'collectivist', which was the general term then in use for one who sought collective (not necessarily centralised) ownership of the means of production. The term was most often opposed to 'mutualist'. 'Socialist' still denoted anyone seeking social improvement, including both mutualists and collectivists. During the 1880s, however, as the collectivists gained the upper hand in the working-class movement, the word 'socialist' replaced 'collectivist' and took on its modern meaning. During the late nineteenth century there were as many as five French socialist parties. All the parties of the 1890s, with the exception of the 'independent' socialists and the Vaillantists, traced their origins back to the first collectivist party, the Fédération du Parti des Travailleurs Socialistes de France ('Federation of the Party of Socialist Workers of France') founded in 1880. At its beginnings, the Federation included all the collectivists as opposed to the mutualists, all the politically minded socialists as opposed to those who sought the improvement of society through social or economic channels. It included the Communard doctor Paul Brousse, who was prepared to enter coalitions with

Radical republicans; the Communard printer Jean Allemane, who emphasised the class base of the socialist movement; and the man who has gone down in socialist mythology as the founder of modern French socialism, Jules Guesde. While the formation of the Federation in 1880 represented a victory of all the collectivists over the mutualists, Guesde provides the best focus for our purposes because he was the most theoretically inclined of all the collectivists.

Guesde was born Jules Bazile in 1845, but when he became a republican journalist he changed his name to protect his father from the consequences of his political activities. When the Commune was declared in Paris, he wrote articles supporting it in a provincial newspaper. After the fall of the Commune, he went into exile at Geneva, where he came into contact with many leading members of the International. After a period of more or less anarchist views, he came to consider himself a collectivist.[26]

Upon Guesde's return to Paris in 1876, he joined a group of collectivists who met regularly at the Café Soufflot in the Latin Quarter, Guesde's great merit was to carry collectivist ideas out of this circle of intellectuals and into the arena of practical working-class politics. Guesde was distinguished from other collectivists by what Bernard Moss calls his 'pedagogical conception of leadership': his conviction that the workers needed intellectuals like him to teach them the way to rebuild society. Guesde began his half-century propaganda campaign with a newspaper which appeared in November 1877. The first issue stated baldly his beliefs: 'We believe, with the collectivist school, to which now belong nearly all the serious minds of the proletariat of the Two Worlds, that the natural and scientific evolution of humanity leads inevitably to the collective appropriation of land and of the instruments of labour.' Guesde expounded this message ceaselessly throughout France. Within a decade he would build the most important socialist party in the country.[27]

Guesdism, as it came to be known, passed for Marxism in France, but in fact Guesde had developed his ideas before he read Marx. What he heard at the Café Soufflot led him to see Marx as endowed with the halo of scientific authority. When he did read volume I of *Capital*, between 1877 and 1880, he found in it only what he was seeking: scientific justification (as he thought) to pursue one aim to the exclusion of all others — the collective appropriation of the means of production. Marxism provided Guesde not with insights but with single-mindedness. 'Anti-capitalism is enough,' Guesde used to say. Women's rights were one of the many causes which he came to look upon as diversionary. Legal rights, the suffrage, in short equality within bourgeois society — Guesde would tell women that these rights were meaningless under capitalism and that they should therefore simply wait for the revolution. Moreover, to struggle for them in the present meant to practise reformism, to accept bourgeois society. The only acceptable struggle for Guesde was against capitalism.[28]

Marx, Bebel, and Engels on the woman question

This was not consistent with Marx's thinking on the woman question, as the problem of the condition of women was then known. To be fair to Guesde, one should note that the paucity of Marx's references to women still troubles Marxists today. In any event, Guesde could not read German, and the two key Marxist works on women were not translated into French until the 1890s: Bebel's *Woman Under Socialism* and Engels's *The Origin of the Family, Private Property, and the State*. With a knowledge of Marx's method and a sense of his historical vision, Guesde could have overcome these problems, as did a number of the German socialists, but Guesde had neither.

Marx clearly believed that women were subject to a special oppression. As early as the *Economic and Philosophic Manuscripts of 1844*, Marx mentioned in an aside that marriage was 'incontestably a form of *exclusive private property*' (italics orig.). This idea was developed in the famous passages on the family in part II of the *Communist Manifesto*. There Marx argued that bourgeois marriage was a form of private property, but that among workers the pressure of proletarianisation was destroying the old form of marriage based on private ownership of the small domestic production unit.[29]

In later writings, Marx developed this second insight. In the first volume of *Capital*, he noted that these new pressures also provided a basis for women's future independence:

However terrible and disgusting the dissolution of the old family ties within the capitalist system may appear, large-scale industry, by assigning an important part in socially organised processes of production, outside the sphere of the domestic economy, to women, young persons and children of both sexes, does nevertheless create a new economic foundation for a higher form of the family and of relations between the sexes.[30]

Marx here recognised both the hardship created in the present by proletarianisation and its potential to liberate women in the future. Woman's work in the household economy put her doubly under the thumb of her husband: she was not only his wife, but also his worker. Wage labour made her less dependent upon her husband, particularly when it drew her out of the house and into the factory. She then had the same status as her husband. She was then dependent, like him, on the capitalist who employed her. She could then struggle, like her husband, to end this dependence and become her own person.

This historical vision, however, did not clarify things for women in the present. Wage-earning did not give women independence from their husbands in the present society. The wages they earned in industry they contributed to the household, in what Scott and Tilly call the family wage economy. Marx, to be sure, spoke only of laying the 'economic foundation' for future emancipation. But what were women to do in the present, when working for a wage simply caught them in a double dependence, upon the capitalist as well as the husband, in the factory as well as the home? Were they simply to wait for the revolution? Or should they in the meantime heed the call of the feminists and struggle for their formal, legal rights, however limited they might be under the capitalist regime?

In 1878, August Bebel, one of the foremost leaders of the German social-ist party, the Sozialistiche Partei Deutschlands (SPD), published what was intended to be the party's definitive statement on the woman question: *Woman Under Socialism*. It ran through fifty editions before the First World War and was translated into fifteen languages.[31] It is hard now to understand the excitement raised by Bebel's thick and heavy book. Although it included a demonstration of Marx's analysis of the woman problem, it also included everything else considered scientific at the time. To us it seems an endless potpourri in which all kinds of arguments are jumbled together. But to social-ists of the late nineteenth century, it seemed to be proof that they had science and history on their side.

Bebel's book lent the authority and prestige of the SPD, the largest social-ist party in existence, to women's rights. It endorsed unequivocally every imaginable reform, from the right for women to vote, to enter university and the professions, all the way to divorce and married women's property. Bebel thus brought the nascent socialist movement to accept feminist demands in their entirety. He went further, however, and posed radical new demands, such as the right to dress for freedom of movement and the right to sexual satisfaction. And while most feminists hesitated to play down women's tra-ditional roles in the home, Bebel dismissed contemptuously the idea that raising a family was women's 'natural calling'. That idea, he said, was 'twaddle'.[32] Finally, the book had great impact in restoring women's self-esteem and encouraging them to act. The German socialist leader Ottilie Baader recalled the impact of Bebel's book on her life in these terms:

I lived resigned and without hope . . . News came of a wonderful book that . . . Bebel . . . had written. Although I was not a Social Democrat I had friends who belonged to the party. Through them I got the precious work. I read it nights through. It was my own fate and that of thousands of my sisters. Neither in the family nor in public life had I ever heard of all the pain the woman must endure. One ignored her life. Bebel's book cour-ageously broke with the old secretiveness . . . I read the book not once but ten times.[33]

However inspirational it may have been, Bebel's book did not provide an answer to the problem of tactics. He did not really link Marx's analysis of the economically dependent situation of women to the problem of their lack of formal rights, but rather talked about each problem on its own terms. Thus the logical implication of his sections on women's rights would be support for the feminists and indeed at one point he even stated that 'women should expect as little help from men as workingmen do from the capitalist class'. The basic message of the book, however, was that the party should support women's rights and women should join the party: 'it is the part of the working woman to make common cause with the male members of her class . . . in the struggle for a radical transformation of society'. But if women were oppressed so much more than men and so differently, how would the party help them? What was the relationship between women's rights and socialism?[34]

Insofar as this question was ever answered in nineteenth-century Marxist theory, it was Engels who outlined an answer in *The Origin of the Family, Private Property, and the State*, which he published in 1884, six years after Bebel's book. Like Marx and Bebel, Engels recognised the problem posed by women's dependence upon men. Indeed, some of his observations have become clichés in certain circles today: 'The modern individual family is founded on the open or concealed domestic slavery of the wife'; 'Within the family he is the bourgeois, the wife represents the proletariat.' But Engels went on to make explicit what had only been implicit in Marx's scattered references to women: women's formal rights in bourgeois society were an essential condition for their emancipation. Engels argued by analogy with universal manhood suffrage:

It provides the clear field on which the fight can be fought out. And in the same way, the peculiar character of the supremacy of the husband over the wife in the modern family, will only be seen in the clear light of day when both possess legally complete equality of rights.

This suggests that equal political and legal rights for women were to be realised in bourgeois society, before the social revolution. Implicit in this, however heretical it may seem, is approval for women to act on their own to obtain their formal rights, with the support of the socialists, just as Marx and Engels themselves had supported the republicans in the revolutions of 1848, seeking to push them to achieve full political democracy.[35]

To be sure, Engels justifies his support for women's legal rights, as he does that for democratic liberties in general, in terms of providing a 'clear field', that is, exposing the more fundamental economic oppression. There can be no doubt that Engels, like Marx, believed that class oppression was primary, sex oppression secondary. But Engels quite clearly suggested that legal equality was to be sought within the present, bourgeois society. Guesde would tell women to wait for the revolution. Marx implicitly and Engels explicitly told them that they had a duty to struggle for their formal rights in bourgeois society.

Marx, Engels, and Guesde could all agree that legal equality with men was useless if women still depended on men to feed them. For these rights to become meaningful, women would have to achieve economic independence. For Marx, economic independence did not mean just the right to take the same jobs as men in present society, even at equal pay, but rather the right to realise one's full human potential through one's work, which was possible for most people only in the future, socialist society. The point here, how-

17

ever, is that formal legal rights could appear more meaningful than they were so long as women had not experienced them. Precisely for that reason, women must not wait for the revolution, but must struggle now for their rights. Only after women enjoyed legal rights would it 'be plain that the first condition for the liberation of the wife is to bring the whole female sex back into public industry, and that this in turn demands that the characteristic of the monogamous family as the economic unit of society be abolished'. But if it is only after women obtain formal equality that they can begin effectively to seek full self-realisation on the social and economic planes, as Engels seemed to suggest, then women must act first as women to obtain legal rights before being able to act in accord with men of their class.[36]

Does this mean separate groups for women? Engels did not really consider the question. Indeed, the passages which we have been analysing are virtual asides in Engels's development of the historical implications of Morgan's anthropology. One would hesitate before suggesting that Engels meant to endorse what today is called separatism. He did not mention, here or elsewhere, the possibility of women's groups, but he certainly did not rule them out. It is clear that he did endorse the battles of women for their legal rights, battles which of course were to be undertaken primarily by feminists.

What would be the role of socialist women toward the feminists according to Engels's analysis? Presumably the analogy with the republicans would obtain here. The duty of the communists during republican revolutions was to goad the republicans into achieving their whole programme. By the same reasoning, the duty of socialist women would be first to support the feminists and then, once they had exhausted their limited programme of formal equality, to go beyond it, toward socialism. Would they join with the feminists as well as the socialists? Would they have their own women's groups within the socialist party? Marx and Engels gave no answers to these tactical questions. It is clear, however, that Engels never made the mistake of assuming that women could simply ignore their lack of rights and act in the socialist party as if they were on the same footing as men, but it is also clear that neither Marx nor Engels ever envisaged socialist groups specifically for women. The socialist women's movement arose out of particular historical circumstances at the level not of theory, but of tactics.

The German socialist women's movement

Indeed, the German socialist women's movement, source of inspiration for all the others, arose out of a minor historical accident. In 1890, when the SPD reorganised following the abolition of the anti-socialist laws, a number of German states had laws which prohibited women from joining political groups or attending public meetings. To get around this prohibition, the party authorised women 'to elect female delegates to Party conferences at special women's meetings'. In 1892, this privilege was abolished at the request of Ottilie Baader, who argued, much as would French socialist women: 'we don't want privileges, but equal rights'. However, the system was reintroduced in 1894.[37]

Thus the SPD created a women's organisation separate from but parallel to the party itself. Women enjoyed their own groups throughout Germany, even in states where it was legal for women to join the party on the same footing as men. Women thus had groups in which they felt comfortable and in which they could learn to speak in public and think for themselves. Clara Zetkin, the leader of German socialist women and indeed of the international socialist women's movement, pointed out in 1913 that this was a key condition for the success of the socialist women's movement:

it must with all firm organisational connection to the movement as a whole, nevertheless possess a certain measure of independence and freedom of movement . . . This is such a vital necessity for the socialist women's movement that its realisation absolutely must prevail, whatever the form of organisation. If the male comrades are not judicious enough to provide this vital necessity, it must be fought for.[38]

The German socialist women's movement benefited not only from circumstances which enabled the party to create such an organisation, but also from a dynamic leader and a solid bi-weekly newspaper. The newspaper was *Die Gleichheit* ('Equality'), which was founded in 1891 and reached a circulation of 125,000 by the eve of the First World War. The leader was Clara Zetkin (1857–1933), who was the editor of *Die Gleichheit* and one of the most influential socialists of the late nineteenth century. Her brochure, *The question of women workers and women at the present time* (1889) became the basis for German social-democratic policy toward women through the Weimar era. Under her leadership, the women's movement developed a large core of women tough enough to brave semi-legality and the dictates of custom in order to act as socialist militants. By 1908, there were nearly 30,000 women members, 5.6 per cent of the total party membership.[39]

In 1908, new legislation granted women the right to join organisations. Women thereupon took their place formally as full-fledged members of the SPD. They kept, however, their parallel organisation structure with women's conferences, separate educational sessions for women, and representation of women at all levels of the party executive. The combination of an existing core of women, women's groups, and full and legal membership, together with the trade-union base of the SPD, enabled women's membership to skyrocket in the six years before the war. By 1914, there were 175,000 women in the SPD, 16.1 per cent of total membership, while the party itself had well over a million members in all. The German socialist women's movement had become the yardstick by which all others would be measured. The French movement, however, arose out of French historical realities. It is to these that we turn now.[40]

19

Part I Feminism and socialism 1876 – 1900

1. Women and the beginnings of the socialist movement 1876 – 82

In the early years of the Third Republic, there was no socialist movement, let alone an organised socialist party. There had grown up during the 1840s what the French called the 'social movement', but this broad term designated all those who sought greater social justice, from republicans and Freemasons to syndicalists and members of the International. The social movement was painfully reconstituted during the Second Empire, only to be crushed again. The repression of the Commune deprived the social movement of its working-class leaders and many of its followers in Paris, the traditional centre of the movement. In the decade following the Commune, a more specifically working-class movement began to emerge through a series of congresses which laid the basis for the parties which, during the following decade, became known as 'socialist' and began to distinguish themselves from the republicans.

The social movement of the Second Empire had not been notable for its support of women's rights. Although the utopian socialists of the 1840s, like Cabet and Fourier, had been ardent champions of equality between the sexes, the sentiments of most republican and working-class militants in regard to women's roles were probably better expressed by Proudhon. In the 1870s, nothing indicated that the social movement if reconstituted would take a stand for women's equality with men. How it did so, how within a decade of the Commune the nascent socialist party came to take a forceful stand for complete equality between the sexes, is the first problem before us. Coupled with it are two related developments: on the one hand, the first effort (and the first failure) to ally feminism and socialism; on the other hand, the first attempt to build a women's movement linked to the socialist party.

The liquidation of the mutualist heritage

Traditional French historiography has suggested that the death or exile of most of the leaders of the social movement following the Commune enabled

21

the French to slough off the mutualist vision which had been so much a part of the social movement during the Empire. In fact, the rank and file sloughed off mutualism on their own, as they re-formed the movement. When the exiles returned in 1880, they found the movement already well beyond mutualism and on the road to the organisation of a political party, collectivist if not Marxist in its aims.

The movement during the Empire had been largely unstructured and such organisation as there was did not survive the Commune. The movement had to be rebuilt from the centre: its first existence after the Commune was through 'worker congresses', which were national meetings of working-class militants. These militants were particularly concerned with the entry of women into the industrial workforce and discussed this problem at length. While opposition to the new roles for women, though consistent with Proudhonism and mutualism in general, was not necessarily linked to mutualism, support for women's new roles was usually linked to the new collectivist ideas which were to displace mutualism by the end of the 1870s. Therefore we can follow the progress of collectivist ideas at the same time as we trace the evolution of attitudes on women's rights.

The first worker congress was held in Paris, in October 1876. In that year a republican government was installed in the place of the monarchists who had crushed the Commune. Political action was once again possible. The congress was organised by a radical republican newspaper; the republicans still thought of the working classes as their natural allies and sought to encourage their organisation in the hope of increasing their own political base. The congress placed the question of 'women's work' first upon the agenda and spent a day on it. An otherwise unknown woman, Valentine Raoult, made the most important and most typical speech. She called for the creation of 'co-operative workshops', to be financed by 'people's banks' and run by the 'fathers, brothers or husbands' of the women working in them: 'it would be more natural for men to provide a living for their wives and daughters'. Co-operatives, people's banks, and women's dependence on men: all these ideas are typically mutualist.[1]

The men at the congress agreed: 'Men being stronger and more robust should earn enough to support the costs of keeping up their household', said one Irénée Dauthier, whose speech was greatly admired.[2] He and the other men recognised, however, that men could not earn enough and so they reluctantly accepted the idea of women's working, but only with the restriction that they do so at home: for women to work in factories meant 'the destruction of morals [which are] the veritable religion of workers'. The resolution on the question suggested such measures as the eight-hour day and the prohibition of night work for women (but not for men), the creation of co-operatives and 'women's trade associations [*chambres syndicales*]'.[3]

At the next workers' congress, held in Lyons in February 1878, 'women's work' was again the first question on the agenda. Men delegates favoured equal pay for women as a means of eliminating them from factories, on the argument that the economic attractiveness of female employees came from their much lower wage scales. Some women delegates, however, had different ideas. One even went so far as to argue for women's right to work: Marie Finet, a delegate from Lyons: 'Should women work? Yes, even if they do not absolutely need to do so. They should work in order to be free, to be independent, they should work in order to be men's equals.' If women were inferior to men, it was society which had made them so. The solution was 'equality of solidarity and of rights between all the members of the proletarian class'.[4]

Her speech received 'prolonged applause and bravos', but her views were not reflected in the congress's resolution on women's work. It did admit that home duties were 'at least equivalent to men's work' and that they 'require[d] all the day's labour', which represented a change from Proudhon's argument that the total worth of women could be assessed at one-third that of men, but it explicitly confirmed that women should be confined to their traditional roles. They should be able to support themselves, but only 'until the day when, embracing a new condition, they become wives and mothers, that is women of the hearth [*la femme au foyer*]'. 'Women of the hearth' — the French equivalent of 'woman's place is in the home'. This notion dominated thinking about women's roles at the second congress, as at the first. Success in bringing the working-class movement to accept the idea of new roles for women came first from outside the movement, from a feminist.[5]

The conservative climate which had prevailed after the repression of the Commune had forced the feminists to suspend their activities. In 1872, Maria Deraismes and Léon Richer decided to begin the monthly meetings of their small feminist group once again. But although they changed its name to eliminate the word *droit* (right),[6] which annoyed the government, and although their meetings rarely gathered more than ten or twelve persons, the government dissolved the group. The occasion for the rebirth of feminism was the Paris Exposition of 1878. These expositions involved numerous congresses, open gatherings to discuss a given subject. Richer and Deraismes decided that an 'international congress of women's rights' would be feasible within the framework of the Exposition so long as it limited itself to discussing civil rights. By ruling out any mention of political rights they hoped to obtain tolerance of their activities from the newly installed republican government.[7]

One militant feminist refused to accept this limitation. She was Hubertine Auclert. Born in the Allier in south central France, on 10 April 1848, of well-to-do parents who left her a modest independent income, Auclert came to Paris shortly after the Commune. In 1876 she founded a new feminist group, Le Droit des Femmes ('Women's Right'), using the word *droit* as if to show that Richer had been a coward to abandon it. The group took the motto 'no duties without rights, no rights without duties'. Auclert decided to speak at Richer's congress on the forbidden subject, women's political rights. Terrified of renewed governmental repression, Richer and Deraismes refused to relax their prohibition. Two weeks before the congress, Auclert was forced to concede defeat. She resigned from the 'initiating commission' and, with four others, from the organising committee. She published as a brochure the speech she had intended to deliver: 'Women's political rights, a problem which is not dealt with at the International Women's Congress'. Having been rebuffed by the feminist leaders, she took her case to the workers.[8]

The working-class movement was still unusually open to outside influence. The worker congresses of 1876 and 1878 had not created any formal structure for the movement. There was still no political party claiming to represent the working class. There was a newspaper, however. After the government's suppression of Guesde's newspaper (in July 1878), the congress of Lyons had arranged the creation of *Le Prolétaire*, which appeared in November 1878. Dominated by collectivists, *Le Prolétaire* distinguished itself in its support for women's rights. In December 1878, it ran a series of articles on 'The woman question' which described the many restrictions to which women were subject and came out unequivocally for complete emancipation. Following the publication of these articles, which may have drawn the newspaper to her attention, Auclert began to place her group's announcements in *Le Prolétaire*. This link enabled her to attend the third workers' congress, held at Marseilles in October 1879, as a delegate of Le Droit des Femmes.[9]

At the congress, Auclert presented her feminism in the most uncompromising terms. She praised the congress for admitting 'a woman, not because she is a worker [she was not], but because she is a woman'. This marked, she went on, the beginning of 'a pact of alliance . . . against our common oppressors'. She emphasised that she was talking about an alliance between two independent forces. Some men, she said, expected women to merge their demands with those of the socialists, who would build a society of equality for all, including women. 'I fear', she said, 'that human equality, preached by all the socialist schools, will again be only the equality of men among themselves, and that women will be duped by the men of the proletariat as the proletarians were by the bourgeois.' She warned against those socialists 'who extol a future equality and who, in the present, oppose women's bringing to bear their intelligence, their ideas, their tastes upon the arrangement of this future society . . . Those who deny our equality in the present, will deny it in the future.' Her speech, concluded with great oratorical flourish, was enthusiastically received. It was the first on the question and set the tone for the rest of the debate.[10]

Those who opposed women's emancipation were thrown on the defensive.

Irénée Dauthier, who in 1876 had argued that women's place was in the home, now added that, although confined to the home, she should enjoy the rights of citizenship. But this modification did not get him elected to the committee. Another delegate provoked a storm when he began to read a report which opposed women's emancipation. The chairman responded by reading a statement to the effect that the delegate's own group had voted against his ideas. The congress voted to deny him the floor and not to include his report in the published account of the proceedings.[11]

Although a minority opposed women's rights, the great majority of speakers came out for complete civil and political equality.[12] Subsequently, Auclert was chosen chairwoman (*présidente*) of a plenary session of the congress, a distinction she was the first woman to receive from such a gathering. She was also named chairwoman of the committee on women. Inside the committee, she recalled many years later, 'I managed by sheer tenacity to obtain a resolution in favour of the complete emancipation of women.' This recollection should probably be tempered in view of Auclert's subsequent break with the socialists. After all, six of the nine members of the committee had spoken for complete equality. None of them had been among those with reservations about women's rights. Nevertheless, Auclert does seem to have been the guiding spirit of the resolution. It reflected her vision in two respects which distinguished it from all subsequent socialist resolutions on the question of women.[13]

In the first place, it was not so much a socialist statement on women as a pact between women and socialists as equals. 'Considering all the advantages there are for the proletariat if it assures itself of women's support in its struggles against the privileged classes', the resolution guaranteed women equal rights with men within the working-class movement: 'Men will admit them in their meetings, study groups, socialist electoral committees, where they will be entitled to speak and to vote.' (Twenty-three years later the Groupe Féministe Socialiste was unable to obtain such guarantees from the Parti Socialiste Français.)[14]

In the second place, the resolution went far beyond most of the speeches, spelling out every conceivable aspect of equality and not just the formal equality with which the socialists would thereafter content themselves. It neatly disposed of the old idea that men should support the family, demanding instead 'that an equitable division be made in the workforce; that work which requires skill devolve upon the weaker persons, men or women; that work which requires great muscular force devolve upon the strong'. Within this perspective, women had a duty to work. 'Rights bring responsibilities: women must work . . . since they consume.' Thus women's right to work was stated in the broadest possible terms, along with legal and political rights. But beyond all the rights enumerated, the resolution left open for women whatever the future experience of humanity might offer:

Men and women . . . will govern this society together and will share in the exercise of the same rights, in public life as in private . . . in all circumstances, women will have their freedom of action like men. The congress, considering that a role must depend on the choice of the individual who fills it, if it is to be fulfilled, assigns no special role to women, they will take the roles and the places in society to which their vocations call them.

Overwhelmed, perhaps, at the scope of Auclert's vision, the delegates hesitated: they passed the resolution only after nine minor objections, two procedural votes, and a second reading. But pass it they did, amid 'prolonged applause'. The socialists never again produced a statement of women's rights to equal this in breadth and profundity, nor did they ever again sign such a 'pact of alliance' between their movement and the feminists.[15]

The apparent reversal of attitudes which passage of Auclert's resolution represents was not simply the result of Auclert's eloquence, howevermuch this may have helped. It was a result too of the progress of collectivist ideas among working-class militants or of collectivist militants within working-class organisations. These ideas were founded on acceptance of the industrial economy and of the democratic republic as the battlegrounds on which would be fought the struggle for improvement of the conditions of workers. Rejection of the mutualist nostalgia for the old domestic economy implied rejection of women's old roles. Acceptance of new roles for women in the economy and the republic was conversely a corollary of collectivist ideas in general. Auclert's success with *Le Prolétaire* was a sign of this. So was the fact that the delegates at Marseilles not only supported Auclert's resolution but also rejected in general the trade-based approach of the mutualists in favour of a political orientation for the working-class movement: the congress called for the creation of a 'Parti Ouvrier', a worker party. They gave the party the name 'socialist' in the old, broad sense of the word, but as the party developed on a collectivist base, the term 'collectivist' gradually fell into disuse, to be replaced by 'socialist' in its modern sense. As a consequence of the congress of Marseilles, then, the Fédération du Parti des Travailleurs Socialistes de France ('Federation of the Party of Socialist Workers of France' FTSF) was founded in 1880 and became the main ancestor of the twentieth-century French socialist and communist parties.

Initially, Auclert's group was faithful to the alliance they had proposed and collaborated actively in building the party. Auclert herself helped found the party's Paris section. Her second in command of Le Droit des Femmes, Clémence Kéva, a lace and trim-maker, was elected treasurer of the party's Paris region federation, the Union Fédérative du Centre (UFC). Nevertheless, the alliance soon foundered on the bourgeois class base of the feminist movement. Le Droit des Femmes was limited to a small number of bourgeois women (there were only eighteen dues-paying members), whose position on social matters was innately conservative. Thus when faced with a choice between collectivist socialism and Proudhonist mutualism, Le Droit des Femmes chose mutualism despite its hostility to women's rights.[16]

The choice presented itself at the next national congress, held in Le Havre in 1880. At Le Havre, the mutualists sought to make a last stand against the collectivists who had routed them at Marseilles the year before. On the opening day, the organising committee, under mutualist control, invalidated the mandates of a number of collectivists and excluded them from the congress, which then passed a resolution violently attacking collectivism. The move was too late. The government had finally amnestied the Communards, who returned from prison and exile in time to celebrate the 14 July 1880. They provided new leadership for the collectivists. At Le Havre, Paule Mink, one of the most famous Communard women, led the battle against the mutualists with the same forcefulness she had shown during the Commune.

Mink had revolution in her earliest background. Her parents were Polish nobles who had supported the revolution of 1830 and fled to France after the revolution was defeated. She was born Paulina Mekarska on 9 November 1839, at Clermont-Ferrand, where her father was reduced to working as a clerk for a tax collector. She went to work in Paris, giving language lessons and sewing, and became an ardent republican at the age of sixteen. In 1868, she founded a women's mutual-aid society and collaborated with Maria Deraismes in a series of public lectures on 'women's work', which became famous because they were the first public meetings allowed under the Empire. In 1869 she founded a republican newspaper, *Les Mouches et l'araignée*: the flies were the French people, the spider was the Emperor. True to form, the spider closed the enterprise down after the second issue. When the war broke out in 1870, Mink organised the defence of Auxerre, south-east of Paris, for which, she later claimed, she was subsequently offered the Legion of Honour, but refused. During the Commune she proved herself an energetic propagandist both in Paris, in the revolutionary clubs, and in the provinces, where she sought in vain for support for the Commune. She was on such a mission when the 'Bloody Week' of repression began. She fled to Switzerland, hiding in the tender of a locomotive, and returned to France only when amnesty was declared.[17]

At the congress of Le Havre, Mink refused to accept the resolution against collectivism. She started to speak in favour of collectivism. The chairman tried to stop her, saying that the question had been resolved and that she was out of order, but she went on. She occupied the podium until, amidst an incredible uproar, the congress was forced to adjourn. The next day, the collectivist delegates organised their own congress in another hall.[18]

Kéva, the delegate of Le Droit des Femmes, remained with the mutualists, whose support for private property apparently mattered more to her than their anti-feminism. They were led by Auguste Keufer, who was to be secretary of the Fédération du Livre (the printers' union) from 1885 to 1919. Like most opponents of women's rights, Keufer spoke of women in the singular, as an abstraction: 'Woman is destined for the home [*foyer*], she must not leave it at all.' The other delegates agreed. Against Kéva's ineffective opposition, they restated the conservative ideals of the first two worker congresses, confining women to be 'the soul of the home [*intérieur*]', taking jobs outside the home only if they had no man to support them. The congress declared itself ready to use 'any means' to prevent married women from working.[19]

The schism at Le Havre marked the end of mutualism as a force in the working-class movement. The mutualists held two more congresses, both of which were dismal failures, and then sank into oblivion. The schism had immediate repercussions for Le Droit des Femmes. Shortly after the congress, the UFC excluded the group, presumably for having sided with the mutualists in the schism. Le Droit des Femmes quickly lost its social concerns and drifted into a comparatively narrow suffragism. By 1883 it had changed its name to Le Suffrage des Femmes ('Women's Suffrage'), which, Auclert's sister remarked, 'better expressed its fundamental concerns'. Auclert's newspaper, *La Citoyenne*, scarcely ever dealt with social issues. Her last book, published after her death (she died on 8 April 1914), included a chapter entitled 'Socialism would not result in women's emancipation'. Despite her disillusionment, Auclert had made an important contribution to socialism. She had written into the socialist heritage a statement of women's rights which was never surpassed, she had brought the alliance between feminism and socialism nearer to realisation than ever before or after, and she had helped liquidate the mutualist heritage. But she left the movement before it became a party, broke the projected alliance, and refused to accept the implications of her support for the collectivists. Others were left to struggle for realisation of women's rights within the party and, in default of the alliance between feminism and socialism, to build a socialist women's movement.[20]

Women's rights: reform or revolution?

The rout of the mutualists confirmed the political orientation of the working-class movement as well as the theoretical support for women's rights voted at Marseilles. The new party was formed during 1880. Its position on women's rights was not clear, despite Auclert's resolution. In the first place, the resolution was not part of a programme. Indeed, there was as yet no programme at all. Thus women's rights had no assigned place in comparison with other demands of the party. In the second place, Auclert's resolution did not ensure practical support for women's rights, but represented only a reversal of theory. Was equality of the sexes a reform to be sought within the present society, and hence a goal to be included in the party's minimum programme? Or was it a fundamental change which only the socialist revolution could achieve, and thus a subject only for theoretical support until then? The party was collectivist, but it had not decided whether the path to collectivism, or socialism as it was beginning to be called, lay through reforms or through revolution. This general policy question was linked to the specific problem of women's rights. New forces within the party brought sharply differing answers to both questions. On the one hand, a new women's group was founded within the party. On the other hand, Jules Guesde was beginning his efforts to impose his brand of Marxism on the party. His interpretation of Marxism seemed to exclude women's rights until after the revolution. The women and the Guesdists were soon locked in bitter struggle, which ended only with the split of the party in 1882.

The new group was L'Union des Femmes ('The Women's Union'). It differed from Le Droit des Femmes in being socialist (they still used the term collectivist), but it was also feminist. It was the first group of socialist women in France. The undisputed founder and leader of the Union was Léonie Rouzade.

If Mink was a revolutionary, Louise-Léonie Camusat was a republican. She liked to boast that her grandfather had been a deputy of the Third Estate in 1789. Born at Paris on 6 September 1839, she absorbed republican and Voltairian sympathies from her father. After a brief period living alone and working as an embroiderer, in 1860 she married Auguste Rouzade, chief municipal accountant for the quiet little town of Meudon, where they spent the rest of their lives.[21] Léonie Rouzade came to socialism only after her marriage, through study and reflection. Even though she had known hardship, she had the luxury of reflecting upon it from a relatively comfortable position. Unlike Mink, she was never a revolutionary. While Mink was ardently engaged in the Commune, Rouzade was absorbed in writing two incomprehensible pamphlets on metaphysics.[22]

In 1872, Rouzade published three novels which she had probably written during the 1860s. All three were inspired by the utopian socialists Cabet and Fourier. One, *Le Monde renversé* ('The World Turned Upside Down'), might tempt a publisher today: it tells of a beautiful woman named Célestine who was abducted into a near-eastern harem where she led a successful women's revolt and set up a new code of laws, the first article of which was 'man owes obedience to woman'. The role of women was also the theme of *Voyage de Théodose à l'île d'Utopie* ('Théodose's Voyage to the Island of Utopia'). The story began, like every utopian novel, with a sudden change of environment. Théodose was shipwrecked on an island 'next to the sun'. He discovered to his amazement that everyone worked only four hours a day, in complete harmony and equality. Before long the question of women's role came up. Chastity was held in abhorrence and marriage blessed, but marriage was an affair of complete equality. Théodose eventually returned to France, having learned the true nature of love from the Utopians, and wooed and married a beautiful woman of great charm, tact, and dignity. But she insisted on maintaining her independence while he slipped back into the old ways. After a showdown, Théodose fell into a coma, repented his attempt to dominate his wife, obtained her forgiveness, and died.[23]

Like Auclert, Rouzade came to the working-class movement through feminism. She attended the feminist congress of 1878 and then joined Auclert's Le Droit des Femmes, thereby entering into contact with the socialists of *Le Prolétaire*. Her talent as an orator was soon appreciated in the small world of the nascent socialist movement. From the summer of 1879, she began giving lectures in the company of Guesde and other socialist leaders — once even of Blanqui, the grand old man of revolution. For the anniversary of the Commune, she spoke at a 'people's fête', organised to raise funds for *Le Prolétaire*. Her speech, noted the newspaper, 'carried off the honours of the evening'. Given her feminism and her sudden activism in the socialist movement, it is hardly surprising that she sought to form a group to bring the two together.[24]

Two women joined with Rouzade in founding L'Union des Femmes. Their backgrounds corresponded to the two forces which the group sought to combine. Eugénie Pierre, born 5 November 1844, had been an active feminist during the 1870s, working on the staff of Léon Richer's newspaper and acting as secretary of the 1878 feminist congress. Marguerite Tinayre, on the other hand, had been active in the Commune. Born in 1831 in Issoire, a subprefecture in the central highlands of France, she inherited 'a certain fortune', which enabled her to publish two novels in the 1860s. One was about the plight of a peasant family uprooted to Paris. The other was in the utopian style Rouzade favoured: it told of a noble who turned model capitalist under his wife's influence. Like Rouzade, Tinayre favoured the nice methods of social change and tended toward the utopian socialists. In 1867 she organised a study group with Saint-Simonian tendencies, Les Equitables de Paris ('The Just of Paris'). She was instrumental in its decision to join the International, to which she herself still belonged at the time of the Commune, but it must be remembered that this did not necessarily imply more than solidarity with downtrodden workers — the First International did not appear collectivist, still less Marxist, from the French point of view. The Commune appointed Tinayre an inspector for girls' schools in the twelfth arrondissement of Paris. Her husband was shot during the repression of the Commune and she was exiled.[25]

The announcement of the founding of L'Union was printed in *Le Prolétaire* of 28 February 1880, side by side with the group's programme. The programme began by paraphrasing the famous brochure of 1789, 'What is the Third Estate?': 'What is woman in present day society?' asked the Union;

'Nothing'. Unlike the feminists, however, the Union tried to link women's emancipation to socialism: in order for women to 'live . . . to be free', the programme continued, 'it is necessary' not only 'that women enjoy all their civil and political rights', but also 'that the soil, raw materials, means of exchange, and instruments of labour be the collective property of all those who work'. 'When these reforms have been accomplished, women will cease to be: [*sic*] the slaves of their parents or their husbands; the slaves of their employers; the slaves of their society.'

With the mutualists out of the way, no one was going to object in theory to women's rights or to collectivism, which even the most reformist members of the party postulated as an aim, however far off they put its achievement. But the Union's programme contained in fact two separate if parallel analyses rather than one integrated one. It was both feminist and socialist; it did not demonstrate a link between feminism and socialism. At the Union's first public meeting, on 13 April 1880, Jules Guesde spoke and Rouzade presented a 'development' of the programme, in which she attempted to link women's demands to those of the working class. Workers had to free women, she said, because 'the root' of clericalism 'is in our ignorance'. So long as it persists, 'we will only be used . . . to reduce your salaries without earning enough to live ourselves'. This argument might have been persuasive if used in favour of admitting women to a trade union, but in the context of a political group it was unlikely to lead to support for women's rights, since it was the very fear of clericalism that led socialists and republicans in general to be reluctant to give women the vote. Rouzade did not pursue her argument to show how equal rights might help get women out of the hands of the priests. Instead she left such problems behind, taking flight in oratory: 'Thus we must all, men and women artisans, organise ourselves in a great family, the family of the proletariat', she concluded, leaving the inference open that women would organise with men on a basis of class solidarity without changing the relations between men and women until the advent of socialism. But when the Guesdists took this position explicitly, Rouzade recoiled in horror.[26]

That Guesde supported women's equality in the abstract was beyond doubt. Returning to France from exile after the 1876 workers' congress, he violently attacked its resolution that men should support women. If women must look to men for support, he argued, they would be in the same position toward men as workers toward their employers:

She [woman] will only exist conditionally, to the extent that pleases man — or what is worse yet — *to the extent that she pleases him* [italics orig.] . 'Prostitute or housewife!' . . . if . . . she must be a housewife, [if] she cannot subsist outside of the family, she will necessarily be a prostitute, what constitutes the latter being the subordination of sexual relations to considerations foreign to these relations themselves.

The idea that women should remain at home offended Guesde's sense of justice:

Why, by what right shut her in, pen her up in her sex, transformed, whether one wishes or not, into a profession, not to say a trade? Man too has functions which derive from his sex; he is husband and father, which does not prevent him from being . . . a worker . . . Why, by what right — howevermuch one wants her to be wife and mother — not to speak of the one who is neither — could not woman also appear in society in the form which suits her?

Moreover, these prejudices facilitated a 'super-exploitation' of women. Men, argued Guesde in terms close to Marxism (which was just beginning to be an influence upon him), were at least protected by the necessity to pay them enough to assure their survival or, from the capitalist's point of view, their continued ability to work. Even this slender guarantee, which male workers found 'in the very greed of capital', did not obtain for women, who were supposed to be nourished by their husbands and who, by virtue of this prejudice, could be paid lower wages perceived as a supplement to the family budget: 'Assured that the *woman* will maintain the *worker* [italics orig.] . . . industrial exploitation can have a free hand.' The answer? At this point in his development Guesde did not simply take refuge in the socialist future. He called for women's complete right to self-fulfilment on the social as well as the economic plane, in terms Auclert herself would have approved: 'To assure to woman as to man the full development and the free application of her faculties. To assure . . . to the worker, without sex distinction, the full product of his labour.'[27]

Guesde's articles of 1876 constituted the most sustained and coherent analysis of women's oppression ever produced by French socialists. Neither Rouzade, nor any of her successors, nor even Guesde himself in later years would ever equal it. As Guesde completed his conversion to Marxism in the years before 1880, it ceased to be a source of insights and became instead a sterile dogma, a simplistic economism of the sort which passed all too commonly for Marxism in the late nineteenth century. By 1880 Guesde had abandoned any vision of emancipation except the economic one. The 'full development' of women's faculties (as of men's) would follow only from their receiving 'the full product' of their labour. Since this could occur only under socialism, concluded Guesde, the struggle for women's rights had to be subordinated to that for socialism. From this perspective any effort to secure rights for women within capitalist society was at best futile and at worst distracting.

This was made explicit in the resolution on women's rights presented by the Guesdists to the founding congress of the UFC, held on 18 July 1880, in preparation for the congress of Le Havre. The resolution stated that the emancipation of women 'in the workshop' was 'dependent upon the emancipation of labour'; the emancipation of women 'in the family . . . upon the transformation of the individualistic family', by which the Guesdists meant only 'social guarantees' for children. While the resolution proclaimed the equality of the sexes, it declared 'that the question of women's rights . . . can

32

only be resolved with the question of labour by collective appropriation'. Not only did women's rights have to await the revolution, but also they were devalued: the resolution argued that the rights which women sought had not emancipated the proletariat.[28]

This was to become a stock argument, but it was scarcely relevant. The problem was precisely that the male proletariat did already enjoy the rights women were seeking. Logically, therefore, women could obtain them in capitalist society. Engels would argue that legal equality was necessary to expose the nature of the real oppression of women. But this position was beyond Guesde, who was already reduced to waiting for the revolution, an attitude he mistook for Marxism.

To the women the Guesdist resolution was tantamount to a denial of the rights voted at Marseilles. Both Le Droit des Femmes and L'Union were represented at the UFC congress: Le Droit by a man named Bal and by Kéva, who was still treasurer of the UFC; L'Union by Tinayre, Pierre, and of course Rouzade, whose profession was given as 'housewife—producer'.[29] They submitted a counter-proposal. It reaffirmed the complete equality envisaged at Marseilles: 'political, civil equality; equality of wages . . . of education; in short complete and immediate equality for both sexes'. It stated that these rights would be obtained 'legally', that is before the revolution. Here was the heart of the problem: from the Guesdist point of view, this was reformism, but from the women's point of view, to put off equal rights until after the revolution was to deny them.

More than a dozen delegates spoke on the two resolutions, including Kéva, Pierre, and Rouzade. The women's proposal passed by thirty-two votes to nineteen for the Guesdists'. Since the congress accepted all the other resolutions presented by the Guesdists, including their programme, this defeat indicates that they were out of line with the majority only on the specific question of women's rights. They were forced to reconsider their position on women's rights and ultimately to move nearer to the very reformist position they abhorred. The women's resolution at the 1880 UFC congress began the process by which all the currents of French socialism, even the Guesdists, came to include women's rights within their programmes of minimum demands. The next step in this process was taken at the collectivist congress of Le Havre in 1880.[30]

As we have seen, the congress split between the mutualists and the collectivists. Rouzade followed Mink to the collectivist congress, while Kéva and Le Droit des Femmes stayed with the mutualists. Rouzade supported Mink fully on collectivism; the rich, said Rouzade, should consider themselves lucky to be expropriated rather than hanged. Mink uttered similar sentiments. They disagreed, however, on the question of women's roles, particularly with regard to motherhood. Rouzade thought that the obligations of motherhood as defined in capitalist society constituted a fundamental link in the chain of women's oppression. The Union's mandate called for the 'collectivity' to assume the costs of raising children and had given Rouzade 'a special mission to develop this question at the congress'. The committee on 'instruction and education' passed a resolution in line with the Union's demands, but Mink defeated it on the floor of the congress, arguing that it did not mention the role of the individual mother. She countered with a proposal which insisted not only on 'instruction in common' to teach children 'equality and the practice of civic virtues', but also on the need for 'the wife-mother' to develop their 'affective faculties'. It called for 'civic instruction, complete and identical for all boys and girls . . . [to be] given by the collectivity', but specified that 'the first education must be left to the family' reimbursed by the state.[31]

However radical this may appear today, it represented a reaffirmation of women's traditional roles in comparison to Rouzade's proposal. It may seem strange that such an argument should come from Mink. After all, she had been a feminist in her earliest political activity. Her lectures on 'women's work' in 1868 had included a vigorous statement of the case for women's political rights. Moreover her personal life was scarcely a model of traditional roles, in contrast with Rouzade's and Tinayre's: after the barricades of the Commune, Mink had borne three illegitimate children while in exile. Anyone who could name an illegitimate child 'Lucifer Blanqui Vercingétorix Révolution Mink' would hardly qualify as a traditionalist.[32]

In fact, however, Mink's lack of concern for women's rights was typical of the Communard women; Tinayre's collaboration with the Union was exceptional. One may guess that the comradeship of the barricades seemed to transcend the differences between the sexes. In any case it is clear from her speech at Le Havre that Mink saw herself as a revolutionary, not as a woman. While Rouzade spoke of herself as a woman and used the first person plural when speaking of women's condition, Mink used the third person. It was only when she spoke of the barricades that she passed into the first person. The need she perceived was not to give women rights in present society but for them as mothers to create revolutionary men and as wives to support them at the barricades:

The Republic must be established in the family as in the society; woman must be independent, so that she is moral, so that she is the veritable companion of man, so that she says to him: 'March, march on, and if you die, I will avenge you or follow you.' ([Caught up in the military metaphor himself, the stenographer added:] Double salvo of applause. Tumult.)[33]

Rouzade was helpless in the face of such revolutionary rhetoric, coming as it did from one who had proved herself in action. Mink's revolutionary speech carried her not so revolutionary resolution. To be sure, to argue so long before the revolution over whether the family or the state should give children 'first education' was to put the cart before the horse. But this was not what was at issue. It is clear from the debates that the participants were arguing about the role of women as mothers, Mink putting the case for maintaining the traditional role, Rouzade suggesting that the burden should not rest exclusively on women. With Mink's defeat of Rouzade's position, the social movement arrived at a narrower definition of women's rights than that set out by Auclert at Marseilles.

Nevertheless, the congress of Le Havre did reaffirm women's rights. The Guesdists presented no opposition to a compromise resolution which forcefully proclaimed women's rights: 'woman must be man's equal and possess like him all her civil, political, and economic rights'. In exchange, the resolution conceded the Guesdists' point that these rights could not be obtained in capitalist society: 'it is impossible to hope that the unjust holders of social wealth will ever consent to grant [these rights]'. Only 'from the social Revolution' could women expect 'the consecration of equality between the sexes'. It is unlikely that this was satisfactory to the Union: aside from the unexpected phrasing 'consecration', which gave some hope of partial reforms before the revolution, the resolution still left women's rights to an uncertain future. In the last paragraph, however, the Guesdists arrived at a position which solved the problem for the women (and which incidentally was both more Marxist and closer to Guesde's 1876 articles). If they could not accept that women's rights were possible under capitalism, they could accept the need to push for them so as to attract women to the party:

Nevertheless, it is important that, in order to attain this end [the social Revolution], all socialists employ their activity to persuade women citizens of the need for them to join together to demand their emancipation, so that it may be shown that they intend to march side by side with men citizens in the claiming of their rights by revolution, peaceful if possible, violent if the bourgeoisie forces them to violence.

The resolution passed without a negative vote, although there were four 'motivated abstentions' and three recorded absences. Everyone was satisfied, the Guesdists because the resolution took a revolutionary line, the women of the Union because it reaffirmed the party's commitment to their emancipation.[34]

This commitment was not integrated into the party programme, however, even though the party did adopt a formal programme at Le Havre. It was the programme which the Guesdists had pushed through the UFC congress. It became known thereafter as the 'Programme of Le Havre'. It was the second Guesdist programme. The first, which Guesde had written while in prison early in 1879, did not contain a single word about women. The second, which Guesde had written during a trip to London in May 1880, with the help of Marx and Engels, and which became the Programme of Le Havre, demanded equal wages for women and, in the preamble (written by Marx), stated that 'the emancipation of the producing class is that of all human beings — without distinction of sex or of race'. The Union had obtained a commitment to women's rights. The next step was to get this commitment included in the party programme.[35]

The Union in action: women and the schism

Before the Union was able to obtain inclusion of its demands in the party programme, the general question of reform or revolution was resolved by a split in the party. This split was directly linked to the question of women's rights as a result of the activities of the Union in the party, and in particular Rouzade's candidature for the Paris Municipal Council.

By the end of 1880, Rouzade and Pierre were putting most of their energies into party activity, leaving the leadership of the Union to others: the new secretary was named Elise Roger; she was seconded by one Ismène Legall as assistant secretary.[36] The Union took its place alongside other constituent groups of the UFC. Eugénie Pierre represented the Union on the UFC federal committee. In April 1881, she was even nominated for committee secretary. Although she received only three of the twenty-six votes cast, this does suggest that she was accepted and taken seriously as a committee member.[37]

Rouzade too was becoming an established party leader. Having spoken frequently in Paris, she began making extensive tours of the provinces: in March 1881, she gave lectures in eight provincial cities in every corner of France. For this she was paid 60 francs; Chabert, the man who lectured with her, received 250. In May she lectured with Guesde at Lille and several nearby towns; in June again with Guesde at Rennes and other cities of the west. Given the state of transports at the time, this was quite a feat for the respectable wife of a no less respectable municipal accountant.[38]

Rouzade was also establishing herself in the party hierarchy. Writing occasional articles for *Le Prolétaire*, she was elected to its editorial committee in October 1881. At the same time, the formation of a national committee of the party was being discussed. The Union insisted that it include a woman and proposed Rouzade. At the party congress of Reims, 30 October to 6 November 1881, she was elected to the newly formed national committee and to the sub-committee named to write its manifesto, even though she did not attend the congress. In December, she was joined on the national committee by another woman from the Union, Floret Pignon. The Union had thus obtained significant representation for women at every level of the party hierarchy.[39]

In December 1881, the Union took another step forward: through its initiative, the party nominated Rouzade as candidate for the Paris Municipal Council, thus making her the first Frenchwoman to stand for elected office as a candidate of a regular political party.[40] This battle marked the high point of the Union's activities, because the tensions which ensued strained

The Union in action

relations among the different factions of the party and ultimately led in part
to the schism in the party and the decline of the Union. The possibility of 'a
feminine candidature' in the 1881 municipal elections had been raised at the
congress of Le Havre by two men: Chabert, Rouzade's friend and lecture
companion; and Roblet, delegate of the Cercle d'Etudes Sociales du 12e
Arrondissement ('Circle of Social Studies of the Twelfth District [of Paris]').
The Circle had mandated Roblet 'to demand woman's civil, civic, and economic emancipation'. But Roblet, something of an anarchist, suggested that a
'feminine candidature' would not only advance this cause, but would also
prove 'that parliamentary government will not achieve anything worthwhile':
the bourgeoisie would deny the candidate her seat after she won the election
(he assumed she would win) and this would show that democracy was an
illusion.[41]

Although the Union did not share Roblet's anti-parliamentary aims, it
certainly supported his idea. After the congress, it asked the UFC to endorse
women candidates 'in the arrondissements where they would not prejudice
the success of the Party'. The UFC took the easy way out. It declared that
such candidatures were not contrary to the party's principles, but that it was
up to each local group to decide for itself if it would nominate a woman.
The Guesdists opposed even this timid position. There was no love lost
between them and the Union after the 1880 UFC congress. The Union in
general and Rouzade in particular were becoming increasingly identified with
the reformists led by Paul Brousse, with whom the Guesdists were virtually
at war for control of the party: *Le Prolétaire*, to which Rouzade was closely
linked, was officially the newspaper for all the party but in reality was
dominated by the reformists. (One wonders how Rouzade and Guesde got
along during their long train rides on the way to lecture together.) Worse, the
idea of feminine candidatures had originated with a reformist (Chabert) and
an anarchist (Roblet). Emile Massard, one of Guesde's original comrades,
wrote in their newspaper that the idea of women candidates was one of
many 'eccentricities' for which the Guesdists could not be held responsible.
There were, he explained, 'madmen and grotesques everywhere'. Women
candidates would at best be 'ineffective' and at worst expose the party to
ridicule. Ismène Legall, the Union's assistant secretary, replied on its behalf,
reminding Massard of the moderation which the group had showed. The
Guesdist paper did not print the reply.[42]

Meanwhile, the Circle contacted Rouzade with a view to her being its
candidate in the municipal elections of January 1881, but failed to follow
up her positive reply. In August, the Union wrote to the Circle seeking an
explanation for its loss of nerve and offering to share the costs of any campaign. Having received no answer, Roger, the Union's secretary, published
the letter in *Le Prolétaire*. Perhaps this stung the Circle into action, for on
the first occasion thereafter it made good its promise. In November a seat on

the Paris Municipal Council fell vacant in the twelfth arrondissement. The
Circle now offered to support Rouzade as candidate for this seat and she
accepted.[43]

The election was to be held on 11 December 1881. Five days before,
Roblet introduced Rouzade at an election meeting of 650 men.[44] It was a
disaster. Roblet began by placing Rouzade's candidature squarely within the
framework of his own anti-parliamentary ideas. Denying any value to political action, he warned the audience that the time had come for drastic
measures: 'We, workers, we do not see any other possible solution except to
seize what belongs to us to prevent the bourgeois from speculating any
longer on our muscular and intellectual strength.' Without transition from
this statement, hardly calculated to induce the predominantly bourgeois
audience to vote for Rouzade, Roblet went on to present 'the candidate
chosen by the socialist group. This candidature', he added, 'is a step towards
the equality of the sexes.'

Rouzade mounted to the rostrum. 'Everyone's turn to laugh and make
more or less grotesque innuendoes', noted the police agent. Rouzade
managed to speak six sentences for women's equality with men, reminding
the audience that thirty years earlier (she meant before the 1848 revolution
had introduced universal suffrage) they had had no more rights than she.
After all, she went on, women created men. Then the interruptions began.
The police agent shyly recorded the less vulgar ones, such as 'Go knit your
stockings.' Someone called out, 'The joke's lasted too long. Get on with
your programme.' This she did, but she chose the aspect of the programme
least likely to be acceptable to such an audience, for it struck at their most
basic conception of themselves as fathers: she returned to the ideas of the
family and society which she had not even managed to get through her own
party at Le Havre. ' "We want", she takes up again [still the police agent's
account] , "society to take responsibility for children". A voice: "You'd
have too many!" ' Exasperated, Rouzade abandoned the podium, telling the
audience that they did not deserve the liberty they enjoyed. Roblet added
that the 'bourgeois' refused to listen because Rouzade had 'too many truths
to tell'. After their departure, the meeting settled down and the 'incident'
was forgotten.[45]

With workers of the neighbourhood, Rouzade was more successful. On 9
December, two nights after the disastrous meeting, the Comité Electoral
Socialiste du 12e Arrondissement ('Socialist Electoral Committee of the
Twelfth Arrondissement' — the Circle under another hat) sponsored an open
meeting to support her. Over 1000 persons attended, including some 200
women. Rouzade spoke on the need for the municipal council to control
rents, to prevent land speculation in areas where it carried out improvements,
and to support children and elderly persons. She was frequently interrupted
by applause and 'warmly acclaimed' at the end of the meeting.[46]

The same day, Rouzade later recalled, a few 'good libertarians' (presumably Roblet and his friends) put up posters of her campaign statement, which was published in *Le Prolétaire* the next day. It was signed by seven women of the Union. It called for an alliance between women and proletarians, the 'last outcasts of modern society'. Both were 'oppressed . . . exploited. They will work effectively toward their common emancipation only if they march together against the ruling class.' The statement accepted the Guesdist position that 'to seek emancipation in present-day society . . . would be to delude oneself' and that 'only by the advent of socialism' could women achieve their full rights. But having made this concession to the Guesdists, the Union warned them that they could not make the revolution in opposition to women and concluded with a plea: 'Help us to bring our sisters to understand that they should come to socialism as to a new liberating religion and, to do that, defend our rights as we defend yours.'[47]

The Guesdists did not heed this plea. They had both a weekly and a daily newspaper at their disposal, but neither printed the statement, although Rouzade sent a copy to Guesde four days before the election. The Broussists, on the other hand, did print it in *Le Prolétaire*. Moreover, on 10 December (the day before the election), *Le Prolétaire* published a front-page article by Brousse supporting Rouzade and arguing that her candidature showed that the proletariat would be a faithful ally of women and would not betray them as the bourgeoisie had betrayed the proletariat. The wording suggests that he was answering the arguments Auclert had made at the congress of Marseilles. He detailed the extent of women's oppression by the law and warmly praised 'our eloquent lecturer'.[48]

These efforts did not suffice to obtain the victory which Roblet had assumed was certain. Brousse, more realistic, said that the campaign was symbolic. Rouzade received 57 of 1122 votes cast; the winning candidate received 631. However, as both Brousse's *Le Prolétaire* and Auclert's *La Citoyenne* noted, this was significantly better than the workers' candidates had done in previous elections in the same district (sixteen votes in 1878, ten in January 1881). Moreover, despite Rouzade's being ineligible (as a woman), her votes were counted by officials, recorded as results of the election, and printed by the newspapers of record. Women were even permitted to witness the counting of the votes. They seemed to have taken a major step toward citizenship. *Le Prolétaire* concluded: 'The question of women's emancipation has been raised; — the party has increased its votes, — women have taken part in the electoral battle . . . We have no reason to complain about the result.'[49]

The Guesdists struck the only sour note. Rouzade castigated them for not printing her campaign statement and ridiculed Guesde's excuse that the printer had mislaid it (four days in a row). They answered her, strangely enough, with a note by Henri Brissac opposing not only women's candidatures but even women's suffrage, on the grounds that women would be subject to anti-republican influence from the clergy. In a misguided attempt to soften the blow, he added, 'If everyone thought — as I do — that women should be eligible [to stand for elected office], and if they were so eligible by law [this from a self-styled revolutionary], I, for my part, would support the candidature of Mme Léonie Rouzade, because of her ideas, her courage, and her talent.' This support meant little, for he himself had just invoked these 'ifs' against women's candidatures. Rouzade replied the same day in a furious letter to Guesde. Her candidature, she said, had been 'uniquely posed as a class candidature'. 'The men who seek to monopolise the control of the worker Party', she added, were forgetting that 'a class candidature lies neither in pants, nor in skirts.' Moreover, in proportion to the votes cast, her candidature had been just as successful in three days of campaigning as Guesde's far more elaborate one.[50]

All this occurred in the context of an increasingly venomous dispute between the Broussists and the Guesdists. The issue at base was reform or revolution: whether to seek improvements in the present society, as the Broussists tried to do, or whether to prepare the revolution, as the Guesdists thought they were doing. Women's rights would become a focal point for this dispute, but during 1881 the focal point was the Programme of Le Havre. At the congress of Reims, in November 1881, it had been the only subject of dispute, because it was the symbol of the adoption of the revolutionary line (as the Guesdists saw it) over the reformist line. The Broussists blamed the programme for the disastrous results the party had suffered in the municipal and legislative elections of 1881. Although the Broussists had the votes to defeat the Guesdists, they did not wish to provoke a schism by scrapping the programme. They passed a resolution maintaining it until the next congress, but expressing serious reservations about it. Shortly after the congress of Reims, Jules Joffrin, a Broussist, became a candidate in a legislative by-election to be held in Paris on 18 December 1881, one week after Rouzade's effort. The Guesdists denounced Joffrin for diluting the programme and withheld their support from him. He in turn castigated the Guesdists for their failure to support Rouzade the week before, even though she had 'fought under the banner of the minimum programme [the Programme of Le Havre]'. The programme was only a pretext, he went on; in reality Guesde opposed him and Rouzade because they were not part of his 'clique'. There was some truth in this observation.[51]

In mid January 1882, the UFC voted to expel Guesde's faction for failure to follow party decisions in not supporting Rouzade and Joffrin. Not surprisingly, the Union voted with the Broussist majority. Rouzade announced that she would not speak at any meetings in which the Guesdist 'men' participated. Thus was prepared the showdown which occurred the following autumn at the congress of Saint-Etienne. The Broussist majority (with the support of the Union's delegate, Claudine Gillier)[52] denied all the Guesdists' procedural motions. The Guesdists walked out. The Broussists reconstituted themselves as the Fédération des Travailleurs Socialistes de France ('Federation of Socialist Workers of France' FTSF) and voted to expel the Guesdists, citing among other factors their violation of party decisions 'in attacking feminine candidatures'. The Guesdists retreated to the nearby city of Roanne, where they founded the Parti Ouvrier (later called the Parti Ouvrier Français ['French Worker Party'], POF). The Guesdists voted to expel Brousse from their new party: he had violated party principles by advocating 'sex struggle' instead of class struggle.[53]

Thus was established the fundamental schism of French socialism, which was to last until 1905, only to give way in 1920 to another schism, that between socialists and communists, which was not without resemblance to the earlier one. The question of women's rights provided a focal point for the fundamental disagreement which led to the schism. In their attitudes toward Rouzade's candidature, to which both sides referred explicitly, they expressed not only their feelings about women's rights but also their disagreement about method and reform in general.[54]

Decline of the Union

After the expulsion of the Guesdists from the UFC, in January 1882, Rouzade remained close to Brousse and to Malon, the leading reformist theoretician. In February they nominated her to make a lecture tour in the Lyons region on behalf of the party. But at its 12 March meeting the national committee took note of a letter from Rouzade indicating that she could not make the tour. This apparently coincided with her departure from the committee itself: thereafter she was no longer listed among its members. She continued, however, to write for *Le Prolétaire* during most of 1882. In a lead article in March she denounced the idea of 'fatherland' as a chimera which inspired proletarians to die in defence of their exploiters. In August she wrote a laudatory review of Malon's latest book (which included a favourable chapter on the Union and her campaign). She also continued to give lectures. At Lille in May, she and a male leader spoke before a reported 3500 persons.[55]

Despite these activities, which in any case tapered off during 1882, she was turning away from the Union and from the party. Perhaps the Guesdists had wounded her more than she cared to say. Certainly the cares and struggles of day-to-day politics were a sorry contrast to the utopian worlds she had created in her peaceful study in Meudon. In this connection it is worth recalling that she never noticed the Commune: when revolution was occurring on her doorstep, she was writing metaphysics. Indeed, one of the novels she published in 1872 could be read as a condemnation of the Commune. It was called *Le Roi Johanne*. Johanne was not a king, but a drunkard who dreamt of being king. Upon awakening from his stupor, he was thrown into jail. It is only fair to add that most of the novel is about his dream, which portrays Rouzade's utopia once again. Still, there were more flattering ways to get to utopia than through a drunkard's visions. One cannot help suspecting that Rouzade felt uneasy about mass action, even as a path to her utopia, and wondering if her rhetorical flair had not carried her beyond her own intentions and far beyond what was comfortable for the wife of a municipal accountant.

After a period of silence and inactivity, Rouzade appeared in print in 1885 with an article which sidestepped any idea of a struggle: she argued that socialism was inevitable because 'it is the search for the best way to live in a society'. She still used the word revolution, but seemed to mean by it something quite different from what she and Mink had meant at Le Havre. By 1887 she denied that there was any need at all for revolution.

When the sacrificed people are guided by reason and united by solidarity, they — who are the immense majority — will have neither to struggle nor to crush anyone to make way for well-being, justice, and right. They will only have to say: we found such a new social order, and the new society will be made according to their will . . . they have only to wish with the same will.

She participated in a feminist electoral campaign in 1885, but it was such a disaster that thereafter she avoided politics altogether, except for attending occasional feminist congresses. She wrote two more pamphlets in the 1890s. One was in the metaphysical style of her 1871 pamphlets. The other, a 'Little catechism of lay and socialist morals', was successful enough to induce her to print at least five editions between 1895 and 1906. It was a charming piece which set out in straightforward language the case for collective ownership of the means of production. The socialist parties could have made good use of it. In fact, however, Rouzade died in October 1916 without making any further contribution to the socialist parties after her work with the Union.[56]

Pierre and Tinayre also turned away from the Union and the party. In 1881 Pierre married a pacifist historian named Edmond Potonié. He seems to have been cool toward political activism. Eugénie Potonié-Pierre (as she henceforth called herself) ceased to participate in the federal committee of the UFC after her unsuccessful candidacy for secretary in April. She was not involved in Rouzade's campaign. From her experience in the Union and her contact with Rouzade, however, she retained a sense of social concern and a taste for utopian visions: she and her husband later contributed still another utopian novel to the piles.

Marguerite Tinayre was also putting her energies into novels. Between 1881 and 1883, she collaborated with Louise Michel, the heroine of the Commune, who had already become a symbol of revolution and anarchism. Out of their collaboration came two long, sentimental novels. Like Tinayre's first novel, these were stories about the plight of innocent victims of urbanism and industry, full of starving children, wronged women, and exhausted workingmen, plus a handful of villainous capitalists. Yet despite her participation in the Commune, Tinayre was anything but a revolutionary. A Protestant schoolmistress, she was republican and anti-clerical. This had sufficed to bring her to support the Commune and to accept from it a position as district school inspector, in which she distinguished herself by trying to bring the nuns to heel, but it did not suffice to make her a socialist once socialism came to mean an organised political party aiming to put the means of production in the hands of workers. In 1883 Louise Michel and Tinayre broke off their collaboration. Michel accused Tinayre of hoping for 'ameliorations of the old social edifice' rather than seeking to demolish it. But by this time Tinayre, like Pierre, had long since ceased to work for the Union.[57]

What did Rouzade, Pierre, and Tinayre have in common which might explain their turning away from the Union and from the party? They all came from relatively well-to-do families and established petit bourgeois to bourgeois lives. Tinayre, like Auclert, inherited a modest fortune, though she lost it after the Commune. Rouzade and Pierre married into comfortable circumstances. Only Rouzade (and she briefly) had experienced the life of a worker, though Tinayre had known hardship as a teacher and governess in exile. They had sympathy for the dispossessed, but they were not of them. Their novels reflect sorrow, not anger; dreams, not action. Indeed, it is significant that all three wrote or would write utopian novels. Not only did their utopianism reflect a distaste for the mechanics of politics which are part and parcel of social change, but also their socialism was limited to their utopian vision. It did not extend to taking sides in class conflict.

All of them shared the republican vision inherited from the 1848 revolution, a vision which is often ascribed to the petit bourgeois, the shopkeepers and tradesmen, even the schoolteachers, who were deprived of the vote under the July monarchy's restriction of the suffrage to the wealthy and were thus staunch republicans and anti-clericals, but who were also close enough to the working classes to sympathise with them, without wishing to take their side in conflict.[58] This vision was shattered in June 1848, when the new republican government dismantled its public works programme and crushed the resulting insurrection, but it was restored by two decades of common opposition to the Empire, which lumped all republicans together under the name they began to take from 1849 on, 'democratic-socialists'.

Rouzade, Pierre, and Tinayre all came to socialism with this vision and left it when they were forced to perceive it as a party taking one side in a class conflict. They all came to the socialist movement after the beginning of 1879 and left what had become socialist parties before 1883, when the traditional republican ideal was breaking down as republicans governed without social concern and socialists created parties seeking to represent the interests of the working classes against the bourgeoisie, now perceived as controlling the republican government. Returning from exile or coming out from their studies and schoolrooms, such women could hardly see the direction the movement was taking; indeed, it hardly knew itself (hence the intra-party disputes we have discussed). When they saw where it was going, they left it. To do them justice it should be noted that they left gracefully. They all remained sympathetic to the spirit of socialism, if not to the parties which sought to embody it, and they all remained staunch anti-clericals and republicans.

They also remained staunch supporters of women's rights. Indeed, they all became feminists. Their feminism did not stem from a direct experience of oppression as women in the family. They all had sympathetic parents who gave them freedom as well as private incomes and they all found husbands who shared their concerns and allowed, even encouraged them to express them in writing and action. Of the three, only Tinayre had children to look after (she had five) and she did not begin her political and literary careers until they were past infancy and an inheritance enabled her to obtain domestic help. All three were feminists precisely because they were free enough to chafe at the oppression they experienced under law, to desire to be citizens. All this they shared with Auclert, who might be taken as a somewhat more clear-cut case of the same tendencies. The title of Auclert's newspaper, *La Citoyenne* ('The [Woman] Citizen'), reflected their most fundamental concern.

They left the Union to a new generation of leaders, about whom we know little, mainly because they accomplished little. Floret Pignon remained on the national committee when Rouzade left it. In May 1882, Elise Roger, the Union's delegate to the federal committee of the UFC, was unanimously elected assistant secretary of the UFC. She was also the Union's delegate to the UFC congresses of 1882 and the national congress of Paris in 1883. In the autumn of 1882, she was elected by a wide margin to the national committee, on which she served two years, apparently without contributing much. The Union delegated three women to the UFC congress of 1883, where they read a report demanding 'the socialisation of international commerce', and two to that of 1884, where they said nothing. The Union, in short, made little progress under its second generation of leaders: women's rights in the FTSF remained at the point Rouzade had left them and the Union made no progress in enlarging its narrow base.[59]

The Union's association with the party came to an abrupt end in September 1884, after a dispute of unspecified nature between Elise Roger and the party newspaper (now *Le Prolétariat*). At the 2 September meeting of the national committee, Roger asked for and obtained the nomination of a committee to arbitrate the dispute, after a lengthy debate in which fourteen delegates spoke. The following week, the committee had not yet met, but Joffrin resigned from it because Roger would not answer his questions. Brousse spoke against the UFC's interfering in the newspaper's affairs. The arbitration committee was thereupon disbanded. A week later the Union des Femmes resigned from the UFC and thus from the party. For all practical purposes, it ceased to exist. There is no further trace of it.[60]

Women's rights and party programmes

There is considerable irony in the fact that the Union's efforts bore fruit only after it had severed its links with the socialist parties. Both the Guesdists and the Broussists agreed to include women's rights in their party programmes as soon as the Union had left their parties. The Guesdists incorporated women's rights into their programme at the breakaway congress of Roanne in 1882, after they had left the Broussist congress where the Union's delegate remained. The Programme of Le Havre called for the 'suppression ... of all the articles of the Code establishing the inferiority of workers vis-à-vis employers'. To this the congress of Roanne added the phrase, 'and of women vis-à-vis men'. Thus the compromise position taken in the resolution on women's rights passed at Le Havre in 1880 was integrated into the POF programme.[61]

Since the debates of this hastily organised congress were not recorded, not even by the police, we do not know who was responsible for this addition. It is clear, however, that it came as a result of the demands which the Union had made on the party in the past. From the UFC congress of 1880 through the congress of Le Havre, the Union had forced the Guesdists to backtrack from their simplistic stance of revolution or nothing and to support at least in principle women's rights as a demand to be made of the present society. The inclusion of women's rights as a demand in the party programme was only the final step in a process the Union had carried on from Auclert's beginning, although this final step probably owed something to the arrival in France of Marx's son-in-law, Paul Lafargue, whose role we will consider in the next chapter. The Programme of Le Havre as amended at Roanne became not only the definitive programme of the POF for the remainder of its existence, but also the basis for the programmes of most other French socialist parties.

The Broussists had scrapped the Programme of Le Havre at Saint-Etienne in 1882, following the departure of the Guesdists, and had replaced it with a preamble to which each electoral district was to add its own programme. In practice, many of these programmes borrowed parts of the Programme of Le Havre. At the UFC congress held in the spring of 1885, less than a year after the departure of the Union, the Broussists finally passed a legislative programme and included women's rights. In words similar to those the Guesdists had used, the programme called for 'revision to make them more egalitarian of the articles of the Code which establish the political or civil inferiority of workers, of women, and of illegitimate children' and for 'equal pay for equal work'. In the municipal programme passed at the same congress, they called more specifically for 'civil and political equality for women'. These provisions were incorporated into the corresponding national programmes at the first subsequent national congress, which was held in 1887.[62]

The programme meant less to the Broussists than to the Guesdists, for the Broussists were pragmatic reformists whose programme was only window dressing. Nevertheless it was a fact of some importance that by 1885 the two major socialist parties had both made equality for women one of the minimum demands in their programme. Yet one cannot help noticing the oblique and negative wording used and the inclusion of women's rights alongside those of workers rather than as an independent demand. Women's rights were in the programmes of both parties, but they were presented grudgingly, in a way which contrasted dramatically with Auclert's generous formulation at Marseilles in 1879 and even with the forceful statement for formal rights passed at Le Havre in 1880.

The Broussists were more favourable to women's rights than the Guesdists in the period from 1880 to 1882. In the longer range, however, the situation was more complex. The Broussists' reformism made it easy for them to support women's rights: equality between the sexes was just one of the many reforms they sought to realise. Yet after Rouzade's campaign in 1881 they showed no more support for women's rights than the Guesdists. In 1884 Joffrin and Brousse made no effort at all to placate Roger and thus keep the Union in the party. Indeed, they virtually sabotaged the arbitration committee. Malon was much more reserved about women's rights in his last works than in 1882. As the gulf widened between them and the Guesdists, they became more republican and thus more wary of women's suffrage for fear of the clerical influence.[63]

On the other hand, the Guesdists' concern with doctrine vastly complicated their support for women's rights. Guesde was determined to avoid the illusion that significant reforms could be obtained within capitalist society. He thus ruled out all reforms, including those concerning women's rights. Naturally, the Union — and Rouzade in particular — were repulsed by this and confirmed in their support for the Broussists' reformism, which in any case corresponded better to their vision than Guesdism. But by joining with the Broussists, they became enemies of the Guesdists as the party split. This enmity made the Guesdists all the less likely to support the Union, particularly on such anarchist—reformist ventures as Rouzade's candidature. Ironically, as we shall see in the next chapter, a clear understanding of Marx and

Engels's positions would have led them closer to the Union. But such an understanding was rare.

For both parties, the demise of the Union meant the end of practical concern for women's rights. But even before its demise, the Union had ceased to be an effective group. Its narrowness and lack of rank-and-file base were the real causes of its demise, not the dispute with the party. It was only a handful of dynamic leaders who hardly even sought followers. They were more interested in passing resolutions and in influencing the party than in recruiting women. Recruitment seems to have been foreign to their political vision. We know what the Union wished to do vis-à-vis the party but not vis-à-vis women. It did not announce its meetings in the socialist press. A woman wishing to join would have had to make an effort to find the group. The result was that it had money but few members. On at least four occasions it gave from 5 to 40 francs to strike and campaign funds: others were giving in centimes. Roughly a dozen women are known to us as leaders of the Union over the five years of its existence. We do not know how many members they represented, but there is no indication of any significant membership base.[64]

The Union played a key role in the setting of French socialist doctrine on women, but it was never more than a precursor. It left no traces in terms of organisational framework and none of the militants of either the Union or Le Droit des Femmes returned to act subsequently in any socialist party. The near disintegration of the Broussist FTSF after 1890 completed the effacement of the Union in socialist memories. Others had to start anew. They did have, however, a firm theoretical commitment on which to build and this commitment was expressed not only in past resolutions but also, if less strongly, in party programmes which were constantly referred to. This was the lasting contribution of Le Droit des Femmes and L'Union des Femmes.

2. Socialist parties in search of women 1882 – 99

The schism of 1882 inaugurated an era of sectarian competition between the Broussists and the Guesdists, competition so intense that the French embarrassed international socialism by holding rival congresses to found the Second International at Paris in 1889. At the same time, still more socialist parties were emerging. In 1889, the Comité Révolutionnaire Central (CRC) came under the leadership of Edouard Vaillant and began to emerge as a socialist party in its own right. In 1890, the Broussist FTSF split in two, leading to the creation of Jean Allemane's Parti Ouvrier Socialiste Révolutionnaire (POSR). Finally, during the 1890s, the socialists who considered themselves 'independent' of the organised parties became an important current and began to form their own party, under the inspiration of Jean Jaurès.[1]

The sectarianism of the 1880s nevertheless prepared the basis for socialist success. In the first place, the sectarian parties clearly distinguished socialism from republicanism, even radical republicanism, by virtue of their distinct organisation, working-class orientation, and insistence on public ownership of the means of production. In the second place, the socialist sects organised at the local level, trained militants and diffused propaganda. These pure and untainted little parties had the advantages of faith and enthusiasm. They spread the socialist message throughout the country, which paid off in the 1890s.

The industrialisation of France, in full swing since the Second Empire, was gradually swelling the ranks of propertyless workers who could find a more relevant approach to their problems in socialist analysis than in that of the radical republicans. More important, however, were the political circumstances which brought the socialists to the fore as spokesmen not only for these workers, but also for all those who believed that the republicans in government had not fulfilled their stated aims. France had enjoyed nominally republican government since 1870 and really republican government since 1876–9, when the republicans had successively wrested the Chamber of Deputies, the Senate, and the presidency from the monarchists. Yet the working classes appeared to be left out of the relative prosperity of the period. Even on the political level, such traditional republican demands as the suppression of the Senate and the separation of church and state seemed to have been forgotten by the republicans in power. Discovery of venality not just among deputies but even on the part of the family of the president of the republic led to further disillusionment. Such republican failures contributed to the mass movement against the republic headed by General Boulanger in the late 1880s. Boulangism collapsed in 1889, when the General lost his nerve for a *coup d'état*, but the frustrations to which he had given vent continued. The bankruptcy of the Panama Company in 1889 led to the discovery of shady dealing between its directors and many republican politicians who had been bribed to help the company or to cover up the scandal. Some of the ensuing dissatisfaction found expression in socialism. In the legislative elections of 1893, the various socialist parties increased their representation from fourteen to thirty-nine deputies. By 1902 there were fifty-one socialist deputies in all.[2]

All the parties except the Vaillantist CRC shared a common inheritance going back to the worker congresses of the 1870s, including the resolutions in favour of women's rights. In the years from the schism to the end of the century, as the parties developed from small sects to real political organisations, there were efforts in various parties to give practical support to women's rights and to attract women into the parties. These two aims were rarely distinguished.[3]

Not all the parties shared the same concern for women. The Vaillantist CRC never considered the question. The CRC was founded by the followers of Auguste Blanqui upon his death in 1881. Its very name suggested its original aim: a 'central revolutionary committee' to carry on the revolutionary tradition incarnated in Blanqui. In 1889, however, under the leadership of the Communard Edouard Vaillant, the CRC moved toward becoming in effect a socialist political party and the traditional Blanquists broke away. In 1898 it changed its name to Parti Socialiste Révolutionnaire (PSR). Nevertheless, the CRC was always distinguished from the other parties by its perceived connection with the revolutionary tradition and with the Commune. It never did hold congresses or have such open proceedings as the other parties, which rendered it inhospitable to women interested in women's rights. Despite the involvement of Paule Mink after 1893, the CRC does not seem ever to have taken a stand on women's rights, still less to have sought to attract women.[4]

Similarly, the Broussist FTSF found nothing to replace L'Union des Femmes. Indeed, although women's rights remained part of its programme, the FTSF became increasingly cool toward women's suffrage. By the 1890s, Malon, who passed for the party's theoretician, had arrived at a bizarre analysis of the history of the family which justified delaying women's emancipation. Drawing on Paul Lafargue's vulgarisations of Engels's work and on the conservative anthropologist Charles Letourneau, Malon argued that women had once dominated men in 'matriarchal' societies and as a result were now particularly susceptible to Catholicism, because the cult of the Virgin Mary satisfied their nostalgia for their lost supremacy. This 'scientific' explanation justified caution in giving women the suffrage. Indeed, the position of the 'Worker Group' in the Chamber, which was close to Brousse and Malon, was 'progressive emancipation of women' – not a word on the suffrage. If the Broussists, like the Vaillantists, avoided the woman question, other parties found themselves confronting it directly in practice.[5]

The Allemanists

By the 1890s, however, the FTSF was a spent force. As the Broussists became increasingly oriented toward municipal and parliamentary reform, they were hard put to distinguish themselves from the radical republicans who called for many of the same reforms. One faction of the FTSF rebelled against the party's reformism and emphasised instead its working-class base. This faction was led by Jean Allemane, a printer and former leader of the Commune. He insisted upon the direct action of the working classes rather than political activity. His party would support the idea of the general strike as opposed to political action. It aimed at 'the mine for the miners' rather than at a centralised economy.

During the 1880s, Allemane's supporters came to dominate the Paris region federation (the UFC), while the national body, the FTSF, remained under Brousse's control, which led to frequent clashes between the two. The situation was further complicated by the fact that the UFC was a stronger and more vigorous organisation than the FTSF to which it was nominally subordinate. Indeed, the UFC accounted for more membership in the FTSF than all other member federations together. In 1890 the disagreements came to a head. The FTSF excluded Allemane. His supporters left with him, taking the whole of the UFC and leaving Brousse the FTSF, now a hollow shell which disintegrated during the 1890s. The Allemanists founded the Parti Ouvrier Socialiste Révolutionnaire (POSR), which continued the vitality and the working-class emphasis of the UFC.[6]

Of all the socialist groups at this time, the Allemanists were the only one in which feminists as such participated. This was true both of the UFC in the 1880s and of the POSR in the 1890s. This feminist participation was un-doubtedly a result in part of the real concern which Allemane sometimes demonstrated for women's rights. But it seems reasonable to suggest that in any case feminists preferred the Allemanists to the more hard-line parties. The Allemanists' emphasis on the local action of workers could seem a version of self-help, consonant with the charities which the feminists were used to supporting, and it certainly seemed less threatening than the Vaillantists' revolutionary traditions or the Guesdists' insistence on political

action to expropriate the owners of the means of production, with whom so
many feminists identified.

Two feminists were active in the UFC in the late 1880s, when it was
already 'Allemanist', though technically still a part of Brousse's FTSF: Marie
Bonnevial and Astié de Valsayre. Marie Bonnevial was a pioneer of many
causes from free thought to feminism. A primary-school teacher at Lyons in
the 1870s, she was one of the founders of the Syndicat des Membres de
l'Enseignement (teachers' union), which organised lay teachers in private
schools, including independent municipal schools. As a major figure in this
union, she was delegated to be a member of the organising committee for an
international worker congress planned by the Lyons worker congress of 1878
for September of that year but prohibited by the government. The members
of the organising committee were prosecuted for 'unauthorised association'.
Guesde, the star of the committee, organised a common defence: a powerful
political attack on the capitalist state. His speech, later printed as a brochure,
gained much notoriety for socialism. But Bonnevial dissociated herself from
Guesde's defence and presented her case on legal grounds. She was acquitted,
while Guesde and the others were sentenced to six months in prison. Having
moved to Paris, she was a delegate of the teachers' union to the 1886 UFC
congress. At the following UFC congress, she was joined by a more flam-
boyant feminist.[7]

Marie-Rose Astié de Valsayre was best known for having challenged an
Englishwoman to a duel on the site of the battle of Waterloo: she wounded
her adversary. Her patriotic poem 'The Exile's Return', dealt with the return
of a Parisian soldier captured at Sedan without even mentioning the Commune, which, after all, had been largely a patriotic uprising against a government which had concluded peace instead of calling on the masses to continue the war. She came late to feminism. In 1882 she wrote a scurrilous
pamphlet, 'The amazons of the century (Gambetta's loud-mouths [*Gueulardes*])', which vilified a number of feminists, including Auclert, Pierre, and
Rouzade. But a year later, in May 1883, she was refused permission to teach
a free course in grammar for women. Perhaps this turned her toward the
feminists. In any event, they forgave her for her pamphlet and in 1885 she
began writing for Auclert's *La Citoyenne*.[8]

She attended the 1887 UFC congress as a delegate of Auclert's group, Le
Droit et le Suffrage des Femmes. Apparently no one recalled that Le Droit
had been excluded in 1880. Bonnevial was again a delegate of the teachers'
union. She was named chairwoman of the committee on women's work.
According to Astié, they wrote its resolution together. Whatever their
respective roles, it was a hard-hitting statement in favour of equal rights
which called upon the party to militate in favour of equal pay for equal
work. It passed unanimously.[9]

Bonnevial and Astié were again delegated by their respective groups to the next UFC congress, in 1888. This time, Allemane apparently remembered that Le Droit had been excluded. He expressed reservations about its admission and the case was sent to committee, where a compromise was worked out: Astié represented Auclert's newspaper, *La Citoyenne*, instead of her group. Astié sat on a committee which prepared a resolution on women's work calling for the suppression of convent and prison work and for an eight-hour day for women. She also made a strong speech demanding the re-organisation of the Syndicat des Dames (ladies' union), which was an ineffective women's auxiliary of the Bourse du Travail (the labour exchange, the heart of the trade-union movement in Paris). It was time, she concluded, for the party to prove by effective action 'its sympathies for the feminine cause'. The congress gladly passed the resolution which Astié presented (she gave credit to Eugénie Potonié-Pierre for help in drafting it), but it was a long way from resolutions to effective action.[10]

Following the congress, Astié obtained the nomination of a committee to reorganise the Syndicat des Dames. It included herself, Allemane, Chabert, and a figure from the past — Léonie Rouzade. The four of them met at the Bourse du Travail on 15 November, but they were unable to agree on a single concrete measure. This failure seems to have marked a reduction in socialist activity for both Bonnevial and Astié.[11]

Bonnevial devoted herself henceforth to the syndical movement and to feminism. She was a leading figure in the federation of Bourses du Travail from its founding in 1892; already active in the Ligue Française pour le Droit des Femmes, she became its vice-president in 1894 (and would be president from 1904 until her death in 1918). Astié did attend the Broussist—Allemanist international congress in 1889, but she was already striking out on her own. During the winter of 1889—90, she founded a Ligue de l'Affranchissement des Femmes ('League for Women's Emancipation'). She and two other women represented the League at the UFC congresses of 1890—1, which passed a resolution calling for the admission of women to the committee of the Bourse du Travail, but by this time she was turning away from both feminism and socialism.[12]

By 1891, she had ceased to write for *La Citoyenne* and embarked on a new career as secretary of the Patronage des Jeunes Filles du 6e Arrondissement ('Young Ladies' Club of the Sixth District'). The word *patronage* denoted a charitable institution usually run by the local priest for the moral redemption of some class of person likely to be led astray. Astié's *patronage* aimed 'to take care of the young ladies whose families cannot keep surveillance over them Sundays and holidays, and to procure for them the moral recreations necessary to the spirit, as well as exercises and games'.[13]

As a delegate to the Allemanists' first national congress in 1891, Astié devoted her efforts to a resolution calling on socialist municipalities to subsidise such *patronages*. Not surprisingly, given the clerical connotations of the word and the anti-clericalism of the socialists, the resolution was not even brought to a vote. Its failure marked the end of Astié's socialist activity. She turned to writing a practical guide for housewives aimed at 'ease by economy' and dedicated 'to intelligent working women'. Her penchant for charity won out over her socialism. Her place in the Allemanist POSR, so to speak, was taken by a feminist with keener perceptions.[14]

Mme Vincent (she never used her first name, Eliska) was the daughter of a Saint-Simonian republican sufficiently sincere to have been imprisoned in June 1848. Left a reasonable fortune on her husband's death, she turned her attention to the lot of women and workers. In 1888 she founded a feminist group of her own, L'Egalité d'Asnières ('Equality of Asnières', the Paris suburb where she lived and died). She represented L'Egalité to the 1889 women's rights congress, where she obtained passage of a resolution calling for the participation of women in the local charity boards (Bureaux de Bienfaisance).[15]

In the same year, Mme Vincent attended her first socialist congress. Like Astié, she was a delegate to the Broussist—Allemanist international congress held at Paris in 1889. Neither spoke there. Her active participation in the party began in 1892, when Jean Allemane published an article on the women's palace planned for the Chicago Exposition of 1893. He urged women to participate and solicited a feminist contribution to the working-class movement. Mme Vincent, Eugénie Potonié-Pierre, and a certain M. du Bellay answered Allemane's invitation by attending the 1892 UFC congress as delegates of Potonié-Pierre's group, La Solidarité des Femmes, Mme Vincent receiving another mandate for her own group, L'Egalité. M. du Bellay participated in the committee dealing with the Conseils de Prud' hommes (conciliation boards for disputes between workers and employers). The committee resolved to seek women's right to vote for and be elected to the Conseils. Mme Vincent liked the idea and began fifteen years of agitation, which ultimately succeeded.[16]

Potonié-Pierre's group ceased to participate in the POSR, but Mme Vincent continued. She attended the POSR national congress of 1892, at which the Allemanists adopted a legislative programme which took up much of the old Broussist programme of 1885, including the articles on equal rights and equal wages for women. Allemane commented that the POSR demanded equality for women on the grounds that all human beings were equal. 'Any law establishing an inequality', he added, was 'tyrannical, an act against which it is everyone's duty to protest by refusing to obey it'. In regard to equal wages, he argued that instead of being penalised vis-à-vis men, women should not only be paid for work on the same basis as men, but in addition should be remunerated for 'the arduous role of maternity'. Mme Vincent was undoubtedly gratified.[17]

At the next POSR congress, in 1894, she called for a resolution requiring all party candidates to put 'civil and political emancipation of women' in their electoral programmes. Logically, this was the next step after including women's rights in the general party programme. But since the Allemanists kept a tight rein on their elected representatives, there would have been no way of getting round such a provision if it had been passed. Party candidates would have had to mention women's rights in their campaign literature. The committee on resolutions apparently found this an upsetting prospect, for it asked the congress to consider not whether to introduce such a requirement but whether to maintain 'civil and political equality' in the party programme or reduce it to 'civil equality' alone. The congress decided to maintain the article intact, leaving things exactly as they had been before: a theoretical commitment with no prospect of action.[18]

The inference to be drawn from all this was that women's rights were not a major priority of the POSR. It is thus hardly surprising that Mme Vincent did not attend the next two POSR congresses. An unnamed delegate of L'Egalité did attend that of 1897 (along with Paule Mink, who was delegated by a feminist group), but Mme Vincent had given up on the socialists. This was the end of female participation in the POSR and another failure for the projected alliance between feminism and socialism.[19]

Neither Astié nor Vincent obtained any specific gestures from the party which might have facilitated the recruitment of women. Still less did they force the Allemanists to undertake a fundamental theoretical consideration of the problems of women. The Guesdists, on the other hand, took theory seriously and thus did discuss women's issues, even during the 1880s, when there were no women in the party to raise them.

The Guesdists: theory

Guesdist theory was something of a paper tiger. The POF saw itself as the French exponent of 'scientific socialism'; indeed, it presented this as its distinctive characteristic. But scientific socialism meant German socialism. The POF depended entirely upon Marx, Engels, and later the leaders of the German SPD for its theoretical development. This may have fostered a tendency to neglect theoretical work. It certainly resulted in an incomplete grasp of Marxist theory, because of all the Guesdist leaders, only Gabriel Deville could read German and not so well at that: he worked from the French translation when he published a résumé of volume I of *Capital* in 1883 and Engels had serious doubts about the quality of his work. Moreover, Deville left the party by 1889.

As a result, the Guesdists were dependent upon personal contact and translations for their theoretical notions. The basic programme of the POF, the Programme of Le Havre, had been virtually dictated to Guesde by Marx and Engels. Thereafter, the Guesdists depended upon Paul Lafargue to keep abreast with the Germans. He could not read German either, but he maintained an assiduous correspondence with Engels and his views carried weight because he had married Laura Marx.[20]

Personal contact and correspondence, however, lent themselves more to the superficial aspects of Marxism than to its profundities. One finds in the Engels–Lafargue correspondence the trenchant judgements, the definitive watchwords, the acerbic remarks about opponents which for Marx and Engels were the tip of an iceberg of extensive theoretical work but which for the Guesdists were the whole of Marxism. This situation reinforced Guesde's personal predisposition towards cut-and-dried formulae rather than dialectical investigation. The Marx who inspired Guesde was the Marx of the *Communist Manifesto*. Guesde did read volume I of *Capital* in translation in 1878, but all he got from it was the conviction that science was on the side of socialism. The main source of his economic knowledge was Lassalle, whose 'iron law of wages' Guesde attributed wrongly to Marx (Lassalle believed that under capitalism real wages could only decline).[21]

If Guesdist economics were weak, their philosophy was still weaker. Lafargue, for all his contact with the masters, displayed a mechanistic materialism which would have horrified Marx. For example, in 1893 he argued that Darwinism 'is only the reflection in their brains [the Darwinists'] of what is occurring in the economic world'. Indeed, the Guesdists referred not to historical materialism but to economic materialism. It followed that there was no point in trying to change ideas. 'Let us set to work resolutely to uproot the capitalist tree', Guesde told anti-clerical workers in 1894; 'the day the tree is cut down, religions and the other forces which come from it will disappear forever'.[22]

Where did women's rights fit in all this? An obvious answer would be that, for the Guesdists, they were dependent upon and would follow automatically from the overthrow of capitalism, a position taken by the Guesdists in 1880. Nevertheless, the answer is more complex. In the early years of Guesdism, the leaders of what was then a faction oscillated between the anarchist tendencies from which they were emerging and the rigid socialism at which they were arriving. Traces of anarchism, discernible in Guesde's 1876 articles, persisted well into the 1880s. In 1882, for instance, Gabriel Deville published an article provocatively entitled 'Free love'. The two daughters of the eminent geographer Elisée Reclus had excited the bourgeois press by contracting, with their father's approval, 'free unions' instead of marriage. Deville argued that this was insufficient because it did not get to the problem of property which was at the root of the hypocrisy of marriage. Socialists, he wrote, would install 'free love', which he did not define, unless it were by his rather Bohemian way of life. He wrote a number of similar articles.[23]

Guesde himself was not immune from these tendencies. In an article written as the Chamber was considering restoring divorce, he wrote of the 'absolute necessity of demolishing the Bastille of marriage'. 'But', he hastened to add, for he disapproved of the kind of life Deville led, 'this revolution in the relations between the sexes, which is commanded by the more and more numerous revolts of the prisoners in this Bastille, cannot precede; it can only follow the economic or social revolution.' Free disposition of oneself would be possible under communism, but only then, he argued, when children would belong not to one family, but to the entire community. Thus while Guesde's anarchist past occasionally led him to sound quite daring on women's rights, his economist version of Marxism led him to list equality for women among the many reforms which could only follow the revolution. After the early 1880s, however, Guesde ceased to write on the woman question. It was Paul Lafargue who became the party's theoretician on this issue.[24]

Lafargue arrived back in France early in 1882 and was deeply involved in the 1882 congress at which equality for women was included in the POF programme and in the preparation of the official party 'commentary' on the programme. While there is no way to distinguish Lafargue's contribution from Guesde's, it seems certain that he was largely responsible, both because the programme took a position which Guesde had been avoiding until then and because in subsequent years all the POF writing about women came from Lafargue's pen. The commentary accepted that socialists had to support women's rights: 'Although civil and political equality cannot emancipate women any more than they have emancipated the proletariat, women have a right to demand them just as the worker party has a duty to associate itself with their demands.' The commentary even went so far as to boast that already 'the working class has given women an equal place in its ranks . . . Women are chosen and elected on the same basis as men.' Technically the claim was true, although Rouzade might well have objected that her equal place in the ranks of the party had not assured her the Guesdists' support.[25]

Support for women's rights was not new for the Guesdists, however. It was in line with Guesde's 1876 articles. It seems ironic that Guesde's conversion to Marxism led him away from this position and that the POF only adopted it after Marx's son-in-law had come to certify its orthodoxy, but such was the case: it is a commentary on the schematic, rigid nature of what Guesde took to be Marxism and on the party's total dependence on foreign socialists for theory.

Lafargue, however, did not just resurrect Guesde's earlier positions. He also provided a more sophisticated position on the problem of working women. Guesde in 1877 had supported women's right to work for reasons of justice. Lafargue now explained that it was the basis for the future society: 'If it is an evil today, in the capitalist regime, industrial work for women will be, in the new society . . . a benefit for women by removing them from economic dependence on men and by enabling them to live for themselves by living by their own efforts.'[26]

Lafargue got this idea from Engels, who was writing *The Origin of the Family, Private Property and the State* during 1883. For Lafargue, however, it was only one idea among many contradictory ones. Indeed, Lafargue had not fully understood Engels's position. Engels did not believe that industrial work was an evil which would become a benefit, but rather that it was a reality which was the 'first condition for the liberation of the wife'. Lafargue confused moralising with historical analysis and failed to grasp the implications of Engels's position. Engels argued that women's legal equality with men was necessary to expose their social and economic inequality, just as the democratic republic provided the battlefield for class war. In this sense, legal equality with men was a first step, a precondition for social equality. This argument could provide a basis for common action between feminists and socialists, since socialists could thus support women's rights as a first step in their own struggle, but it was never understood by the leaders of French Marxism. This was in part because of delays in translating the German works, but more because of Lafargue's limitations in interpreting them.[27]

The Origin of the Family was published in October 1884, but was not translated into French until 1893. During this period, Lafargue's writings were the only source of Engels's ideas available to the French. Before he read *The Origin of the Family*, Lafargue had not seen the implications of Lewis Morgan's *Ancient Society*, which was the starting place for Engels's work. When he finally read *The Origin of the Family* (not, of course, in German, but in an Italian translation), he called it a 'revelation'. In 1886 he summarised the book in a series of articles in the official newspaper of the POF. Fully half of his series was devoted to an analysis of Aeschylus' *Oresteia* which took up only a page in Bebel and Engels's works. Lafargue always felt more at home with literary criticism than with history and economics. The remainder of his articles presented in extremely broad strokes the idea that women had been forcibly subject to men in order to install a regime of private property, for monogamy and assured paternity were necessary for the inheritance of property, keystone of the new regime. Carried away by his own enthusiasm, Lafargue had his last sentence deleted when the article appeared in a respectable journal: 'The patriarchal family made its appearance in the world escorted by disorder, crime and degrading force.'[28]

The other socialist classic on the woman question was August Bebel's *Woman under Socialism*, which was first published in 1878. It lacked the profundity of Engels's work, but it did lend the prestige of German Marxism to the entire array of feminist demands. The impact of the book, however, was limited by problems of translation. It did not appear in French until 1891 and then the translation verged on the unreadable: full of 'mistakes and slovenly renderings', noted Engels, fearing for his own book, which was in the hands of the same translator.[29]

P. Argyriadès, a leading member of Vaillant's CRC, if something of a maverick, undertook to remedy the situation with a twenty-four page 'analytical translation' which was published during the winter 1892–3.[30] It presented deftly the major points of Bebel's book likely to interest party militants: women were once the equals of men; monogamy and Christianity enslaved them and enabled capitalist industry to use them as a cheaper source of labour; socialist society would abolish marriage and Christianity and support maternity as a social function, thereby permitting women to realise their full potential of equality with men. Unfortunately, Argyriadès's broad strokes emphasised sensational elements and obscured the book's impact as a socialist work supporting women's rights.

The Origin of the Family appeared later in 1893, in a French translation 'entirely reviewed by Mme Laura Lafargue' and checked by Engels himself. But neither Engels's nor Bebel's works were to have any influence in France compared to that of their vulgarisers, Lafargue, Argyriadès, and Charles Vérecque, a young Guesdist who began to write on the woman question in 1893, drawing mainly on Bebel. The impact of these writers was at best uneven. All of them, particularly Lafargue, tended to exalt motherhood rather than to seek to reduce the burden it posed for women. Once the excitement surrounding Engels's and Bebel's books died down and once Engels's death in 1895 had removed all restraints from Lafargue, this tendency came to the fore.[31]

In 1904 Lafargue wrote a short pamphlet, 'La question de la femme' ('The woman question'), explaining the political consequences of matriarchal theory in somewhat tongue-in-cheek fashion. Drawing on his medical background, he argued not only that women had originally been thought to be superior to men in intelligence, but also that they lived longer and had more 'vital' organisms. Women, he concluded, should do the thinking and leave men to do the physical labour. This was good fun, but it had a serious counterpart in Lafargue's exaltation of maternity, which amounted almost to a secular cult of the Virgin Mary. The most extreme formulation of this tendency came in 1906, but it was always present in his work: 'Maternity and love will permit women to reconquer, in the communist society of the future, the superior position they enjoyed in primitive societies.'[32]

Lafargue did, however, remain a supporter of women's rights. Others in the POF went so far as to limit women's role to motherhood in the spirit of exalting it which they got from reading such works as Lafargue's. Henri Ghesquière, a major figure of the POF at Lille, wrote a short pamphlet ostensibly to popularise Bebel's work, but he completely misunderstood it. He argued that the greatest hardship women suffered was not to be able to remain at home. Socialism, he suggested, would deliver them from the horrors of factory labour and return them to home and hearth.[33]

This hardly squared with the POF programme, still less with the official commentary. But then Lafargue's veneration of maternity hardly squared with the programme he himself had written and flatly contradicted the ideas of Engels he had imported into France. Neither Engels nor Bebel envisaged maternity in the glowing terms of Lafargue. They expected socialism to free women from its burdensome aspects, permitting them to become full persons in their own right. Far from a 'superior position' resulting from maternity, they hoped for a position of equality and full self-realisation for both sexes resulting from the de-mystification of maternity and the end of women's economic dependence on men.[34] In all the vulgarisers who passed for theoreticians in the POF, and especially in Lafargue, who was supposed to be the authority on Marxism, there remained, beneath the surface froth of Marxism, an undercurrent of ideas one is tempted to call Latin, Catholic, or Proudhonist. The real impact of these pamphlets was to reinforce traditional concepts of women's role by clothing them in advanced language and bestowing the authority of socialist theory upon them. Aline Valette, the only woman to play a major role in the POF, was herself an example of similar tendencies.

The Guesdists: action

Aline Valette was a martyr-figure among socialist women: she died of tuberculosis shortly after being named the first full-time secretary of the POF. Since she was also an original thinker in her own right and the only woman ever to serve on the POF national council, one could glorify her on the basis 'first woman to . . . '. For our purposes, however, it is not her firsts that are important, but her failures: failure to bring the POF to a more profound conception of the problems of women; failure to overcome her own sex and class limitations; failure, ultimately, to bring women into the party.

Born at Paris in 1850, Valette became a vocational schoolteacher in Paris. She was elected secretary of the teachers' union in which Bonnevial was active at its tiny founding congress in 1878. She gave up her teaching position upon her marriage to a well-to-do lawyer. He died before she was forty, leaving his young and attractive widow in comfortable circumstances. In 1883, she published a very successful homemaker's guide which ran through thirty-four editions in ten years. It outlined a vast programme of housework which, if followed, would have kept a woman tightly locked in traditional roles.[35]

This was not accidental: Valette insisted upon the importance of women's role as mothers. She had nothing but scorn for women who wished to avoid their maternal duty. To a woman who wrote that she did not want children and that 'humanity won't die of it', Valette replied acidly, 'On condition, Madame, that all women . . . do not think like you.' The springs of Valette's action were morality and charity. She was a member of the 'Charity for Women Discharged from Saint-Lazare Prison', for which she wrote a fund-raising brochure. The Charity attempted, not too successfully, to entice prostitutes released from prison into the paths of virtue.[36]

Valette embraced socialism at the age of forty, drawn to the left by her humanitarianism. During the 1880s, she became one of the first women's labour inspectors for the Paris area. Such positions were unpaid, volunteer work. Initially it was just another form of charity for her. But once brought face to face with the realities of industrial life, she was shaken and began to seek further for solutions to the problems she saw. She joined a Guesdist study group and thus, as its delegate, went to the international socialist congress of 1889. Subsequently, the historic May Day of 1890 (the first in Europe) greatly impressed her. The strike movement was the result of a resolution she had seen passed at the congress. It was highly successful and it replied directly to her concern for women exhausted by twelve and even fourteen-hour days. It seemed to show that the Guesdists were addressing themselves successfully to the issues that concerned her. By the time she attended the Brussels international congress of 1891, she was a confirmed Guesdist. Ironically, however, it was only through feminism that she became a party leader.[37]

In January 1892, eight Parisian feminist groups, under the leadership of Eugénie Potonié-Pierre, created a Fédération Française des Sociétés Féministes ('French Federation of Feminist Groups'). The Federation organised a congress for May 1892. Valette joined the organising committee and attended the congress as a delegate of an ephemeral seamstresses' union. The congress voted to put the Federation on a permanent basis. Scarcely a month after the congress, however, on 17 June 1892, Potonié-Pierre abruptly resigned as secretary of the Federation in a dispute over her personal control of the group. Valette replaced her as secretary. In this capacity she attended the POF congress of 1893, where she was named to the party's national council.[38]

The Federation was responsible not only for her elevation in the POF, but also for the creation of her newspaper. The major task which the congress had set the Federation was the preparation of a 'Feminist grievance list' (*Cahier des doléances féminines*: the name was taken from the lists prepared for the meeting of the Estates-General in 1789). In the hope of reaching out into the world of working women for the preparation of the list, Valette founded a newspaper, *L'Harmonie sociale*. The first issue appeared on 15 October 1892. It was a weekly tabloid. The masthead proclaimed, 'The emancipation of women is in emancipated labour', but most of the contributors were feminists more than socialists: Mme Vincent, Marie Bonnevial, and a newcomer, Marya Chéliga-Loevy, who contributed a sentimental serial novel about how an innocent young girl reached socialism through suffering.[39]

L'Harmonie sociale was certainly socialist in its intentions. It even serialised Bebel's *Woman Under Socialism*. But it was not exempt from confusion and ambiguity. The first issue included a number of Guesdist texts on women, among them the resolution defeated by L'Union des Femmes at the 1880 UFC congress and the resolutions of several international congresses. The former, however, was no longer Guesdist policy: it had been repudiated at Le Havre and contradicted the final version of the party programme. More surprisingly, Valette's version of the resolution of the 1891 international congress contained two clauses which were not in the official version: 'the same civil and political rights as men'; 'equal pay for equal work'. Valette had simply fabricated them by wishful thinking.[40]

She was hardly a Marxist: she cited Henry George as a key thinker. Her writings on women showed tendencies similar to Lafargue's work, but had even less of a Marxist veneer. In the lead article of the first issue of *L'Harmonie sociale*, she argued that women had neglected their 'natural role of reproducers' in favour of the 'artificial role of producer'. What would Bebel have said, having decried in *Woman Under Socialism* 'the twaddle about the "natural calling" of woman . . . assigning her to domestic duties and the family'? What would Engels have said, having stated unequivocally in *The Origin of the Family* that 'the first condition for the liberation of the wife is to bring the whole female sex back into public industry'?[41]

To be sure, Valette found the roots of the problem in the economic conditions, but she meant by this the low salaries which forced women to work in order to supplement their husbands' salaries. She certainly did not envisage class struggle: her remedy was to 'study the conditions of labour' in an effort 'to re-establish equilibrium, to harmonise [work]'. In this aim, the newspaper would help women to choose their professions suitably, seeking work which would help them regain the lost harmony of family life. But work was only a necessary transition preceding 'the happy era when women will be returned to their biological role of creator and educator of the species'. This position, which was neither Marxist nor feminist, corresponded to Lafargue's tendency to envisage a 'superior position' for women because of their maternal role. What was implicit in Lafargue's thought, however, was explicit in Valette's.[42]

A certain 'Dr Z.' began to collaborate with Valette in *L'Harmonie sociale*. Marilyn Boxer has identified him as Dr Pierre Bonnier, whose brother Charles was a leading member of the POF and 'an intimate friend' of Guesde.[43] Dr Bonnier joined with Valette in a series of articles seeking to make of her ideas a coherent though still conservative theory they called 'sexualism', which they intended to be the feminine counterpart of socialism.

As man's role was to produce, and socialism was the ideology by which his production would be restored to harmony; so woman's role was to reproduce, and 'sexualism' was the ideology by which her reproduction would be restored to harmony. Capitalism had not only distorted the productive relations for women (as for men), but also it had degraded women in their sexual role, 'not in their relations with capital as workers, but in their contacts with masculinism [*sic*] which has deformed and sterilised human evolution for centuries'. Just as the capitalist held legal title to the product made by his worker, so did the male hold that made by his wife, that is the children. These ideas were the basis of a brochure published by Valette and Bonnier in 1893. The cover showed a hermaphroditic angel helping a nude woman to rise from her shackles while the sun rose in the background. The text expanded the ideas advanced in the articles. Women were the first slaves because of their 'physiological servitude'. As the poor, burdened with badly paid work, wished to be rich, so women, burdened with unjustly treated maternity, dreamt of being men. When women became conscious of their exploitation and freed themselves, they would return with joy to their natural destiny: motherhood.[44]

Obviously Engels's ideas had not yet reached Valette and Bonnier. One wonders if they had read Bebel's book as they serialised it. 'Sexualism' was really only a play on the words 'producer and reproducer'. To take it seriously would be to do what Guesde had denounced in 1876, to 'pen [women] up in their sex, transformed . . . into a profession'. It assumed that child-rearing was exclusively incumbent on women and implied that production should be exclusively incumbent on men, which amounted to accepting the prevailing idea of women's role. It did not even raise the possibility of community support for child-raising, which played a major part in Bebel's thinking. The interesting comments on 'masculinism' were drowned in a torrent of adulation of motherhood. Strangely, no one noticed the traditional bent of Valette's thinking, except Potonié-Pierre, who of course had an axe to grind after the struggle over the federation; she denounced 'sexualism' in 1894 as an attempt to force women back into subordination.[45]

Although Valette believed in an eventual return to maternity as women's essential role, in the short run she sought reforms which would admit women into civil, economic, and political equality. The brochure included in an appendix the 'Feminist grievance list', which Valette herself had prepared and submitted to the first (and only) general assembly of the Federation, held on 16 March 1893. It passed unanimously. The 'Grievance list' was less exotic than 'sexualism'. It amounted to a bill of rights for middle-class women. It called for women's access to all levels of education and to all professions, including government and public office, and demanded, in the words of the socialist party programmes, the abolition of all articles of the Napoleonic Code putting women in an inferior position. On the first of May

1893, the Federation sent delegates to the offices of the mayors of each of the twenty arrondissements of Paris, where they solemnly deposited copies of the 'Grievance list'. This was the Federation's only major action.[46]

At the general assembly, Valette announced that the Federation was now composed of sixteen groups with a total of 35,000 members, a figure presumably based on Marya Chéliga-Loevy's claim that all the feminist groups of the world were members of her Union Universelle des Femmes ('Universal Women's Union'), which in turn was a member of the Federation. But these were phantom groups. Without Potonié-Pierre, the Federation had no reason for existence and soon fell apart.[47] Valette had no group of her own to back her up. *L'Harmonie sociale* ceased publication in July 1893. Valette was left with only her title as secretary of the Federation and her mandate to the coming POF congress. Her nomination to the POF national council at this congress was the result of ties she was already developing with the POF and of events within the party.

In January 1893, Valette supported the call of the Comité des Femmes de Lille ('Lille Women's Committee') for free lunches for schoolchildren. This programme had been decided at the 1891 POF congress in connection with a resolution inviting workers to demand women's rights. Guesde and Lafargue hoped that such a campaign might help recruit women into the party, where they were virtually an unknown species (between 2 and 3 per cent of the total membership). But the Comité des Femmes withered away shortly after issuing its appeal. Its only enduring act was the publication of Ghesquière's pamphlet exalting home and hearth discussed above.[48]

Guesde and Lafargue were disturbed by the failure of their efforts in Lille, which was one of their strongholds. Charles Vérecque proposed that the POF include a woman in its leadership in order to 'prove that, among the socialists, if we demand the same rights for women as for men, we also know how to treat them on an equal footing'. At the same time, the party decided to reorganise the national council at the congress to be held in Paris during October 1893.[49]

So it was that when Valette appeared at the congress, she came at an opportune moment. There were no other women of leadership calibre in the POF. Potonié-Pierre and Vincent, who also attended the congress, were primarily known as feminists and, to the extent they were socialists, were associated with the POSR. Paule Mink had left the POF for the Vaillantist CRC. Laura Lafargue always remained discreetly in the background.

Valette, on the other hand, was increasingly known as a Guesdist. In April 1893, she had been invited by the party to lecture in another of its strongholds, the industrial town of Roubaix, near Lille. Although she had never before attended a national POF congress, she had been at both international congresses (1889 and 1891) and had endeared herself to Guesde by choosing the Guesdist one in 1889: she was, he used to tell Vérecque, 'the only woman who has understood socialism'. She was elected to the new national council and remained a member until her death in 1899. In November 1896, the council chose her as the first full-time, paid secretary of the POF. The party installed its headquarters in her dining room.[50]

During her stint as a member of the council, before she was burdened with the administrative tasks of the party, Valette apparently went through a period of acquiring Guesdist (if not Marxist) thought. In 1895 she began writing regularly in the official party newspaper. Her first article there took a straight Guesdist line. Women's incorporation into the workforce, she now argued, would bring their 'emancipation': *'so long as women are economically dependent on men nothing will be done'* (italics orig.). But 'sexualism' still persisted in Valette's thought. The 'emancipation' she had in mind was a return to home and hearth after the revolution. Economic independence was only a means to this end.[51]

Valette's thought intertwined perfectly with Guesde's and Lafargue's. Following Guesde, she argued that women's duty now was to 'adopt resolutely the masculine tactic, that is, as proletarians and with the proletarians — being themselves proletarians — work toward the *appropriation of the instruments of production by the collectivity'* (italics orig.). In other words, forget about women's rights for the moment and join the POF. Following Lafargue, she argued that the revolution would free women to fulfil themselves most naturally, in the home, where they would find 'maternity and love' the most satisfying functions possible. Despite her earnest efforts to study Marx (she appears to have read *Capital* in 1897 or 1898), her thought remained within the limits of 'sexualism'.[52]

In May 1897, Charles Bonnier, Dr Z.'s brother, published a long article outlining a complete legislative programme to grant women their rights. Perhaps encouraged thereby, Valette submitted a resolution to the 1897 POF congress calling upon the party 'to elaborate a feminine programme'. This was needed, her resolution stated, because 'women's aptitudes and sexual burdens' created for them 'a situation distinct from that of men': women, it went on, were not only 'dispossessed of the fruit of their labour as wage-earners' (like men), but also 'dispossessed of the product of their flesh as mothers, . . . doubly enslaved as producer and reproducer'. The resolution was supported by Paul Lafargue and Paule Mink (who, though now a member of the CRC, was the delegate of a feminist group). Guesde, however, seems to have had reservations about the resolution, probably because of its manifest 'sexualist' tendencies, which scarcely fitted in with the POF orthodoxy of which he was more than ever the guardian. He agreed that 'a new affirmation' of women's rights would be useful, but argued that there was no need for new doctrine (as Valette's resolution clearly implied), since that had been settled in previous congresses. The resolution was tabled for study until the next congress.[53]

Although Valette's declining health prevented her from participating in
the preparation of the 1898 congress, a draft resolution on women's rights
was drawn up for it. It was far removed from 'sexualism'. It called on socialist municipalities (or party sections where the party did not control the
municipality) to institute an unofficial ballot for women beside the official
one for men and, in addition, to give women the vote in municipal referenda.
This was a striking departure from the usual abstract statements of rights. As
the resolution explained, the unofficial vote would create pressure to grant
women the suffrage. Moreover, it would make effective use of the power the
socialists already enjoyed in local government. It was the only concrete plan
of action for women's rights ever submitted to a socialist party, with the
possible exception of Mme Vincent's call for inclusion of women's rights in
campaign literature. It never reached the floor of the congress. There was not
one woman among the 190 delegates.[54]

Valette was already dying of tuberculosis. During the winter of 1897–8,
her constant coughing had been a source of worry to her friends. In April
1898, she went to Arcachon, south of Bordeaux, for the traditional (and
traditionally ineffectual) cure of warm climate and mineral water. Although
she convinced herself that she would recover and continued to write until
September 1898, she was too ill to attend the congress. She died at Arcachon
on 21 March 1899. No one took her place in the POF, which, in any case,
was by now preoccupied with the Dreyfus affair and socialist unification.[55]

Even had Valette lived, she could not have altered the course of events,
because of the party's inertia, because of the limitations of her own thinking
(limitations which she shared with the other party leaders), and because of
the difficulties she, like any bourgeois woman, faced in relating to the mass
of unpoliticised working women who constituted the obvious target for her
efforts. The party's inertia lay in its refusal to consider the particular situation
of women in the society of the time. It was typified by Guesde's refusal to
entertain any resolution which went beyond an 'affirmation' of equality
between the sexes. The POF refused to offer anything to working women
beyond what it offered to men. Yet, unpoliticised, burdened with housework
as well as factory labour, working-class women could not and did not come
to the party as if they enjoyed the conditions of men. Valette never came to
grips with this problem.

Indeed, the limitations of her thinking and of her class origins compounded the problem. Her thinking was always based on traditional ideas
about women's role. Hidden at first under the jargon of sexualism, her ideas
were later covered with standard Second International Marxist rhetoric. In
one of her last articles, written in July 1898, she stressed that the evolution
of society was preparing a revolution. If it were violent, the bourgeoisie
would have only itself to blame, for it had already destroyed the working-
class family and left behind 'torrents of blood'.[56] But there is no indication

of her abandoning her conviction that motherhood was the ultimate ideal toward which socialism would carry women. Indeed, one of her last acts, the draft resolution for the 1897 POF congress, still reflected all the 'producer and reproducer' rhetoric of 'sexualism'. While it is possible that working women whose factory jobs were even less gratifying than their domestic toils might have responded to Valette's ideas, sexualism was not relevant to the problems women faced. At best Valette held out an ideal for the future while working women needed ways to cope with the present. At worse she presented a restrictive, traditional conception of women's role as the emancipation of women and the aim of socialism.

Secretary of the Fédération Française des Sociétés Féministes, she never conceived of a meaningful role for women beyond maternity. Secretary of the POF, she remained bourgeois: two years after attaining this position, she wrote of her difficulty in obtaining the confidence of the women workers at the Bourse du Travail: 'This core ["200 women workers"], we will find it all ready for us . . . [*sic*] on condition that we are very diplomatic: for how they mistrust bourgeois women, poor things.' In the last analysis, Valette was cut of the same cloth as the feminists.[57]

The difficulty of the socialist parties in the era before socialist unification was that women like Valette and Vincent were the only ones they could bring into leadership positions. Revolutionary women like Mink preferred to concern themselves with the revolution, like men; women who were workers, on the other hand, could scarcely take part in serious political work. Even if they did not have, as most of them did, the double burden of factory and housework, the political concerns which enabled some working-class men to become active in the parties were not part of their roles.

All this resulted in a vicious circle of limited leadership and lack of constituency: there were no leaders who could effectively draw women into the parties, and since there were few women in the parties, there was no demand for effort in this direction, thus no demand for female leadership. This vicious circle spun within a larger one: the parties were concerned with votes, whatever their rhetoric. And women did not vote. How was this vicious circle to be broken? Some feminists believed that they could organise working women. But could they overcome the workers' suspicion of their bourgeois origins? 'How they mistrust bourgeois women, poor things.'

3. Feminists in search of a mass base: the rise and fall of social feminism 1889 – 1900

'We are accused, indeed, of *never concerning ourselves with the misery of working women* [italics orig.] and of concerning ourselves only with the woman voter, lawyer or doctor', complained Maria Pognon, president of the Ligue Française pour le Droit des Femmes. Pognon was one of those who sought to correct this situation, realising that feminism could not become an effective force unless it reached beyond the narrow circle of bourgeois women to whom it had so far been confined. Earlier, during the 1890s, women like Eugénie Potonié-Pierre also endeavoured to expand the horizons of feminism, but without perceiving the need to enlarge its base: thinking in humanitarian rather than political terms, they tried simply to incorporate their social concern into feminism, much as they had attempted in the 1880s to bring their feminism into socialism. Their 'social feminism' (to coin a phrase not used at the time) paved the way for more conscious efforts to bring working-class women into the feminist movement. The failure of these efforts in turn left the field clear for an authentically working-class women's movement within socialism.[1]

The mainstream of feminism was still timid and legalistic. When it manifested itself in two congresses held in 1889, after more than a decade of dormancy, it reflected the conservatism of its social base. One of these congresses had semi-official sanction within the framework of the Exposition of 1889 and was organised by a committee which included some of the wealthiest families and best-known politicians of France. The other congress was organised by Richer and Deraismes in much the same spirit as that of 1878: firmly republican, but just as firmly determined not to rock the ship of state by discussing controversial problems. Rouzade and Potonié-Pierre attended this congress but remained aloof.[2]

Potonié-Pierre still retained the social concern which had impelled her to join with Rouzade in founding L'Union des Femmes. She was disturbed by the narrow approach of Richer and Deraismes's congress and in response began a lifelong effort to create a broader feminist organisation, one which would embody her social concern. Her first attempt followed immediately after the congress, in the autumn of 1889. She joined with Astié de Valsayre to found a Ligue des Femmes ('Women's League'), sometimes styled Ligue Socialiste des Femmes. This was not a propitious time to collaborate with

Astié, who was more unstable than usual: she was still involved with the Allemanists, but was on the threshold of shifting the focus of her work to the Patronage. The League was stifled at birth with quarrels.[3]

Potonié-Pierre nevertheless persisted in her efforts. 'The social question is coming toward us', she remarked, 'let us go toward the social question.' In 1891 she founded Le Groupe de la Solidarité des Femmes ('Women's Solidarity Group'). She was aided by Maria Martin, editor of *Le Journal des femmes*, successor to Auclert's *La Citoyenne*.[4] They were joined by a wide range of social feminists, Rouzade first among them. Even Nathalie Lemel, the bookbinder and syndicalist reputed to have been the first Frenchwoman member of the First International, deported with Louise Michel after the Commune, later claimed to have been involved in founding the group. It proposed 'to demand women's economic, civil and political rights' and in general to champion 'the whole cause of women's economic and social emancipation'.[5]

The next step in Potonié-Pierre's campaign to enlarge the feminist movement was the founding of the Fédération Française des Sociétés Féministes ('French Federation of Feminist Groups') at the beginning of 1892. With the feminist congress organised by the Federation, 13–15 May 1892, Potonié-Pierre hoped to establish social feminism in its own right, competing with if not taking the place of the more conservative strands of feminism. On a symbolic level, the congress was highly successful. In the absence of any other feminist congress on the horizon, it attracted not only all the social feminists, such as Bonnevial, Chéliga-Loevy, Pognon, Valette, and Vincent, but also a number of mainstream feminists, including Deraismes herself. Moreover it brought them together with a number of socialists: several socialist militants attended the congress and, in addition, several well-known socialist leaders lent their names to it, though not their presence: Edouard Vaillant, leader of the CRC (this was the only time he was ever involved in women's issues); P. Argyriadès, editor of *La Question sociale* and populariser of Bebel; Emile Pasquier, secretary of the free thought federation; and the independent socialist deputy Chassaing. To link Deraismes, the respectable anti-Communard dean of feminism, with Vaillant, whose very name stood for the Commune, was no mean achievement.[6]

On a practical level, however, the congress was less successful. Instead of a coherent policy to integrate social concern into feminism, the congress produced a disparate variety of proposals reflecting the delegates' pet concerns. The one exception illustrated the depth of the problems involved. Georges Diamandy, co-founder and president of a revolutionary socialist student group, proposed that 'the Congress, considering that its demands are closely linked with those of the international proletariat, supports the demands of this proletariat'. This was splendidly militant in tone and caused some of the delegates to balk, but it could hardly be said to clarify the issues. It passed, however, much to Potonié-Pierre's satisfaction. 'For the first time', she rejoiced, 'women, finally accepting the outstretched hand of the social cause . . . have united . . . their demands with those of the pro-letarian party.'[7]

In fact, however, the resolutions of a few dozen leaders without followers scarcely sufficed to unite the two causes. After the congress, the Federation was torn by strife partly arising from the dim and hazy recognition of this fact by some of the members. Potonié-Pierre resigned as secretary and the Federation passed into Valette's hands, where it soon withered away. La Solidarité, however, continued on its way under Potonié-Pierre's leadership, a stable group but henceforth limited to a relatively small circle of concerned bourgeois women.

Potonié-Pierre never perceived that the logic of her own efforts implied enlarging the base of her movement. Indeed, her aim was not so much to encourage working people to be active as to forestall such activity; 'to join the two causes of women and the proletariat', as she put it, 'in order to make of them one single cause, the humanitarian cause, so that social evolution may proceed peacefully'. She owed more to her husband's pacifism than to a vision of women in action. The basic source of her thought, as of her husband's, was Saint-Simon, whose sayings appeared throughout their utopian novel, sometimes in the most unexpected places: when the hero flushed the toilet, a coin rolled out of a box. It was marked, ' "To each according to his works", — St-Simon.'[8]

Like most utopians, Eugénie and Edmond Potonié-Pierre wanted the stork to bring the new society without the sordid political midwifery normally attendant upon social change. The novel began with a denunciation of socialist party politics. The hero fell into a coma not through hypnosis, but as a result of fatigue and exasperation caused by attending 'those mass meet-ings [*réunions populaires*] where there swarm, amidst the just yearnings of the workers, lurking ambitions neither more nor less repugnant than those which abound in the highest political circles'.[9]

Eugénie shared her husband's distaste for political action. Her innumer-able short stories were peopled not with activists but with victims: mothers driving out their children for want of food, pregnant women starving in the streets, unemployed workers committing suicide, etc. She had real sympathy for such cases, but she never conceived of urging them to take action into their own hands. Her political ideas were those of the charitable bourgeois she always remained.[10]

La Solidarité, like its leader, never got out of its bourgeois mould. It met in the town hall of the sixth arrondissement, one of the most religious and reactionary of Paris, on Wednesday afternoons. A weekday afternoon was a time when middle-class women could come and get back in time for dinner, without having to explain to their husbands. A working woman, however, could come only by giving up her afternoon's wages. What would she get in return? A typical meeting involved a letter to the prefect of police protesting against the round-ups of prostitutes, a letter 'to the press' protesting against 'pernicious literature and imagery', and a resolution calling on women to seek places in the civil service. Even when social problems were discussed, the tone remained bourgeois: polite, well-to-do women writing polite, respectful letters to the authorities; the problems of the common people being discussed by their betters. It all took place in a sphere far removed from that of ordinary workers. They were not really expected to come and they did not come.[11]

After the failure of the Federation, the group turned to attending socialist congresses and to planning a woman's candidature (shades of Rouzade). Neither effort was successful. La Solidarité's delegation to the Allemanist congress of 1892 (Potonié-Pierre, Vincent, and a certain Monsieur du Bellay) was able to obtain support for their demand for the entry of women into the Conseils des Prud'hommes, but Potonié-Pierre, who was the sole representative of La Solidarité at the POF congress of 1893, had no apparent effect there. (Valette and Vincent attended this congress with mandates from the Federation, from which Potonié-Pierre had withdrawn; the congress did, of course, elect Valette to the POF national council.)[12]

La Solidarité's effort to promote women candidatures was still less successful. In October 1892, the group decided to ask all the socialist parties to present 'a feminine candidature'. Potonié-Pierre wrote to all five parties in the group's name, explaining that they would accept any districts, however hopeless, since the object was propaganda. She argued that, pending the installation of a 'rational economic system', women, like proletarians, should use the suffrage to reduce their burdens. Of course the suffrage alone was insufficient, but this was no reason for not seeking it at all. In her letter to Guesde, she also asked that he publish her request and that four members of La Solidarité be delegated by the POF to explain the project to socialist municipalities. (She proposed herself, Maria Martin, Maria Pognon, and Mme Vincent.) Guesde never replied, nor did any of the others. By February 1893, Potonié-Pierre was discouraged. She published the correspondence. 'Name women candidates, citizens', she demanded. When this too went without reply, the group named its own candidates: Deraismes, Rouzade, and Séverine (well known as editor during the 1880s of the pioneer socialist newspaper, *Le Cri du peuple*). All three refused, but a fourth nominee accepted: Paule Mink.[13]

This marked a major change in Mink's thinking. In 1884 she had raised a storm of protest by standing up after a lecture by Auclert and speaking against women's suffrage on the grounds that women were too subject to clerical influence. In 1889 she had written to a Guesdist congress that 'even if women could vote for women, that would not free them from exploitation, from prejudice, from the misery by which they are bent and broken'. In 1891 she still denied the very existence of the 'woman question' and opposed women's suffrage as irrelevant. Exploited for their work and their sex by their employers and their men, women would be free only when socialism ended exploitation, at which point 'laws and customs will consecrate equality of rights for them'. Thus, she concluded, women should 'throw in their lot sincerely with the socialists'.[14]

In her report to the congress of the Federation, in 1892, Potonié-Pierre challenged Mink directly, referring to this article: 'There is no woman question, we've been told a thousand times, there is [only] the social question. Yes, certainly! . . . but to resolve it . . . we need the participation of everyone.' And so, she argued, there was a woman question: women must participate in the construction of the new society and rights in present society were prerequisite to such participation. Within a year, in a startling reversal, Mink came to accept Potonié-Pierre's analysis.[15]

This resulted in part from Mink's disappointment with the Guesdists over the issue of the general strike. The idea that one day all the workers would go out on strike and bring down capitalism with one great blow originated with the anarchists and was taken over by the Allemanists and the revolutionary syndicalists. The Guesdists argued, like the German socialists, that the general strike would not succeed unless the vast majority of the workers supported it and that when the majority did support the strike it would be unnecessary: they could vote the socialists into power. But despite her membership in the POF, Mink was an ardent partisan of the general strike. Provincial militants (she lived in Montpellier now) were interested in action, not in ideological subtleties, she had told the reformists in 1882. Now she said the same to the Guesdists. She and others in the POF who had been impressed by the powerful May Day demonstrations of 1890 and 1891 sought to persuade the party to support the idea of the general strike. In 1892 Mink wrote, 'The general strike is here, just around the corner'; she called upon the party congress of that year to 'decide it', 'this powerful revolutionary act'. Instead, however, the congress rejected the principle of the general strike after a long struggle, thus conforming to Guesde's line. This was a great blow to Mink. She accused the party of lacking revolutionary courage and of delaying the revolution for several years.[16]

Shortly after the congress, Mink moved back to Paris, where her contact with the feminists and her disappointment with the Guesdists led her to believe that women's rights were more important than she had previously thought. Early in 1893 she accepted the offer of La Solidarité to be a candidate in the legislative elections to be held in August. Now she argued like any feminist that women would reduce corruption in politics and improve the administration of education and charity. But unlike most feminists she claimed to have accepted the candidature as a 'disciplined soldier of the Worker Party [the POF]', to which she still belonged. The POF, however, made no move to support her candidature. She now had a second grievance against the party.[17]

Her feminism was further stimulated by the publication in *L'Harmonie sociale* of the *Cahier des doléances féminines*, which was distributed on May Day 1893. Mink praised this act and concluded that economic equality for women would be impossible without civil and political rights. By the summer of 1893 she had quit the POF and joined Vaillant's CRC, whose links with the revolutionary tradition satisfied her still unslaked thirst for revolutionary activity: unburdened by dogmatism, the Vaillantists did not rule out the general strike and seemed in general a more active and energetic group than the Guesdists. Having made this decision, Mink took up the question of her candidature again. In August, just before the elections, she published a second letter of acceptance, stating that she had waited till the last minute to see if any socialist party would support her. None had done so. Without party support and without preparation, Mink's candidature had no impact, but the socialists' failure to support her drove her closer to the feminists.[18]

Mink soon became active in La Solidarité and became Potonié-Pierre's closest collaborator, both in La Solidarité and in Argyriadès's magazine, *La Question sociale*, for which both wrote in most issues and of which Mink was editorial secretary from September 1894 until April 1897, when it ceased publication. Potonié-Pierre tapped hitherto unsuspected wells of sentimentality in Mink, who took to writing vignettes in Potonié-Pierre's style: a jobless worker killing himself so that his children would receive public support as orphans; a hotel keeper seducing the servant girl and, upon her becoming pregnant, telling her to 'get rid of it'; an old worker dying of starvation at the door of the factory where he had laboured forty years; a worker drafted into the army losing his arm because of an officer's cruelty and shooting himself rather than face his fiancée . . . Mink showed a keener sense of social reality than Potonié-Pierre, but, like her, portrayed victims, not activists.[19]

It is a measure of Potonié-Pierre's success that the Ligue Française pour le Droit des Femmes, so timid under Richer's leadership, was now in the hands of social feminists: Maria Pognon had become president in 1892 and Marie Bonnevial was vice-president. They co-operated with Potonié-Pierre in organising the 1896 feminist congress under the joint sponsorship of the League and La Solidarité. It is a measure of her failure, however, that the congress, like that of 1892, was unable to work out any coherent policy. There were a number of progressive resolutions: Argyriadès obtained passage of a resolution calling for the state to bear the cost of raising children (shades of Rouzade); Marie Bonnevial and Mme Vincent secured one for the eight-hour

day for both sexes and one for equal wages for equal pay; others passed one
for a minimum wage. These resolutions, however, were thrown up in a
jumble, along with everyone else's pet reforms; Marya Chéliga-Loevy —
women's right to choose or refuse the nationality of a foreign husband;
Edmond Potonié-Pierre — the 'inviolability of human life'; Mink — 'free
union', and so on.

Two incidents illustrate the difficulties the congress encountered. On the
one hand there were personal differences. When Maria Pognon was elected to
the chair for a session, Rouzade raised a storm of protest: Pognon, though
married to a wealthy businessman, kept her own pockets lined by running a
hotel of furnished rooms near the Champs-Elysées. Since such establishments
frequently served businessmen for illicit sex, Rouzade accused Pognon of
gross immorality and stalked out in a huff. On the other hand there were
ideological differences. As in 1892, a revolutionary student introduced the
notion of class struggle: his speech threw the congress into an uproar. Mme
Vincent, 'herself a socialist', noted *Le Figaro* maliciously, 'begged the
collectivist student not to ruffle the feelings of the assembly'. Social concern
could mean many different things, but it could not, must not mean class
struggle. Despite their differences and their confusion, the feminists were
clear that their principles must be maintained even if in conflict with those
of the socialists. The congress, for example, resolved that 'women's work
hours be limited only when men's are', in opposition to the socialist position
in favour of special regulations for women, which had been reaffirmed at the
1893 international congress.[20]

The real significance of the congress was in establishing Mink and Potonié-
Pierre's leadership of mainstream feminism and in preparing the succession
of other social feminists. Their leadership was confirmed at the international
feminist congress of Brussels, in 1897, where they were the real powers of
the French delegation, which included Bonnevial, Vincent, and most other
prominent feminists. The Belgian feminists sparked Mink's old fire by their
extraordinary conservatism. When one expressed the hope that women
would not embark upon careers which would take them away from their
home and hearth, Mink retorted:

It is not we who tear women away from home and hearth, it is exploitation, it is capitalism which takes not only women, but also children, to create competition for men. In
order to rekindle our hearths and make humanity happy again, we must suppress capitalist exploitation, there is no other way . . . And, while we discuss whether women should
or should not work, there are thousands of women workers who are working and dying
of exhaustion.[21]

The partnership of Mink and Potonié-Pierre, however, was nearing its end.
Eugénie Potonié-Pierre died unexpectedly of a cerebral haemorrhage on 12
June 1898. Her funeral brought together several dozen social feminists with
Mink and a token male socialist, the maverick Argyriadès. Even Léon Richer

tottered along as if to represent the acceptance by mainstream feminists of
Potonié-Pierre's contribution. In the autumn, Edmond Potonié-Pierre called
La Solidarité together. At a meeting presided by Rouzade, the group chose a
new secretary: Caroline Kauffmann, founder of the Ligue Féminine
d'Education Physique ('Feminine League of Physical Education').[22]

For a time Mink continued to collaborate with La Solidarité, even co-
signing a report on women's physical education which Kauffmann delivered
at the international feminist congress held in London in 1899. Mink was La
Solidarité's delegate to the congress of socialist organisations in December
1899, at which the unification of French socialism began. (Rouzade and
Kauffmann were also delegated, but did not go because the group received
only one mandate.) In 1900, apparently dissatisfied with the direction La
Solidarité was taking, Mink ceased to attend its meetings. She lent her name
to a short-lived Groupe Socialiste Révolutionnaire des Citoyennes de Paris
('Socialist Revolutionary Group of Women Citizens of Paris', a name which
suggests links with the Vaillantists). This group delegated Mink to the
second congress of socialist organisations held in September 1900. (La
Solidarité was in theory a member of the Fédération Socialiste Indépendante
and could therefore have sent a delegate but did not.)[23]

It was the last such meeting in a life crowded with militant activity. Mink
died at her home near Paris on 28 April 1901. In death as in life she remained
a militant and a woman of the people. Her funeral, quite unlike Potonié-
Pierre's, was a mass popular demonstration, for she was known as a heroine
of the Commune. The ghost of the Commune still inspired fear of revolt: the
government deployed 1300 troops and countless police to keep order.
Behind her red-draped cortège, Vaillant and several other socialist deputies
associated with the Commune led the long procession. It continued until
nightfall.[24]

The Groupe des Citoyennes died soon after Mink, but La Solidarité continued on its way under Kauffmann. It had ceased, however, to embody the
social concerns of feminists. That task fell to Marguerite Durand.[25]

The most ambitious attempt to create a movement of 'social feminism' was
also the last: the international women's rights congress of 1900. The secretary and guiding spirit of the congress was Marguerite Durand. Actress
turned journalist turned feminist, founder of the famous dog cemetery at
Asnières, Durand was called 'the muse of Boulangism': she had been married
to a Boulangist deputy and her salon had been a centre of the General's
parliamentary intrigues. She had been converted to feminism while covering
Potonié-Pierre's congress in 1896. She became vice-president of the Ligue
Française pour le Droit des Femmes. In December 1897, she used part of her
large fortune to found the world's first daily newspaper 'directed, administered, edited, [and] typeset by women', *La Fronde*.[26]

La Fronde's politics were the essence of social feminism. It was republican, anti-clerical, and progressive on social issues, but within the limits of a spirit of charity and conciliation rather than class struggle. In Durand's hands, social feminism was not just an expression of concern, it was a means to feminist ends. Durand understood what Potonié-Pierre had ignored, that feminism needed a mass base. She believed that, if feminism showed sisterly concern, it would become more attractive to working women, among whom she sought the desired base. She stated this aim with astonishing lucidity, not to say cynicism: 'Working women are the only ones yet to have shown bravery ... it is they who will make the revolution for their bourgeois sisters.' Durand made it quite clear that the 'bourgeois sisters' would retain control of the movement: 'But what good are arms which flail about', she went on, 'when there are no brains to guide them?' All of Durand's efforts were characterised by her dual concern to attract working women and to remain at the helm of the organisations to which she attracted them. She was active in support of women's *syndicats*, giving large donations to many and founding three herself. But she gave donations only when she was assured of her influence over the leaders and the three *syndicats* she founded were company unions, grouping employees of her own newspaper.[27]

The same two concerns characterised her preparation of the international women's rights congress of 1900. She intended that the congress should take positions on social issues which would help feminism attract working women, but she expected the newcomers to follow her leadership. Thus she included in the organising commission five persons more or less associated with socialism as well as with feminism, but also linked to her personally as well. René Viviani was a prominent socialist deputy, but a well-bred one who could be counted upon not to shock the ladies with talk of class struggle. He was on excellent terms with Durand because he had helped force the Ecole des Beaux-Arts to provide studios for women, a cause ardently championed by *La Fronde*. Marie Bonnevial was now the secretary of the Syndicat des Membres de l'Enseignement (the teachers' union which she and Valette had helped found). But she was also a vice-president of the League, alongside Durand, to whom she was devoted. Stéphanie Bouvard constituted with her mother and sister the core of the Syndicat des Fleuristes Plumassières ('artificial flowermakers' union') and was thus indebted to Durand, who patronised the Syndicat liberally. The other two socialists on the commission were Caroline Kauffmann of La Solidarité and Mme Vincent of L'Egalité, neither of whose socialism went beyond the bounds of respectability and both of whom were better known as feminists than as socialists.[28]

The composition of the organising commission was important because its tasks included the preparation of the draft resolutions on which the congress would act. In this respect Durand's minute preparation was to pay off. The commission prepared resolutions supporting some major reforms, such as the eight-hour day and a minimum wage, and a number of minor ones, such as minimum rates for piecework, the nomination of women work inspectors by women's unions, the extension to commercial employees and to domestics of the labour laws of 1892 and 1900 (which limited the working day to eleven hours with a reduction to ten promised for 1904), and of the right to have disputes judged in the Conseils des Prud'hommes. Although the congress rejected the minimum wage and was ambiguous about the eight-hour day, it accepted enough reforms to lead Bonnevial to argue that the feminists had adopted 'the socialist solutions'.[29]

Nevertheless, instead of inaugurating an era of co-operation between socialists and feminists and opening up feminism to working women, the congress consecrated the split between them and brought an end to efforts to bring working women into feminism. No agreement on specific reforms could bridge the class differences which separated the vast majority of the delegates from working women. Most of the 500 delegates to the congress were women of wealth and elegance, like Durand and Pognon. At the opening day, 5 September 1900, the feminists were joined by a host of official and semi-official personalities, including several deputies and the representatives of no less than six governments, whose presence seemed to constitute official recognition of feminism (as the organisers of the congress happily noted). In this respect the congress was indeed a great success, the greatest success of French feminism before the First World War and perhaps the greatest ever. But the presence of the wealthy and the powerful threw into sharp relief the contrasts between the feminists and the few working women delegates.[30]

Not all the working-class women at the congress were under Durand's thumb. Despite some reluctance, she had to admit a group over which she had no control and which had not always shown her the respect she demanded, the Groupe Féministe Socialiste (GFS). It had been founded less than a year before (as we shall see in chapter 4). *La Fronde* had welcomed its founding cautiously: 'Socialist feminism, especially economic, will render great service to the cause by complementing in a way [the feminism] which is concerned with legislative reforms.' But the two socialist women delegates, Elisabeth Renaud and Louise Saumoneau, did not intend simply to 'complement' Durand's efforts. Their intervention highlighted the class differences she sought to bridge by abstract resolutions.[31]

The delegates were humanitarian enough to accept reforms in principle, but they balked when such reforms threatened their own way of life. They found it easy to vote for a resolution supporting the eight-hour day for industrial workers: it was adopted without discussion. But while few of them were industrial employers (though many of their husbands were), all of them had servants at home. Their benevolence did not extend to their maids.[32]

The proposal that domestics have a full day off a week gave rise to one of the toughest and longest debates of the congress. The socialist woman delegate, Elisabeth Renaud, made this proposal explicitly from the point of view of a servant. She reminded the delegates that she had worked for others and had 'lived these humiliations' while they saw the matter from their point of view as mistresses. The following exchange was typical of the majority's desire 'to maintain their class privileges' (as the socialist women later reported to their group):

Mme Wiggishoff.[33] — . . . You're asking for an entire day off. But where will these little girls of 15 or 16 go? Where will they eat?
Mme Renaud [delegate of the GFS]. — At your house [*chez vous*].
Mme Wiggishoff. — So I'm to cook lunch for my maid? I'm not a saint and it's more than likely that her lunch won't be ready. That's not practical.

This resolution was nevertheless adopted, but by a slender margin.

There was even greater hostility to the amendment, 'and in regard to minors, that they be submitted to inspection concerning the hours of work'. Mme Avril de Sainte-Croix (a feminist whose wealth was worthy of her titled name) evoked the spectacle of prostitution: 'If you protect minors, no one will want to employ them and the result will be a great quantity of girls whom you will drive into prostitution.' Nevertheless this too was passed, 'after two votes declared doubtful by the chair', by 110 to 70.[34]

Throughout the congress, class differences appeared in the tone of the debates more than in the actual results. When Stéphanie Bouvard (who was very much a worker, though linked to Durand) proposed that 'an annuity of 800 to 1000 francs be granted to every working woman over fifty', the dignitaries of the congress jumped on her:

Mme Marguerite Durand, Secretary General. — I believe that the bill [presently pending] for a workers' pension fund answers Mlle Bouvard's wish and that, consequently, it is not necessary to pass a special resolution . . .
Mme Chairwoman [Maria Pognon]. — Is Mlle Bouvard aware of this bill?
Mlle Bouvard. — I'm perfectly aware of it, but I believe that it does not fulfil the conditions of my resolution.
In the bill, it is not society itself which pays the retirement fund, it is the worker.

Surprised by Mlle Bouvard's refusal to yield (after all, she had just given 500 francs to Bouvard's *syndicat*), Mme Durand called upon authority:

Mme Marguerite Durand, Secretary General. — Mlle Bouvard is confusing the question of workers' pensions with that of old-age pensions. Very well, I repeat, these questions are presently before the Parliament and we do not, therefore, have to worry about them ourselves . . . It is, I believe, M. B[e]auquier's bill.
M. B[e]auquier, Deputy of the Doubs. — The pension fund for disabled workers has been before the Chamber for a number of years . . .
Consequently, I believe that, for the Congress, it is useless to go on talking endlessly about these questions which will shortly be resolved by the Parliament.

In fact Mlle Bouvard was right. The law on workers' pensions (which was not passed until 1910!) provided for a fund to be taken out of wages. And it was

Beauquier who was confused: he was not talking about this bill, but about another providing for invalids from industrial accidents. No one jumped on him for this confusion. The scarcely veiled disdain of which Bouvard was the object made class differences obvious.[35]

Elisabeth Renaud scarcely fared better, despite her age and her forceful expression. The Doctoresse Edwards-Pilliet urged workers to marry young. Renaud objected, 'But they don't earn enough to feed a wife and children!' The Doctoresse replied:

I realise that the economic situation is indeed very difficult. Young men of 20 or 25 who are not married get into the habit of spending money, they live at the café, drink absinthe [and] aperitifs, and then have women; but these women have to be paid, and the money they spend for that, they would spend much more usefully on their wives and children.

Renaud retorted, 'Workers don't keep mistresses.' She turned on the delegates and addressed them as a 'daughter of workers, representing workers', speaking to the bourgeoisie: 'You can't blame proletarians for going to cabarets, because that's all you've left them.'[36]

This fell on deaf ears. The delegates could see the working class and its problems only in terms of drunkenness and laziness; workers were responsible for their own problems and required the stern guidance of the bourgeoisie to be delivered of their woes. Against Renaud's strenuous objections, the congress voted (for example):

That a stay of at least one month in special hospitals . . . be imposed upon any mother who, after childbirth, cannot show that she has sufficient means for herself and her child. This measure aiming to eliminate all financial aid . . . which rarely profits the mother and child.

The word 'imposed' infuriated Renaud. It implied, as did the second sentence of the resolution, that the working-class father drank away the money given the family. But despite Renaud's eloquent opposition, the word 'imposed' was easily maintained, after six pages of debate.[37]

One major newspaper called Renaud 'one of the most influential *"oratrices"* ' (the feminine form of the word was rare and probably implied condescension). Although the socialist women could not reverse the dominant trends of the congress, they did succeed in stiffening the resistance of the other working women present such as Bouvard. By the end of the congress, they had formed a compact group which clearly and forcefully challenged the right of the bourgeoisie to make decisions about workers. The organisers of the congress felt this resistance and resented it deeply. In the closing speech, Maria Pognon protested:

We have been told, bourgeois women are mistaken in trying to regulate conditions for working women; that is possible, but nevertheless we bring, we who are designated by the title of bourgeois women, such compassion and such good will that it grieves us deeply to discover, what sadly we do sometimes discover, that working women believe themselves to be and want to be the enemies of bourgeois women. Bourgeois women, for our part, are not the enemies of working women, they are their friends. (Repeated applause.)

Pognon had an explanation for the problem: it was caused by the socialist doctrine which Renaud was spreading around the floor of the congress:

I know that there is a certain party that preaches class struggle; well then, I censure that party, I do not accept class struggle, I accept class harmony! (Bravos.) Those who preach hatred do ill: hatred can destroy, only love can build! (Brisk applause.) . . . We must tear down this wall of hatred you want to establish between us. We extend our hand to you, loyally, with all our heart, why don't you want to clasp it and did you come here sometimes to carry on systematic opposition because you are working women and you call us bourgeois? (Applause.)

(Mme Renaud protests.)

I didn't say that for you, Mme Renaud, but I have seen what's been going on in the hall.

Pognon's speech undoubtedly reflected the sentiments of the other leaders of the congress. She herself was speaking as chairwoman of the congress. She was one of Durand's closest collaborators and president of the League. Her speech created a sensation. Although she subsequently apologised in the popular socialist newspaper, *La Petite République*, and although Durand removed the offending passages from the official account of the congress, nothing could mask the split between feminists and socialists, of which Pognon's outburst was only the symbol.[38]

The socialist women addressed a protest to *La Petite République*. The congress had ended, they wrote, 'like any self-respecting bourgeois assembly, with a diatribe against socialism'. Saumoneau, the other socialist woman delegate, reported to their group that the speech had 'established much better than we could have ourselves the barrier which separates bourgeois feminism from socialist feminism'. The congress, she added, had demonstrated 'the desire of many feminist leaders to bring the women of the people [i.e. working women] behind them [into their groups]', which, she warned, 'would constitute a very great danger'. Fortunately their plans had been exposed and thwarted.[39]

So they had been. Not so much through the action of the socialist women's group, but rather because the events of the congress had exposed the contradictions involved in Durand's effort to enlarge the social base of feminism. Even before the congress, she had felt constrained to defend herself against the charge that she was facilitating the infiltration of socialism into the respectable feminist movement. It was now clear that her conservative supporters were unhappy with the concessions she made, while conscious working women felt them insufficient. The congress demonstrated the existence of real conflict of interest as well as of ideas which even Durand, for all her sophistication, could not reconcile.

Thereafter Durand's influence declined rapidly. The following year, French feminists finally managed to set up an umbrella organisation: the Conseil National des Femmes Françaises. But the Conseil formalised Durand's failure to unify the feminists on her terms. Her counterpart from the conservative feminists was among its founders; she was not. While half of the founders were social feminists, the other half were staunchly conservative. They could agree only by excluding political considerations and restricting themselves to a narrower feminism than Durand's. (In fairness it should be noted that this displeased the Catholic feminists as well and they kept aloof from the Conseil.)[40]

Nor did Durand succeed with working women. A police informant told a revealing story. Sometime before the congress, Durand had given 500 francs to each of her four favourite *syndicats*. In December (after the congress), the leaders of the *syndicats* were approached and asked to contribute 125 francs each for the purchase of an 'objet d'art' as a gift for Mme Durand. After some hesitation, they refused and offered her flowers instead.[41]

Durand's patronising and occasionally disdainful attitudes lost her further sympathy. Upon the founding of a Syndicat de Femmes de Lettres et d'Artistes (for which she had not been consulted), she wrote rather sniffily, 'Are they planning to pretend . . . that a tart of a café singer should be paid like Yvette Guilbert [the Edith Piaf of the day] ?' The café singers resented the word 'tart [*grue*] ' and the ensuing polemic ended before a court, with a great deal of attendant publicity for Durand, much of it unsympathetic. In 1901 Durand made a similar error. On the occasion of a printers' strike at Nancy, she urged members of her Syndicat des Femmes Typographes (the women typographers' union of employees of *La Fronde*) to replace the strikers, on the grounds that the male *syndicat* had refused to admit them (which was true). The women had a good case: just before the strike, the male *syndicat* had obtained the ouster of a number of women typographers from a Parisian newspaper. But to most unionists, the action of going to Nancy constituted scabbing. It created much hard feeling. The Bourse du Travail excluded the female *syndicat*, which went to court to obtain reinstatement. Once again there was much unfavourable publicity.[42]

None of this helped Durand recruit working women for feminism. After the congress, she had reached a dead end. By 1903 she ceased her efforts in this direction. In August of that year she stopped publication of *La Fronde* as a daily newspaper (though it continued for two years as a monthly). She returned to traditional feminist activities and left working women to themselves.

Social feminism had failed. Social concern would henceforth express itself in more traditional ways. Feminism would henceforth content itself with its traditional bourgeois clientele. What would socialist women do?

Part II Origins of the socialist women's movement 1899 – 1914

4. The Groupe Féministe Socialiste 1899 – 1905

Thus far we have seen the elimination of a number of possibilities for the political organisation of working women and their sympathisers. The attempt at a feminist alliance with socialism failed, although it made an important contribution to socialism. The attempts of individual women of feminist (and sometimes socialist) tendencies to work within the socialist parties failed too and left few traces. Finally, the attempts of feminists themselves to organise working women failed completely and were never to be renewed. Could working-class women be organised on a socialist basis by their fellow working women? The experience of the Groupe Féministe Socialiste (GFS) founded in 1899 suggests that they could.

Like its predecessors, the GFS sought to combat the oppression which women suffered both as women and as workers. It was, however, more successful than they had been. There were three reasons for this. First, it articulated effectively the experience and concerns of working women themselves. By its class-based approach and its links with the socialist parties as well as its authentically working-class origins, it identified itself with the most profoundly felt aspects of working women's experience. Second, by functioning within the socialist movement, it gave women the feeling that they could have some impact on reality, through a significant organisation. Third, at the same time, the GFS remained sensitive to the particular difficulties public life presented to women: it was autonomous from the socialist parties, functioning as a kind of women's section parallel to party organisations but separate from them and free of their intimidating male atmosphere.

These were precisely the characteristics of the German socialist women's movement which was already flourishing. In the French case, however, these factors of success were accidental and temporary. The GFS's combination of functioning within socialism but autonomously as a women's section was the result of circumstances, not design. These circumstances ceased to exist in 1905, when the competing socialist parties were unified into the Section Française de l'Internationale Ouvrière ('French Section of the Workers' International', SFIO). Before unification, the loose organisation of French

81

socialism permitted flexibility. Afterward, equivocacy became impossible: either one was a member of the party through its duly constituted organs or one was not. The GFS failed to defend its position within the independent socialists' movement and thus did not become a party organ when the independents created the Parti Socialiste Français (PSF) during 1901—2. Like the men, the socialist women accepted implicitly a policy of integration of women into the regular (male) sections, a logical consequence of the theoretical equality which women enjoyed within the party. The result was that in 1905 the GFS found itself outside the unified SFIO.

Bereft not only of resources (the German socialist women's movement had party support) but also of a framework within which to function, the GFS quickly withered and died. Its failure meant that there would be no socialist women's organisation at all until 1913. Moreover, when in that year was founded the Groupe des Femmes Socialistes (GDFS), which remained the basis of the organisation of women in the SFIO throughout its existence, it was crippled by the failure of its predecessor. It was only an auxiliary for those few women already in the party. This is a large part of the explanation for the small number of socialist women in France as compared to Germany. The organisation of socialist women in the Third Republic was vitiated by failings whose origins are to be found in the failure of the GFS.

Origins

The GFS may be said to have begun at a meeting of Potonié-Pierre's group, La Solidarité des Femmes. In February 1897, a young seamstress painfully conscious of looking like the 'simple provincial just arrived from the country' that she was, left her work one Wednesday afternoon (thus foregoing half her daily earnings of 2 francs) to attend a meeting of La Solidarité. Ill at ease among the bourgeois women in whom she recognised employers and customers rather than sisters, she listened to a long debate on the morality of the custom of bestowing a dowry. In families like hers there was no question of dowries. Reflecting bitterly on the debate's irrelevance and her lost wages, she determined to create a movement for working-class women like herself and in fact devoted the next fifty-three years to that task. Her name was Louise Saumoneau.[1]

Louise Aimée Saumoneau was born on 17 December 1875 near Poitiers. Late in 1896 she and her parents followed her married elder sister to Paris. There she found life difficult. She was young, poor, and without any source of income beyond her own earnings doing piecework as a seamstress. Her father and brother-in-law were cabinet makers employed in large workshops. It was all they could do to provide for her elder sister's family of four children and for her younger sister.[2]

Not only did Saumoneau live entirely in a working-class milieu. She was a worker even to her physical aspect. Jeanne Halbwachs, a socialist student who was to become a leader of the French section of the Women's International League for Peace and Freedom, went to see Saumoneau once, around 1910, to ask her help for a feminist project (she refused). Halbwachs' reaction: 'she had something of an unattractive appearance, the simplicity of a woman of the people — dull, dreary, truly a woman of the people'.[3]

What displeased the middle-class student, however, attracted others. Among them was Elisabeth Renaud, who was to become Saumoneau's mentor and with whom Saumoneau would found the GFS. Renaud was born on 8 August 1846 in the Doubs. Her family practised a strict Protestantism, from which she retained a severe moral sense (and to which she ultimately reverted, becoming a Seventh Day Adventist at the age of seventy-five). Her father was a worker in the Japy watch factory, where she worked as a girl, delaying her education until she could pay for it. She received her school certificate in 1870. Thereafter she worked for several years as a governess for noble families in St Petersburg. In 1881 she married a printer who died after five years, leaving her two children and numerous debts. To support herself and her family, she ran a *pension de famille* (boarding house) where she gave French lessons to foreigners.[4]

She held republican views before her marriage. She used to tell her grandchildren that her Russian pupils had at first insisted that she bow to them and call them by their titles, but that she had refused. Their father bore her out, but upon her departure told her, 'You are too republican to stay in Russia.' Whether true or not, the story reflected her own image of herself: a republican above all, in the 1848 spirit which linked the republic with social justice. She evolved logically toward socialism in the decade following the death of her husband in 1886, a period during which she herself encountered the difficulties of workers and of women. The result was a generous, optimistic socialism with faith in the future and frequent use of words like 'reason' and 'light' giving an enlightenment veneer to a sense of morality and justice:

We, children of proletarians, direct descendants of those slaves who disappeared in the night of time without having even glimpsed justice, we see glimmering the dawn of complete emancipation by *rehabilitated labour* [italics orig.]. Yes, labour, cursed by those who are overwhelmed with it, despised by those whom idleness corrupts, will become the keystone of a new society.[5]

Our records of Renaud's activity as a socialist begin with a police note of May 1897, citing her presence at a private meeting of the Guesdist student group. In this group she met many socialists who were to figure in her life subsequently: Jean Longuet, secretary of the group at this time, was to be a close friend for thirty-five years; Léo Guesde (son of Jules) was to marry her daughter; and Jean Allemane, who was often a speaker for the group (party divisions were still fuzzy), was to print her works and to be her last political collaborator — together they broke from the SFIO in 1914. These acquaintances became intimates at her Friday evening teas, which they and other socialists frequented assiduously.[6]

The result of these diverse contacts was a socialism one could describe as eclectic. Her name appears among the delegates to both the Guesdist and the Allemanist congresses of 1897, but she spoke at length only at the latter. The Allemanists would seem to have been a more likely choice than the Guesdists, for she favoured the general strike (which was one of the key issues dividing the two parties, the Allemanists having made it an article of faith, the Guesdists having maintained the total rejection of it which had so angered Paule Mink). In 1898, however, Renaud followed Longuet and a number of other members of the Guesdist student group when they quit the POF and joined the independent socialists.[7]

The independent socialists were relative newcomers, but they were gaining on the older socialist parties. In the 1893 elections, they elected eighteen of the thirty-nine socialist deputies. Their socialism had deeper roots in French traditions, emphasising as it did the need to perfect the republic and fulfil its promise of social justice rather than overturn it. Their greatest leader, Jean Jaurès, began his parliamentary career in 1885 as a republican. Defeated in 1889, he returned to his career as a university philosophy professor and completed his two doctoral dissertations (one in Latin on the origins of German socialism). His intellectual development combined with his concern for justice to bring him to socialism: 'Even if the socialists extinguished all the stars in the sky, I would walk with them toward justice, that divine spark which alone will rekindle all the suns of the firmament.' Quaffing a glass of red wine as he mounted to the podium, Jaurès spoke brilliantly for two or three hours, conveying to his hearers both the profundity of his thought and the greatness of his heart. Students thronged to the Chamber to hear his speeches (as one of them told me in 1971); workers — as many as 30,000 — came to hear him at open-air meetings. Before the end of the century, Jaurès had become the spiritual leader of socialism. In addition to his activities as party leader in the Chamber and outside it, he found time to lead the campaign for Dreyfus, to write one of the great histories of the French Revolution, to produce almost daily newspaper columns, and to found and edit a major new party daily, *L'Humanité*.[8]

Renaud, who shared Jaurès's generous republicanism, settled comfortably among the independent socialists, although she still remained close to Allemane, who published as brochures two public lectures she had given in 1898.[9] She was thus a militant of some note when she met Saumoneau. Saumoneau's youth, ardent convictions and working-class aspect must have pleased Renaud, who was past fifty, but burning with faith herself and proud of her working-class origins. Saumoneau soon became a regular at Renaud's

Origins

Friday evenings and, for a time, her protégée. The founding of the GFS was
the logical outgrowth of their encounter.

The 'Call' for the constitution of a socialist feminist group appeared in the
socialist press on Sunday, 2 July 1899. It was signed by four women, all of
them workers: Saumoneau ('seamstress'), Renaud ('governess [*institutrice*] '),
Estelle Mordelet and Florestine Malseigne ('clothing makers [*confection-
neuses*] '). It outlined the 'double oppression' of women, 'exploited on a
large scale by capitalism, subjected to men by laws and *especially* [italics
orig.] by prejudice'. The 'Call' suggested, however, that class oppression was
fundamental, sex oppression secondary. The GFS would seek 'to develop
women's intellectual and moral faculties in order that they may aid in the
emancipation of labour'. The 'Call' recognised the 'legitimacy' of feminist
demands: the group would defend them 'as reforms whose realisation would
improve women's situation' but it insisted that the basic 'struggle' was between 'exploiters' and 'exploited'.[10]

Even in this founding document, however, there were ambiguities fore-
shadowing the differences which would separate Saumoneau and Renaud
within a few years. Was the group to struggle for women's demands from the
start, or did it first have to 'tear women out of this passivity degrading for
them and dangerous for the triumph of social demands'? Saumoneau clearly
thought that education must come before women's rights: 'we, women of
the people, we would be failing in all our duties . . . if we sought, uniquely,
to break women out of the narrow circles where they are enclosed to throw
them into the social conflict in all their ignorance', for (as the GFS would
state in its 'Statutes') 'women *especially* [italics orig.], having been kept out
of public matters . . . are not in condition to fulfil their duties toward
society'. Renaud, on the other hand, never lost sight of feminist demands.
Indeed, she had what today we would call a sense of sisterhood: 'Women?
They are the slaves of the slaves. Some of them have the privilege of being
the slaves of the masters, but they are none the less subjects.' Saumoneau's
harsh tone was thus tempered by Renaud. If Saumoneau provided a hard
core of class consciousness, Renaud emphasised the concrete, daily problems
of women's experience. So long as it lasted, their partnership was a source of
strength for the GFS, for only by taking into account both the primacy of
class and the importance of sex roles could such a group succeed.[11]

How many women responded to the 'Call' and met to found the group?
A handful, perhaps. Renaud wrote to Marguerite Durand later in 1899 that
the group had started slowly because 'the season' had not been 'propitious';
in after years Saumoneau referred to 'the disadvantageous conditions in
which the movement was born'. Nevertheless, as she put it drily, 'the meeting took place and the first socialist feminist group was created'.[12]

At this meeting, the group drafted statutes which provided that it would aim to educate women and, in addition, 'to obtain all the economic, political and social advantages which can bring about an improvement in women's situation and increase their means of action in the struggle for the emancipation of the proletariat'. Reforms were seen as strengthening the proletariat for further action in the class struggle. This was the language Jaurès used to defend his reformism against those who preached revolution and who complained that reforms simply prolonged the life of capitalist society. Not surprisingly, the GFS decided at the same meeting to join the Confédération des Socialistes Indépendants of Jaurès and Millerand.[13]

Yet this was only two weeks after the so-called Millerand affair had blown up, a result of the evolution of the Dreyfus affair. Dreyfus had been convicted in 1894. Serious public doubts about his guilt began with Zola's 'J'accuse' in January 1898. That summer, a series of articles by Jaurès had forced the minister of war to review all the documents of the case. He discovered that the most important evidence had been forged. The arrest and suicide of the officer charged with the forgery put the right on the defensive. It responded by violent attacks on the government. By 1899, the very existence of the republic seemed to be under threat from reactionary forces. In June of that year, a dynamic business lawyer named René Waldeck-Rousseau formed a ministry of 'Republican defence'. To assure support from the left, he included Alexandre Millerand, one of the best-known socialists after Jaurès. To conciliate the right, he named as minister of war a general who had been particularly brutal in the repression of the Commune, the Marquis de Gallifet. That a socialist should sit alongside 'the butcher of the Commune' was intolerable to the older generation of socialists, who saw their parties as inheritors of the Commune's revolutionary traditions, while the younger generation of independent socialists accepted it in the interest of the republic. This disagreement — the Millerand affair — delayed socialist unity, which had seemed close at hand. For the GFS to decide in favour of the independents at this time demonstrated a reformism without complexes.[14]

Having made the choice for reformism, what would the group actually do? In September, Renaud gave a talk on the Dreyfus case. The Waldeck-Rousseau government had assured a second trial for Dreyfus, but the military judges had found him guilty again, though this time 'with extenuating circumstances'. Renaud made a plea for justice for Dreyfus which the group voted to have Allemane print as a flyer for public distribution. It was vaguely humanitarian and in no way related to the problems of working women. Two weeks later, the GFS decided to seek by petition the abolition of courts martial, of religious orders, and of the death penalty, as well as the transformation of youth prisons into 'humanitarian schools'.[15]

This grab-bag of reforms hardly constituted the 'advantages' the GFS had originally spoken of seeking for working women. They had still to put into practice their working-class consciousness. Whether because it therefore failed to attract members or because (as Renaud herself suggested) it had no centrally located meeting place, the GFS floundered by November. Renaud may even have given it up for lost. She attended the first congress of socialist organisations in December with a mandate not from the GFS, which had not yet followed up its intention to join the independents, but from a male group.[16]

The problem of a meeting place was solved by Longuet's student group, which found a hall in the Latin Quarter and offered the use of it to Renaud.[17] The GFS announced in the socialist press that, as of 31 December, it would meet every Sunday. The programme: lectures by Renaud or Saumoneau (sometimes both) and discussions of current events. Weekly lectures by such women ('they didn't smile very much', recalls Renaud's granddaughter) would seem forbidding, but the group did meet weekly and finally got off the ground. In February 1900, it became a recognised section of the Confédération des Socialistes Indépendants. In March it demonstrated its vigour by a successful public meeting presided by Allemane. It remained, however, to cater in reality to the needs of working women, to clarify the ambiguity between its feminist and socialist positions. During 1900, the first year of its working existence, the GFS struggled to do so, without great success.[18]

The GFS took part in the violent debate over the Millerand—Colliard law of 30 March 1900, the main result of Millerand's efforts to obtain concrete reforms through his participation in government. The law of 1892 had set the working day at twelve hours for men, eleven for women, and ten for children. Millerand argued that this law had not been enforced (which was true) because it was too cumbersome (which was not certain). He therefore proposed an eleven-hour day for everyone, with the promise of the ten-hour day for 1904. The independents supported him, but the Guesdists fought bitterly against this 'backward step'. The GFS came down on Millerand's side, arguing that the 1892 law would remain 'illusory without the new law', children having 'always worked eleven hours and more', and that the new law represented 'a step backward . . . only in order to arrive at real progress'. To this standard reformist argument, the GFS added a point which the men had overlooked in their debates:

In regard to women, there is an unquestionable advantage in their being assimilated to men in work, given that the great number of women whom capitalism has industrialised should not be differentiated from men because this aggravates the condition of inferiority to which they have been reduced by the laws and the prejudices accumulated by centuries of ignorance.

This position corresponded to that of the feminists, who opposed all restrictions on women's right to work (except insofar as men were subject to the same restrictions). It was diametrically opposed to the position of the

Socialist International, which had resolved in favour of special regulations for women at its 1893 congress.[19]

In a second case, the GFS managed to strike a balance between feminism and socialism. In June 1900, there began a strike of cabinet-makers demanding 'the exclusion of women' from their shops. The GFS passed and distributed a resolution terming the demand 'profoundly unjust' and explaining to the strikers that the only way to avoid women's undercutting their wages was to persuade women to join the union and demand equal wages. This position coincided with that of the feminists but it was consistent with socialist theory and, more importantly, with the interests of the working women concerned. Such balance was difficult to achieve: thirteen years later, faced by a similar problem (the Couriau affair), the socialist women would refuse to support a woman's right to work for fear of betraying the principle of class struggle.[20]

In a third case, the ambiguity in the group's position led it into confusion. The anti-Dreyfusard forces waged a major battle in the municipal elections of May 1900. The GFS termed the elections a struggle between 'the partisans of the democratic regime' and the reactionaries who, 'under the cover of nationalism, seek only to strengthen the power of the military'. This was simply the reformist socialist position. But the GFS added that the elections were of special interest to women, 'the relentless opponents of militarism'. Such optimism about women's political positions hardly squared with the talk about women's ignorance and passivity, still less with a class-based analysis. The statement went on to ask women 'to use their rights as women and as mothers to make their ideas penetrate the minds of voters'. Women were to use feminine wiles on their men? This was consistent neither with feminism nor with socialism. This statement may have been due to the influence of new members, a number of whom had joined during the spring of 1900. Nonetheless it betrayed the continuing ambiguity within the GFS, torn as it was between sex-based and class-based analysis.[21]

This ambiguity was resolved by the socialist women's confrontation with the feminists at Marguerite Durand's congress. The experience of the group's delegates[22] seemed to confirm Saumoneau's argument of a year before:

> The bourgeois feminist movement . . . represents . . . economic interests, but not those of the masses of women.
> We know that among the bourgeois feminists, there are women who have excellent intentions with regard to social problems . . . But as they want to maintain their class privileges and consequently the organisation which develops and perpetuates the miseries [they seek to alleviate], . . . they are condemned to exhaust themselves in vain criticisms and useless lamentations.

To Pognon's closing speech accusing the socialists of preaching class hatred, the GFS responded with a vigorous resolution affirming that it would be 'puerile to deny' the existence of the class struggle and reminding 'the

women of the people . . . [that] their individual emancipation can only be
the result of the economic emancipation of the working class in all its
entirety and that, consequently, they must not abandon the terrain of class
struggle which is theirs, to run after a chimerical . . . emancipation on the
bourgeois terrain'.[23]

For the duration of their collaboration, Renaud accepted Saumoneau's
view. She had another clash with the feminists which helped confirm her in
this position. In February 1902, she went to a meeting of La Solidarité to
get signatures on a petition calling for a militia to replace standing armies,
which 'serve only to defend the capitalist order, witness the use made of
them in strikes'. La Solidarité forbade her to circulate the petition, deeming
it too 'political'.[24]

Saumoneau's opposition to the feminists grew more violent even as the
danger of their seducing working women into their ranks grew fainter. A
year later, in 1901, Saumoneau told the GFS that nothing could 'permit
them to jump over the ditch which separated the whole proletariat from the
capitalist bourgeoisie'. She warned them against the 'danger' of heeding 'that
lying phrase: "women's emancipation" '. Never again, after the experience
of the congress, would the women of the GFS take the risk of being (as
Saumoneau put it in a veiled reference to Bonneval) 'a few socialist indivi-
dualities [*sic*] astray in this bourgeois movement'. The GFS was henceforth
committed to the primacy of class struggle. Yet the presence of Renaud
enabled the group to keep in sight women's problems as women alongside
those as workers. On this basis it enjoyed surprising success.[25]

Expansion

The expansion of the GFS began as a result of the feminist congress. The
GFS resolution condemning the feminists and affirming class struggle had
brought it warm praise from both the independent socialist and Guesdist
newspapers. Its meetings were regularly announced in all the socialist press.
Most of all, it was attracting new members. It decided to cater for them in
two ways: first, to create a *syndicat* for seamstresses; and, second, to create
sister groups of the GFS in other neighbourhoods.[26]

The creation of women's *syndicats* had been one of the original aims of
the GFS. One trade was of particular concern to the group. Many of its
members, including Saumoneau, were seamstresses, working at least ten
hours a day by the piece making up garments, most often underwear. The
work was seasonal and badly paid: employers gave it on a take-it-or-leave-it
basis and the women, sweating alone at home, isolated and unorganised,
took it at virtually any price. The GFS issued a call for seamstresses to attend
its regular Sunday meeting on 18 November 1900. Enough came that it
seemed feasible to launch a Chambre Syndicale des Travailleuses de l'Aiguille

('Women Needleworkers' Union') at a special meeting the following Wednesday. Louise Saumoneau was elected secretary, her younger sister Berthe assistant secretary, one Alice Foreau treasurer, and Estelle Mordelet (another founder of the GFS) assistant treasurer.[27]

It was not a propitious time. In mid February 1901, tailors and seamstresses began a month-long strike which, despite a massive campaign of support in the press, ended in a very thinly disguised defeat. This strike did not directly concern the seamstresses doing piecework at home, but rather those who made outerwear, work done in shops. The Chambre Syndicale was not trying to organise these women. Nevertheless, the socialist women were troubled that women workers, who were in the majority in the industry, had clearly been 'refractory to the strike movement'.[28]

This was doubly discouraging because the strike had received not only massive coverage in the press but also extensive financial support, especially from *La Fronde*. The high degree of feminine participation in the clothing trade, both as workers and as customers, made it a natural test of Durand's social feminism. *La Fronde* assured its readers that the strike was worthy of their support, that it was led not by 'agitators' but by honest workers who did not mean to threaten social institutions. The paper carried the strike on its front page every day for a month. Durand gave 500 francs to open a subscription for the strikers, which ultimately raised 4359 francs, a massive sum in the eyes of the seamstresses, whose wages were usually between 2 and 3 francs a day.[29]

For Saumoneau, support from *La Fronde* was proof that the strike represented only 'the first stirrings' of workers who lacked class consciousness. 'This bourgeois faction [the feminists] acts, penetrates workers' ranks, defends the interests of their trades, hoping thereby to turn them away from the great social movement and to separate them from the whole of the proletariat, *especially* [italics orig.] from the conscious part.' Following this logic, Saumoneau soon came to oppose women's *syndicats* as such, because they facilitated this 'bourgeois influence'. By the summer of 1901, she argued that only joint men's and women's *syndicats* were acceptable. Even if male *syndicats* refused to accept women, they should found not female *syndicats* but their own mixed *syndicats* 'to set the example'. 'Working women must', she explained, 'give to their action the class character which suits it rather than the sex character with which it seems marked.'[30]

The Chambre Syndicale soon followed Saumoneau's thinking. It began negotiations with the *syndicat* which had led the strike. The latter agreed to open itself to workers in all aspects of the garment industry and to revise its statutes to provide explicitly for its leadership to include women as well as men. Saumoneau's Chambre Syndicale disbanded in September 1901, its members entering the other *syndicat*, which kept its promises.[31]

Saumoneau's hostility to bourgeois feminism was leading her away from

sensitivity to women's problems. If separate women's *syndicats* were dangerous because subject to bourgeois influence, what about separate socialist
groups for women? In fact, by 1913 Saumoneau would reach a position of
condemning women's sections within the party; she would accept only a
limited kind of auxiliary for women already in the party, with disastrous
consequences for the movement. In 1901 and 1902, however, this was not
yet a problem because Saumoneau's point of view in the GFS was balanced
by Renaud's.

Shortly after the founding of the Chambre Syndicale, the GFS decided to
create sister groups to accommodate members who came from other neighbourhoods. In December 1900, sister groups were founded in the thirteenth
and seventeenth arrondissements. That of the seventeenth met in a co-
operative called La Ménagère ('The Housewife'). It elected a woman named
Mme Dumoulin as its secretary. It seems to have functioned effectively as a
circle for informal discussion among women of the neighbourhood. They
met twice a month, holding in addition an occasional concert or dance
('sauterie'). Sometimes they had a lecture. In May 1901, for instance, we
find the following note in a republican newspaper: 'The Groupe Féministe
Socialiste du 17e after having, in its last meeting, been informed of the
Russian revolutionary movement, vows scorn on the activities of the tsar and
addresses all its sympathies to the Russian people'.[32]
     The GFS of the seventeenth arrondissement continued to meet through
December 1901. At the beginning of April 1902, the police spy reported
that Mme Dumoulin had given up her efforts to reconstitute it. She blamed,
he wrote, 'the anarchists who frequent the People's University [which also
met at La Ménagère] and who will only tolerate mixed groups'. Apparently
the women had wished to keep men out of their discussions and the anarchists had not accepted this. If so, this would bear out our point that, to be
successful, a socialist women's group had to provide a specifically feminine
centre, a kind of women's section, where women would not be intimidated
by male dominance. But the GFS of the seventeenth arrondissement seems
to have suffered also from its lack of hold on political reality. The women
do not seem to have felt a part of the socialist movement. After a while, they
tired of their resolutions without effect. This would bear out our point that
such a group must function within the party.[33]
     The experience of the group formed in the thirteenth arrondissement
bears out both these points. The direction it took was toward greater participation in the socialist movement and it ultimately became a section of the
Parti Socialiste de France (PSDF, formed in 1902 by the union of the
Guesdists and Vaillantists), but it was nevertheless dominated by women,
most of all by Adèle Kassky.
     Kassky was born in 1848 of an impoverished Norman noble (she claimed)

and a working woman who earned the family's living by painting manufactured objects. Her father, a ferocious Freemason, led her to republican meetings when she was still a child (this was during the Second Empire, when such activity was illegal). At sixteen, she became a laundress. At nineteen, she married a blacksmith, Edouard Kassky. Active in the Commune, arrested and released by luck, she retained a Communard, insurrectionary spirit all her life.[34]

Kassky called a meeting at her home on 16 December 1900 at which a group was founded. The treasurer was Kassky and the secretary was a certain Mme Duvignaud, a friend of Kassky from the Commune (said Kassky). The group called itself the Groupe Féministe Mixte (GFM) because there were some men among its members, notably the Communard poet-printer Achille LeRoy.[35] The GFM was less suspicious of feminism than the original GFS (which henceforth styled itself the GFS of the fifth arrondissement to distinguish itself from its siblings). For example, it supported a campaign to facilitate divorce while the GFS of the fifth arrondissement kept aloof from it. The GFM was also less austere than the GFS of the fifth arrondissement, holding frequent *fêtes* to attract new members. Here is the programme of one, for Christmas, 1901. It was more elaborate than usual, but typical in content:

Mass lecture-concert. Talks: by Citizen Félix Boisdin, on 'Feminism and solidarity'; by Citizen Andrée Téry, on 'Women and socialism'; by Citizen Rama, on 'The ideal which we seek to realise'.
Concert by the Aurore Social of Plaisance.
Property is the Right to Murder, social play by F. Boisdin, performed by the Lyre Sociale of Belleville.
God is Not, by a student of the anticlerical *pensionnat* [boarding establishment] of Montreuil.
Pierrot's Madness, mime drama by L. Marsotteau, performed by Citizen M. Surani.
Invitations may be found in all the co-operatives of the 13th [arrondissement].[36]

The GFM was the most successful of all the groups. Its success was the result of its providing a predominantly women's atmosphere, or at least one in which women felt comfortable (though this was not its conscious purpose, witness its ultimate evolution into a regular party section), at the same time as it was unequivocally class-based and functioned within the socialist movement.

The rapid expansion of the GFS into a *syndicat* and three groups,[37] accomplished despite its lack of resources, encouraged the women to establish their own newspaper. It would be class-based, like the newspaper of the German socialist women's movement, *Die Gleichheit* ('Equality'), 'valiant organ' of a movement which 'has only gained by a clear and frank separation from all bourgeois elements'. In mid February 1901, the 'Tribune feminine' of the Guesdist daily, *Le Petit Sou*, announced the imminent appearance of *La Femme socialiste*. The first issue was dated March 1901. It was an attractive four-page newspaper in a large format, printed by Allemane. Renaud was director, Saumoneau secretary. The masthead proclaimed, 'There can be no antagonism between the men and the women of the proletarian class.' (Fact or desire? Had they forgotten the cabinet-makers' strike?) The publication of *La Femme socialiste* was an indication of the groups' success: it was funded by membership dues. Another sign that they were reaching a certain number of women was Renaud's furious protest in the June issue against a rumour being spread among the seamstresses that Saumoneau was not a worker.[38]

The newspaper itself in turn further aided recruitment to the groups. It provided a rallying point, with calendars of meetings and descriptions of other activities. Its fundamental purpose, however, was to educate women for socialism. It provided standard party literature, serialising speeches and brochures by leaders such as Guesde and Jaurès. It also attempted to acquaint its readers with the significance of the manoeuvres of the various socialist parties. But it gave particular emphasis to issues of interest to women, especially to strikes in which women were active. Thus, for example, a major strike of coal miners at Montceau-les-Mines (near Le Creusot) received much attention: articles from a local woman in July and September 1901; a first-hand report by Renaud in November 1901, upon her return from a special trip to Montceau; and again articles from the local correspondent from December 1901 through March 1902.

Apart from such strikes, two issues received particular, indeed passionate, attention in *La Femme socialiste*: militarism and clericalism, which Renaud called 'the two main pillars' of the regime. Both were topics of predilection for republican socialists like Renaud, especially now that they were major public preoccupations. The Waldeck-Rousseau government, having pardoned Dreyfus in September 1899, sought to channel feverish public opinion against the more overtly seditious and anti-republican religious orders. Under his successor, Emile Combes (prime minister from 1902 to 1905), this policy gave way to a struggle for total laicisation of education and complete separation of church and state. Combes's government, like that of Waldeck-Rousseau, relied on a coalition of 'left' and 'radical' republicans with the independent socialists. The other socialist parties disapproved of such distractions from the class struggle but refrained from voting against Combes.[39]

Renaud and Saumoneau saw the anti-clerical struggle not only in terms of perfecting the republic, but also of educating women. 'Clerical women are the mill-stone about the neck of progress', wrote Renaud; 'the last rampart of capitalism', said Saumoneau. When Combes closed the church schools, in July 1902, *La Femme socialiste* applauded. Renaud elaborated in reply to a protest from Mme Jules Lebaudy, the fabulously wealthy heiress to the Lebaudy sugar trust, who claimed that the church schools were needed to 'moralise' men and thus combat prostitution. Not at all, retorted Renaud: the church schools were in fact the 'principal suppliers' of prostitutes. On the one hand, 'the "Good Sisters" ... by exploiting children ... provide mortal competition to the workers outside [of the convents] '. On the other hand, they taught their charges neither reason nor a trade, thus rendering them unfit for anything but prostitution. In freeing women from clerical influence, Combes was doing them an invaluable service.[40]

Anti-militarism was also a public issue as a result of the Dreyfus affair. General André, Gallifet's successor as minister of war (1900–5), sought to eliminate clerical and monarchist influence from the army. In addition, he implemented such humanitarian reforms as the abolition of irons in military prisons. *La Femme socialiste* was fortunate in having a collaborator who could write on these matters with passion and first-hand knowledge: Gaston Dubois-Dessaulle had spent three years in the disciplinary corps. His articles make shocking reading even today, when we are accustomed to atrocity stories.[41] An issue of *La Femme socialiste* rarely passed without an article by him or by Renaud attacking the army on moral grounds. Renaud sought to push General André to undertake more reforms and to educate women about the 'pernicious' influence of the army on the young men they nurtured so painfully: it deprived men in their formative years 'of their conscience, their responsibility, [which are] the only way to make moral men of them'.[42]

The newspaper did not limit itself to educating women about general political issues. It also took up specifically feminine issues. It attacked the prohibition of paternity suits, the most flagrant example of the double standard built into the Napoleonic Code: the woman was left burdened with the moral and financial responsibility for an illegitimate child, powerless to obtain aid from the father, who was legally blameless. Similarly, it attacked the system of regulated prostitution: 'Only the woman is scorned, punished, labelled', noted Renaud, not 'the clients, who are always sheltered from all the humiliations reserved for the women, although they carry the contagion'.[43]

These issues preoccupied the groups as well as the newspaper. The GFS of the fifth arrondissement had an ongoing committee on prostitution and the GFM had devoted one of its first meetings to the subject. Despite a moralising tone, they saw the issues in terms of economic reality and class oppression. 'Wealthy women, men of letters', complained Renaud, 'claim that it is laziness ... that engenders prostitution.' But those who talk this way, 'never having known the anguish of tomorrows without bread and without shelter, are incapable of understanding the state of mind of those in the grasp of misery'. It 'never occurs' to such wealthy women that 'while they are jealously guarding their daughters, it is the daughter of the poor man, whom nothing and no one protect, who is the prey of the passions of their sons'.[44]

Thus *La Femme socialiste* always brought women's problems back to socialism. 'You may wonder what our feminism consists of', said Renaud and Saumoneau in the first issue. They answered:

Persuaded that socialist doctrine opens all the gates of the future to women as well as to men, but recognising on the other hand that women remain attached to the furrows of the past and that they are thus in a state of unquestionable inferiority compared to men, and judging it necessary that women enter, for the regeneration of our society, into the path of the ideas which are shaking the world, our aim is to put women in a position to enter by the gates which socialism has opened to all those oppressed.

Socialism would open these gates through 'the abolition of classes, [which] alone can enfranchise humanity in its entirety'. And so the newspaper, like the groups, sought 'to ensure that the women of the proletariat struggle for the emancipation of their class in the ranks of the Socialist Party'.[45]

Whenever there was a conflict, the interest of the party was more important than any specific women's rights. *La Femme socialiste* supported enthusiastically the decision of the Belgian socialist women to cease agitation for women's suffrage in order to facilitate the party's effort to obtain universal male suffrage:

We can only congratulate the Belgian socialist women who have, by this decision, demonstrated a class consciousness which we would like to see imitated by the socialist women of France. By placing above one of their individual rights the interest of the Worker Party [which] is at the same time the interest of the proletariat of both sexes, they have given to all socialists an admirable example of solidarity.[46]

However unappealing this position may seem today, it was successful at the time, at least in combination with sensitivity for women's position within the party. In the summer and autumn of 1901, the GFS seemed on its way to becoming an authentic movement. The newspaper spoke for three flourishing groups. Presumably there would soon be more. What was needed was a central organisation to co-ordinate their action and give them direction as the movement grew.

In August 1901, *La Femme socialiste* issued a call for the formation of a Union Féministe Socialiste of the Paris region. In response, representatives came to a meeting on 25 August from the two GFS, the GFM, and from a hitherto unknown organisation, Le Groupe Féministe d'Etudes Socialistes des 10e et 11e: l'Egalité Humaine (POSR) ('Feminist Group of Socialist Studies of the Tenth and Eleventh [Arrondissements] : Human Equality'). L'Egalité Humaine sent four representatives, including its founders, M. and Mme Pasquier.[47]

L'Egalité Humaine met every Monday night at a room it shared with another Allemanist group. Its meetings were limited to informal discussion, apart from a *fête* at which Allemane spoke and an occasional petition. It remained a faithful member of the Union and used *La Femme socialiste* for its announcements so long as both lasted. Thereafter, it apparently continued to meet just as before, but functioned only on a local basis.[48]

The Groupe Féministe Socialiste

L'Egalité Humaine made a total of four groups which constituted the Union Féministe Socialiste and elected a council of eleven, including Renaud and Saumoneau for the GFS of the fifth arrondissement and three for each of the other groups. It was decided that the Union would be non-partisan, welcoming groups linked to any socialist party, and would hold quarterly meetings to determine how to facilitate socialist propaganda among women.

From the outset the Union demonstrated the hostility to feminism increasingly characteristic of Saumoneau. In August, a bevy of pupils from the socialist school of Gent (Belgium) innocently provoked the wrath of the Union by accepting a bouquet of flowers from 'the bourgeois newspaper, *La Fronde*'. At its first meeting, on 25 August 1901, the Union protested:

Our direct adversaries are those men and women who . . . want in the name of a so-called sex struggle, to enrol . . . the women of the proletariat, in order to make of them auxiliaries of the women of the bourgeois class . . . The members of the General Committee [of the party] . . . have increased . . . this confusion [by permitting *La Fronde* to offer the flowers].[49]

The Union asked the general committee to vote 'regrets'. But although Adèle Kassky was a member of the committee, it did not reply.

The Union was soon preoccupied with enemies further to its right. Upon the founding of the reactionary Ligue des Femmes Françaises ('Frenchwomen's League') in the autumn of 1901, the Union reacted with a vigorous condemnation: 'The [forces of] reaction and the church are trying to seize power again.' Women were the instrument they hoped to use. 'Reaction had made them its secret agents, but . . . today apparently the confessional is not enough; it is by public appeals that reaction calls them, exploiting their lack of political and social knowledge and the prejudices with which the church has saturated their brains, in order to draw them into a movement of religious and capitalist defence.' The Union explained: 'These ladies declare that they love France. That is understandable: France represents, in their eyes, something very concrete: castles, estates, forests, millions.' At its next general meeting, on 29 December 1901, the Union resolved 'in order to reply more effectively to the nascent nationalist feminist movement to employ a great part of its activity to combat it'.[50]

During the spring of 1902 the Union held four meetings (all well attended) at which Renaud and Saumoneau denounced the League and the audience passed resolutions 'congratulating them' on their action. In June the pro-clerical forces planned a demonstration against the imminent closure of church schools. Since the demonstration was to be led by women of the League, the Union made a point of marching in the republican counter-demonstration. It then challenged the League to a debate, but received no reply. It held four more meetings against the League in the autumn, but the need had passed: Combes had closed the church schools without serious opposition. And the Union, despite appearances, had already attained the peak of its development.[51]

Before we examine its decline, let us try to evaluate the success of the 'socialist feminist movement'. During the period from 1900 through 1902, three neighbourhood groups functioned successfully and supported a newspaper and a rudimentary central organisation. Their membership can be estimated at between fifty and one hundred, a respectable number in view of the fact that there were less than one hundred and fifty socialist women in the whole Paris region in 1905 when the unified party (the SFIO) was founded,[52] while the groups functioned in only three of the twenty arrondissements of Paris proper (four or five if one includes L'Egalité Humaine) and without party help. Moreover, the audience they could draw was significantly larger than their formal membership, judging from attendance at *fêtes* and major lectures. Renaud and Saumoneau were no longer leaders in search of a movement. If they still dominated the Union, it was in large part because of the difficulty most women had in speaking before mixed audiences of any size. Even Kassky shrank from being a delegate to the congress of socialist organisations in 1901 — the GFM was represented by a man.

In the autumn of 1901, two provincial groups were founded: a Groupe Féministe Socialiste of some twenty members at Sens (a city on the border between Burgundy and the Paris basin) and L'Avant-Garde Féministe at Marseilles. The movement was still 'very weak' wrote Saumoneau, 'but given its modest beginnings, the mounting path it has followed and its rapid progressive development are tokens to us of its future development'. This was a fair assessment.[53]

Decline

Unfortunately, this development was cut short during 1902. During the period from 1899 to 1905, the socialist parties moved toward unification. Autonomy would no longer be possible once the parties were unified into one national structure. Only the confusion of the several conflicting, manoeuvring parties made it possible for groups like the GFS to be members of a party and yet retain their autonomy. The competing parties, abysmally organised, accepted the membership of all kinds of groups which had sprung up on their own: study groups, co-operatives, *syndicats*, etc. But a unified national party strong enough to constitute its own local sections would require membership through them. If there were to be exceptions such as women's or youth groups, special provision would have to be made for them.

As the independent socialists moved toward more rigorous organisation, it became imperative for the GFS to carve out a formal position within the

party or else be left out. But the leaders of the GFS, like the men of the
party, accepted unquestioningly the idea of integration of women individually into the regular sections. Moreover, they feared that separate organisations could facilitate bourgeois influence (witness Saumoneau's opposition
to feminine *syndicats*). As a result, they did not seek a formal position within
the party when they were in a position of strength. Only upon unification,
in 1905, did the GFS request inclusion in the party. By then, however,
weakened by other factors, it was unable to impose itself and met with a
refusal which gave it the death blow.

The GFS had joined the Confédération des Socialistes Indépendants in
February 1900. Renaud, who represented the group to the independents'
congress in March, was there elected to their federal committee. The GFS was
represented (no name was given) at the congress which united the two wings
of the independents, in August 1900, and (by Saumoneau) at the congress of
socialist organisations, in September. The party was more than willing to
accord places to individual women.[54]

It was not, however, prepared to grant a place to women collectively. The
project of unification prepared early in 1901 by the party's general committee included no reference to women or to women's rights. The GFS of
the fifth arrondissement resolved in response:

to demand that the Socialist Party add to its principles that of equality between the sexes
and word as follows the Party's declaration of principles . . .
The groups . . . adhering to the Party must admit women in their ranks on the same
basis as men.
In all the meetings of the Party where the voter registration card is required, this
measure cannot be applied to women [who of course had no cards].

to demand the creation of an exclusively socialist and working-class women's column in
all the newspapers which have placed themselves under the control of the Party . . . [as
in] Germany.

The GFM gave this resolution its vigorous support: 'Considering that women
. . . will do their duty in the avant-garde just as during the great revolution
. . . [the GFM] demands for women the place which is due them in the
revolutionary movement.'[55]

Both groups missed the point. They perceived the problem in terms of
doctrine and not in terms of organisation. They fought the old battles of the
1880s over again to obtain declarations of women's rights as individuals,
instead of fighting for the inclusion within the party of a specific organisation
for women. The failure of the French socialist women's movement began
with this error, which was to be repeated by the definitive women's group in
1913. The problem of the twentieth century was not doctrine but organisation.

At the congress of Lyons, in May 1901, the women lost both on doctrine
and on organisation. This was not for want of representation. The GFS of

the fifth arrondissement was represented by Renaud, who, having just been elected assistant secretary of the Seine federation (i.e. the Paris region), was now a well-known militant. The GFS of the seventeenth arrondissement was represented by Saumoneau, who also received a mandate from the co-operative in which the group met, La Ménagère. The GFM was represented by a man named Morby. The delegates submitted the resolution quoted above. It went to the resolutions commission which, 'overloaded with work' (as Saumoneau later put it), shelved it until the following congress.[56]

The overload of work was the problem of Millerand's participation in a bourgeois ministry alongside General Gallifet. This raised such passion and so preoccupied the congress that Renaud, who herself had intervened at length in favour of Millerand, accepted the postponement, adding that during the coming year 'we will have the time, by words and by deeds, to demonstrate the solid bases on which we rest in demanding an equal place for women'. Nevertheless she was unhappy that the commission had not even had the time to propose the simple addition of the words 'of both sexes' to the phrase 'emancipation of the proletariat' in the first sentence of the party's 'Declaration of Principles', the more so in that both the Guesdist and the Allemanist programmes included the phrase. Renaud protested:

Révelin has said that the word proletariat applied to both sexes; that's possible, but we want it to be stated. In 1789, the Rights of Man were drawn up, and the rights of man then were equally the rights of woman. Yet women are still waiting for the rights of men ... No socialist man can refuse to grant us what we ask, we want it written 'proletariat of both sexes', because we don't want to be duped any longer. (Applause.)

'The applause which we have just heard completely satisfies Citizen Renaud', noted the chairman rather smoothly, for the applause did not satisfy her: the phrase was not added. In reality this was only a partial defeat and not the most important. The next year, at the congress of Tours, some of the points of the GFS would be incorporated into the party platform. The most important battle had been lost without anyone's fighting it or even noticing it.[57]

Apart from the Millerand affair, the main problem confronting the congress was to make a disparate collection of reformist organisations into a party (the PSF) capable of confronting the PSDF which the Guesdists and Vaillantists were organising. To this end the congress adopted statutes providing for a uniform, hierarchical structure of town or arrondissement groups linked within each legislative district. To be sure, 'study and propaganda groups', *syndicats*, and co-operatives were still recognised as component parts of each federation, but the days of such groups within the party were clearly numbered. Only the federations would be represented on the general committee and in party congresses. These measures reflected an understandable concern to create a durable party structure, but they meant that the GFS would soon be unable to participate as groups in the party. It seems obvious in retrospect that the GFS, devoted as they were to party activities, could hardly function outside the party. Thus for the GFS to survive would have required a specific decision of the party to constitute women's groups on the basis of the existing GFS. But neither the party nor the GFS themselves recognised the need for women's groups. During the half day of debate on the new party structure, the problem of women was never mentioned and no women intervened.[58]

It seems hard to imagine how the leaders of the groups could have overlooked the need for a separate women's organisation, given that they were leading one. But in fact they did not consciously intend to create separate women's sections. They had no clear idea of the organisational relationship between their groups and the party, which was understandable in view of the confused situation obtaining before unification. Moreover, their very success within the party as individuals on the basis of integration blinded them to the difficulties ordinary women encountered in the ranks of the male organisations.

In the year following the congress, women obtained important and effective representation at the highest levels of the party. On 1 July 1901 the Seine federation delegated Adèle Kassky as one of its three representatives to the PSF general committee. Upon the expiration of her term in November, Elisabeth Renaud and (three weeks later) Marie Bonnevial were appointed representatives. At the beginning of 1902, the term of office was lengthened to a year. Bonnevial served for one year, Renaud two. Thus during 1902 two of three representatives of the Seine federation to the highest body of the party were women. Moreover, Saumoneau had been elected archivist of the federation and Renaud assistant secretary and, in virtue of these offices, both sat on the federal committee. Socialist women would never again be in such a good position to make themselves heard within the party. But they continued to struggle for abstract principles rather than concrete organisation.[59]

The congress of Tours, in May 1902, drew up the first party programme of the PSF. A special commission of the general committee (which included Bonnevial, but not Renaud) had drawn up a draft which was submitted to the congress. It contained some of the demands the GFS had made in 1901, but not the guarantee of admission to meetings or the 'women's column' in party newspapers. It did, however, include 'universal direct suffrage without distinction of sex' and a call, in almost the words of the Guesdist programme of 1882, for the 'repeal of all laws which establish the civil or political inferiority of workers, of women, and of illegitimate children'. It also mentioned a need for new divorce laws, legalisation of paternity suits, equal pay for equal work, and the by now traditional prohibition on work done in convents.[60]

At the congress, the draft programme was sent to the commission, of which Jaurès was chairman. While the commission met, the congress addressed itself to other matters, often bordering on the trivial. Renaud herself wasted time (she should have been lobbying the commission) with a pet project she had introduced with Longuet and Saumoneau at the last congress to prohibit socialist deputies from soliciting official decorations. It met a hostile response.[61]

The programme came back from the commission shorn of several articles on women's rights. The call for universal suffrage remained, as did divorce, paternity suits, and the convent prohibition. Equal pay, however, had disappeared without a trace. The article for 'repeal of all laws which establish civil or political inferiority' had been reduced to 'civil inferiority of women'. By the omission of the reference to workers, women were no longer assimilated to workers as an oppressed group in their own right. More important, of course, was the suppression of the word 'political'. This was partially corrected by Viviani (the socialist deputy who was Durand's friend). He proposed the addition of an article, 'admission of women to all public functions', which was adopted, but which seems less categorical than the original wording; it avoided the word 'political'. The commission had brought its version back so late that the congress had no time for further discussion. It is not even sure that anyone noticed the omission of equal pay. The delegates meekly voted the revised text and the congress was closed.[62]

The groups had suffered a serious setback. The draft programme had already been weaker than the old POF and POSR programmes even before it lost equal pay and before the call for women's political rights was diluted. Moreover, the GFS had not obtained the individual women's rights it had sought within the party, the guarantee of admission to meetings and the 'women's column'. Still worse, the statutes passed the previous year had been put into practice. Renaud and Saumoneau had attended as delegates not of the GFS but of the Seine federation. The same was obviously true of Bonnevial, who was not a member of the GFS and who ceased her participation in the socialist movement after this congress. And Renaud and Saumoneau owed their place in the federation not to their standing as leaders of the GFS but to their individual merits. The GFS was on its way to being shut out of the party.[63]

The congress had a more immediate consequence. It led to the departure of the GFM from the PSF and from the Union. Kassky and the other veterans of the Commune in the GFM had been uncomfortable in the company of Millerand. The frankly reformist bent of the programme adopted at Tours was too much for the GFM. Immediately after the congress, it held several meetings on its 'orientation'. At its meeting of 15 April 1902, the subject announced was membership in the PSDF. Five days later, in a communiqué to the Guesdist newspaper, it styled itself a member of the party. It ceased to communicate its announcements to *La Femme socialiste*, although Kassky's address continued to be listed as a depository of the news-paper. In January 1903, her home became the office of both the GFM and of the thirteenth section (i.e. that for the thirteenth arrondissement) of the PSDF. By 1904, Kassky was secretary of the combined fifth, thirteenth, and fourteenth sections of the party as well as treasurer of that of the thirteenth. The GFM had provided the cornerstone for an important party section. This was, at least institutionally, the most enduring contribution made by the groups.[64]

The Union faced a difficult situation at its June 1902 quarterly assembly. Responding to the dissolution of the GFS of the seventeenth arrondisse-ment and to the departure of the GFM, it voted to admit individuals from neighbourhoods which had no group and recalled that the Union, 'founded outside of all socialist organisations, admits groups into membership . . . whatever may be the socialist organisation to which they belong'. This may not have been altogether convincing. Renaud and Saumoneau, who domi-nated the Union, were ardent members of the PSF, which was now charting a purely reformist course. The GFM did not return to the Union, which was thus reduced to L'Egalité Humaine and the sole GFS of the fifth arrondisse-ment. The provincial groups were not heard from after Tours, although a letter was received from a new group in Lyons.[65]

Perhaps it was because Renaud sensed that the project had lost its momentum that *La Femme socialiste* 'disappeared with the issue of September 1902', as Saumoneau put it drily some thirty years later. Renaud seems to have realised that the group could hardly proceed outside the party and in the face of its indifference, for if she was fuzzy on the problem of organisation, she was clear on that of doctrine and was evidently dis-appointed by the programme of Tours. The quarrel which was to keep Renaud and Saumoneau from ever again speaking to one another began at this time. It is easy to imagine a scene between them at which Renaud suggested that, given the lack of funds and the difficulties with the party, it would be well to suspend efforts for a time and Saumoneau reacted to this as defeatism and employed in anger some expression which Renaud could never forgive. In any event, Renaud ceased to participate in the meetings of the group. They were no longer held at her new *pension*, where they had been moved in the spring when she added a large assembly room, but at the 'People's University' of the rue Mouffetard in the Latin Quarter.[66]

Without Renaud's sensitivity to women's problems, without her warmer, more supple approach, Saumoneau's position degenerated into sectarianism. The GFS became more a weapon in the battle against the feminists than a positive movement in its own right. The more progressive feminists, 'the bourgeois feminists grouped around the newspaper *La Fronde*' (as Saumoneau later specified), became for her and her followers, as the socialists for the communists of a later day, 'their natural adversaries'. By the end of 1902, Saumoneau classed all the feminists with the reactionaries:

The nationalist women's movement, although it does not place itself on the terrain of feminist demands, is one of the factions of bourgeois feminism. Socialist feminism, which is the adversary of all these factions, which in any case are united on the terrain of bourgeois property, will combat them all without distinction, as it has always done.[67]

On this basis Saumoneau struggled on, holding monthly meetings of the GFS through 1904. The group, however, showed no vitality beyond the announcements of its meetings. In August 1904, *L'Humanité* (which Jaurès had founded in April and which was well on its way to becoming the official organ of the unified party) carried an appeal for all socialist sections to ask the secretary of the GFS to give a lecture '[on] the Socialist Feminist Movement, its aim, its principles, its usefulness'. This lecture, which Saumoneau delivered to several sections during the autumn of 1904, began with an admission of failure: 'our Party too often holds itself aloof . . . from feminine questions'.[68]

Saumoneau fared little better as an individual without a power base than as sole leader of the GFS. She had been a member of the interfederal committee (which replaced the general committee) in 1903, but only for a few months. She lost her positions as archivist and member of the federal committee of the Seine federation in the reorganisation which followed unification in 1905. She was named assistant treasurer of the federation in April of that year, but held the position only temporarily. She was elected one of the federation's twenty-one delegates to the congress of unity, but by the slimmest of margins. Thereafter she was unsuccessful in party politics and still more unsuccessful in persuading her comrades of the usefulness of the GFS.[69]

'This movement went under during the tempest preceding the realisation of socialist Unity', she wrote in 1924. 'Our men comrades . . . did not understand the usefulness of the movement and did not want to recognise the sole group remaining.' In the summer of 1905, Saumoneau requested admission of the GFS to the newly unified Seine federation. After countless difficulties, the question was finally decided at the federal congress of December 1905. The committee on this question, chaired by Achille Cambier,[70] recommended admission of women's groups on the same basis as the youth groups already constituted. The congress, however, voted against the committee's recommendation and refused to recognise the GFS. In January, the national committee at its quarterly plenary meeting refused to overrule the federation.[71]

This decision was the death blow. The GFS ceased to meet. But it had already ceased to represent a genuine movement and, from this point of view, the party's refusal to take it seriously was hardly surprising. In a forlorn attempt to alter the unalterable, Saumoneau once again delivered her lecture on the 'Socialist Feminist Movement', in February. The entry fee was 30 centîmes. Few indeed they must have been who paid it, for not only did the GFS not rise from its ashes, but also Saumoneau withdrew from party politics for seven years.[72]

So it happened that, at the very time the German socialist women's movement was going from strength to strength, the French socialist party (the SFIO) decided not to have any women's movement at all. The GFS had proved that such a movement was feasible, provided it fulfilled three conditions. Obviously, it had to work within the party in order to give its members a grip on reality. The original GFS and the GFM had done this, although the GFS of the seventeenth arrondissement had not (which was one of the reasons for its failure): instead of the abstract wishes of the feminists, they had posed concrete questions about real public issues to their members and had offered them the opportunity to influence them through the party. A second condition of success was that, while taking account of women's oppression both as workers and as women, such a movement respond to the primacy of class experience over that of sexual role: the women of the working class identified more easily with their fathers, brothers, and husbands, however difficult they may have found them, than with the views of their employers. This too the GFS had done, by speaking to its constituents in working-class terms and on a socialist basis.

The success of the GFS was also due, however, to the fact that it knew how to address working women on their own terms as women, because it was distinct from the party and provided a kind of women's section: if the feminists could not reach working women because their organisations were uncomfortably bourgeois, so the socialists had difficulty because their groups were uncomfortably male. The fact that working-class women identified more readily with proletarian men than with bourgeois women did not mean that they could participate easily in political activity with these men. Politics was a sphere they were accustomed to leave to men. To take political initiative as a rare woman in a male socialist section required extraordinary self-assurance and even courage. The very experience of the GFS makes this clear. As we have suggested, the groups at their peak probably had between fifty and one hundred members in three arrondissements, almost as many as there were women members of the SFIO in the entire Paris region when the party was unified in 1905. If all the former members of the GFS had joined the party, they would have doubled the number of women in the Paris region; if every arrondissement and suburban town had provided as many women as each of the arrondissements did for the GFS, the number of women in the party's Seine federation would have been more than a thousand instead of between one hundred and one hundred fifty. Thus it is clear that many former members of the GFS did not join the unified party on an individual basis. They had been willing to participate in a women's group but were not prepared to enter the regular (male) party sections alone.

Madeleine Pelletier was to provide a perceptive analysis of this problem, key to the subsequent weakness of the French socialist women's movement. After three years in the newly formed SFIO, she realised (so she wrote in 1908) that there were two fundamental obstacles to women's joining the regular sections. The first was the preoccupation of the sections with electoral problems. How could one expect women to interest themselves in questions of the first and second round of balloting when they could not even vote? The second obstacle was less tangible, but if anything more important than the first: the male atmosphere of the sections. Pelletier explained:

In the feminist organisations in which I am involved, there is an important contingent of women either socialist or ready to become socialist; I have tried to bring them into the Parisian sections [of the SFIO], I have not succeeded. Accustomed to women's groups, even to free thought groups, where they feel at home, they feel themselves to be intruders in the sections, where no one thought of drawing them out of the corner where they had humbly hidden; thus the result was negative: the conclusion of women was that, socialists or not, men were still masculinists [*sic*].

One can imagine the tobacco-filled air, the male complicity troubled by the presence of a woman, in short the male club atmosphere of the socialist sections, which would only increase as socialism became more and more a party involved in contemporary politics and less and less a movement. The solution Pelletier suggested was to form 'feminine sections': 'There, women will feel more at ease, the section will be *their* [italics orig.] section, they will speak there, will draw up resolutions, in short [they] will bring the section to life as they themselves will be born to socialist life.'[73]

This was exactly how the GFS had worked (unlike any subsequent French socialist women's organisation) and the secret of its success. Yet the GFS had functioned on this basis only accidentally. None of the leaders perceived the problem in these terms, not even Saumoneau when she was seeking admission to the SFIO for the GFS. The women of the GFS agreed with the men of the party on a policy of integration: indeed, insofar as they had sought organisational guarantees from the party, they had been those of individual rights within the male structure. Women would enter the party (or in fact not enter it) individually, on the same basis as men, through the same party sections. This policy would be a dismal failure.

Why did both men and women of the party cling to it nevertheless? Part of the answer lies in the very advances of French socialism. It had inscribed the equality of the sexes in its programmes virtually from its founding. It had admitted women into its ranks on an equal footing with men from the very beginning. Women had often played important roles in the parties,

105

sometimes at the highest level, from Rouzade through Valette to Renaud. These individual examples appeared to justify the policy of integration. More fundamentally, they blinded their beneficiaries to the difficulties of ordinary women. From the exalted perspective at the top of the party, a woman leader could easily forget about the women who were not in the party at all. Separate groups for women could even seem a retrograde step, a denial of the very principle of equality and of the success these individual women had achieved. Yet underneath their individual success there would remain a pattern of collective failure. Women did not represent more than 2 to 3 per cent of the membership of the SFIO from its founding in 1905 through the fall of the Third Republic in 1940. This was the lowest percentage of any European socialist party. In Germany, women represented 16 per cent of the membership of the SPD on the eve of the First World War.[74]

A comparison between the German and French socialist women's movements, although beyond the scope of this work, would suggest that in Germany the creation of an autonomous socialist women's movement was forced upon the SPD because women were prohibited from joining political parties. Indeed, after 1908, when the prohibition was lifted, the SPD moved away from autonomy and toward integration. As early as 1890, the SPD created separate women's groups and a complete women's organisation parallel to the party, which it financed and supported and which had formal links with the party itself. The peculiarities of the German situation further favoured the organisation of women. The inclusion of trade unions in the party meant that there were already women enrolled in the party who provided a core for the organisation of women. In France, unions were completely separate from the parties. Finally, in Germany, the SPD, moving in an incompletely democratic regime, maintained a revolutionary posture in words if not in deeds, which made the suffrage seem less important. This was compounded by the fact that men themselves did not have full voting rights or effective control of government by their votes.[75]

French socialism, however, had moved in an environment of political democracy since its founding. The SFIO was a party of citizens, devoted essentially (whatever its rhetoric) to participation in the political processes from which women were barred. Women were not citizens and the use of this term of address in the party was an irony. To pretend that women should enter the party on the same basis as men was to ignore all the handicaps under which women laboured.

The refusal of French socialism to envisage an autonomous women's movement and the failure of the GFS were to entail the general failure of French socialism to attract women members. The party's decisions in 1901 and 1902 (of which the refusal in 1905 was only the logical consequence) destroyed not only the GFS by depriving it of its base in the party, but also the possibility for the SFIO to have an autonomous women's movement in

Decline

which women could participate comfortably. The split between Renaud and Saumoneau which ensued from these decisions was largely personal at the outset, though stemming from a significant difference in outlook. But by 1913, when the definitive organisation of French socialist women was finally constituted, their split represented a division in the ranks. The possibility of synthesis was lost. The definitive socialist women's organisation would either be, under Renaud (its first secretary), a kind of advanced arm of feminism, or it would be, under Saumoneau (its second secretary), a women's auxiliary of the party. The latter, as we shall see, is what it became. In the interim between 1905 and 1913, however, during the 'heroic years' of French socialism, the failure of the GFS deprived socialist women of a field on which to act.

5. Women and the SFIO 1905 – 14

The entire political landscape was transformed by the unification of all the socialist groups into one Parti Socialiste (Section Française de l'Internationale Ouvrière), the SFIO. Whereas in the past socialist women had dealt with small, competing parties, they were now faced with a large, united organisation on its way to becoming one of the four main forces on the political spectrum. In 1906, the SFIO received 878,000 votes and elected fifty-two deputies (of a total of 591); in 1914, 1,398,000 votes and 103 deputies. It was a party of national stature, a far cry from the tiny groups within which Rouzade, Valette, and even the GFS had struggled.

Despite its electoral success, the SFIO did not resolve the problem of mobilisation of militants, always the Achilles' heel of French socialism. (Only the communists would eventually organise a mass party of committed militants and that only in the 1930s, around the Popular Front.) The SFIO began with 34,688 members in 1905 and reached 90,725 in 1914. By that time, the German SPD already had a million members, of whom 175,000 were women.[1]

What would the SFIO do about women? We have already seen that it would not have a women's organisation. It remains to be seen what it would do to attract women individually and to seek women's rights. Would it make use of the national stature it was gaining to work for women's emancipation? And, inversely, what would women do in and about the SFIO?

The SFIO and the politics of women's suffrage

Like many movements which become major political forces, the SFIO was a very different affair from its predecessors. Some felt that the party was betraying its revolutionary heritage. Others felt that it was taking on national responsibility. The fact was that support for the republic was the most important element in the party's heritage and that as a national political party it worked within the republic's political structure, not to overthrow it but to perfect it. Once unity was assured, one of the party's first major policy concerns was to obtain proportional representation in the Chamber of Deputies.

Such a reform would seem to lead logically to women's suffrage. But proportional representation was a 'serious' matter, a reform which could interest male voters and which might even be realised. Women's suffrage was beyond the pale of practical politics, unlikely to be realised and still less likely to interest voters. Electoral statements of socialist candidates rarely mentioned women. Apart from general party programmes — and even these were occasionally doctored to leave out women's rights — only one or two socialists mentioned women's suffrage in their individual programmes for each election.[2]

Not only did socialists avoid the issue of the suffrage, but also some actually opposed women's suffrage, fearing that women would bring the clerical influence out of the confessional and into the voting booth. After the international socialist congress of Stuttgart in 1907, the socialist deputy Bracke wrote that, despite the quasi-unanimity obtained in the vote on the resolution for women's suffrage, he found in the corridors 'the old arguments that stop more than one comrade at the moment of action. Women's suffrage, to be sure! But later, when they've been educated.' Even many feminists, following in Richer and Deraismes's tradition, thought it advisable to leave women's suffrage aside until the question of proportional representation was settled.[3]

Thus it was that in 1906, as we shall see, the party voted to present a bill for women's suffrage which was never written and that in 1907 the SFIO deputies named a sub-committee on women's rights which never met. The socialist deputies were hardly unique in this. Marguerite Durand's friend Beauquier had formed a group of deputies for women's rights (over 200 signed up), but Madeleine Pelletier was chagrined to discover that in ten years it had not met once. (Durand herself might have been similarly chagrined had she realised that Beauquier did not trouble his electors with women's rights: his 'profession of faith' did not mention them, even as late as 1906.)[4]

Nevertheless, the SFIO did more for women's rights than any other party. It was the only party formally open to women.[5] When the Buisson–Dussaussoy bill for women's suffrage in municipal elections was tabled, it bore 198 signatures, including those of seventy-three socialists, all but three of the party's deputies. Such leaders as Sembat, Tarbouriech, and Bracke worked hard for women's rights and co-operated sincerely with the feminists (a point of annoyance for socialist women like Saumoneau).[6]

The question of women's suffrage, which, as Madeleine Pelletier argued, was the keystone of all women's rights, was first posed before the Chamber of Deputies in 1901. The moderate Radical Gautret proposed to give the right to vote to those women who had no husbands to represent them. This bill was promptly forgotten. Five years later, in 1906, another moderate, M. Dussaussoy, presented a bill giving all women the right to vote, but only in municipal and cantonal elections. Fearing that this was the best that could be expected, the feminist congress of 1908 came out strongly for this bill. Sembat made a forceful speech for it in October 1909, at which point it was still in committee. In the summer of 1910, the socialists presented a resolution demanding consideration of the bill. Ferdinand Buisson, a Radical deputy who was chairman of the committee to which the bill had been referred in 1906, finally reported it back favourably in 1911. By this point even such staunchly uncompromising suffragists as Auclert had come round to accepting the bill's piecemeal approach rather than get nothing at all.[7]

But the nearer the socialists got to obtaining proportional representation, the more they hesitated to jeopardise it by allowing it to be linked to women's suffrage. By January 1912, they felt — wrongly as it turned out — that they were nearing the decisive moment on proportional representation. Jaurès noted in an article that it was just around the corner. He did not even mention women's suffrage. Although the socialist group in the Chamber discussed women's suffrage three times during 1912, they were probably trying to see how they could do something about it without involving proportional representation. When a group of women led by Auclert asked Sembat to propose a women's suffrage amendment to the proportional representation bill, he demurred, saying it would be 'inopportune'.[8]

It was not until 1913 that Buisson formally tabled the Dussaussoy bill, with the support of the socialist deputies. But the Chamber was preoccupied with the proposal to increase the term of military service from two to three years. (Three-year service was finally voted in the summer of 1913 despite an intense and courageous campaign led by the socialists.) A much diluted version of the original proportional representation bill was finally passed late in 1913, leaving the way clear in theory for women's suffrage. Only in February 1914, however, was the Dussaussoy bill put on the agenda of the Chamber. By the outbreak of the First World War it had still not been assigned a date for debate. The Chamber was doing little better than the Senate, whose committee on women's civil rights, named 19 May 1890, had not produced a single report in twenty-four years. The Chamber did finally pass women's suffrage in 1919, but allowed the Senate to kill it in 1922.[9]

Thus, even if the SFIO did more for women's rights than any other party, it could hardly be said to have put them at the forefront of its preoccupations. What could women do in the party? Until the founding of the Groupe des Femmes Socialistes (GDFS) in 1913, most socialist women would either be inactive, like Saumoneau, or active independent of their sex. Before 1913, one woman alone personified the woman question in the SFIO: Madeleine Pelletier.

Madeleine Pelletier

Anne Pelletier — she took the name Madeleine when she became an adult —

was born on 18 May 1874 'in a fruit and vegetable shop on the rue des
Petits-Carreaux' in Paris. Her mother was extremely religious, known it
seems as 'the Jesuit' in the neighbourhood. Her father, by contrast, was
down-to-earth. It was he, she said, who 'initiated' her 'in sexual matters'
when she was twelve. What this meant is not clear, for Pelletier always maintained that she was a virgin, but it does not indicate a good overall relationship with her parents. She made this statement in 1939 to Hélène Brion,
who alone of all her friends remained faithful to her and visited her in the
asylum where she was interned on court order after having been convicted
of practising abortions. Brion attempted to take an autobiography by dic-
tation, but Pelletier, paralysed by a stroke and broken by her internment,
could speak lucidly only for short periods. What she did say, however, was
revealing:

I never loved my mother but I felt a certain respect for her; I lost it the moment I pic-
tured her as being like me and I felt a disgust which remained with me for a long time.
    I wasn't liked at school. I was dirty. I was badly dressed. Horror! I had lice. They
swarmed over my head and fell on the table. [Here the ms breaks off.] [10]

It would be an error to over-psychologise and to attribute Pelletier's
feminism and even her masculine attire to her relations with her parents.
But it would be fair to say that her childhood provided the emotive base, the
cutting edge of her feminism. She felt a visceral and conscious resentment of
the injustice she suffered from being a woman and she detested the pretty
feminists like Marguerite Durand who did not: she called them 'half-
emancipated'. For her, feminine clothes were signs of 'servitude', of being a
'sex' and not an 'individual'. Her masculine attire, her 'short hair, detachable
collars, ties', etc., were 'exterior signs of liberty' in a world which was essentially male and in which, as she put it, 'women don't believe in themselves'
for they were taught from childhood that 'only men have personalities that
count'. Her male attire was thus not only a sign of liberty, but also a passport into the male universe, which from her earliest childhood had seemed
the only meaningful one. In her black dress surmounted by a man's jacket
and tie, complete with bowler hat and cane, she set out to challenge the male
world on its own terms. Or rather several male worlds: medicine, Freemasonry, and — while remaining a feminist leader — socialism. [11]

To undertake a medical career, Pelletier had to open up a number of previously all-male fields. In this she was highly successful. In 1899 she became
the first woman doctor to be appointed to the staff of the Assistance Publique (welfare board). This marked the start of a scientific career during
which she published numerous articles in medical journals. In 1906, after a
long feminist campaign, she was permitted to take the competitive examination for doctors in insane asylums. She was the first woman to do so and
she passed with flying colours. But already, as she later recalled, 'I was

111

sacrificing my scientific career to this propaganda' for the admission of women to the regular Masonic lodges. In this she was less successful than in her medical work.

There were in France two Masonic lodges open to women: Le Droit Humain (founded by Maria Deraismes) and La Grande Loge Symbolique Ecossaise. While the two regular obediences did not formally recognise the mixed lodges, they tolerated them tacitly. In April 1904, Pelletier's hospital supervisor convinced her that she would be able to work for the admission of women to the regular lodges by entering one of the mixed ones. She thereupon joined the lodge La Philosophie Sociale of La Grande Loge Symbolique Ecossaise. In the summer of 1904 she brought into her lodge Louise Michel, one of the last remaining symbols of the women of the Commune now that Mink was dead, 'in order to make use of her universal notoriety as a powerful lever for spreading my ideas'. At the end of her first year as a Freemason, Pelletier felt confident of success in the near future in her effort to gain admission for women to the regular obediences.[12]

In fact she was on the verge of failure. Her campaign was soon discredited by several unpleasant incidents. One brother wished (by her account) to bring a woman 'of questionable morals' into the lodge. She regarded this as a threat to the lodge's integrity. She fought a losing battle which ultimately resulted in her quitting La Philosophie Sociale for another lodge, Diderot. But she had enemies everywhere by now. In the spring of 1906, a woman at another lodge brought a judgement against her at which (by her account again) she was accused of being uncooperative in sexual matters. She was deeply embittered against Freemasonry, the more so in that the protest letter she wrote about the affair was used to justify the policy of exclusion of women from the regular obediences. Despite all this, she remained a Mason and continued to encourage women to join. But it ceased to be the centre of her activity. She gave more of her energies to feminism, in which she was already deeply involved.[13]

After the death of Eugénie Potonié-Pierre in 1898, La Solidarité des Femmes, now under the direction of Caroline Kauffmann, rapidly changed character. By the end of 1900, such old-guard members as Léonie Rouzade and Paule Mink ceased to attend, both apparently because they thought the group was becoming insufficiently anti-clerical. During 1901 Mme Vincent also quit the group, because it joined the Conseil National des Femmes Françaises, which she denounced as 'clerical'. La Solidarité was certainly drifting away from Potonié-Pierre's social concern and toward a more single-minded feminism, although it was probably unfair to accuse it of clericalism.[14]

The group's new secretary, Caroline Kauffmann, was a soft socialist and a hard feminist. She did join the SFIO, but if she believed in 'the levelling of classes', she thought it would be 'the fruit of integral education'. As a feminist, however, she was unbeatable. When the centenary of the Napoleonic Code was celebrated in 1904, most feminists were content to make speeches denouncing it; Kauffmann took action. From the spectator's gallery at the official celebration banquet, she tossed upon the tables balloons half a yard in diameter and bearing the slogan, 'The Code crushes women; it dishonours the Republic.' When the man she had paid to inflate the balloons ran out of breath, she began to scream her slogan and was promptly arrested.[15]

Kauffmann was compelled to make frequent trips to the provinces to supervise her business affairs. In 1906 she began to look about for a successor as secretary of La Solidarité. Pelletier had been to a few meetings of the group and she was known for the energy with which she had demanded the right to take the examination for asylum doctors. Kauffmann appeared one day in the office where Pelletier waited forlornly for clients. Point-blank, she asked Pelletier to succeed her. Recalled Pelletier: 'I had no illusions about the value of such an offer; I knew that the group was small; I had been to several meetings; everyone spoke at once and the most preposterous ideas were put forth under the pretext of feminism.' Nonetheless she accepted and became the third secretary of La Solidarité.[16]

Kauffmann was not always away from Paris. When she was home, she and Pelletier co-operated in a number of feminist activities. During the 1906 elections, while other groups put up posters with elaborate justifications of women's right to vote, Kauffmann and Pelletier went about sticking up a small piece of paper which stated simply, 'Women should Vote, They are Subject to the Laws and pay Taxes.' Two years later, Kauffmann and Pelletier supported Hubertine Auclert in her last and most forceful public protest: they stormed a town hall where voting was taking place in the municipal elections and Auclert smashed the urn and stamped on the ballots. Inspired by Auclert's act no doubt, Pelletier smashed the windows of another polling booth during the second round of voting, the following week. Both acts became legendary as the only violent demonstrations ever undertaken by French feminists. During the winter of 1907—8, Pelletier also founded a monthly newspaper, *La Suffragiste*, in which Kauffmann collaborated assiduously. Yet despite all this feminist activity, Pelletier gave most of her energies to the SFIO.[17]

Women in the SFIO

'A woman', wrote Pelletier in 1908, 'cannot sacrifice feminism to any masculine political party whatsoever, without betraying her own cause.' Why then did she devote herself to socialism rather than to feminism? She thought (or pretended to think) that she was using the party to achieve feminist ends, but this proved to be an illusion. Women's suffrage, she claimed in another article written in 1908, was the only cause that counted. To obtain it, women should simultaneously 'create vast feminist organisations' and 'penetrate the existing political parties'. Although she denied that it mattered which party one chose to enter, she did suggest that the SFIO was a good target because its statutes called for the admission of women on an equal footing with men. She gave tactical advice in Machiavellian tones. One should speak little of feminism and 'aim above all to be a *good militant* [italics orig.] , a member whose opinion counts'. To this end, it would be useful to join a minority faction of the party because, 'especially if it lacks [people of] ability, [it] will overcome its repugnance [to women] and call upon our militant'. This was exactly what Pelletier did in the SFIO. She joined factions which made use of her political talents and she thereby acquired a certain notoriety, if not real influence in the party. But after promising beginnings, she gained nothing for women's rights. The factions she joined used her, she did not use them.[18]

Shortly after unification, Pelletier joined the SFIO and sought to become a recognised militant by using her scientific credentials to attract attention as a lecturer. She then allied herself with the Guesdists, 'the faction generally considered the most revolutionary'. By the summer of 1906, she was well known as a Guesdist. With their aid, she steered a resolution for women's suffrage through the fourteenth section of Paris, which in turn proposed it to the Seine federal committee. They in turn referred it to a sub-committee whose chairman (G. Renard) strengthened it to a specific demand upon 'the elected representatives of the party to present, this year if at all possible, a bill to the Chamber' for women's suffrage.[19]

In November 1906, Pelletier presented this resolution at the party congress at Limoges, to which the Guesdists had delegated her from their stronghold of the Nord. With deft phrases she laid aside one by one the arguments invoked against women's suffrage, not, as she told the delegates, because she feared they might not vote for the resolution, but because she knew that behind their votes would lurk many reservations, all tied to one question: would women be used by the priests? On the contrary, she argued, once they were able to participate in political life, they would follow their economic and class interests and leave the priests behind, especially since the socialists would then have an incentive to propagandise them, a task now left to the priests. She could have invoked Engels's authority for this argument, but she does not seem to have read *The Origin of the Family* any more than her fellow Guesdists.

Only one delegate spoke against the proposal. Lapicque (Vosges) argued that women would indeed give votes to the enemy and that his federation would therefore vote against the proposal, not liking 'that one present a bill with the secret hope of seeing it rejected'. After two brief speeches in support of the resolution, it was voted 'unanimously less six votes' (those of the Vosges). But the very brevity of the debate lent credence to Lapicque's insinuation that many who voted for the resolution hoped to see women's suffrage rejected. Events bore him out.[20]

Pelletier suspected that the resolution would not suffice to move the socialist deputies. She organised direct action. On 21 December 1906, seven weeks after the congress, she led a deputation of seventy members of La Solidarité to the Chamber. They demanded admittance at the regular meeting of the socialist group. They were received cordially, by Pelletier's account. After she and Kauffmann had spoken, 'Citizen Jaurès assures the delegation that what is needed will be done and in the very near future.' The indifference with which women had accepted the defeat of clericalism by the Combes government had proved, Jaurès added, that the socialists had nothing to fear from women's suffrage. After the women left, the deputies voted to set up a sub-committee whose task it would be to prepare a bill for women's suffrage. Louis Dubreuilh, general secretary of the SFIO, wrote in *L'Humanité* that the party would do its duty. 'Feminism', concluded Pelletier in her account on the front page of *L'Humanité*, 'is no longer alone; it has backing from the Socialist Party.'[21]

She was being over-optimistic.[22] It took the deputies three months just to name the members of the sub-committee and they did so only when pushed by Delory, a Guesdist leader who had supported Pelletier's resolution at the congress of Limoges. Moreover, the committee when named included none of the deputies known for their support of women's rights. It was composed of Carlier, Constans, Jaurès, and Willm. Of these, only Carlier had even a distant connection with feminism (he had collaborated with the prominent feminist Odette Laguerre, but only on a book of anti-war readings for schoolchildren).[23] Sembat's absence is particularly surprising, since he had distinguished himself in supporting feminism: he and Coutant were the only SFIO deputies whose personal programmes called for the 'civil and political emancipation of women'. (Many deputies used the SFIO programme, which of course did contain articles supporting women's rights.) In any event, the committee never met and the bill was never written. When the socialist group prepared its annual report for the party congress of 1907, it made no mention at all of women's suffrage, in complete disregard of the resolution passed at the previous congress.[24]

Surprisingly, Pelletier never made an explicit attack on this failure. She continued to campaign for women's suffrage as if nothing had happened. She even bent over backwards to give the party the benefit of the doubt. In May 1907, she wrote that she could understand socialist distaste for the feminists, because they were indeed 'bourgeois women'. But exactly for that reason, she argued, the feminists posed no threat, for they needed drawing rooms to make demands and carriages to demonstrate. 'Proletarian feminism', by contrast, would speak in meetings and march in the streets.[25]

On 17 June 1907, she and Kauffmann did march in the streets. Not, however, with proletarian women, but with a group of English suffragist women. After the demonstration they went to the Chamber and had an interview with Jaurès. Did they remind him of the promises made six months before and as yet unkept? From the Chamber they proceeded to the offices of *L'Humanité*, on whose front page they received a photo and a two-column story the next day.

In July, Pelletier spoke at the Seine federation's congress and obtained a vote to present the same text as that voted in 1906 at the coming congress of 1907 to be held at Nancy. This congress was thus a replay of Limoges. Not only was the same resolution voted, but also no one, neither Pelletier nor any other orator, alluded to the failure of the deputies to act upon the resolution during the year since it had been voted the first time. Yet it made no sense to vote the same text over again without giving a reason for doing so. Pelletier simply stated that she was asking the congress to 'confirm' the resolution of Limoges. Then, in addition to refuting the clerical argument at greater length than at Limoges, she dealt with an argument she was encouraging in the ranks of the 'insurrectionalists'. They opposed the electoral and parliamentary action which was becoming the mainstay of the SFIO. Consequently, they disdained the suffrage and those who sought it. Pelletier had no difficulty in demonstrating that this was a fallacious argument. The proletariat had shed blood to obtain universal suffrage and the party now made it the focal point of its action. How then ask women to renounce it in advance? It would be quite another matter, she pointed out, to ask women once they had conquered the right to vote to renounce it as a revolutionary tactic.[26]

She spoke in vain. At the end of her speech, 'numerous voices' were heard calling 'vote!', impatient, presumably, to get on to serious business. After a short speech by one of those who had supported her the year before (another replay), Pelletier was stabbed in the back by a woman named Gauthiot, from Paris. She argued that Pelletier's resolution was 'of no interest; it's one of these numerous diversions'. Pelletier then received unexpected support from another woman, Citizen Sorgue, a former Vaillantist now in the ranks of the 'insurrectionalists' of the SFIO.[27]

Sorgue reminded the congress that she had always denied 'that women will emancipate themselves by the ballot . . . proletarian women will emancipate themselves only by engaging in the syndical struggle'. But, she went on to tell the delegates, 'since you're in favour of political action, you haven't the right to refuse women the right to vote'. A Guesdist delegate attempted to resurrect the resolution defeated at the 1880 UFC congress! When this was defeated, the congress proceeded without further ado to vote the Limoges resolution a second time. This 'confirmation' was in fact its burial. No one, not even Pelletier, made any further effort to implement it.[28]

Women did win one small victory, though accidentally. Sorgue asked why there was not a single woman on the governing body of the party, the Commission Administrative Permanente (CAP). After all, she pointed out, every faction of the party was represented proportionally on it. She demanded 'the representation of the feminine sex on the Commission'. The chairman replied that the congress could not directly name a woman as such, but that the different factions of each federation should take it upon themselves 'to see if they want to include the feminine element' in their nominations to the CAP. As it happened, the Seine federation already had a woman on its list. She was Angèle Roussel (no relation to the feminist Nelly Roussel), a Guesdist who had distinguished herself chiefly by assiduity in attending party functions. She had been elected to the executive of the Seine federation in June and had therefore been included among its nominees to the CAP. She was duly elected from the Guesdist faction. In the autumn of 1907 she became assistant secretary of the CAP.[29]

Why was Roussel chosen in preference to Pelletier or Sorgue, both better known? Both Pelletier and Sorgue were members of the 'insurrectionalist' faction (Pelletier having just quit the Guesdists). This faction was not beloved of the party hierarchy and as a young group did not have as many votes as the other factions. Roussel, by contrast, was a faithful Guesdist of long standing. One must also point out, however, that Roussel was far more docile than Pelletier and Sorgue and that she never raised the question of women's rights. Indeed she seems to have been of the opinion that they were a diversion from the class struggle. Roussel was an inoffensive, conscientious, hard-working militant, always willing to act as secretary at meetings, always assiduous in attendance: between 1905 and 1914, she never missed a single national council or congress. Yet she never spoke at a congress except for one sentence in 1908 and a statement on her resignation from the CAP in 1913. One suspects that these were qualities which many men still found endearing in a woman. Is there not a parallel with the fact that when, in 1908, the German SPD put a woman on the party executive, it chose not Clara Zetkin, who was known world-wide as the forceful and energetic leader of the socialist women's movement since 1890, but rather the docile nonentity Luise Zietz?[30]

On 17 August 1907, three days after the congress of Nancy, there took place (in conjunction with the international socialist congress at Stuttgart) the first international conference of socialist women, under the leadership of Clara Zetkin. The French made an effort to be well represented and managed to come up with a delegation of eight women, more than attended most national congresses.[31] They included the wives of two male leaders, Lagardelle and Tarbouriech; two women whose names do not appear elsewhere in party affairs: Melgrandel and Moiret; and Gauthiot, Pelletier, Roussel, and Sorgue.[32]

Of these, only Pelletier and Gauthiot played roles in the conference, which was dominated by the Austrian and German women, who insisted upon a complete separation of socialist women from the bourgeois feminists. Pelletier objected, somewhat timidly: 'Our women's movement is socialist through and through . . . but it must stand a little way outside the party . . . and concentrate on one goal, the conquest of women's suffrage.'[33]

Gauthiot once again stabbed Pelletier in the back. She insisted that French socialist women, contrary to Pelletier's claims, would fight only within the party for the liberation of all the proletariat together. Pelletier lost. The conference passed a strong resolution stating that 'the socialist parties of all countries have a duty to struggle energetically for the introduction of universal suffrage for women', but adding: 'socialist women must not ally themselves with the feminists of the bourgeoisie, but lead the battle side by side with the socialist parties'.[34]

Women's suffrage was on the agenda for the congress, which followed the women's conference. The French were represented on the congress committee on women's suffrage by Pelletier, Roussel, and two men, one of whom had supported Pelletier with forceful speeches at the last two national congresses. Following a German initiative, the committee voted to adopt the resolution passed by the conference, to which the Austrian Victor Adler added an effusive greeting to the conference. Adler then proceeded to destroy the sweet harmony he had just helped create. He proposed an amendment to the effect that each national section should determine for itself the right time to begin the struggle for women's suffrage.

Everyone knew that the Austrian party had postponed agitation for women's suffrage until the achievement of universal manhood suffrage. The women's conference had unequivocally rejected this tactic. Adler's amendment, however, would have legitimated it, thus vitiating the effect of the women's resolution. Pelletier, who had seen that even where men already enjoyed universal suffrage the party was all too ready to postpone the fight for women's suffrage, led the fight against Adler with a violent statement which caused him to withdraw his amendment. The women's resolution passed as it stood. Subsequently, no national section could subordinate the struggle for women's suffrage to that for universal men's suffrage without violating an official resolution of the International. Pelletier could claim much of the credit for this victory.

She could also claim some credit for the other major accomplishment of the women at Stuttgart. She had proposed to the conference the creation of an international socialist women's office to be organised through Clara Zetkin's newspaper, *Die Gleichheit*, and to function through the Brussels secretariat of the International. The conference had rejected this proposal following the opposition of Rosa Luxemburg, who considered the Brussels secretariat a drag on the movement. But the congress voted to set up an independent women's secretariat with Zetkin at its head.[35]

The creation of the international secretariat of socialist women implied the creation of women's sections within each national party. In France, however, there was only one forlorn effort to implement this decision. The thirteenth section of Paris (Kassky's) had set up a 'feminine commission' the previous April. After Stuttgart, its secretary, Louise Napias Chaboseau, called in *L'Humanité* for all socialist women to come to a general assembly in October 1907, to form a women's section. But the assembly was never held and the commission soon disappeared.[36]

The commission was doomed from the start. In the first place, it took an approach which would prove disastrously restrictive to all subsequent socialist women's groups. It did not address itself to women outside the party, but rather only to those already in it or associated with it through men. The problem, however, was that there were too few women in the party. The solution had to be to draw more women in from outside the party rather than to organise the handful who were already members. But in the second place, the commission did not even address itself to women, at least not directly. Instead it aimed at them only through men. For its first public meeting, in the spring of 1907, Paul Lafargue had lectured on 'Proletarian women and socialism'. The announcement of the lecture invited 'all comrades accompanied by their women companions'.[37]

Pelletier remained completely aloof from the commission. She may well have disapproved of its dependence on men, but it is surprising that she did not voice her disapproval or initiate an effort more in line with her own ideas. One might reasonably have expected her to do so once the commission had disappeared by late 1907 and the party's foot-dragging on women's suffrage had demonstrated that women would have to organise themselves to get anywhere. Pelletier clearly understood this and she was certainly thinking about women's groups. Early in 1908 she was drafting the article in which she called so eloquently for 'feminine sections' and analysed so brilliantly the intimidating male atmosphere of the regular sections. She understood, better than anyone else, the need for women to have 'their own sections'. Her analysis confronted the real, human problems which prevented women from entering the SFIO. Why did she never act on it? We will address ourselves below to the profound reasons underlying Pelletier's failure to act on her analysis. The reason she did not do so at this time (the winter of 1907–8) seems to be simply that she was embarking with another faction of the party, to which she gave all her energies, the 'insurrectionalist' faction led by Gustave Hervé.

Hervé was a socialist history teacher dismissed for his ferocious anti-militarism and anti-patriotism. In 1906 he came to Paris and founded a weekly newspaper, *La Guerre sociale* ('social war'). It is hard to judge his activities fairly because upon the outbreak of the war he switched to an authoritarian patriotism equalled in virulence only by his previous anti-patriotism. It does seem, however, that his articles and speeches tended toward demagoguery and did not help the party to combat the real forces which were preparing war. Nevertheless, *La Guerre sociale* was highly successful.[38] It was the only journal at this time which had a direct appeal to syndicalists and anarchists as well as to socialists. Pelletier's switching to this faction foreshadowed the anarchist strain which would soon dominate her thinking.

Pelletier left the Guesdists for the Hervéists around July 1907. At the Seine federation congress held that month, the Guesdists submitted a resolution urging that the *syndicats* co-ordinate their action with the party. This was yet another in the long series of vain efforts which the Guesdists made to subordinate the *syndicats* to the party, blindly following the German model. The move was all the more badly received in that the Confédération Générale du Travail (CGT, the equivalent of the TUC or AFL-CIO) had only the year before passed a resolution known as the Amiens Charter which reaffirmed the independence of syndicalism from all political parties. Pelletier had not realised that subjection of *syndicats* to the party was an essential part of Guesdist doctrine. She was just as shocked as Mink had been to discover that opposition to the general strike was crucial to Guesdist dogma. As Pelletier put it herself a year later, 'most often the woman militant will go astray at the beginning'. The Guesdists, she now realised, had 'looked to their left; beneath the attenuated form of the CGT, they recognised anarchism and their terror was such that they are still running, all the way to the extreme right'. Pelletier wrote this in an article in *La Guerre sociale*, thus making it a public declaration of her changed allegiance.[39]

At the 1907 national congress, which came immediately after her break with the Guesdists, Pelletier began her career as a Hervéist by speaking against the Guesdists' motion on anti-militarism. They argued that one could not prevent war so long as capitalism existed. Pelletier argued that they were discouraging workers from undertaking the very activities which prepared the revolution. They were saying to the workers, she quipped sarcastically, 'no agitation, no demonstration'; let them 'satisfy their revolutionary sentiments by taking out membership in the party'. The Guesdists were thus part of the processes which were moving the workers away from action and integrating them into the capitalist society they had sought to destroy.[40]

With a profound sense of psychology, Pelletier analysed these processes of integration. A perfectly honest militant entering into the regular political life of the party was subjected to social and psychological pressures which rendered him less revolutionary: 'constantly preparing elections and never insurrections, he ends up by seeing nothing in socialism except parliamentary activity'. The higher he rose, the more it was in his interest that there be a proletariat whose party could send him to the Chamber (at 15,000 francs a year) rather than that the proletariat disappear. Pelletier was careful to make clear that it was not a question of honesty but of situation. She was the first French socialist to analyse the process involved instead of blaming individual leaders for betrayal.[41]

The only solution, she argued, was 'to make the party always keep its finger on the Revolution'. If socialism did not come by violent revolution, it would be only a change of names. Prisons would become socialist prisons, but they would still be prisons. The bourgeoisie (whose great flexibility she underlined) would continue to run the show. She carried her argument to its logical, anarchistic conclusion, supporting 'propaganda by deed' (i.e. violent acts), though only in periods of widespread unrest, and urging the party to direct its efforts toward 'thugs': 'to prepare the revolution, to encourage these skirmishes which make the revolutionary education of the masses, we need people who are not afraid of illegal activity'. If the socialists were not for civil war, she concluded, they were no better than the radical republicans. She joined the Hervéists because they attacked the republic instead of defending it like the Jaurèsists.[42]

Pelletier's Hervéism was entirely consistent and self-sufficient. Feminism had nothing to do with it. She could hardly have ignored that, in the spring of 1907, *La Guerre sociale* published two articles extremely hostile to feminism. In any event, in June 1908 (a year after her switch), she certainly noticed a column in *La Guerre sociale* criticising the English suffragist women with extraordinary violence: the following week her protest appeared side by side with Hervé's reply. He defended the right of his collaborators to oppose feminism, adding that he himself thought there was no reason to refuse political rights to women if they wanted them, though he thought them worthless: some of us 'follow your campaigns, even your campaign for women's political rights, if not with enthusiasm, at least with sympathy'.[43]

Pelletier nevertheless continued to support Hervé. Soon she was leading his greatest battles for him. It was she, she claimed in 1910, who had had the idea of grouping the 'insurrectional' faction (as the Hervéists were called) in a caucus so as to have more influence over party politics. The police reports bear her out. Subsequently, she became the faction's tactician. At its first meeting, on 26 February 1909, she was the one who presented the draft resolution on conduct in the second round of voting in national elections. It provided that SFIO candidates maintain their candidature in the second round instead of stepping down in favour of the best placed republican, even if this meant dividing the republican vote and thus electing a reactionary.[44]

Having virtually single-handedly steered the resolution through the Seine federation congress, Pelletier defended it brilliantly at the national congress of Saint-Etienne in April 1909. She held her own, even in debate with Vaillant and Jaurès, the party's most forceful leaders. 'To ally ourselves with you reformists to defend the Republic', she told them, 'would be yet another dupery.' 'The Socialist Party must not be a party of social peace', she added, 'but a party of social revolution, a party of revolt into which, along with the working class, we enter, we who are of no class [déclassés].' Though she did not succeed in getting the resolution passed (no one could have done that), she did succeed in manoeuvring so that the Hervéists obtained seats on the CAP. She herself was listed a deputy member next in line to succeed Hervé on the CAP.[45]

The following autumn, Hervé resigned from the CAP because he could not participate in its meetings. He was in jail. Pelletier thus took his place. Member of the party's national executive body and leader of the 'insurrectional' minority of the Seine federation, she was now in a position to work effectively for women's rights. In fact, however, she did very little for this cause.[46]

Yet there was surely occasion to recall to the socialist deputies the promises made in 1906, if not the resolution passed at Limoges and again at Nancy. In the autumn of 1909, two years after Nancy, there had still been no socialist bill for women's suffrage. During the crucial debate on proportional representation that year, Sembat spoke at length to urge the introduction of such a bill. The feminists seized hopefully upon his speech, but *L'Humanité* probably gave it its due with a single sentence preceding the text of his speech on proportional representation, which was spread over two columns. In any case, with no bill on the agenda (or even written), his statement was necessarily academic. In the new legislature following the elections of 1910, the socialists presented a resolution describing women's suffrage as an urgent reform, but this was all they did during Pelletier's tenure on the CAP and they did it without any action from either the CAP or Pelletier herself.[47]

The CAP named Pelletier and Roussel as delegates to the international socialist congress of Copenhagen held in 1910 and to the second conference of socialist women, held in conjunction with the congress, but only Roussel went. Even this was a last minute effort. Three weeks before the conference, Clara Zetkin wrote to ask whether there would be any French delegates at all. Jean Longuet commented with some embarrassment that the federations should try to find some women who could go. He followed his own advice, bringing his sister-in-law. Another militant brought his wife, and Sorgue finally came, making with Roussel four French women delegates to the congress and presumably to the conference. The conference passed a resolution on women's suffrage virtually identical to the one adopted at Stuttgart in 1907. It also called for social security for women and children and for a struggle against the high cost of living. The Frenchwomen did not distinguish themselves.[48]

Pelletier's failure to attend was probably due to her disillusionment with socialist politics. In June 1910, three months before the congress of Copenhagen, she announced that she was breaking with the Hervéists. She explained that Hervé had always been a Jaurèsist at heart, that though he talked of revolution he really worried about lay control of education and such reforms. Now, she predicted, he would return to the Jaurèsists. (She was right.) She, on the other hand, was moving back to the Guesdists, but her heart was not there. Indeed, her heart was no longer in the party. She began to miss CAP meetings. Her break with the Hervéists meant naturally that they did not nominate her for the CAP at the 1911 congress. As the Guesdists were hardly ready to do so either, she lost her place on the CAP. Within a year, the CAP was without any women: Roussel resigned in January 1912, denouncing waste in the party finances.[49]

Socialist women on the campaign trail

Pelletier was on her way out of the party, but she was still able to make use of her membership in the party for feminism. Like Kauffmann and Renaud, she undertook feminist election campaigns. All three stood as SFIO candidates in the 1910 and 1912 elections.

Legislative elections were to be held on 24 April 1910. La Solidarité decided in March to pose women candidatures. By the beginning of April they had ten names on their 'Parti Féministe' poster. Only Pelletier, however, actually ran a campaign. She decided to stand in the fifth arrondissement because it was 'the most intellectual district'. But perhaps because the party feared she might draw off socialist votes in a district where it could hope to win (for even if she stood as a 'Parti Féministe' candidate, she was known as a socialist), the Seine federation offered her its nomination in the eighth arrondissement, one of the most reactionary of all Paris. Fearing exclusion if she maintained her 'Parti Féministe' candidature in the fifth, she accepted the SFIO nomination in the eighth.[50]

She campaigned seriously, holding three public meetings. Even a hostile reporter conceded that she was well received at her first meeting. She herself commented that the audience had been so preoccupied by social problems that they had swallowed her feminism without noticing it. In deference to the local party committee, which was concerned with getting more votes than at the last election, she tried to avoid speaking of her anti-militarist and insurrectional ideas, but determined not to preach the Jaurèsist reforms. This proved more difficult than she expected.[51]

At the last campaign meeting, Hélène Brion, a feminist primary-school teacher, took complete notes of Pelletier's speech. Pelletier began with a feminist preface devoted mainly to attacking the party for giving her a hopeless district. Thereafter she launched into a classic political speech, attacking her opponents vigorously and seeking to interest the domestics who constituted the majority of the district's population. 'That the rich vote for M. Denys Cochin [her opponent], that's natural . . . But what is not understandable, is that the proletariat . . . should vote for M. D. Cochin . . . against their own interest as domestics.' Cochin had opposed a weekly day off for servants, she said: 'he claimed that they're part of the family. That reminds me of a Jew who said to his domestic, "My friend, now you're part of the family, so I'm cutting off your wages." ' The more Pelletier got into the swing of this sort of speech, the more she found herself preaching the very reforms she detested: the day off, the eight-hour day, the minimum wage, free education, even the income tax. She was a politician despite herself.[52]

She received 340 votes of 8698, which was better than the SFIO candidate had done in 1906. She wrote that she had received these votes as a revolutionary and an anti-militarist (which seems unlikely from the reports of her speeches); had she stood as a moderate republican, she claimed, she would have got 2000 votes. But it seems reasonable to assume that formal party endorsement was an important part of her success, and only Jaurès' paper, *L'Humanité*, had supported her and only the SFIO would endorse women candidates at all.[53]

Kauffmann also stood as an SFIO candidate in the same election, but her candidature was a last minute affair. Her name did not even appear on the 'Parti Féministe' poster. *L'Humanité* did not begin carrying her name as a party candidate until 17 April, a week before the election. She held only one meeting. She did not even have a committee to count votes for her (the officials would not do so). *L'Humanité* estimated that she had received seventeen votes, *Le Journal des femmes* 150. She herself claimed nearly 200.[54]

Elisabeth Renaud's astonishingly successful campaign in the Department of the Isère — she received 2869 votes, more than one-fifth of those cast — was the product of the convergence of two local forces: a strong feminist movement and an active socialist federation sympathetic to women's rights. The former was focused in the local section of the Fédération Féministe Universitaire (FFU). The FFU was founded in 1903 by Marie Guérin to promote such women's demands as co-education and equal wages within the primary-school teachers' mutual aid groups, the Amicales d'Instituteurs. (Public servants were not permitted to constitute *syndicats*.) The FFU section of the Isère was an especially active one. Its secretary, Venise Pellat-Finet, was a national leader of the FFU and associate editor of its magazine.[55]

The SFIO Isère federation was also unusually energetic. The prefecture of the Isère, Grenoble, was the seat of one of the three provincial dailies which the SFIO controlled, *Le Droit du peuple*. The federation was powerful and responsive to women. Pellat-Finet herself was an important party member. It was the Isère which gave its mandate to Angèle Roussel for national councils and congresses. Renaud stood in the town of Vienne, a sub-prefecture some twenty miles south of Lyons, where the local socialist section displayed the same sympathy to women's rights as did the federation. The city council, entirely socialist after the elections of 1912, was to distinguish itself by passing a strongly worded resolution in favour of women's suffrage in 1913, when there was hope of getting the Dussaussoy–Buisson bill onto the floor of the Chamber.[56]

After her break with the GFS, Renaud had despaired of the possibilities for action within the party. She had collaborated instead in the Ligue Française pour le Droit des Femmes. When the FFU offered her the chance once again to combine feminist and socialist action, she replied enthusiastically. On 10 April 1910 the local socialist committee gave her its nomination in the hopelessly reactionary second district of Vienne, composed of the tiny villages on the outskirts of the town. The FFU, the League, and the party joined together to prepare Renaud's campaign, spending a total of 391 francs for posters and travel.

A week before the election, Renaud came down from Paris and began an energetic campaign. She drew up an electoral statement which was widely posted. Arguing the essential injustice of women's subordination to men, she claimed that women were subject to laws, taxes, and capitalist exploitation as much as men, if not more. If men's rights were based on their military service, women's could be based on ' "Maternity Service", no less arduous than "Military Service" . . . Soldiers give death, Women give life. And while barracks will disappear with standing armies, Maternity will remain.' Like Valette's 'sexualism', this kind of thinking seems retrograde today, but it appealed to peasant audiences in 1910.[57]

Renaud spoke every day in two and sometimes three villages. A reporter from *Le Droit du peuple* wrote that the peasants, having come out of curiosity, were finally conquered by her speeches. They must have been good if they held the audience's attention, for they invariably lasted two hours. While the opposition papers ignored her, *Le Droit du peuple* announced and covered her meetings every day. In Paris, *L'Humanité* and *Le Rappel* (a radical republican paper for which Auclert sometimes wrote) gave her sympathetic attention.[58]

The results far exceeded Renaud's expectations. She received 2813 ballots cast in her own name, to which should be added the 56 cast in the name of the man who had signed her formal declaration of candidature in order to permit her to stand. The winner received 10,421. Her success can be judged by comparing her 2869 votes with the 202 received by the SFIO candidate in 1906 and the 1519 received by that of 1914 (when, however, an indepen-

dent socialist also stood and drew off 2637 votes.) *L'Humanité* ran a dithy-
rambic report: 'The success increased with each meeting. In tiny hamlets of
2 to 3000 inhabitants, the halls were packed, and many voters remained outside when 6 to 800 persons had occupied halls that were too small.'[59]

Renaud followed up this campaign with a candidature in the municipal
elections of 1912. She stood in the district of the Odéon. Two weeks before
the election, *L'Humanité* announced that, 'at the same time as she will speak
in the name of our Party, [she] will demand the right to vote for women'.
She held only one meeting, but nevertheless obtained 519 votes of 2821
cast. *L'Humanité* wrote of 'the very appreciable result that she has obtained
in a clearly reactionary district'.[60]

Pelletier also stood as a party candidate in the same elections, in the
equally reactionary district of Saint Thomas d'Acquin. She held two meetings. She estimated her total at 306 votes of 3610 cast. But this was her last
effort as a socialist. Her vital energies were already in other causes. She had
been leaning toward the anarchists more and more since she broke with
Hervé in 1910. She was developing ideas which she could propagate more
easily among the anarchists than among the socialists, ideas on the right to
abortion, the right to sexual fulfilment for women, and even the need to go
beyond the nuclear family. She remained a member of the party, but her
heart was elsewhere.[61]

Pelletier's anarchism was the logical consequence of her development since
entering the SFIO. Her whole orientation was toward the revolutionary
aspects of socialism and not toward its proletarian class basis. She thought
like a 'déclassée', which she rightly believed herself to be. She demonstrated
continued hostility toward the working class: 'Bourgeois milieux are the
least refractory to feminism'; 'The working class will be the last to come to
feminism. It is in the natural order of things; the ignorant respects only
brute force.' She performed veritable feats of casuistry to maintain this
belief. In 1905 she argued that the Freemasons were amenable to women
and women's demands because they were bourgeois. Having found them
not so amenable, she argued in 1910 that they were hostile to women
because they were peopled by the working class and the *petite* bourgeoisie.
Nor did her good receptions from working-class audiences in her campaigns
alter this opinion. She affirmed in 1912, 'as for liking the working class
such as it is, no! a thousand times no!'[62]

Yet she was a sincere socialist for a time, and for the same reason that she
would become an anarchist: because, as she put it in 1912, 'I love justice
passionately.' For this love of justice she continued to agitate in the SFIO,
even though by 1908 she had decided that the socialist leaders were 'shame-
ful anti-feminists' who, 'for the question of women's suffrage', demonstrated
only 'a great scorn'. For this love of justice she continued to serve Hervé's

faction with all her power even though he had made it clear that he was at best lukewarm on women's suffrage.[63]

Yet her love of justice does not explain why she never sought to create separate women's sections. She said nothing about Chaboseau's abortive efforts in 1907, did nothing to follow up her own call for women's sections in 1908, and said nothing when, in 1911, the party's national council, of which she was a member, quietly pigeonholed a motion presented by the Ardèche federation to create a women's section of the party. Was it not that to operate in the male context of the party as a whole raised her self-esteem? We have suggested that from her childhood she had perceived the male universe as the only one that mattered. In 1907, at Nancy, she had pointed out that 'by giving them [women] the title of citizen, one immediately raises them in their own esteem, up to a higher rank'. In the SFIO everyone was called citizen. In a women's section, this would make no sense.[64]

The SFIO gave her the title of citizen and the chance to work for justice. Her action in the party contradicted her Machiavellian precepts. She was a socialist despite herself, and a deeply committed one. It was not the party's anti-feminism which led her to quit it, but its reformism. And she left it not for feminism but for anarchism, although her experience with *La Guerre sociale* had taught her not to expect support for her feminism from these quarters. In a short story written after the war, she judged the socialists from an insurrectional standpoint rather than a feminist one. She found them all wanting:

Intellectuals were numerous in the party, but most of them only came to make a career, [and] had very little sincerity.

. . . Far from pushing the workers to revolt, they held them back. When, by chance, violent incidents did take place, the intellectuals never approved them; they limited themselves to excusing those who had committed them. To be sure, they spoke of revolution, but without believing in it and without wanting to do anything serious to prepare it.

Indeed, they insidiously turned the masses away from revolution by presenting it as something inevitable which could not take place before the expiration of the economic process. They invoked the need for breaking the bourgeois order with a proletarian majority obviously impossible to obtain.[65]

Pelletier remained all her life a revolutionary. She fought one more battle in the party in support of the Third (communist) International. She was a delegate to the congress of Tours in 1920, where it voted to join the Third International. Full of hope in the Russian revolution, she was quickly disillusioned. By 1925 she had quit the party to return to the anarchists. She ended her life as a martyr for a contemporary cause. She put her belief in the right to abortion into practice and was arrested in April 1939. Half paralysed by a stroke since 1937, she must have seemed strange to the judge, who had her examined and committed to the asylum at Vaucluse. The faithful Brion consulted a lawyer, who advised her that the case was hopeless. She visited

Pelletier four times at Vaucluse in the summer of 1939 and then ceased to go, finding her state too sad to bear. Toward the end of the year, she paid two more visits to Pelletier, at one of which she took the brief autobiographical notes. Pelletier died alone at the asylum on 29 December 1939.[66]

Nothing remained from the struggle she had waged in the SFIO before the First World War. She had failed to orient the party towards women's rights and she had failed to create a women's organisation of the party. The implications of this failure extended far beyond Pelletier's personal tragedy. No other socialist leader would understand so well the social and psychological problems women faced in the party. No other leader would perceive the link at the organisational level between these problems and the recruitment of women for the party. No other leader would articulate so well the need for a separate women's group in terms of overcoming these problems to facilitate recruitment. Pelletier's failure left the definitive socialist women's organis-ation, when it was finally founded, in the hands of leaders who refused to take these problems into account. In this sense Pelletier's failure is linked to the general failure of the French party to develop a strong women's movement.

6. The Groupe des Femmes Socialistes 1913 – 14

One evening shortly before Christmas 1912, the wife of a young army captain gave a dinner. It was not a typical military affair: all the guests were women, and socialists into the bargain! Captain Comignan was not put out, however. He was accustomed to his wife's unusual interests. When he had been stationed in Brittany, she had written imitation Celtic verse. In Paris, it had been feminism: she had even written in *La Française* and had considered herself a disciple of the beautiful 'neo-Malthusian' feminist, Nelly Roussel. Then she had wangled a lunch invitation from Paul and Laura Lafargue, shortly before their joint suicide in 1911. On her return from their country home south of Paris, she declared herself a socialist. This was a bit much for an officer's wife. However, understanding her husband's position — she herself was proud of being the 'daughter, granddaughter, great-granddaughter, wife and sister of French officers' — she took a pseudonym for her public affairs. Born Marie-Anne-Rose Gaillarde (at Paris on 20 September 1875), she called herself Marianne Rauze: 'a Rose by any other name'.[1]

Rauze had invited her guests with one purpose: to create a socialist women's group. Among the half dozen women were Elisabeth Renaud and Adèle Toussaint-Kassky (Adèle Kassky had married the Allemanist deputy Edmond Toussaint, in 1905). They were now aged sixty-seven and sixty-five, but still ready for action. All the guests agreed in principle that there should be a women's group in the SFIO. They decided to meet again on 5 January 1913 at Renaud's *pension*. There they wrote an appeal for women to come to a public meeting on 23 January to found a socialist women's group, the Groupe des Femmes Socialistes (GDFS).[2]

Madeleine Pelletier was not of the company at either gathering. She had been invited to the dinner, but refused: 'Madame Rauze has written to tell me that the dinner will not be held at the Palais Royal but at her home; I have therefore asked her to excuse me. My stomach . . . ' If Pelletier disliked Rauze's cooking, Renaud detested Pelletier's masculine attire, Freemasonry, and libertarian ideas on sexual matters. Pelletier was not invited to Renaud's *pension*. She complained bitterly at being left out after all she had done for women and for socialism, but in fact she made no effort to be included. These personal tensions masked fundamental disagreement about the direction the group should take. 'I fear', Pelletier explained, 'that the socialist women's group will only be the kindergarten of the socialist party and that it will leave feminism behind to please the men in the Party.' In fact, the group would become explicitly anti-feminist within a year, thus confirming Pelletier in her decision to stay aloof from it. This anti-feminist approach was due to the action of Louise Saumoneau.[3]

Saumoneau had not been invited to either gathering: she and Renaud were still not speaking to each other. But she was not one to be deterred. She had been preparing for the leadership of the socialist women's movement for almost a year. In March 1912, she had brought out a newspaper called once again *La Femme socialiste*, but resembling the old paper only in name. Its format was four small pages. The first six issues contained nothing but documents from the 1899 GFS and an advertisement: 'French lessons for foreigners . . . Mademoiselle Saumoneau'. She was still working hard as a seamstress (now doing alterations for a dress shop), but following Renaud's example she supplemented her income and increased her political contacts with lessons. She had at least half a dozen Russian socialists among her students. The paper thus served to advertise both her lessons and her politics: the documents presented were an effort to set the record straight about what she and Renaud had done a decade earlier and to stake her claim in any future group.[4]

Saumoneau was determined to put the GDFS on the course the old GFS had taken under her leadership: unremitting hostility to the feminist movement. We shall thus refer to her faction as anti-feminist. They were women who often supported women's rights in principle, but who would not be caught dead in a feminist group. They believed that sex oppression was secondary to class oppression, that feminism was bourgeois as a movement, and that it represented the class interests of the bourgeoisie. Their opponents, on the other hand, agreed with Pelletier that at least some measure of feminism was essential within the socialist party. Virtually all of them were active in feminist groups. If they were often ready to recognise that many feminists were bourgeois, they refused to dismiss the feminist movement as bourgeois in nature. Believing that the problem of sex oppression was important in its own right and independent of class oppression, they denied that feminism represented one class interest. We shall refer to this faction as feminist. Between these two factions were moderates like Renaud and Toussaint-Kassky. In the end they too, like the feminists, would fall victim to Saumoneau's determination.

Left out of the earlier sessions, Saumoneau came to the formal founding meeting of the GDFS on 23 January 1913 in a fighting mood. 'A great number of women citizens', she reported, engaged in 'a heated discussion' on the aims of the group. The appeal had specified that the group's aim would be 'to organise working women, to give them an exact notion of their social rights and duties and thus to lead them to come and militate in the socialist

130

groups'. The feminists sought to broaden the aims beyond the mere function of recruitment for the male socialist groups which this statement implied. They obtained a revised statement of the aims: 'to support and defend all the demands of the feminine proletariat (political, syndicalist, and co-operative)'. But while they were winning abstract principles, Saumoneau was obtaining concrete organisational bases which would render their victory illusory.[5]

For this founding meeting the party membership card had been required for voting. Saumoneau, however, demanded that party membership be a prerequisite for joining the group in the future. In the heat of the debate over the aims, this request was accepted virtually without opposition. Yet it was fraught with disastrous consequences. It meant that the group would not recruit women from outside the party, but only from within the party. A woman who responded to the group's propaganda would have to go first not to the group but to a regular male section. But as Madeleine Pelletier had made clear, the male atmosphere of the regular sections was the biggest stumbling block to the recruitment of women.[6]

The import of Saumoneau's victory was not recognised at the time. The feminists thought they had won the day with their new statement of the group's aims. At first, events seemed to justify their interpretation. At the group's first regular meeting, four of them were elected to the executive commission. Two of them were prominent feminist leaders: Marie Bonnevial, who had succeeded Maria Pognon in 1904 as president of the Ligue Française pour le Droit des Femmes; and Maria Vérone, who was secretary of the League and who, upon Bonnevial's death in 1918, would succeed her as president. Vérone was also well known as the only really active woman lawyer in France.[7] The other two feminist members of the executive were schoolteachers: Pelletier's friend, Hélène Brion;[8] and the suffragist Marguerite Martin.[9] Only two of those elected to the executive shared Saumoneau's views: Louise Couteaudier and Suzanne Gibault, though two others (Alice Jouenne and Wally Grumbach) might be expected to put the party's interest before other considerations.[10] Most of the others had feminist connections, however insufficient Pelletier thought them: Rauze had been a feminist before her conversion to socialism; Renaud was still active in the Ligue Française — Vérone called her 'one of our oldest and most zealous members'. Renaud was elected secretary of the GDFS, Toussaint-Kassky treasurer. Saumoneau did not even get a seat on the executive commission, but she continued her struggle undaunted.[11]

She won her second victory at the April meeting. A proposal was made for the women to go in a body to the commemoration of the Commune in the Père Lachaise cemetery, but it was rejected because this would constitute competition with the regular sections. Instead, each woman was to go individually, with her section, alongside her male comrades. This decision set a precedent which the group subsequently respected. Thus not only would it not recruit women directly, but also it would not provide a focus for women's activities in the party. This meant that women were not able to make an impact as women and that they were not able to create a more comfortable environment for themselves within the party, since they were scattered among the men and isolated from each other. There would be no sisterhood, even within the party.[12]

These policy problems absorbed most of the group's energies at the outset. They were compounded by factionalism. At the April meeting, for example, Renaud asked Caroline Kauffmann (yes, Pelletier's colleague from La Solidarité) to preside in her stead because, she complained, some persons had called her 'an authoritarian Guesdist'. Preoccupied by these differences, the group was unable to organise a celebration of the 'international women's day' which the German socialist women held each March. Indeed, the group made little headway during its first six months. Its only direct action was an expression of support for women striking at the Lebaudy sugar refineries: Renaud and Saumoneau went — separately — to express the group's solidarity. The GDFS also held three lectures: Jouenne on the 'three-year law' — the bill to increase military service from two to three years, which the SFIO was opposing vigorously; Renaud on 'utopian socialism'; and Vérone on 'the vote for women'. Its first season of action was closed by a walk in the forest of Meudon organised by Suzanne Gibault. On 29 July, the executive met at Renaud's *pension* and set the next meeting for 2 October. During this interval, there occurred two events which crystallised Saumoneau's anti-feminism and enabled her to take control of the GDFS: her debate with Hélène Brion and the Couriau affair.[13]

Theory . . .

During the summer of 1913 Saumoneau engaged in a passionate debate with the feminist Hélène Brion. It began in Rauze's newspaper *L'Equité*. The paper first appeared in February 1913. Though its stated aim was to educate women to be 'in solidarity with enslaved men', it was open to feminists as well as to socialists.[14] By its fourth issue, it had carried articles from nearly every woman prominent in the two movements. In June there appeared a long article on 'Feminism and Socialism'. It was written by a provincial militant, a schoolteacher named Suzanne Lacore, who used the pen-name 'Suzon'. She was the secretary of the SFIO federation of the Dordogne, of which she was the only woman member.[15]

Lacore's analysis was the same as Saumoneau's. Feminism, she argued, was a movement toward justice based on 'natural right', on women's desire no longer to be considered 'housekeeper[s] and mother[s] above all', but persons in their own right. Although this would be nice for proletarian women, it was secondary to their economic oppression. Feminists were 'educated, enlightened women, most often of the bourgeoisie, who will . . . use the ballot . . . in support of the capitalist regime'. Their emancipation was irrelevant to that of proletarian woman, for they were on the opposite side of the barrier in the class struggle. All efforts to cross this barrier were doomed to failure: 'the deeper is dug the abyss between wage earners and possessors, the more are felt the effects of the condescending protection of rich women toward their "enemy sisters" '. The only course of action for proletarian women was to join the party.[16]

During the following year, Lacore developed these ideas in subsequent articles. As her ideas would correspond to the practice of the socialist women's organisation throughout the life of the SFIO, they merit our attention. Lacore continued to insist that proletarian women had nothing in common with even the most advanced feminists, for by virtue of their being bourgeois the latter could not 'conceive of a society based on this community of labour and of wealth which the future will impose, and which remains the sole condition for worker, feminine and human liberation'. She used Lafargue's articles to argue that the origins of women's subordination to men were economic, although her formulations of this idea were sometimes ambiguous. 'The day when masculine domination will no longer have interest in keeping women in bondage, this sex slavery will disappear by itself.' This could only occur, however, after the revolution had built the new society of which the bourgeois could not even 'conceive'.[17]

'Class struggle', Lacore went on in the very words the GFS had used in 1900, was 'a hard fact it would be puerile to deny'. There were only two classes. Between them 'a buffer class' was getting thinner every day. Bourgeois women such as feminists could help proletarian women only if they deserted the ranks of their class and joined the socialist party. Proletarian women had a duty to steer clear of the feminists. Indeed, like Saumoneau, Lacore was cool toward women's groups even within the party for fear that they might foster feminist influence. Women in the party were not to be sisters among other women, but citizens among men and women even if, as in her own case, they were alone among men. For those women who had not her talent and courage, Lacore had little concern.[18]

Lacore's arguments won the approval of Saumoneau and of a number of socialist men.[19] But *L'Equité* also published a feminist reply by Hélène Brion, entitled 'Feminine solidarity'. Brion argued that the difference between the sexes was more important than that between the classes. Even in working class and peasant families a girl assumed household tasks from her earliest childhood 'while the boy blossoms in liberty'. Girls became conscious of their subordination to men long before they experienced the class struggle. Indeed, Brion went on, Proudhon's famous phrase, 'housewife *or* prostitute', should be changed to 'housewife *and* prostitute' (italics mine), for what was the difference between the prostitute and the 'poor housewife well and truly married who, each Saturday, despite all her attempts to flee, must undergo the ignoble beating administered by her proprietor, followed by "caresses" (?) [sic] just as ignoble'? Whatever the title, women were slaves to men. The true solidarity, therefore, was not within one's class but within one's sex: 'there can be no question of class struggle between bourgeois feminists and women who work'. If bourgeois women sought the right to vote, it was to reform society 'in the interest of their sex . . . to protect women, poor women in the first instance, working women'.[20]

Marguerite Martin supported Brion. In alliance with the feminists, socialist women could obtain useful reforms. They would be free subsequently to take up their own struggle. Moreover, she added, one often came to socialism through feminism, as in her own case. Other leaders of the GDFS, however, came down on Lacore's side. Suzanne Gibault argued that the group could not reach working women directly: 'we will encounter first the father, the brother, the husband'. Thus they should not take men as adversaries but instead 'above all *remain women* and *be pleasant*' (italics orig.). Feminism was out of the question for socialists.[21]

Marianne Rauze also argued against co-operation with the feminists, despite her recent involvement in their ranks. The SFIO, she now believed, would suffice to achieve women's emancipation, if only enough women joined. If proletarian women were to help the suffragists obtain the vote, the latter would use it in their class interest against the workers. The suffrage would not emancipate proletarian women; it had not emancipated proletarian men (an old Guesdist argument). The only hope was economic independence for women, which could only be achieved by 'an expropriator revolution [sic] . . . to transform this regime into communism'. Rauze did admit, nevertheless, that 'masculine arbitrariness' was an oppressive force in its own right, although rooted in economic conditions. She left the door open for the feminists.[22]

Saumoneau, however, slammed it shut, hurling invectives against 'that amalgam of intriguing, naïve, deranged and hysterical women which is bourgeois feminism'. Her reply to Brion ran in serial form in *La Femme socialiste* for nearly a year. Feminism was a 'metaphysical' remnant of the past, Brion a 'scatterbrain'. Among the working classes, boys worked as hard as girls; if Brion thought otherwise, it was proof of her bourgeois origins. Socialists had always acted in the interest of women; for proof she listed all the socialist statements on the woman question since 1848. Bourgeois women should therefore join the SFIO. If they chose instead to act as feminists, it was because socialism threatened their class privilege. Feminism was at best a diversion, feminine solidarity a myth created to fool working women and draw them away from socialism. Heartened that Lacore had come along to

support these arguments, which (as she pointed out) she had been making
for fifteen years, she renewed the call she and Renaud had used as the masthead of the old *Femme socialiste*: 'There can be no antagonism between the
men and women of the proletarian class.' This theory was put severely to the
test by the Couriau affair.[23]

. . . and Practice

Emma Couriau and her husband Louis were both typographers. In 1912 they
moved to Lyons, where Emma obtained a job at union wages. At her husband's urging, she applied to join the local section of the printers' union, the
Fédération du Livre, in virtue of a resolution passed at its 1910 congress
which provided that women might join if they were paid union wages. The
Lyons section, however, not only refused admission to Emma, but also
expelled Louis for allowing her to work.[24]

The 1910 resolution had not really signified a change in the printers' traditional hostility to women in their trade. The influence of Proudhon (a
printer himself) and the use of women as strike-breakers (common during
the Second Empire) had led the federation, in the words of its original
statutes, 'to oppose, by all legal means, women's working in composing
rooms'. Keufer, the secretary of the federation since 1885, had been the
principal spokesman of the anti-feminists at Le Havre in 1880. By the end of
the century, he and other members of the central committee were 'embarrassed' by their policy of opposition to women workers. 'In order to put a
stop to disobliging criticisms', they began efforts to modify the policy and
finally succeeded in 1910 in obtaining the admission of women as a principle.
They made no effort, however, to change the mentality of their rank and file.
Indeed, to obtain passage of the resolution, they had promised at the congress that the employment of women 'will remain rigorously limited to the
printing houses which employ them now' and that members would still have
the right to strike if women were introduced into 'shops where there aren't
any at present'. Moreover, the central committee had supported a resolution
'that workers who are heads of families aid in the application of the principle,
"women's place is in the home" and engage their companions to refuse all
work outside the home'.[25]

Small wonder then that, at a general assembly on 27 July 1913, the Lyons
section confirmed its executive's decision to refuse membership to Emma
and to expel Louis. Small wonder too that the federation refused to force
the section to conform to a resolution which had only been meant as
window dressing. In August the national central committee refused to
review the decisions. Emma constituted a women's *syndicat* and demanded
its admission directly to the federation, but the central committee hemmed

and hawed throughout the autumn and finally adjourned consideration of the question indefinitely. In the meantime, the affair had taken on national importance.[26]

L'Humanité had carried a protest by the Fédération Féministe du Sud-Est, Pellat-Finet's section of the FFU, the one which had supported Renaud's candidature in 1910. Thereafter the socialists kept silence, reticent before the syndicalists' traditional hostility to external interference. The syndicalist left, however, soon joined the feminists in protest. Alfred Rosmer wrote a series of eleven front-page articles in *La Bataille syndicaliste*, the official organ of the CGT. He concluded that the printers had failed in their most elementary duties of working-class solidarity and pleaded with them to recognise the need for women to join in the syndical struggle.[27] His articles brought the issue home to the mainstream of the syndical movement: by the autumn the leadership of the CGT and even many sections of the Fédération du Livre had disowned the Lyons decision. In November, Louis was admitted as an individual member attached directly to the federation. Emma's case, however, proved intractable.[28]

By this time, the affair had become a major preoccupation for socialist women, despite all their efforts to avoid it. The hard-core anti-feminists like Saumoneau refused all discussion of the affair. But even Rauze and Renaud hesitated a long time before coming to grips with it. Although *L'Equité* had published Louis's account of the affair in July, it was not until September that Rauze wrote about it and not until December that *L'Equité* took it up as a major cause, although the journal then devoted virtually the entire issue to the affair.

Renaud made no effort to raise the problem until the GDFS resumed its meetings on 2 October, when she brought it up after the scheduled lecture. The group decided not to discuss the affair until representatives of the Fédération du Livre could be invited. To this end a special meeting was scheduled for 20 October, at which two representatives of the Fédération du Livre were present. After a long debate, the group passed a resolution 'energetically' censuring the Lyons section. This decision left everyone dissatisfied. Brion wrote to Marguerite Durand that Stéphanie Bouvard and Elisabeth Renaud had led an 'abject surrender'. Saumoneau, on the other hand, was furious at what seemed to her an anti-worker position. She mounted a campaign to put the group back on a 'class basis'.[29]

The triumph of Louise Saumoneau

Saumoneau soon turned the dispute over the Couriau affair into a personal victory. At the regular meeting held on 6 November 1913, Marguerite Martin passed on an invitation from the feminists for the GDFS to participate in the protest meeting on the affair planned for 15 December. Saumoneau succeeded in persuading the group to reject the invitation, apparently by mobilising a number of seamstresses. The group had thus affirmed 'its determination to remain a class-based group', she commented; she had eliminated the danger of a triumph of 'the feminist or "anti-masculinist" tendencies'. She had completely reversed the group's position on the affair. Rauze, Renaud, and Vérone nevertheless spoke at the protest meeting, but only as individuals disavowed by their group.[30]

Renaud's loyalty to the party and the group was already strained to the breaking point. Since May 1913, she and her old friend Jean Allemane had collaborated in the newspaper *La Lutte de classe* ('class struggle'), published by two militants of the extreme left of the party, Achille and Gabrielle Cambier. Mme Cambier had been the director of a party summer camp. Ousted from her position as director in 1911, she had created a fuss by accusing a number of leading socialists of misuse of funds destined for the camp. She and her husband began a campaign against the party leadership which quickly broadened into an attack on general party policy. In July 1913 the national council of the party prohibited members from collaborating in the Cambiers' newspaper. Renaud and Allemane ignored the prohibition. The matter came before the council again in October. One participant wrote to Renaud that the council had considered excluding her and Allemane as well as the Cambiers. Moreover, her informant told her, forgetting that she was the secretary of the GDFS, he had suggested in another debate that the group have a column in *L'Humanité*. The reaction had been 'Let [them] keep to the cooking.' Renaud, stung to the quick, published the letter – in the Cambiers' newspaper. Finally, the party added further insult: *L'Humanité* listed all the men present at a ceremony in memory of Benoît Malon, but omitted the names of the women who attended, among them Renaud and Toussaint-Kassky. Both protested bitterly in the Cambiers' newspaper against what they felt to be a slight to women.[31]

Meanwhile, Saumoneau renewed her offensive. She initiated proceedings for a revision of the statutes to include the requirement that the executive 'always and in as large a measure as possible be composed of a majority of working women'. Disavowed by the group and insulted by the party, Renaud resigned in the face of Saumoneau's offensive. At the next meeting, on 10 December, Saumoneau was elected provisional secretary and given charge of the elections to the executive commission, to be held in January 1914.[32]

The elections confirmed Saumoneau's hold on the group. There were twenty-two candidates for secretary, including Saumoneau herself, Gibault, Jouenne, Martin, Toussaint-Kassky, and Renaud (who apparently considered trying to win back control of the group before she quit the party in solidarity with the Cambiers, who were excluded on 20 December). Renaud may have withdrawn her candidature before the elections; once out of the party, she could not stand. In any event, she was neither elected secretary nor even a member of the executive. Saumoneau became the second secretary of the GDFS. Toussaint-Kassky was re-elected treasurer, but she left the party (and thus the group) early in February to join Renaud and Allemane in the Cambiers' new Parti Ouvrier (PO).[33] The feminists were routed. Bonnevial, Brion, and Vérone disappeared from the executive, leaving only Martin. Most of the members of the new executive were newcomers, comparatively unknown. Those for whom we have information, such as Stéphanie Bouvard and Louise Couteaudier, were workers and friends of Saumoneau. She was firmly in control.[34]

This was demonstrated by her success in blocking Marianne Rauze's attempts to regain influence in the group. Rauze had followed her husband to Chartres, where he had been transferred toward the end of 1913. Her experience with provincial women quickly discouraged her about their revolutionary potential. She now felt the need for specifically feminine groups to educate women for party membership. In February, she took the train to Paris to speak in favour of a new structure of the GDFS which would cater to this need. Only Marguerite Martin supported her.[35]

Later in the spring, Rauze offered to make her newspaper into an official organ of the GDFS. This would have been a good deal for the group: *L'Equité* was an attractive publication and it was doing well – it had become bi-weekly in March and was planning to publish weekly in the autumn. Saumoneau, however, would not tolerate any division of her authority with a woman she suspected of being insufficiently anti-feminist. Before Rauze could submit her proposal formally, Saumoneau persuaded the executive to found its own organ (which never appeared) rather than take over *L'Equité*. Rauze termed Saumoneau's actions 'rancorous manoeuvres against a personality'. It was true that no love was lost between the attractive, vivacious officer's wife and the plain, hard-working seamstress. But for Saumoneau at least, these differences were symbolic of their differences of class and her fight with Rauze a struggle against bourgeois domination of the group. When Rauze submitted her proposal to the group as a whole, the rank and file agreed with Saumoneau. After two long meetings on the question, the group voted in July to support Saumoneau's stance. The group authorised the executive to plan its own newspaper, to appear in September 1914.[36]

Saumoneau's control over the group is surprising in the light of the Couriau affair, which had been a clear defeat for the partisans of proletarian solidarity. One must conclude that the mass of working women who attended the meetings but did not speak identified with Saumoneau and supported her with their votes.[37] One must also suppose that these women provided new energies which Saumoneau was able to tap, for no sooner did she take office than the group began an unprecedented round of activity. Within a week of her election, the executive was organised into three sub-committees (education, propaganda, and legislative studies), each of which showed energy and vitality. In the six months before the outbreak of the First World War, scarcely a week went by without one or more meetings of some part of the GDFS.[38]

Unlike Renaud the year before, Saumoneau was able to organise a rally to celebrate international women's day for the first time in Paris, on 9 March, in co-ordination with the German socialist women. The group made extensive preparations, putting up posters and inserting large announcements in *L'Humanité*. On the day of the rally, *L'Humanité* also ran a front-page story on the German activities, urging the French to follow their example that evening. The rally was a great success. With Saumoneau presiding, over 2000 men and women heard speeches by Jouenne, Martin, and Rauze, by the socialist deputies Compère-Morel and Bracke, and by Jean Longuet for *L'Humanité*. Inessa Armand, one of Lenin's lieutenants, spoke for Russian socialist women. Clara Zetkin sent a telegram: 'a socialist women's day at Paris, that's good news indeed'.[39]

During the legislative elections of May 1914, the GDFS even sent delegates to the electoral meetings of socialist candidates to speak for women's suffrage. Since it carefully kept its campaign aloof from that of the feminists,[40] even Saumoneau participated. The group put up posters all over Paris calling on women to join them in bringing both economic and political demands to the attention of the electors. After the elections, the group organised systematic distribution of handbills for recruitment. During May and June it organised neighbourhood 'chats'. For May Day, it called on women to strike and sent a delegation to the syndical meeting. The GDFS was finally functioning and obtaining recognition as an organ of the party (though officially it had no such status). Saumoneau could send a telegram of solidarity in the group's name to a demonstration of German socialist women at Berlin, just as Zetkin had done for the women's day at Paris. This was Saumoneau's achievement.[41]

There was, however, a negative side to the balance sheet. The policies which Saumoneau initiated prevented the group from coming to grips with the basic problem of the mass of non-politicised women, whom it would be hard enough to bring to a women's group, let alone to the regular sections. To be sure, no one since Madeleine Pelletier had clearly formulated the problem. Rauze, for example, complained of the lack of women in the party at the same time as she argued for limiting the GDFS to recruitment from within the party, without perceiving the contradiction: if the problem was the lack of women *in* the party, how could it be resolved by recruiting from within the party where there were so few women? To bring more women into the party, one would have to go outside it. But women like Rauze, Renaud, and Toussaint-Kassky were at least sympathetic to the difficulties women experienced in approaching the party and Rauze gained much understanding after her contact with the women of Chartres. Saumoneau, however, had no patience with timid women. Having overcome many difficulties herself, she expected other proletarian women to do the same. For her the problem was to keep out the feminists, to maintain the group's class basis.

By limiting the group to recruitment from within the party and by prohibiting it from acting in parallel with the sections, Saumoneau effectively kept out the feminists, but she also kept out the masses of working women. To be sure, she had the support of the working women of the group, who may have resented the domination of the group by bourgeois women like Rauze. These working women, however, were exceptional, like Saumoneau herself. They did not see how these provisions made it difficult for ordinary women to join the party. No matter how many talks were given and posters put up, the woman who was inspired thereby to join the group had first to join her local section. And the sections remained a male domain. No matter how many women were in the group, they found themselves uncomfortably alone in all the important activities of party life.

These difficulties were illustrated in the recruitment campaign of November 1913. The campaign culminated in a big rally. The GDFS, following its earlier decisions, decided not to go in a body, but to advise members to go with their sections or individually. To go in a body, as did the youth groups, would be to 'compete' with the sections. The result was, as even one of Saumoneau's supporters was forced to admit in an article in *L'Equité*, that 'the handful of women disseminated throughout the assembly waited with anxiety for a word from the lips of the orators indicating that this propaganda included women'. The 'word' came only after someone protested. Then the secretary of the Seine federation replied that 'of course' women would not be forgotten. In fact, however, the GDFS was forgotten because it could neither recruit nor constitute itself as a force within the federation, by virtue of its own decisions. The same fifty women who were 'disseminated throughout the assembly', had they been together, would have forcefully reminded the orators of their presence. And they would have drawn strength from being together. For if even an established militant already in the party and writing for *L'Equité* felt uncomfortable, how would a newcomer have felt?[42]

During 1913, two provincial groups provided instructive comparison with the Parisian efforts. In 1911 at Lille a group had been established called the Ligue des Droits de la Femme. It was a front of the kind the communists would later be so successful in building. It was linked to the socialist party in that the members of the executive were all party members, but there was no formal requirement of party membership and indeed the group aimed to draw in women who were not yet connected with the party. The League had built its way slowly to forty active members by the summer of 1913. But in the spring of that year, two prominent socialist women of Lille, Jeanne D. Forster and Marguerite Dupuis-Vérecque, decided to form a new group 'composed exclusively of party members', modelled on the GDFS. The new group was indeed formed in March, but it petered out by July. It seems to have succeeded only in destroying the League.[43]

In contrast to Lille, Lyons boasted a socialist women's group affiliated not only with the party but also with Venise Pellat-Finet's Fédération Féministe du Sud-Est. They credited Madeleine Pelletier with having 'instigated' their group. Founded in July 1912, they had over fifty active members a year later. The secretary attributed their success to their policy of not requiring party membership. Instead, they tried to prepare new members and present them to the sections when they had become accustomed to party life.[44]

The GDFS, however, resolutely barred any such concessions to the difficulties women faced in approaching this quintessentially male domain. The policy of integration was to be applied inflexibly. Women were to enter the party as citizens, not as sisters, on the same basis as men. But women were not citizens. To be sure, they shared the same class oppression as men. Men, however, could combat their oppression through political channels while women could not. Political activity developed bonds which made party life more enjoyable for men: citizenship led to comradeship. It was difficult for women to share this comradeship. The only comparable bond was their common experience as women. Only by an appeal to that experience could the GDFS have recruited women in numbers and made party life attractive to them, but the group refused to make such an appeal because it smacked of feminism.

The origins of the group's hostility to feminism lie in the very real class differences felt so keenly by Saumoneau and apparently shared by the vast majority of the rank and file of the GDFS. Saumoneau's exceptional class consciousness and her painful alienation from the feminists in the early days of her political engagement enabled her to articulate the general class hostility of working women toward the feminists. By so doing, she gained control of the GDFS. But this same hostility then prevented socialist women from capitalising on their own bonds as sisters, even within the parameters of their class and political situation. The sentiment of class overwhelmed that of sisterhood once again.

Through the GDFS, Saumoneau shaped the SFIO's approach to women for the duration of the party's existence. The First World War froze the GDFS in Saumoneau's mould. The prestige she acquired in the anti-war struggle enabled her to keep it that way.

141

Part III Development and decline of the socialist women's movement 1914 – 79

7. The First World War and socialist women 1914 – 20

On 28 June 1914, Serbian nationalists assassinated the Archduke Francis Ferdinand. But it was not until 23 July, when the Austro-Hungarian government published its ultimatum to Serbia, that there seemed to be danger of a major war. In response to the news of this ultimatum, Jaurès turned an election speech near Lyons into what was to be his last plea for peace on French soil: 'We have at this moment against us, against peace, against human life, terrible odds, in the face of which the proletarians of Europe must make every effort at solidarity of which they are capable.'[1]

Saumoneau was one of the first to make that effort. She had already called a meeting of the executive for 22 July, to discuss the measures to be taken in the event of a limited war between Austria and Serbia. The executive authorised an 'extraordinary meeting' of the group for the 24th. Faced with the news of the Austrian ultimatum, the GDFS planned a special meeting for 3 August, but events moved too fast for it. On 28 July, Austria declared war on Serbia. Upon learning of this, Saumoneau brought the executive together for an emergency meeting. That same day, 29 July, the leaders of international socialism met at Brussels in a desperate effort to organise a campaign against the war. Like them, the women could only draw up fiery proclamations, though in Saumoneau's inimitable style:

To Women!

Comrades,

War, horrible war is at our gates and tomorrow, perhaps, your sons, your brothers and your husbands will be struggling with their comrades from beyond the frontiers.

Will you allow this monstrous massacre to take place? No. All of you, you will rise up in a mass to form a living barrier against menacing and murderous barbarism.[2]

This text was meant to be handed out as a tract. But the onslaught of the climate of war quickly rendered such distributions impossible. On the evening of the 31st, Jaurès was assassinated by a nationalist, who had been stirred up by the right-wing papers. French socialism lost its brightest and most beloved star. Thereafter, Paris was virtually on a war footing. One of

Saumoneau's friends, Variot, was arrested for distributing the group's tract.
There was no question of trying to hold the anti-war meeting scheduled for
3 August.[3]

On that day Germany declared war on France. The German socialists,
responding to the threat of a Russian invasion, voted for war credits. The last
hesitations of the French socialists disappeared. They too would vote war
credits, on the very day of Jaurès's funeral (the 4th) and in his name. International socialism had ceased to exist. The leaders of each national party
joined with their governments to support the war upon the nations whose
peoples the International had claimed to join together. Guesde himself
became a Minister without portfolio and the old Communard Edouard
Vaillant supported this war against Germany as vigorously as he had supported that of 1870.

The GDFS and the war

For three months following the outbreak of the war, the GDFS was completely quiescent. Both *L'Equité* and *La Femme socialiste* ceased to appear,
although Saumoneau prepared manuscript editions of her paper which she
circulated among friends. She refused from the start to accept the war,
believing that socialists had a duty to remain faithful to the International.
She held several meetings of the executive at her flat, but it could not muster
the courage to call a meeting of the group until 8 November.

At this meeting, Saumoneau presented a resolution 'of international
solidarity and desire for peace'. This was too much for the group, which
referred it back to the executive. When it met on 22 November to consider
this resolution, Saumoneau presented it with an even more daring one which
declared that the war had been 'unleashed by the frenetic covetousness of
the possessing classes' and extended the group's 'fraternal greetings' 'over the
fields of carnage' 'to the socialist and working women of the belligerent
countries'.[4]

Saumoneau's resolution was outdone by another, presented by a leading
member of the Bolshevik section in Paris, a Russian student named Ludmila
Stigliss. The police thought that Stigliss had been one of the 'five or six
Russians of both sexes, professing socialist revolutionary ideas', to whom
Saumoneau used to give 'French lessons, generally followed by political discussions'.[5] Stigliss wished to condemn the SFIO leaders for their acceptance
of the war. In this she was acting according to Lenin's thinking: there could
be no return to the Second International; it was dead and its leaders had to
be denounced in order to clear the way for a new international which could
use the war to make a revolution. Saumoneau opposed Stigliss's resolution
as 'one-upmanship'. The GDFS, she argued, had no right to make judgements

144

on party policies. This legalistic attitude shaped Saumoneau's subsequent evolution.[6]

A third resolution was presented by Suzanne Gibault, Alice Jouenne, and one Gabriel [*sic*] Rosenthal, a trio whom Saumoneau later blamed for the departure from pre-war policies (she called them 'intellectuals'). Their resolution carefully avoided peace, brotherly greetings, and any other terms which might seem unpatriotic. It was so innocuous that Gibault could say that 'nearly all women' would find it acceptable. The group decided after a stormy debate not to adopt any resolution at all. The mountain had not even given birth to a mouse.[7]

In January 1915, the GDFS held its annual election of officers. While eight of the ten members of the new executive were supporters of the war, Stigliss and Variot managed to get themselves elected. In addition, Louise Couteaudier, soon to be Saumoneau's second in the anti-war movement, became treasurer. Saumoneau, however, did not stand for re-election as secretary, 'desiring', as she put it, 'to have her freedom of action for the anti-war and anti-chauvinist propaganda that the group was refusing to undertake'.[8]

On 3 January 1915, she wrote to Lenin's collaborator, Inessa Armand, that 'a Russian comrade' (presumably either Stigliss or another of her former students, a more important Bolshevik named Debora Gopner)[9] had given her a copy of Clara Zetkin's appeal 'To the socialist women of all countries'. Zetkin was a leading member of the anti-war minority of the German SPD. She now used her position as secretary of the international socialist women's movement to call on her former followers to express their desire for peace. Zetkin argued that women were in an especially good position to struggle for peace: having no political rights, they bore no responsibility for the war. 'If men kill, women must fight for peace; if men keep silent, our socialist duty is to raise our voices.' It was to spread this message that Saumoneau had sought her 'freedom of action'. With the support of anti-war members of the GDFS, she managed to circumvent the censors and distribute the appeal to most of the group's rank and file. The initial reactions were hostile, to say the least.[10]

The new secretary of the GDFS was Alice Jouenne. She was admirably suited to the role she was to play: keeping the GDFS a docile instrument of the pro-war majority of the party. Her main interest was the co-operative movement. She was not much of a socialist and still less of a feminist. In a typical article she argued that 'the Frenchwoman is "a woman of the home" *par excellence*, for while being a good housewife, she knows how to preserve her attributes as a charming woman'. It was therefore obvious that she should shop in co-operatives, where her 'qualities of order, of foresight and of control' would be reinforced. Jouenne's housewifely soul was naturally

145

patriotic. As soon as she received a copy of the appeal, she sent a letter to all members of the group asking them 'to be more than ever united in our great socialist ideal . . . in order to provide a sort of moral and comforting rear guard for our brothers who are struggling against militarism'. She convoked them to a meeting on 7 February, at which she would speak on 'German Militarism'.[11]

Marianne Rauze was even more hostile. Her newspaper, *L'Equité*, had ceased publication at the outbreak of the war. It suddenly reappeared. In the lead article, Rauze wrote in sentimental terms of how 'the voices of these [socialist] women have met above the storm'. But in another article immediately following this one, under the signature of 'Mater' (though she had no children), she went on, 'leaving the general question of sentiment, we enter into the practical question'. And in practical reality, not only were all sisterly and internationalist sentiments cast aside in defence of 'the people of the Rights of Man' who were fighting against 'Prussian feudalism', but also all means were good to oppose the anti-war forces: she argued that 'shady schemers' were peddling 'a doubtful falsification' of a bogus appeal — an insult which infuriated Saumoneau and which Rauze knew was unfair and untrue.

Rauze's attack marked the beginning of a general counter-offensive. At the 7 February meeting, the GDFS even went so far as to censure Saumoneau's conduct. She replied with articles in *La Femme socialiste* and with letters which she trudged round Paris delivering to every member of the group. But she was almost completely alone, except for her Russian friends and Couteaudier. Worse, Rauze had been able to keep her in the dark about the growing international movement. In this same issue, *L'Equité* published correspondence between the Dutch socialist women and Marianne Rauze. The Dutch had written to *L'Equité* on 24 November to ask support for the appeal which Zetkin was then planning to issue. Instead of referring the letter to the GDFS (of which Saumoneau was then the secretary), Rauze replied herself, ruling out any contact with enemy socialists until the end of the war and the 'liberation of republican territory and of neutral Belgium'.[12]

The international conference of socialist women

Despite Rauze's efforts, Saumoneau had eventually been informed of Zetkin's plans and she knew that Zetkin intended to hold an international conference. Having resigned the leadership of the GDFS, she would be free to attend despite the group's opposition. But she would need a group to represent. To this end she constituted the Comité d'Action Féminine Socialiste pour la Paix contre le Chauvinisme (CAFSPC). At the beginning it consisted (according to the police) of three women: Saumoneau, Stigliss, and

Gopner. The other anti-war members of the GDFS preferred to remain in the background.[13] The new group's first action was to congratulate Clara Zetkin — through the Swiss socialist women, who were celebrating international women's day on 7 March 1915 just as if there were no war — on her 'action which will lead to an international conference'.[14]

This conference was the subject of a stormy meeting of the GDFS also held on 7 March. Jouenne read out a letter from Heleen Ankersmit, secretary of the Dutch socialist women, who asked the GDFS to name a delegate to an international meeting of socialist women. The executive refused, on the grounds that the agenda had not been set. This reply brought three letters in return, including one from Clara Zetkin herself, convoking Jouenne to a meeting to be held in Switzerland and offering to pay her expenses. On 20 March, Jouenne held a special meeting of the GDFS to consider this offer. The meeting was designated as 'private'. There were nineteen women and one man (the police informer?) in attendance. Jouenne once more complained that there was no indication of the topic to be discussed and added that the 'insistence of these foreigners seem[ed] highly suspect'. (So much for socialist internationalism.) She herself, in any case, would not go.

Suzanne Gibault proposed that the GDFS consult with the CAP and follow its advice. This would have been tantamount to refusal, for everyone knew that the CAP would not approve, committed as it was to the war effort. Gibault's proposal was voted down unanimously after it was pointed out that it would be an abdication of the group's independence. The group then voted directly against participation by eight votes to three, with eight abstentions. The three were Stigliss, another Russian (presumably Gopner), and a lone Frenchwoman named Charpentier. Jouenne thereupon drew up a reply which declared that 'no member representing the French socialist women' would attend. She explained that Ankersmit had told her Saumoneau would attend and she wished to make it clear that Saumoneau would not represent the GDFS.[15]

And so she would not. But she would go. Indeed, she was already on her way to Berne. For although the police inspector who read the report sent out a notice to prevent her getting a passport, she arrived in Berne to be the delegate of the CAFSPC to the international conference of socialist women before it began on 25 March 1915.

The Berne conference has been neglected by historians, not so much because women were involved as because it did not follow the Bolshevik line: whereas the Bolsheviks could claim that the later (male) conference at Zimmerwald was the starting point for the Third International, Berne did not appear as the direct source of any movement. But there is no excuse for neglecting the heroism involved. While the majority of the twenty-eight delegates were from neutral countries, there were several from Germany and England, a number of Russians (including four Bolsheviks), and one from

France — Saumoneau.[16] These women came to fraternise with representatives of nations which were not only at war with their own countries but indeed were threatening their very existence.

Saumoneau came to the conference with a resolution declaring 'war upon war', the words of the international socialist congress of Basel held in 1912. But Saumoneau meant by these words a struggle for peace and for 'the resurrection of the International', while her Bolshevik allies back in Paris meant a struggle to turn the war into a civil war and to create a new international. They sent her some 'corrections' aimed at bringing her resolution more in line with Bolshevik thinking. The new clauses condemned the socialist parties for voting war credits and for collaborating in bourgeois governments. Saumoneau could not accept the condemnation of her party and the clear implication of schism. She therefore withdrew her resolution.[17]

The resolution ultimately adopted was similar to Saumoneau's original text. If it did not call for the 'resurrection of the International', it did call for its 'reconstitution'.[18] Only the Bolsheviks opposed it. Subsequently the central committee of their party backed them up, expressing disappointment that the conference had failed 'to lay the cornerstone of the future International'.[19]

Lenin had logic on his side, and history too, as it turned out, but Saumoneau had a point when she talked of the impossibility of schism and illegal action in France. The war had reduced the GDFS to a handful, of which only one Frenchwoman had voted for sending a delegate to the conference. There was not one man in the SFIO who was prepared to do as Saumoneau was doing, to go and meet his fellow socialists of the belligerent nations, let alone to bring back, as she would, a resolution calling for immediate peace. To expect her in addition to return with a condemnation of the party within which she found what little support she had was unreasonable.

What she did bring back was enough to raise the hackles of most members of the SFIO: a manifesto addressed 'To the women of the proletariat', with the provocative title, 'Where are your husbands? Where are your sons?', which stated that 'the workers have nothing to gain from this war, they have everything to lose, everything, everything that is dear to them'. It went on to call on women to act, to demand peace. This was strong stuff indeed in France in the spring of 1915, when the country appeared to have narrowly averted a German victory and was felt to be engaged in a life-or-death struggle for survival.[20]

Still, Saumoneau did not intend to go so far as to say this in public. She hoped to confine her work to the party, in an effort to alter its position. But she soon realised that there was little room for action within the party. While *L'Humanité* published a relatively unbiased account of the Berne conference, it thereafter refused to mention anything regarding her activities. When the fifth section of the party (to which Saumoneau and most of the Russian students belonged) sent a protest to the Seine federation 'against the overly chauvinist [i.e. nationalist] attitude of certain elected leaders of the party', the federal executive calumniated Saumoneau violently in its private session and in its official response warned the Russians 'not to interfere in questions relating to the internal affairs of the country' — another blow struck for socialist internationalism.[21]

Following this rebuff, Saumoneau scheduled a 'private' meeting for 25 April to organise the propaganda campaign envisaged at Berne. The police succeeded in preventing it. In a typewritten notice, she finally drew the conclusion that the campaign could not be limited to the party. She also realised that the CAFSPC alone could not make an impact with its meagre resources. She asked for the help of 'all internationalists'.[22]

Results were soon forthcoming. On 10 May, copies of the manifesto were found on the steps of the Saint Ouen church, in the seventeenth arrondissement. This was undoubtedly the work of someone other than Saumoneau, for this was far from her home and church steps were not her style. By June, however, Saumoneau herself redoubled her efforts. The federation of the Haute-Vienne adopted a timid anti-war resolution in May. This encouraged Saumoneau to write a new tract, reminding women that 'the women of Berlin have already demonstrated twice before the Reich[s]tag' and calling in scarcely veiled terms for similar demonstrations in Paris. The police commissioner thought it 'a veritable call to revolution'. The CAFSPC managed to print it and mailed it to socialists, hidden in 1913 issues of *La Femme socialiste*. Distribution of the manifesto also continued.[23]

Throughout the summer of 1915, the discovery of Saumoneau's tracts in different parts of Paris annoyed the police every week or two. The Director of the Sûreté asked, 'could one not take measures against the Saumoneau woman?' But a conscientious official replied that the laws against anarchism could not be applied to Saumoneau, who was a 'pacifist'. He suggested instead expelling Gopner and Stigliss, adding that this would have the further advantage of not troubling the socialist party in the slightest. The government did not follow up his suggestion.[24]

Leaving Saumoneau alone was the government's safest course. Virtually the only direct result of her efforts was to rouse Jouenne to action. She issued a violent statement disclaiming any connection between Saumoneau and the group and she offered Saumoneau a chance to debate the issues within the group. Even this was a surprise: three of Saumoneau's supporters speculated — presumably in conversation with the police spy — that Jouenne was 'following the tactic dictated to her by M. Renaudel', the socialist party deputy who led the pro-war faction of the party. The debate was held on 22 July. After a violent discussion, according to Saumoneau's account, the executive proposed to vote approval of the pro-war resolution passed the

149

week before by the party's national council. Saumoneau demanded a roll-call vote. Jouenne, having forgotten the roll, was forced to put the vote off to the next meeting. She was so angry that she announced her resignation as secretary. But a week later she withdrew her resignation, after consultations with the 'powers' of the party, as Saumoneau noted with regret. The vote was never held. The GDFS did not meet again until November. Perhaps this seemed safer to Jouenne than providing a forum for Saumoneau.[25]

The momentum of the Berne conference had been dissipated without arousing any echo in the GDFS, let alone in the party as a whole. The tracts of the CAFSPC written in August and September 1915 betrayed hopelessness, even bitterness.[26] The head of the police intelligence (Renseignements généraux) summed up the difficulties of the anti-war forces with considerable acuity: 'There does exist a pacifist movement . . . But this movement has not been able to get beyond the bounds of the economic and political organisations [i.e. the CGT and the SFIO] whose membership is moreover greatly reduced, and remains unknown to the masses of the labouring population.'[27]

By the light of Zimmerwald[28]

Only when the government unwisely decided to prosecute Saumoneau was she able to move beyond the narrow limits within which she had so far been confined. The scruples and political worries of the civilian police did not trouble the military authorities, who governed Paris by virtue of the state of siege. At the end of August, they ordered her to be convoked before her local commissariat. She was questioned about the distribution of Zetkin's appeal, for which she took full responsibility. Then she was released. Expecting to be arrested, she asked Jean Longuet to defend her. He agreed 'wholeheartedly'. He himself, however, did not expect her to be arrested. No stranger to the government's thinking (he was now a deputy), he thought the government would avoid giving her publicity and he was right. She might have been left alone indefinitely had not the police discovered, early in the morning on 27 September, no fewer than 109 copies of the Berne manifesto on the tables of cafés and in door handles throughout the tenth arrondissement. Saumoneau herself was probably not involved, but the authorities naturally assumed she was responsible. She was arrested on 2 October 1915 and imprisoned at Saint-Lazare (usually reserved for prostitutes).[29]

Censorship kept Saumoneau's arrest from being mentioned in the newspapers. The first to learn of it were the socialist deputies. They discussed it at their weekly meeting on 7 October. Longuet defended Saumoneau; Renaudel stated that he had already asked the Prime Minister to release her because her arrest was an 'error', 'a blunder which could become dangerous, for it was to be feared that she appear a martyr'. When Saumoneau's rank-

and-file comrades learned of her arrest, they offered no more support than the deputies. On 12 October, Louise's sister Berthe raised the matter at a meeting of her section, the twelfth. The secretary promised vaguely to write a letter of 'moral support' to Saumoneau. There was no talk of a protest. Saumoneau's section, the fifth, decided on 20 October simply to request that she be classed as a political prisoner. There were only three protests, two from Paris sections (the third and Montrouge) and one from the Haute-Vienne federation.[30] The party's Seine federal council, meeting on 8 November, received these protests with something less than sympathy. 'They should have put her in a padded cell', remarked one member. The secretary was instructed to reply 'that the question was being looked into'. There matters might have remained indefinitely had not the Zimmerwald conference given new impetus to the anti-war movement.[31]

The international socialist conference of Zimmerwald, a village near Berne, was held from 5 to the 8 of September 1915. Six months after the socialist women, socialist men finally took up the challenge thrown down by the women and, like them, met together and fraternised with fellow socialists who were their national enemies.[32] In France, however, there was no socialist man yet willing to do what Saumoneau had done: both members of the French delegation were prominent syndicalists and came to Zimmerwald on that basis, though one, Albert Bourderon, was a member of the party as well as secretary of the coopers' federation. The other delegate was Alphonse Merrheim, secretary of the metalworkers' federation. The delegates at Zimmerwald agreed on a condemnation of the war as imperialist, just as the Berne conference had done, but their statement implied a condemnation of the parties which had supported the war and thus left open the possibility of a new international. Although it fell short of their desires, the Bolsheviks could accept it. Zimmerwald came to be seen as the symbolic beginning, the 'embryo' of the Third International.[33]

The first Paris meeting at which Zimmerwald was discussed was held on 22 October, more than six weeks after the conference and three weeks after Saumoneau's arrest. Stéphanie Bouvard, who had taken Saumoneau's place in the CAFSPC, made use of the occasion to distribute the group's latest tract. At the end of the meeting, she asked the chairman if she might speak on behalf of Saumoneau (who was still in prison), but the meeting was already adjourning.[34]

At the next meeting, on 7 November, Bouvard was more determined. After the Zimmerwald delegates spoke for peace, Jean Longuet embarked on one of his tepid centrist lectures. From the floor came a voice: 'As always, neither for nor against.' At this point, reported the police informer, 'a short but ardent speech was pronounced by a working-class woman'. It was Bouvard. She told the audience that women were way ahead of men in the struggle for peace (which was true) and that the CAFSPC had distributed

30,000 copies of the Berne manifesto (which was probably the informer's exaggeration). She went on:

No newspaper says a word about this arrest and they hide the fact that Louise Saumoneau is imprisoned like a common criminal. The socialists don't want to do anything — a conspiracy of silence reigns. With tears in her eyes, the speaker implores the assembly to remember the terrible dance of death. (This speech is drowned out in long and forceful applause.)

Two days later, the twelfth section of the party held its regular meeting, with a hundred persons in attendance (including Berthe Saumoneau). This time, instead of vague talk of letters of 'moral support', they voted unanimously a strong protest against Saumoneau's imprisonment.[35]

The rapid growth of the Zimmerwald movement within the party apparently led the government to release Saumoneau 'provisionally' in order to prevent the movement from having a martyr.[36] Saumoneau went free on 20 November. Only then did Berthe tell her of the death of their nephew on the front. Berthe had known for six weeks, but had taken off her mourning when she went to see Louise in prison. The two sisters had cherished him because he was the only one of their nieces and nephews who shared their political concerns. Louise wrote his epitaph in her own fashion — a typewritten tract:

When 16 months ago, the war broke out, we the mothers, the wives, the sisters of those who left . . . despite our grief, we kept the hope that the being who was so dear to us would return able-bodied.

Not one of us could admit that the young, robust man she took to the station would not come back again.

Since then, alas! how many women in mourning . . .[37]

At the Seine federation congress on 9 December, Saumoneau was honoured by being named to the chair. But she still faced an uphill struggle. She submitted a resolution protesting against the recent police search at the headquarters of the French section of Jane Addams's group, the Comité International des Femmes pour une Paix Permanente ('International Women's Committee for Permanent Peace', CIFPP).[38] Her resolution gained general import from a phrase condemning all such actions, 'which bring our regime closer and closer to the tsarist regime'. Renaudel lost his temper at this phrase and obtained its deletion.

Tensions were high throughout the congress. When Saumoneau interrupted a pro-war speaker, he replied, 'Citizen Saumoneau, go howl outside and bugger off.' Despite its frayed nerves, however, the pro-war majority was still firmly in control. The resolution for war to the bitter end (which Suzanne Gibault supported) received 6121 votes as against 545 for Bourderon and Saumoneau's Zimmerwaldian statement. But Longuet's minority resolution received 3836 votes. It was not, to be sure, what one would call pacifist in intent: it demanded continuation of the war until

Belgium was liberated, Alsace and Lorraine returned to French sovereignty, and the Kaiser dethroned. It also called, however, for contact between the socialists of the warring nations 'independent of the continuation of the war'. Its relative success reflected growing uneasiness about the unqualified support for the war and the abandonment of socialist internationalism which had hitherto been uncontested party policy. This uneasiness was manifested in a similar balance of forces at the national congress a fortnight later.[39]

Thus were established the divisions in the party which would last until the end of the war and, in modified form, until the schism of 1920. On the 'right' was the 'majority', led by Renaudel, which supported all-out war. In the 'centre' was the 'minority', led by Longuet, which supported the war, but also sought an international meeting of the socialist parties irrespective of the continuation of the war. On the 'left' were the Zimmerwaldians. They were agreed in refusing to support the continuation of the war in the name of socialist internationalism, but they were themselves divided between those who, like Saumoneau, wished to 'resurrect' or 'reconstitute' the old international and those who, like the Russians, meant to build a new international.

The growing uneasiness about the party's war policy meant that the Zimmerwaldians could expect to find an audience for their message, even if few were as yet prepared to risk opposing the war and seeming unpatriotic. The Zimmerwaldians had already established an organisation to reach this audience. On 21 November (the day after Saumoneau's release), they founded the Comité d'Action Internationale. An executive committee of twelve was elected. 'A member of the CAFSPC [presumably Bouvard] asked and obtained that her group would have two delegates on the [executive] committee.' They were Bouvard and Louise Couteaudier.[40]

Both were old friends of Saumoneau. Bouvard had met Saumoneau at the feminist congress in 1900. Since then she had given up the trade of artificial-flower maker to become manager of a co-operative. Couteaudier had come into contact with Renaud and Saumoneau in 1899, when she led the wives of strikers at Montceau-les-Mines. During a later strike, she wrote articles for *La Femme socialiste*. After her husband left her with seven children in 1904, she came to Paris and earned a living doing housework. A member of the SFIO since its formation, she was elected to the executive of the GDFS at its first meeting. Upon the outbreak of the war, in which all three of her sons were drafted, she devoted herself to the anti-war cause, faithfully distributing not only Saumoneau's many tracts, but also those of Sébastien Faure, anarchist opponent of the war.[41]

Both Couteaudier and Bouvard were women after Saumoneau's own heart: self-consciously working class and profoundly opposed to the war. Saumoneau herself, exhausted by her efforts, rested for several months, but she could be assured that her friends would represent her views within the nascent Zimmerwaldian movement.

The twilight of women's groups

With the constitution of the Comité d'Action Internationale and the beginning of organised opposition to the party's pro-war line, the struggle against
the war moved beyond the confines of the women's groups to the party as a
whole. Anti-war women had taken advantage of their peculiar status in
society to initiate the struggle. Now that it had begun, they were no longer
in a special position and their organisations lost much of their *raison d'être*.
Some women's groups stayed afloat, but they were only fronts for general
anti-war action and even they were subsumed into regular party activity by
the end of 1917. While the beginning of the war had given women a chance
to play a more important role than usual, its continuation destroyed their
groups. They abandoned them to take sides in the only question that
mattered by 1916: the continuation of the war.

The war divided and finally destroyed the GDFS. During 1916 it continued
to function fitfully before falling apart in 1917, but it was scarcely a shadow
of its former self. In January 1916, the group held its annual elections.
Jouenne was again elected secretary and Gibault was named assistant secretary. But only seventeen votes were cast in all. The group had lost its most
active elements: Saumoneau and her followers on the one hand, Rauze and
her allies on the other.[42]

Saumoneau, Bouvard, and Couteaudier, as well as the Russian women who
supported them (such as Gopner and Stigliss), were devoting all their attention to the Comité d'Action Internationale ('Committee of International
Action'). They had decided not to nominate a candidate for the executive of
the GDFS and to abandon it entirely to the pro-war majority, for they
rightly assumed that without them it would not function. Marianne Rauze,
on the other hand, was preoccupied with her husband. Wounded in the
autumn of 1915, the good captain died a year later. During his agony, Rauze
ceased all political activity. She turned *L'Equité* over to Marguerite Martin,
who managed to bring out six issues between November 1915 and the
following June. While under Rauze the resurrected paper had been a mainstay
of the hard-headed pro-war movement, under Martin it became laden with
pro-war sentimentality. She secured the collaboration of the feminist Nelly
Roussel and together they filled the paper with articles about the courage of
women and the need to respect the weak. This sort of approach did not sell
newspapers in the France of 1916, in the midst of the battle of Verdun. With
the June 1916 issue, *L'Equité* ceased publication.[43]

The GDFS was almost a corpse, but it continued to twitch for a while.
During 1916, reduced to a handful, it concerned itself with such issues as the
creation of state orphanages, the clerical influence, and the right of un-
married women to obtain a pension upon the death in action of the fathers

of their children. In September 1916, Saumoneau noted bitterly that the topic for discussion was Mme Roland, the heroine of the great Revolution. After the elections of January 1917 (at which Jouenne was again re-elected secretary), the GDFS ceased to meet.[44]

Saumoneau and her friends still persisted in their efforts to animate a socialist women's movement against the war, although these efforts remained secondary to their activities within the Comité d'Action Internationale. The CAFSPC decided to celebrate the now traditional international women's day in March 1916. After sending the usual letters of solidarity (to the German, Dutch, and English anti-war socialist women), the group tried to hold a 'private' meeting, but on the appointed day the entry to the hall was barred by police. Some of the women managed to slip away and meet in a private home, where they drew up a protest which Saumoneau typed and distributed as usual. In May, a police agent reported that she was circulating copies of this tract at a meeting of the twelfth section of the party and that a number of women took copies to hand out. At the top of the report, the commissioner scrawled 'Again!', wielding his thick blue pencil with a heavy hand.[45]

Although Saumoneau's tracts could exasperate the authorities, they reached only a very limited audience. Despite all its efforts, the CAFSPC was unable to enlarge its base. To remedy this situation, Saumoneau revived *La Femme socialiste* in July 1916, with the enthusiastic collaboration of Louise Couteaudier. Couteaudier had begun writing in January: she had sent a short but effective anti-war statement to a Swiss socialist newspaper. But though she folded the text in an innocuous magazine, it was intercepted by the authorities.[46] Now that she had an outlet for her blunt eloquence, she wrote every other month on the difficulties the war caused working women.

In a further effort to enlarge their base, and also to bypass the Russians of the CAFSPC, who were continually pushing them toward Lenin's policy of schism, Couteaudier and Saumoneau founded a new socialist women's group, the GDFS of Sceaux. They set up its headquarters in Montreuil, the working-class suburb where Couteaudier lived. In order to give this group greater status, they sought the approval of the GDFS. During the autumn of 1916, Saumoneau began attending meetings of the GDFS, one presumes to the great astonishment of Jouenne and company, for she had kept away for well over a year. She argued disingenuously that the executive was now dominated by petit-bourgeois elements, in violation of the statutory requirement that it should be composed of a majority of working women. To remedy this, she went on, the group should change its rules to permit the constitution of affiliated sections in the more heavily working-class suburbs. New statutes, embodying this suggestion, were approved in principle at the October meeting. Jouenne delayed formal adoption as long as she could, but after a prolonged war of nerves with Saumoneau, she mailed them out to members and they took effect in January 1917. It was the last act of the GDFS for five years.[47]

The GDFS of Sceaux was now a section of the Parisian GDFS — a technicality, since the latter was now defunct, but a useful one in terms of status. Saumoneau and Couteaudier, however, had not waited for the formalities to be completed. As soon as approval in principle had been voted, they had constituted the 'Groupe des Femmes Socialistes de la 1ère Circonscription de Sceaux (Montreuil, Vincennes, Fontenay, Bagnolet)'. Couteaudier was elected secretary and her nineteen-year-old daughter, Emilienne Carré, assistant secretary.[48] Like Saumoneau, Couteaudier displayed a talent for manoeuvring. The situation of the new group was unclear, if not irregular, since the GDFS statutes which would permit its existence had not yet been adopted. To give the group a semblance of official sanction, and also perhaps to reduce Jouenne's opposition, Couteaudier invited Jouenne to speak at the first regular meeting of the GDFS of Sceaux, on 15 October 1916. Jouenne accepted and spoke in her usual inoffensive fashion on the need for women to join the party.[49]

By 1917 the GDFS of Sceaux was a functioning group which gave Saumoneau and Couteaudier a real base. The new organisation prepared to celebrate international women's day in March 1917, in liaison with the CAFSPC, which was not difficult since they shared the same leaders. The CAFSPC printed a new tract. In a surprisingly good presentation, it decried the fact that, 'for two and a half years the war, *unleashed by the capitalist classes and governments of all countries* [italics orig.], has continued its devastating and murderous work'. Why did the workers not act to stop it? 'Are you waiting to be crushed completely?'[50]

This tract was distributed when the GDFS of Sceaux celebrated international women's day, on 18 March. The local socialist deputy, Paul Poncet, gave a speech — on women's suffrage. Saumoneau spoke on the war and read a letter from Clara Zetkin. The group then voted a vigorous resolution in Saumoneau's inimitable style: it found a special source of satisfaction in 'the vitality of the Socialist Women's International, still standing in the midst of the tempest, . . . [by virtue of] the firmness of its conscience and its fidelity to the immortal principles of international socialism'.[51]

In fact, however, both the international and the French socialist women's anti-war movements were on the verge of being completely absorbed in the general socialist struggles. During the spring of 1917, planning began for an international socialist conference to be held at Stockholm in September. The anti-war socialist women decided to hold a conference of their own in conjunction with the Stockholm conference. This was the last attempt to perpetuate the spirit of Berne, to struggle against the war as socialist women. The conference was never held.

The preparations for it, however, gave rise to considerable jockeying for position among the French socialist women. Not surprisingly, the GDFS of Sceaux voted to send Saumoneau as its delegate to the conference. More unexpected, however, was Marianne Rauze's attempt to appropriate the conference for herself. Behind the struggle of personalities lay the difference between the Zimmerwaldians, with whom Saumoneau was fully engaged, and the minority (Longuet and company) with whom Rauze had thrown in her lot.[52]

Rauze's conversion dated from her husband's death, in September 1916. She appeared in the autumn of that year as an important collaborator of the weekly newspaper, *Le Populaire*, which the minority had begun in May 1916 to support their policy of national defence *and* internationalism. In November she and a male member of the minority were named as a 'propaganda committee' of the minority federations. They published a major brochure on their position which they sent to all federations in preparation for the national congress of December 1916. The minority made impressive gains at this congress, which reflected credit on Rauze. During the following year, she emerged as one of the major leaders of the minority, acting as secretary of its executive and treasurer of the fund appeal for *Le Populaire*.[53]

The minority was concerned that the women's conference at Stockholm might be dominated by Zimmerwaldians like Saumoneau and Zetkin. Rauze was the obvious woman to block them. In August 1917, she began to write about the conference, which was still projected for September. She posed as a critic on the left, complaining that a letter from the Dutch socialist Heleen Ankersmit proposed an agenda that did not include the war. (This was the same Ankersmit to whom *L'Equité* had given such a negative reply in December 1914.) A fortnight later, Rauze offered to take the preparation of the women's conference into her own hands in order, she argued somewhat disingenuously, to centralise matters. She made no reference to Saumoneau or the GDFS of Sceaux. By 15 September, she could report replies from fifteen federations, and more still a week later. Her attempt to wrest the leadership of the anti-war women's movement from Saumoneau failed only because the conference aborted in the face of the combined opposition of the government and the pro-war socialists. The GDFS of Sceaux reaffirmed its demand that Saumoneau be the French delegate, but the conference was already dead.[54]

With it died all efforts to use the socialist women's movement as an instrument in the anti-war struggle. The women's conference had never been more than a poor relation of the men's even in the eyes of those who sought to attend it. Saumoneau valued her mandate from the GDFS of Sceaux less than that she held from the successor to the Comité d'Action Internationale, which entitled her to attend the general conference. Similarly, Rauze regarded her efforts to lead the women's delegation as secondary to her work within the minority. The focus of action had shifted from the women's groups to the party as a whole. The socialist women's movement was subsumed within the larger anti-war forces it had helped to initiate. Although Saumoneau and Couteaudier continued to publish *La Femme socialiste*, they brought out only two issues between June and December 1917.[55] They allowed the GDFS of Sceaux and the CAFSPC to cease functioning after the autumn of 1917. Henceforth women acted on their own in the factions of the party which corresponded to their choices in the face of the war and the Russian Revolution. From 1917 until 1922, there was no socialist women's movement in France, there were only individual socialist women.

Women and the anti-war struggle

Saumoneau had been unable to participate in the founding of the Comité d'Action Internationale on 21 November 1915 because she was just out of prison. Neither of her friends on the executive committee was able to hold her own in its intense male atmosphere. Couteaudier, whose suburban home was too far from the centre for her to keep up with events, disappeared from the committee by the end of 1915. Bouvard, although esteemed by the other committee members, ceased to participate after August 1916. In the meantime, however, anti-war socialist women had once again found in Louise Saumoneau their natural representative.[56]

The Comité d'Action Internationale was torn between socialists and anarchists from its inception. To get rid of the anarchists, the socialists dissolved the Committee in January 1916 and fused with the syndicalist opposition to the war, to form the Comité pour la Reprise des Relations Internationales (CRRI). The CRRI sought the resumption of international relations between socialist parties and trade unions of the warring nations, thus effectively excluding the anarchists, long since barred from the internationals.[57]

Although Saumoneau had been resting when the CRRI was constituted, she was active again by January. From the floor at CRRI meetings, she argued in favour of support for Jean Longuet's minority whenever it took effective action to restore relations between the socialist parties. This policy was violently criticised by Trotsky and by Lenin's lieutenant, Inessa Armand, who felt that simply to restore relations between the parties which had betrayed internationalism would be to pardon and perpetuate such treason. 'Have you seen the resolution [of] Loriot-Rappoport-Saumoneau?', wrote Lenin to Armand on 30 January 1917. 'I'd like to write for the French, in order to tear it to shreds.' Saumoneau in turn attacked the Russians for wanting to provoke the schism which she was determined to avoid. Her policy appeared for a while to bear fruit. A second Zimmerwald was held at Kienthal, in Switzerland, in April 1916. Three deputies of the SFIO minority attended. On their return, they broke party discipline and voted against war credits. This act seemed to justify Saumoneau: with proper encouragement, it appeared, the Longuetist minority could be persuaded to take firmer steps against the war. At the plenary meeting on 3 July, Saumoneau rode a wave of enthusiastic support and was elected to the executive of the CRRI, defeating Trotsky, who also sought a seat.[58]

In fact, however, the Kienthalians' vote was a flash in the pan. The Longuetist minority continued to vote for war credits. Saumoneau and Bourderon's policy of supporting the minority led only to a severe defeat of the CRRI at the SFIO national congress of December 1916. The minority came within a hair's breadth of defeating the pro-war majority, having gathered half the Zimmerwaldian votes without making any concessions to them. The minority had the wind in its sails. And it had drama on its side too. In the midst of a pro-war speech, a woman in mourning stood up. Shaking her black veils, she cried, 'enough dead!' It was Marianne Rauze.[59]

Rauze was stealing Saumoneau's thunder, while the minority as a whole was eclipsing the Zimmerwaldians. Saumoneau's policy minimised the differences between the minority and the Zimmerwaldians and thus enabled the minority to co-opt part of the CRRI. Even Saumoneau's friend Bourderon went over to the minority at the beginning of 1917. Saumoneau would not, however, for she could not accept national defence. As a result of these defections, Saumoneau found herself at the head of what remained of the CRRI. When it was reorganised in February, she and Fernand Loriot emerged as joint secretaries. The executive was further reinforced by the entry of a number of left-wing socialists, including Léonie Kauffmann (no relation to Caroline) and Hélène Brion. Brion withdrew almost immediately after an argument with the men concerning women working in munitions factories, but Kauffmann remained a staunch supporter of Saumoneau on the executive until the latter's resignation.[60]

During 1917, things went from bad to worse for the CRRI. The overthrow of the tsarist regime made it possible to present the war in a better light. Hitherto, even the most hardened pro-war socialists had been embarrassed that the fight 'against Prussian militarism' was being undertaken in alliance with the Tsar. In April, the entry of the United States into the war provided the pro-war socialists with Woodrow Wilson's superb propaganda. Slogans like 'Make the world safe for democracy' helped transform the war from a purely national contest for survival to a republican, almost socialist cause, easing the troubled conscience of more than one socialist. Since most of the anguished souls were in or near the minority (the pro-war majority was not prone to doubts), these developments reinforced the minority at the expense of both the majority and the CRRI.

The party's third wartime national congress, held in October 1917, marked the nadir of the CRRI, which was again outflanked by the minority. Saumoneau and Kauffmann took an intransigent stand while the third CRRI delegate, Charles Rappoport, split from them to vote for a left-wing minority resolution. This split provoked a violent quarrel. Saumoneau was especially bitter that she had been kept off the resolutions committee, the more so since Marianne Rauze had been a deputy member. She blamed this too on Rappoport. But while they were quarrelling, the Bolsheviks were preparing a revolution which would soon upset the balance of forces within French socialism, and indeed in the whole world.[61]

The October revolution vaulted the Bolsheviks to the top of the international socialist movement. Before their success, they had been only a minor party in the International. Now they had made a revolution, while the others were still talking. They had succeeded where no one else had and their success seemed to justify Lenin's policy of opposition to the war. But Lenin's thinking was not fully understood. The separate peace of Brest-Litovsk in March 1918 shocked many socialists. The result was, as Annie Kriegel suggests, that while Clemenceau's hard-line policies and the failure of workers' demands were combining with the Bolshevik success to undermine the pro-war majority of the party, Brest-Litovsk set limits on its leftward evolution which favoured the minority more than the CRRI.[62]

By the middle of 1918 it was clear that the old pro-war majority was losing its hold. At the national congress in October, a new CAP was elected. The pro-war forces and the Longuetist minority each obtained seven seats, the CRRI two. Rauze was named a deputy member for the minority. The CRRI's seats went to its joint secretaries, Fernand Loriot and Louise Saumoneau. Saumoneau's fidelity to her faith had finally been recompensed. She had been made a national leader of the party, in virtue, however, not of her leadership of the women's movement, but rather of her position in the anti-war struggle. It was a personal triumph, consistent with the policy of integration that Saumoneau supported. It did not imply recognition of women as a group.[63]

Women and the Third International

It was only after the war that Lenin was able to enforce his policy of creating a new international — the third — to replace the pre-war international which, as Lenin correctly perceived, had ceased to exist when its member parties had supported their governments in 1914. The founding congress of the Third International (though not officially termed as such) was held in

Moscow, from 2 to 4 March 1919. On 17 April, the CRRI formally joined the Third International. Saumoneau, still secretary of the group, approved this decision, exalting 'the real and effective agreement existing between the Committee [the CRRI] and the *Third International*' (italics orig.). For her 'the path of class struggle' lay with the Third.[64]

On 20 April, an extraordinary national congress of the party began at Paris. The CRRI submitted a motion calling on the party to join the Third International and to work for an immediate seizure of power. As floor leader for the CRRI, Saumoneau spoke vigorously for this motion, condemning the new Longuetist majority as hardly better than the old one. The Longuetists proposed to remain in the Second International and talked of orienting it 'toward the social Revolution, following the examples of Russia, Hungary, and Germany'. Saumoneau pointed out to the congress that if one really wished to make a revolution like the Russians, one should join their international. The CRRI lost, but it increased its vote significantly. Three weeks later, it took the step of changing its name to 'Comité de la IIIe Internationale' ('Committee of the Third International'). The Third International, it argued, 'is the successor to the work begun at Zimmerwald'. On this basis, Kauffmann and Saumoneau were re-elected to the executive, but Saumoneau now became assistant secretary, clearly subordinate to Loriot.[65]

Did she regard this as a slap in the face? Was she already involved in the disagreements with Loriot which would become irreparable the following year? Or was she simply overworked? (As well as publishing *La Femme socialiste*, she was collaborating in two Third International organs.)[66] Whatever the reasons, Saumoneau abruptly resigned as assistant secretary on 22 July 1919, barely two months after assuming the position. The resolutions of the Committee disappeared from the pages of *La Femme socialiste*, but she remained a member of the executive and she continued to struggle for the SFIO to join the Third International. In August she wrote of the need for the party to get out of the 'funeral vault of the Second International' and into 'the International of world social Revolution . . . the International which picked up the flag of socialism and of the proletariat which its predecessor had let fall from its debilitated hands on 4 August 1914'.[67]

At the Strasbourg Congress in February 1920, she spoke for the Third International on the grounds that 'we have entered the revolutionary period'. No one bothered to defend the Second International, and by 4330 votes to 337 the SFIO dissolved its ties to the corpse of the International which, in the prime of life, had midwifed the French party's birth sixteen years earlier. Nevertheless, the Zimmerwaldians (of whom Saumoneau was a representative on the resolutions committee) were unable to obtain a vote for joining the Third International. The congress voted instead the motion of Paul Faure's Committee for the Reconstruction of the International, which stipulated that it would join only after obtaining assurances of the independence of central and western European parties. Saumoneau heaped scorn on this resolution and on the 'Reconstructors' themselves, little suspecting that she would soon join their ranks.[68]

Women obtained greater recognition at the Strasbourg Congress than they had since the days of Madeleine Pelletier. Not only did more individual women gain high office in the party (Léonie Kauffmann was elected a deputy member of the CAP, joining Rauze and Saumoneau, who were re-elected deputy and full members, respectively), but also several speakers raised the problem of the lack of women in the party. There was general agreement that more needed to be done, but few solutions were proposed. No one mentioned the GDFS, although both Rauze and Saumoneau were present and active at the congress: concerned with the fundamental question of the Third International (which both supported), they were not interested in women's groups, particularly as the GDFS would be in Jouenne's hands if resurrected and Jouenne opposed the Third International. It was finally agreed that the CAP would seek to remedy the problem by choosing a woman as one of the party's paid propagandists, a simple, indeed superficial expedient, but a feasible one. The choice fell on Saumoneau, by far the most prominent woman in the party. She took up her duties in April, touring the Lot-et-Garonne to explain to peasants, and particularly to women, that the era of revolution had begun.[69]

At almost exactly the same time, Saumoneau resigned from the executive of the Committee of the Third International, following violent disagreements with Loriot. The Committee, instead of accepting her resignation, expelled her for 'acts of indiscipline', a foretaste of later communist practice. Rappoport even accused her of having sold out the Third International in exchange for her job, but this was an unfair accusation, especially coming from such an avowed enemy. (The violence of their quarrels in the CRRI was almost legendary. He called her 'the viper'.) In fact, Saumoneau continued to support the Third International. As late as the August issue of *La Femme socialiste*, she called it 'this veritable synthesis of socialism and of proletarian action' — words which, whatever they meant, were scarcely those of an opponent of the Third.[70]

Yet in August Saumoneau did begin to move away from the Third International. There were two reasons for this change of heart. In the first place, her support for the Third International had been linked from the start with her assumption that the socialist revolution had begun. But by the summer it became clear that, if the final battle had opened, the socialists had lost. The great railway strike of May 1920, which had been the left's great hope, ended in disaster before the month was out. Discouraged, Saumoneau ceased her collaboration with *La Vie ouvrière*, a newspaper closely linked to the surge of revolutionary optimism.

In the second place, and more important, Saumoneau had always opposed schism in the party and expulsion of militants for their past support of the war. At Strasbourg she had refused to believe in the authenticity of a statement attributed to Zinoviev demanding expulsions. 'The Moscow International', she had stated categorically, 'could not and may not demand the personal expulsion of those responsible for the policy we have opposed'. But in August it became clear that Moscow would demand expulsions. The congress of the Third International (19 July–7 August) posed the famous 'Twenty-One Conditions' for national parties which sought to join the Third International. Foremost among the conditions was the exclusion from leadership positions of reformists and centrists, which meant not only the old pro-war majority but also the new Longuet-Faure majority. Moreover, all those who did not accept the conditions were to be expelled from the party. Since the conditions also included centralisation, iron discipline, periodic purges, etc., the expulsion of most of the present leadership of the party would follow when it joined the Third International. And that meant schism.[71]

Saumoneau had struggled since Berne to avoid a schism. Upon learning of the conditions (she wrote the following January), she 'took the firm determination not to join the Party of proscription and of "periodic purges" '. She turned toward the Reconstructors, whose position at least in principle supported the Third International though in practice it meant the reverse: the Reconstructors wished to pose conditions to the Third International, but it was now becoming clear that it was Lenin, not Paul Faure or Jean Longuet, who would pose the conditions. Western parties had to comply or not join. Saumoneau had no choice. On 13 November she signed the Reconstructors' motion for the coming congress at Tours. The decision cost her dear. In the autumn of 1920, she fell ill and remained bedridden through the winter.[72]

Her illness saved her from having to attend the congress of Tours, in December 1920, and there to witness the destruction of socialist unity, whose consecration she had watched fifteen years before with the hope and enthusiasm of youth. The congress decided (as by now everyone knew it would) to join the Third International. The SFIO's record of failure since 1914 now contrasted too painfully with Lenin's success: failure to prevent the war, failure to end it on 'socialist' terms, failure to maintain its parliamentary strength in the 1919 elections, failure to support the great strikes of 1919 and 1920, failure to make a revolution. The decision came too late, however. Lenin's tactics had made a revolution in Russia during the war, but the problem now was to adapt to the failure of revolution in the west after the war. For this, the Third International had no better answers than its opponents. The mass of new members who streamed into the SFIO during 1920, however, could not know the future. Disillusioned by the harsh realities of life in the aftermath of the war, they sought to create a party which would make a revolution as Lenin had done. In accordance with this

desire and with the Twenty-One Conditions, the congress rebaptised the
SFIO as the Parti Communiste Français (PCF), abandoning the old name
with disdain. The right wing of the party (those who had supported the war)
and the Reconstructors (more or less the wartime minority) walked out
separately, later to join uncomfortably under the discarded name to recon-
struct the SFIO. Now there were two parties which claimed to stand for
socialist principles and all socialists had to choose between them.[73]

In the turbulent events of 1920, the leaders of the different factions of
the old GDFS made their own individual choices. Madeleine Pelletier, like
many of her anarchist friends, had been enchanted by the Russian Revolution after years of utter discouragement in the face of the war. In the
winter of 1919–20, she revived her review, *La Suffragiste*, and used it as an
organ to defend Bolshevism. She managed to get a mandate to the congress
of Tours in order to vote for the Third International. (She and Lucie Colliard,
a young elementary-school teacher who also supported the Third, were the
only women at Tours on their own, although there were three women there
with their husbands.)[74]

Marianne Rauze continued her leftward trajectory into the PCF. She was
a woman who moved with the times. In November 1918, once the war was
safely won, she was calling for propaganda for the social revolution, arguing
that its hour was at hand. At Strasbourg she voted with Saumoneau for the
Third International. But this was the only time their positions coincided. In
August 1920, when Saumoneau was having doubts about the Twenty-One
Conditions, the police reported that Rauze was urging munitions workers to
cease production. In the spring of 1921, she was giving lectures on Engels's
theories about women at the PCF's 'Communist Marxist School' near Paris.[75]

Rauze's departure left Louise Saumoneau a clear field in the reconstructed
SFIO. To be sure, the pro-war women were all there, from Jouenne to
Gibault. Now, however, they were on the defensive. To have supported the
war was, in the 1920s, a charge to live down. The SFIO sought constantly to
defend itself against the PCF's accusation that it was a party of class treason,
having collaborated with the government in support of the war. Saumoneau's
impeccable anti-war credentials made her the SFIO's prize exhibit of revolutionary purity. The prestige she had gained in the anti-war movement, the
consequent eclipse of her old rivals such as Gibault who had supported the
war, and the departure of rivals such as Pelletier and Rauze for the PCF
combined to put Saumoneau at the forefront of the socialist women's movement during the 1920s.

Saumoneau made a painful decision to join with women she heartily
despised in the new, reconstructed SFIO, which represented in her eyes the
resurrection of the party of Jaurès. Her tragedy was that it was only the
ghost of the old SFIO. The revived SFIO had the name and the bulk of the
veterans of the old party, but in 1920 it was the PCF which attracted the

vital forces of the French working classes. The rigidity and fidelity which had enabled Saumoneau to remain true to the spirit of Jaurès's SFIO during the war now bound her to its ghost. Yet this ghost, however pale it appeared in the aftermath of the schism, was to prove a surprisingly vital force. Slowly and painfully it took on solidity and became a new party in its own right. And in this party, one woman would stand out above all the others: one woman who had led the socialist women's movement since 1899, one woman who had opposed the war from the outset, one woman who had been the French delegate at Berne, one woman who had been on the CAP since 1918: Louise Saumoneau.

8. Reconstruction, decline, and rebirth 1921 – 79

After the schism, those who refused the conditions posed by the Third International found themselves confronted with the task of rebuilding their 'old house', as they called the SFIO. Although they regarded themselves as the inheritors of Jaurès's legacy, in organisational terms the party of Jaurès, the SFIO, had transformed itself into the French communist party, the PCF. Party members who had walked out — ostensibly to maintain the socialist tradition — had actually quit the party. They had to build one anew. Their task was facilitated, however, by the fact that they had with them nearly all the party 'chiefs'; deputies, bureaucrats, section secretaries, and indeed veterans of the pre-war days in general preferred to rebuild the old republican structure rather than accept the new Bolshevik party.[1]

Most of the pre-war leaders of the GDFS went with them, but the position of women in the new party was not thereby strengthened. Louise Saumoneau had emerged as the most eminent woman of the party, but she had attained her eminence and her seat on the CAP as the representative not of women but of the CRRI. Deprived of her followers, she was named only a deputy member of the new CAP. She did not become a full member until 1927 and then served only three years before resigning in 1930. No other woman sat on the CAP between the two world wars.[2]

We have seen how Louise Saumoneau gave her particular stamp to the GDFS before the war and how she acquired during the war the prestige which would put her in the forefront of the women of the resurrected SFIO. It remains to explain how the GDFS was reconstructed, how it was transformed into the Comité National des Femmes Socialistes, and how Louise Saumoneau controlled both the reconstruction and the transformation, ensuring that the socialist women's movement throughout the life of the SFIO would remain true to the principles she had imposed on the original GDFS: integration of women with men, recruitment exclusively from within the party, functioning as a women's auxiliary of the party.

Rebuilding the old house

Saumoneau and the other veterans of the GDFS believed that their primary function as militants was within the party and that the GDFS was secondary

166

to it. They preoccupied themselves first with rebuilding the party. Only when the party was functioning regularly did they turn their attention to reconstructing the women's group. In the February 1922 issue of *La Femme socialiste*, Saumoneau announced that she would concern herself with the reorganisation of the GDFS — as soon as the next party membership drive was over. She reminded her readers that the members of the GDFS 'must be and remain registered in a section' of the party, because the GDFS was 'a group of women belonging' to the party. On 7 May 1922, a number of veterans of the old GDFS met and reconstituted the group as it had been at its last meeting in 1917, that is with the old executive, including Jouenne as secretary. Saumoneau devoted herself — successfully of course — to making sure that the old bases of membership were retained, that membership in a section remained the prerequisite for joining the group. The only change was a provision for provincial groups which would be related to the Parisian one by correspondence. This measure had few results.[3]

Saumoneau had initiated the reconstruction of the GDFS on her own without consulting anyone else and without even being a member of the executive. In addition to her strength of character and her reputation, she had the advantage of total and absolute control over *La Femme socialiste*, the party's only newspaper aimed at women. With the issue of March 1923 it vastly enlarged its format, becoming a four-page tabloid. It continued thus until the Second World War. Holding all these trumps, Saumoneau soon became the real leader of the GDFS, completely effacing Jouenne. On 11 April 1923 the GDFS celebrated international women's day for the first time since 1914. Jouenne played no role, although she was technically still secretary of the group. Stéphanie Bouvard presided and Saumoneau spoke, reminding the audience of the 1914 women's day which she had organised and which had been the first held in France. A month later, Saumoneau was the delegate of the GDFS and of the party to the conference of the reconstituted socialist women's international (and, with three men, to the congress of Hamburg which resurrected the Second International, or tried to do so). In all this Jouenne played no role.[4]

It was only in April 1924, however, that Jouenne finally resigned as secretary, enabling the group to elect Saumoneau to the position again. As secretary of the GDFS, Saumoneau was ably seconded by her old friend Bouvard and by her old enemy Suzanne Gibault, now remarried to Buisson. The war over, they all shared identical views on the dangers of feminism and on the need to maintain the GDFS as a socialist group, however small, rather than risk the danger of penetration by feminists. They displayed great energy in the task of galvanising the GDFS back to life. But their great activity was condemned to sterility by the very limitations they imposed on themselves.[5]

The GDFS barely managed to regain its pre-war membership, despite its pretension to being a national organisation. In 1930, questioned at the national congress, Saumoneau flatly refused to make membership figures public. The following year, however, Buisson decided to give the following figures: '220 registered in our group, half in the Parisian region, and the other half scattered in the provinces'. This was clearly a failure for a party which claimed 125,000 members, a failure all the more painful in that it came after eight years of hard work (work, to be sure, which received no financial aid and little moral support from the party). It was natural that, by this time, younger women entering the party would begin to question and to criticise the organisation and the leaders that had produced such meagre results.[6]

One of these women, Germaine Picard-Moch (wife of the socialist deputy, Jules Moch, later to be Minister of the Interior), gave a devastating critique of the GDFS at the party's 1930 congress:

The Women's Group, it is Louise Saumoneau — it is a little bit the dictatorship of Louise Saumoneau, but it is above all the action of Louise Saumoneau.

She organises, then, educational meetings, but the pity is that it's always the same women who go there. When for example Louise Saumoneau speaks of the Charter of the Party, she has for an audience: Suzanne Buisson, Marthe Louis-Lévy, Citizen Osmin, Germaine Picard-Moch and some others; when Suzanne Buisson speaks about the CGT, she has for an audience: Louise Saumoneau, Marthe Louis-Lévy, Citizen Osmin, etc . . . [*sic*] and that's the way it always is.

Another young woman, Suzanne Collette, supported Picard-Moch, pointing out that while the GDFS was not efficient at recruiting women, its very existence nonetheless enabled the party 'to be royally uninterested in everything concerning the organisation of socialist women'. Collette was determined to get the party to face up to its responsibilities, to create an official party organisation which would have a mandate to recruit women in substantial numbers.[7]

The Comité National des Femmes Socialistes

Collette had already begun her campaign. In 1928, when a new member of the thirteenth section of Paris, she had presented a resolution calling on the party to create an official women's group. It was accepted by her section and then by the Seine federation (still relatively sympathetic to women, as in the days of Madeleine Pelletier). The federation took the project to the national congress of 1929, where it was accepted unanimously and without debate. This was, however, more an indication of lack of interest than of enthusiasm. Collette was not at the end of her struggles.[8]

Her resolution provided that the CAP would name a commission which would form the new national organisation, but as the 1930 national congress approached, it became clear that the CAP was not going to act. The only woman member of the CAP was Louise Saumoneau, who had her own ideas. She was manoeuvring to frustrate Collette's resolution and to substitute a project of her own. She and Suzanne Buisson consulted the party's parliamentary group instead of the CAP, thereby avoiding any reference to Collette's proposal. They obtained an authorisation to prepare a project for the congress of Bordeaux to be held in June 1930. Collette, however, maintained her own project.[9]

The congress was thus confronted by two competing resolutions emanating from two hostile factions. In themselves, the two projects were surprisingly similar. On the key question of recruitment, Collette agreed entirely with Saumoneau. Her proposal called for the party 'to organise the women belonging to our sections, following the example of the organisations which are already functioning in Germany and Austria'. The reference to Germany and Austria missed the mark: the German and Austrian movements had succeeded precisely because they did not organise only 'the women belonging to our sections', but also recruited women directly from outside, acting as independent women's groups. This is what had enabled them to gain a foothold among masses of women, which the French had yet to do. Nevertheless, Collette rejected this form of organisation: 'It would be', she told the 1930 congress, 'clumsy and inoperative *to create organisations of socialist women outside of the Party*' (italics orig.).

Saumoneau, of course, also rejected this possibility, but more violently, as was her wont. Some comrades, she said in presenting her project to the same congress in the name of the GDFS, wished to create an organisation analogous to the Young Socialists, functioning separately from and parallel to the regular sections and including sympathisers as well as party members. 'This form of organisation', she told the congress, must be rejected 'as being inspired not by the spirit of class . . . but by the spirit of sex, and we think that such an organisation would inevitably become a feminist organisation with some socialist tendencies.' She went on: 'I would even say that, personally, if such a form of organisation were to be accepted in the Party, I would support more easily the idea of not having any organisation at all, rather than that of an organisation which I consider dangerous for the future, for the Party, and for Socialism. (Brisk applause.)'

Collette's proposal, however, did not envisage such an organisation. The only real difference between her project and that of the GDFS lay in the fact that hers involved obligatory inscription of all women members of the party in the new women's organisation and representation of this organisation on the CAP, while the GDFS explicitly rejected 'this idea of obligation' and that of special representation for women 'out of respect for the principle of equality of the sexes'. Women, Saumoneau concluded, should enter the party 'as militants of the Party and not as women'. There should be no difference in the treatment of men and women. This was Saumoneau's most brutal formulation of the principle of integration.

Since both sides agreed on this principle, the debate focused on the one point of difference between the two projects: the question of obligatory versus voluntary registration of women party members with the new organisation. Although several women spoke on the two proposals and although no speaker was happy with the existing situation, no one raised any other suggestions except for one woman who argued that there should be no women's organisation at all and one man who suggested that the tactics his section had employed in Strasbourg should be used: they had gone to the wives of members of the section and had said to them, 'Your husband is in the party, your duty is to follow your husband . . . and to enrol in the party yourself'.

The congress of Bordeaux, faced for the first time with a long if not profound debate on the organisation of women, was unable to choose between the two projects and finally voted to turn the question over to a commission to be named by the CAP. The commission, when constituted, included Saumoneau, Buisson, and Marthe Louis-Lévy from the GDFS, as well as several of the women who had criticised the GDFS, such as Collette and Picard-Moch. In all there were nine women, joined by an equal number of men, among them Léon Blum, the party's leader since 1919 and the man who would be, in 1936, the first socialist prime minister. Other men on the commission were Bracke, a deputy with a long record of support for women's rights, and the two wartime leaders, Longuet and Renaudel. For once the main leaders of the party were going to devote themselves to the problems of women in the party. Their presence would assure Saumoneau of a solid majority if there were any challenges to her conception of the women's organisation.[10]

Her work in the commission was Saumoneau's last contribution to the socialist women's movement. She had already resigned from the CAP. Her resignation took effect in 1930, after the congress of Bordeaux. Subsequently, perhaps stung by the extent of the criticism aimed at the GDFS, she resigned as secretary and devoted herself to her work as paid propagandist and to her two journals (she had founded a quarterly called *Propagande et Documentation* and she continued to publish *La Femme socialiste*). To succeed her as secretary, Saumoneau proposed her assistant, Marthe Louis-Lévy, but Louis-Lévy demurred, wishing simply to remain assistant secretary. She proposed Suzanne Buisson. Although Saumoneau preferred the more pliant Louis-Lévy (perhaps in the hope of retaining direct control of the group's affairs), she found Buisson eminently acceptable. In the autumn of 1930, Suzanne Buisson was elected the fourth secretary of the GDFS.[11]

Suzanne Buisson (or Gibault) was born Suzanne Lévy at Paris on 19 September 1883. Her parents were clothing wholesalers. She joined the SFIO upon its formation and remained a member to her death. She married Gibault and had one child before his death at the beginning of the war. Supporting herself as a clerk in a lace-wholesaler's office, she became archivist of the clerk's *syndicat* (Fédération Nationale des Syndicats d'Employés). After the war, she married the national secretary, Georges Buisson.

Suzanne Buisson was a vivid contrast to Louise Saumoneau, who had almost deliberately avoided traditional women's roles, whose manners with others were harsh and abrasive, and whose appearance was intentionally plain. Buisson cultivated normality. She followed her own advice from her 1913 articles: 'remain women and be pleasant'. She enjoyed a calm and happy family life. Warm and friendly in manner with all kinds of people, she revelled in human contact. Although tall and very stout, she always maintained a 'coquettish', 'womanly' appearance: 'I went to the hairdresser's, so as to reflect credit on the Party', she told Daniel Mayer one day before leaving on a mission for the Resistance. And while Saumoneau was fiercely and self-consciously working class, Buisson represented the new middle classes which were coming to dominate the reconstructed SFIO. Her husband Georges had by now reached the top of the syndical bureaucracy, working as first assistant to the CGT secretary Léon Jouhaux. But despite these contrasts and despite their violent disagreement during the war, Saumoneau and Buisson were both party women. Both saw the GDFS as an instrument for keeping the party free of feminist influence. Buisson had supported Saumoneau in the debate with Hélène Brion and continued to support her after the war. With Buisson taking her place, Saumoneau could rest assured that the GDFS would remain as she had left it.[12]

Nevertheless Saumoneau left nothing to chance. She remained on the commission until it completed its proposal for a new national women's organisation, thus assuring herself that it too would be stamped with her imprint. The basis of the commission's project was that 'women members of the Party belong in the first instance, like men, to their local section'. They would then have the option of participating in the women's organisation, in addition to their section. There would be no obligation for any section to create a women's group. The women's organisation would not be represented on the CAP. Indeed, after Saumoneau's departure in 1930, there was no woman on the CAP in any capacity. Buisson became a deputy (substitute) member in 1939, but not until after the war would a woman again be a full member.[13]

This project was presented to the 1931 congress by Suzanne Buisson and Marthe Louis-Lévy. Both justified the past record of the GDFS and paid homage to Saumoneau. No one spoke against it. Collette did not speak at all. Suzanne Lacore, still living in Perigord following her retirement as a school-teacher, gave a brilliant speech in which she defended the project with reference to her articles of 1913 which had initiated the debate with Hélène Brion. Lacore still opposed feminism, but argued that a more powerful women's organisation was needed to overcome the lack of women in the party and the indifference of men:

Personally, I have always been struck by this indifference, and the scene we have had, this evening, — at the moment when a woman came to the rostrum, giving by her appearance alone a kind of signal of evasion for our comrades — has confirmed me in my opinion on this point. (*Applause.*)

The congress voted the project 'unanimously less one vote', but the indifference and the scarcity of women remained. Could the new Comité National des Femmes Socialistes (CNDFS) make headway against these old obstacles?[14]

In fact the CNDFS was not really new at all. Under the new name there remained the same leaders, the same attitudes, and the same restrictions that had characterised the GDFS. The first committee was appointed at the 1931 congress. It naturally included all the women who were known in the party — and the best-known women were the leaders of the GDFS. Suzanne Buisson thus ceased to be secretary of the GDFS and became secretary of the CNDFS. Marthe Louis-Lévy was her assistant secretary in both organisations. The CNDFS had a second assistant secretary, a younger militant named Suzanne Caille, whose approach was also similar to Saumoneau's. Berthe Saumoneau, Louise's sister, was named treasurer, giving Louise a family connection to the new committee. Thus the leadership of the CNDFS was virtually identical to that of the old GDFS. Although Collette and Picard-Moch were also appointed to the CNDFS, they were far outnumbered by former members of the GDFS who supported Saumoneau and Buisson's policies down the line.[15]

The election of committee members in the spring of 1932 changed nothing. The veterans of the GDFS remained the best-known women in the party. Naturally they swept the field. Buisson came first with 896 votes (of 984 cast), followed by Louis-Lévy (845), Lacore (841), Berthe Saumoneau (809), and Alice Jouenne (799). Apart from Berthe, who did not long remain on the committee (she had no taste for politicking, recalls her niece), and from the addition of some younger militants, such as Berthe Fouchère and Andrée Marty-Capgras, the leadership of the CNDFS would remain virtually unchanged until the Second World War. It was essentially the old leadership of the GDFS minus Saumoneau and, by a quirk of fate, plus Marianne Rauze, who, weary of romantic chimeras, returned to the party and was elected to the CNDFS in 1937. What injection of new blood did take place was largely fortuitous. Berthe Fouchère recalls now her astonishment when, in 1932, a young schoolteacher and a newcomer to the party, she was asked to stand for the CNDFS because there were not sufficient candidates to fill the twenty-one seats.[16]

The same attitudes characterised the CNDFS as the GDFS because all its officers shared Saumoneau's conception of the group and because most women in the CNDFS tended to place their party membership above their commitment to solve the problems of women. This was after all the basis on which they had succeeded in the party: they were party militants, they had chosen the party rather than feminist organisations, and the party had given them apparently equal standing with men — it had made 'citizens' of them. They responded by putting the party first.

Finally, the CNDFS was bound by the same restrictions as the GDFS. Its statutes defined it as an organisation of women belonging to the party. It offered women not a group of their own but instead a task additional to their party membership: to bring other women into the sections of the socialist party. And while it seems that the atmosphere of the sections was more hospitable to women in the 1930s than before the First World War, the sections could hardly respond to women's particular needs. Indeed, by placing women on an equal footing with men, they tended to obscure the special problems of women.

The result of all this was that the CNDFS functioned as a women's auxiliary of the party, just as Saumoneau had intended. Yet this was a period for taking initiatives. The left had the wind in its sails. On 12 February 1934, socialists and communists had marched together in protest against fascist riots of the 6th, giving the left a foretaste of the power it could wield if united. In May the Third International authorised the French communists to concede whatever was required to bring the socialists to sign a 'unity of action' agreement, and this was done on 27 July 1934. In May 1935, the left parties were joined by the Radical Party, whose tradition of republicanism and anti-clericalism had won out over its fear of collectivism. The Popular Front was born. On Bastille Day, 1935, an immense crowd followed the leaders of the three Popular Front parties in a gigantic outpouring of strength. Léon Blum marched arm-in-arm with the communist and Radical leaders, symbolising the new unity of the left, which could now aspire to govern after twenty years of defeat and division.

The Popular Front parties won the national elections in April and May 1936, although this was due more to the three parties' standing together in the run-off balloting than to the overall swing to the left. Nevertheless it was a great victory. It inspired two million workers throughout the country to strike and occupy their factories. When Léon Blum took office in June as France's first socialist prime minister, he was faced with a near revolutionary situation which he channelled into a number of overdue social reforms. In this atmosphere of hope and enthusiasm, the SFIO doubled its membership during 1936, and increased it still further over 1937, reaching a high of 286,000 as opposed to 120,000 two years earlier. (The SFIO had barely reached 90,000 members in 1914, at the height of its glory under Jaurès!)[17]

While the party was forging ahead, the CNDFS was functioning only as a women's auxiliary, without any political life of its own. When faced with political decisions, it scurried for cover. In the winter of 1934—5, the CNDFS was approached by the Rassemblement Mondial des Femmes, a 'women's world rally' against fascism created by the Amsterdam-Pleyel Committee against War and Fascism, which drew together republican, socialist, and communist intellectuals, prefiguring the Popular Front. The CNDFS, unlike the communist women's group and even some feminists, was more concerned to safeguard the interests of the party in its negotiations with the PCF than it was to mobilise women. It turned abjectly to the (male) leadership of the party, deciding that 'only the CAP was qualified to determine . . . the attitude which ought to be adopted, in the face of this "Rassemblement", by our Committee which, as is well known, is only an internal organisation, a sort of vast [party] commission, specialised in feminine recruitment'. As the party was then taking a hard line in its alliance with the communists, the CAP determined that the socialist women should refuse to meet with the delegates of the Rassemblement and the CNDFS devoted much of its energy to enforcing this refusal when rank and file women sought nevertheless to work together with members of the Rassemblement. Similarly, when representatives of the CNDFS did agree to meet with the feminine section of the PCF to plan a campaign against the high cost of living, it was only with the prior approval of the party secretariat and in the presence of a male national secretary acting as a kind of guardian of the seraglio.[18]

The CNDFS was a remake of the GDFS: the same leaders, attitudes, and restrictions. It was a women's auxiliary. Did it succeed in its assigned aims? According to the resolution which created it, it had three aims: '(a) The recruitment of women; (b) their socialist education; (c) the preparation of feminine questions to propose for the Party to study'. How did the CNDFS fare on these points? On recruitment, it is true that the percentage of women in the party increased slightly during the 1930s. The census of women in the party as of 15 March 1933 counted 2995, or 2.17 per cent of the total membership. The next census, in 1934, discovered 3376 women, or 2.57 per cent of the total membership. Thereafter women were slightly more than 3 per cent of the total and this percentage was maintained during the vast increase in membership which followed the victory of the Popular Front in 1936. The CNDFS seems to have been a holding operation, which may have prevented a relative decline in the number of women in the party during the influx of new members but which did not profit from this influx to create a new basis for women in the party.[19]

On education, the CNDFS continued the same old round of lectures as the GDFS, with somewhat more attention to the provinces, mainly because the CNDFS had some financial help from the party (not much: 12,000 francs in 1934 and even this was contested by a delegate at that year's congress: he wished to reduce the subsidy of the CNDFS in favour of the Young Socialists).[20]

On 'feminine questions' the CNDFS was singularly unsuccessful. On 1 March 1934, the Chamber of Deputies approved the bill put forward by the

old socialist Bracke 'granting all political rights to women'. The bill never got
to the Senate, but even so, as the Popular Front began to arouse hope of an
electoral victory, many socialists began to tremble at the thought that the
right might trick them out of their victory by allowing them to grant women
the suffrage: they still assumed that women would vote as the priests told
them and that women's suffrage would thus mean the triumph of the right.
(It is only fair to add that most historians and political scientists have agreed
that women were politically more conservative than men, though probably
not enough so to have altered the results in 1936.) One socialist deputy,
Sixte-Quenin, openly expressed this fear. He presented to the 1935 party
congress a resolution which gave the socialist deputies the option of voting
against Bracke's bill while reaffirming the principle of women's suffrage:
'considering the danger which there could be to public liberties in the
immediate attribution of the right to vote to women, which would run the
risk of leading to the legal installation of fascism in power'. The resolution
was defeated not through the efforts of the CNDFS — no woman spoke on
the question — but through those of Bracke himself. And a sizeable minority
voted for Sixte-Quenin's resolution: 720 mandates as opposed to 2117 for
Bracke's.[21]

It is hardly surprising that the CNDFS obtained virtually nothing for
women from the Popular Front government — it had sought nothing. Blum
did nominate three women as under-secretaries of state. One of them was
Suzanne Lacore, who took Alice Jouenne as her chief of staff. The appoint-
ment of individual women to high office, though not ministries, paralleled
the principle of integration which benefited some women leaders in the
party but left it incapable of reaching the masses of women outside. As
prime minister Blum contented himself with this gesture, sweeping general
reforms — in particular women's suffrage — under the carpet. The CNDFS
acquiesced, making no effort to obtain women's suffrage during the only
time the party was in power, enjoying not only a left majority in the
Chamber but also (still more unusual) the moral and political force to assure
passage of its bills in the Senate, which had killed women's suffrage in 1922.
Thus in a sense it was the women's organisation of the party which broke the
promises made at Marseilles in 1879. It was not Blum but de Gaulle who
would give Frenchwomen the vote. They would get the suffrage not by their
own struggles but by the fiat of one man.[22]

From the Popular Front to the Liberation: the decline of the socialist women's movement

Blum's Popular Front government lasted just over a year. Upon Blum's resignation, French government began to slide to the right, culminating in 1940
with the installation of Marshal Pétain as prime minister and then 'chief of

175

state' in the Vichy government after the defeat of France. Under the strain of these developments, the SFIO virtually fell apart. Léon Blum opposed the policy of appeasement, though rather timidly, while the other principal leader of the party, Paul Faure, declared for the Munich Accords.

Confronted by the problems of war and fascism. Saumoneau saw only a repeat of August 1914. In 1937, she complained that efforts were being made for 'the preparation of people's minds to accept the "just war . . . " as in 1914'. As the party split between Faure and Blum, Saumoneau sided with Faure, who like her had opposed the First World War (he had been part of the Longuetist minority). She moved with him from approving Munich through condemning 'Stalino-bellicism' to supporting the quasi-fascist Vichy regime. Saumoneau's inflexibility, her determination to avoid the mistake of 1914, and her anti-communism all combined to bring about this change, which may seem shocking today but which represented, in the slow march of the real events of the period between the two wars, a path taken by a substantial segment of the French left.[23]

After the Liberation, Saumoneau refused to go back on her commitment. She refused the SFIO's offer of a pension, complaining 'I do not find in your warlike ideologies, your jingoism, and worse, the pure socialism to which I consecrated my days and my late nights.' She signed her refusal, 'Louise Saumoneau, half a century of socialist militancy'. She joined with Paul Faure in founding a splinter party which sought to justify their positions during the war, accusing the SFIO of class collaboration in the Resistance. In *Propagande et Documentation*, which she published again from 1947 through 1949, she condemned the 'émigrés' of the Resistance and their 'so-called "Liberation" '. In 1949 she contracted cancer of the jaw and died at Paris on 23 January 1950. Given her political turns, there were few who chose to mourn her. She herself might well have chosen as her epitaph the words she had written upon the death of Adèle Toussaint-Kassky and Elisabeth Renaud, both of whom (like Fernand Loriot) died in October 1932:

Together they ended their lives as militants as a result of incidents painful for many of us and which affected grievously their sensitivity and their incorruptible sense of justice. Their material lives faded away . . . and they entered into the void, our retirement for all of us.[24]

Saumoneau died as an outcast of her party, but her ghost remained in the SFIO, perpetuated ironically through Suzanne Buisson's Resistance record. For if Saumoneau had been a heroine of the anti-war struggle during the First World War, Buisson was a martyr to the socialist Resistance in the Second World War. After the defeat, she and her husband found a home in Lyons, together with the general secretary of the CGT and his wife. Having as a couple the highest contacts in both the trade union and socialist movements, they became a natural focus of socialist Resistance. Their home was the centre of the clandestine SFIO. When the party took formal shape in secret on 18 June 1943, Suzanne was named 'comrade in charge of relations with the communists'. It was she who nominated Daniel Mayer as secretary general.

On 29 March 1944, the Gestapo seized the headquarters of the Resistance in Lyons. Since the party's Comité Directeur (which replaced the CAP) was to meet there on 1 April, Suzanne Buisson took steps to warn all members so they would not walk into a trap. Unable to reach one member, she determined to catch him at the entry. For forty-five minutes she paced up and down on the footpath before the guarded building, until her large frame attracted attention. She was arrested and taken to Paris by the Germans, never to be seen again. All that is known is that the Gestapo got no information out of her, despite the torture that a Jewish resistant would have suffered.[25]

Suzanne Buisson thus became a martyr figure for socialist women and it is she who is remembered in the party today, while Saumoneau's name has disappeared. Yet Buisson's martyrdom enshrined Saumoneau's ideas. After the war, the CNDFS was not reconstituted. It seemed disrespectful of women's new status as citizens to have a special group for them in the party. Instead of the CNDFS, the party created a Commission Nationale Féminine. The very word 'commission' was indicative of the change (the CNDFS had been a 'committee'). 'Commission' retains some of its original sense: a 'charge or mandate', generally from above, such as the commission of an officer; 'comité' suggests a group elected from a larger group. The Commission Nationale Féminine was the staff which the party mandated to deal with women. There was no longer even a pretence that women had a group of their own or representation as women. Women no longer voted for the national women's leadership and the party no longer took a census of women as it had in the 1930s. The secretary of the Commission Nationale Féminine did have a seat on the Comité Directeur, but this was in virtue of her status as a staff officer, not of any representative quality.[26]

These changes marked the end of the socialist women's movement. Hitherto women had sought to express their socialist aims in groups of their own. Henceforth the socialist party would designate officers to deal with the problem posed by women. This was the logical culmination of Saumoneau's policies, particularly the policy of integration. Saumoneau had based her action on her desire to prevent the feminists from getting a base in the party through independent women's groups. She had not sought to build a socialist women's movement so much as to prevent the feminists from taking over the movement which others created. When the GDFS had been formed, Saumoneau moved in to keep the feminists out. When younger women in the party had tried to create a national women's organisation, she had acted to thwart their designs and to ensure that the new organisation, the CNDFS, would remain within the limits she prescribed. She had stated then that she would prefer not having any women's organisation at all to having one with any independence of the party. She had dreamed that women would be treated as citizens and not as sisters. By giving women the vote, the republic enabled the party to realise her dream. Separate groups for women were no longer needed. Sisters might desire separate organisations, but citizens needed only the party.

Women and the socialist party since 1944

The creation of the Commission Nationale Féminine in place of the CNDFS was not perceived in such dramatic terms by those who lived it. They believed that they were continuing the pre-war tradition of the CNDFS and in a sense they were right. Thus although our story could conclude with the demise of the CNDFS and the end of a socialist women's movement, it seems proper to follow the fortunes of women in the socialist party in the period of the Commission Nationale Féminine and after.

The first secretary of the Commission was Simone Kahn, who had been a deputy member of the pre-war CNDFS. In 1947 the position was taken over by Berthe Fouchère, who had joined the CNDFS in 1932. Fouchère was a tough militant who had achieved notoriety in 1923 when she was dismissed from office at the beginning of her first year as a primary-school teacher in the Nièvre for having written an article hostile to the French occupation of the Ruhr. (She was reinstated in 1925, but in another department, the Oise.) In regard to the role to be played by the CNDFS, Fouchère's ideas had been the same as those of Saumoneau and Buisson. She had accepted Blum's decision that women's reforms (which she regarded in any case as minor issues) had to be subordinated to the fight against fascism. Under her leadership the post-war Commission continued to follow the policies Saumoneau had enshrined in the party's pre-war practice, the more easily in that the Commission did not seek to be an organisation in its own right but only a delegation of the party secretariat.[27]

Did the policy of integration work now that women were citizens of the republic? It is true that there were many women among the men who streamed into the party after the Liberation. Within two or three years they formed 16 per cent of the total membership, according to Berthe Fouchère's informed guess. But while this was certainly better than the 3 per cent they represented during the Third Republic, it does not seem fully commensurate with the expectations aroused by the new status of women nor with the party's great surge of membership in the heady years after the Liberation, especially as it did not increase beyond this 16 per cent, and indeed probably decreased slightly after the initial wave had crested.

The party quickly reached a height of 355,000 members and took its place as the major governmental party of the left, obtaining a quarter of the votes in the elections of the first three years after the war. But the party quickly became habituated to participation in government. The enthusiasm of the Liberation gave way to the sad realities of the cold war and colonial war. Profoundly involved through its participation in government, the party soon tarnished the bright image it had inherited from the Popular Front and the Resistance. Léon Blum himself presided over the beginning of the Indo-Chinese (later the Vietnamese) war, at the end of 1945. In the same year, he was beaten in his efforts to bring the party to drop its revolutionary rhetoric in order to conform with its reformist practice. The hard line 'Marxist' Guy Mollet ousted Daniel Mayer as party general secretary because Mayer was too reformist. Yet when he became prime minister, in 1956, Guy Mollet became a vigorous leader of the colonial war in Algeria.

Berthe Fouchère resigned as secretary of the Commission Nationale Féminine in protest over the war in Algeria. She was replaced, in 1958, by Janette Brutelle. Another generation had taken over the reins, one without any connection with the pre-war SFIO. Brutelle was only three years old in 1932, when Berthe Fouchère was first elected to the CNDFS. Brutelle began a career as a schoolteacher in 1949. After taking the leadership of the Young Socialists' organisation in her native department, the Aude, Brutelle entered the national youth council of the party in 1953. After her transfer to Algeria, she became secretary of the socialist federation of Algiers (which was treated as a French department). From the position of the French colonists, even the socialists, the war made sense. Brutelle had no qualms about taking the position.[28]

The Fourth Republic and the SFIO, which was too closely associated with it, were near the end of the road. In 1958 General de Gaulle took the head of colonial and army elements who sought to assure continuation of the war. By a *coup d'état* remarkably similar in constitutional terms to that of his old enemy Marshal Pétain in 1940, de Gaulle took over as president and pushed through a new constitution, creating the Fifth Republic. The SFIO lost its possibilities of achieving government. As it had lost its other reasons for existence, it now began a precipitate downward slide which culminated in the electoral disaster of the 1969 presidential election: the SFIO candidate received 5.07 per cent of the vote!

During its long decline, slow during the 1950s, rapid during the 1960s, the party made no progress in attracting women. It is probable that the number of women declined even faster than the total membership. From its high of 355,000 members after the Liberation, the party reached a low of 75,000–81,000 members during the 1960s and even these figures represented paper membership in mostly inactive sections. By 1969, women constituted some 15 per cent of this membership, though it is difficult to know how much credence to give these figures.[29]

Brutelle was the last secretary of the Commission Nationale Féminine.

Between 1969 and 1971, the SFIO merged with a number of small centre parties to form a new party, which abandoned the historic name to call itself simply the Parti Socialiste (PS). In 1971, François Mitterand became first secretary of the PS, just three days after his Convention des Institutions Républicaines had been absorbed into the party. He brought in a new group of leaders and made a clean sweep of the party's institutions. The Commission National Féminine was disbanded. The institutions which could trace their ancestry back to Saumoneau and the GDFS thus perished with the SFIO itself.

The problem of women and socialism had not been resolved. It remained and still remains to plague the new PS. In the confusion and excitement of the beginnings of the new party, women were at first ignored. Each year had its immediate preoccupations which eclipsed the problems of women. In 1971, the new party was still being reorganised. In 1972, it negotiated an agreement with the PCF creating the union of the left. In 1973 it fought a long campaign for the legislative elections. These elections confirmed the ascendance of the new party, but the left was still in the minority in the Chamber. The party finally settled down to build new structures which could endure a long struggle.

Among the new leaders who entered the party with Mitterand were several women. One of them was already concerned to make a place for women in the party. She was Marie-Thérèse Eyquem, a career bureaucrat who, as national inspector for youth sport activities, had done much to encourage women's sports. In the 1960s she was president of the Mouvement Démocratique Féminin, a group of women supporting Mitterand's presidential campaign. At the 1973 congress, she fought for the principle of a quota for women in the party, 'a minimum percentage . . . of women at all levels of the organisation: Comité Directeur, Executive, Federation, Section'. This quota was fixed initially at 10 per cent. Eyquem became a member of the national secretariat, but only as the leader responsible for contact with other organisations, not as leader of a women's group.[30]

Formally, the party did have a women's committee, the Commission des Femmes, but it was inactive and not represented at the summit of the party hierarchy. Mitterand's photo-finish loss to Giscard d'Estaing in the 1974 presidential elections confirmed the party's determination to prepare itself for a long struggle. In 1975, Janette Brutelle resigned from the Commission des Femmes, on which she had sat with stoic endurance amidst the new members of the competing Mitterandist faction. Her resignation paved the way for the party to replace the Commission with a new women's organ, the 'delegation to women'. Eyquem, who was past sixty, left the task of heading the delegation to a younger woman, Denise Cacheux. She was a close collaborator of Pierre Mauroy, mayor of Lille and Mitterand's second in the party. As head of the delegation, Cacheux sat on the 131-member Comité Directeur, but not on the 27-member national secretariat. For Eyquem and the other Mitterandist women, this was not good enough.[31]

The PS was now in full swing. Carried along by its electoral success and apparently secure in the union of the left, it had by 1977 a real membership of 160,000, of which women represented between 15 and 20 per cent. At the Nantes congress in 1977, the women sought a greater share in the party's success. First they asked that the quota be raised from 10 to 20 per cent. They believed that women now amounted to almost 20 per cent of the membership and should be guaranteed office in the same proportion. However, in the face of lack of support from the male members of the Comité Directeur, they had to accept a 15 per cent quota, the compromise offered by Mitterand.[32]

They had better luck with their other demands. The congress agreed to upgrade the 'delegation' to a 'Secrétariat National à l'Action Féminine'. This gave it much greater status than any previous women's organisation. The secretary automatically sat on the party's highest leadership bodies, including the national secretariat, and had her own office and staff. Moreover, the resolution setting up the new organisation specified that it was to be paralleled at every level of the party: 'each organism of leadership, from the section to the national secretariat', it read, would include 'a woman – or man – secretary responsible for the problems posed by the feminine condition in society and in the Socialist Party'.[33]

Denise Cacheux returned to municipal responsibilities in Lille. The new secretary was Yvette Roudy, an exceptionally dynamic woman just reaching fifty in 1979 who – unlike all her predecessors – considered herself a feminist as well as a socialist. Roudy combined traits of both kinds of predecessors. Interviewing her, I was reminded of both Saumoneau and Auclert. Like Saumoneau, Roudy came from working-class origins. Her father was a metalworker, her mother a domestic. She ceased formal education at sixteen and became a typist. She escaped from this background, however, by marrying a man who rose to the top of the ranks of secondary education. Like Auclert, Roudy's political beginnings were through feminism. In 1963, Colette Audry asked her to do the French translation of Betty Friedan's *Feminine Mystique*. She found in the book answers to many problems that bothered her. She subsequently joined the Mouvement Démocratique Féminin and became its general secretary, alongside Eyquem, who was president. She thus participated in Mitterand's 1965 presidential campaign and became one of his faithful lieutenants. But her fidelity to Mitterand did not prevent her from holding her own against the men of the party to defend the interests of women, as she did at Nantes, where she led the agitation to obtain the new measures.[34]

Although no one could know it at Nantes, the year 1977 was to be a high point of the party's development. In September of that year, the PCF broke off the union of the left and returned to its traditional ghetto. The ensuing defeat of the left parties at the March 1978 legislative elections inaugurated an era of decline and factional fighting for the PS. Roudy's task became still more difficult: to attract women in a period of general stagnation of membership.

Even without this added complication, Roudy faced an uphill climb. There was still no women's organisation, let alone women's groups at the local level. Roudy's policies still remained within the lines drawn by Saumoneau. Her aim was to promote women within the party and to render the sections more hospitable to women, not to create a separate base for women in the party. Even the seemingly radical quota was based on the policy of integration. Roudy herself compared it with American measures 'to struggle against racial segregation'. She did not take note of the argument that such measures were intended to integrate blacks into white society, an argument put forth by blacks who contested these measures and called for separate organisations in which, they suggested, they might develop a collective identity vis-à-vis whites.

In 1979, Yvette Roudy was elected a deputy to the European parliament at Strasbourg. Her successor was Véronique Neiertz, who took the title 'Secrétaire Nationale aux Luttes des Femmes': no longer just 'feminine action' but 'women's battles'. She herself spoke not of socialist women, but of 'socialist feminists', renewing the terminology of the first GFS, abandoned by the GDFS and hence unknown in the party until now. Neiertz was successful, indeed dramatically so, in getting the party to take feminist positions, but no more than Roudy did she appear to have the answer for organisation at the local level.

For the party's national convention of 12–13 January 1980, a massive new programme was elaborated, representing an attempt to maintain the party's advanced image on a basis distinct from the communists'. An important part of this programme was the party's claim that it represented the heritage of May 1968, including the women's movement, which it attributed to this heritage. The programme stated that 'the women's struggle is not a simple reform movement [*mouvement contestataire*] but an original movement of social transformation, in the degree that it passes through the class struggle but cannot be simply reduced to the class struggle'. The programme went on to quote Mitterand as having said, 'one cannot be socialist without being feminist, and if the French socialists understood this better, socialism and feminism would have long since become indissociable'. Whatever their historical truth, such statements clearly demonstrated a new concern for women's issues among the party leadership, at least in theory.[35]

What this could mean in practice was to be demonstrated in the 1979 parliamentary debate on the legalisation of abortion. In 1975, the law prohibiting abortion was 'suspended' for five years and provision made for legal abortion up to the fourteenth week, reimbursed through social security like any other medical act. In 1979, with the five-year limit running out, the parliament debated the extension or repeal of the 1975 suspension. Under Neiertz's leadership, the PS undertook a major struggle on the question of abortion, submitting its own bill, which provided for abortion on demand up to the twentieth week, with therapeutic abortion subsequently, as well as a massive programme of birth control and sex education. Around this bill, the PS led a very visible and dynamic campaign, with leaflets, brochures, and press statements flooding local sections, which responded so well that Neiertz could claim that 60 per cent of the federations had undertaken major public activity on the issue, organising 'hundreds' of public debates and leafleting in all the major cities of France. When the socialist bill failed, the party's deputies voted solidly for extension of the 1975 law, which was passed largely through socialist and communist support.[36]

Although the PS could take credit for having fought a major battle on an issue which was generally seen as a litmus test of feminism, the problem of male reticence in the face of women's issues nonetheless persisted. In a restrained but forceful post-mortem, Neiertz complained that only ten socialist deputies had stayed in the Chamber during the night of 29 November 1979, when the final outcome of the struggle was decided: 'In the face of the thirty communist deputies who did not cease to intervene and of the hundred or so deputies of the right who succeeded each other at the microphone, the socialist participation in the debate appeared intelligent, to be sure, motivated without any doubt, but a bit lightweight.' And if it was argued that women should take responsibility in this sphere, she went on, then the party had to face the fact that there were only two socialist women deputies, compared to eight communists.[37]

Feminist convictions and actions, even 'battles' or 'struggles', still led back inexorably to the problem of the role of women in the party. In turn the lack of women at the top of the party was still linked to the lack of women at the base. The old problem of a women's organisation still confronted the new PS as it had the old SFIO. Louise Saumoneau firmly implanted in the party the policy of integration and the prohibition of independent groups for women. No one has yet challenged her legacy. The new PS is still a party of citizens, not of brothers and sisters.

Conclusion

Having come to the end of a century of the history of women and socialism, let us try to answer the four questions with which we began: (1) Why did the alliance between feminism and socialism fail after such promising beginnings? (2) What ideals and ideologies governed the socialists' conduct toward feminism and toward women in general? (3) Why did the SFIO never develop a strong women's movement? (4) Would separate women's groups and a more autonomous women's organisation have helped the party to recruit more women? What, in short, is the heritage which weighs upon the new PS today preventing it from attracting women into its ranks, given that at the end of 1977 women constituted less than 20 per cent of the membership of the party? This is roughly the same proportion as in the German SPD — in 1914!

The alliance between feminism and socialism was begun in confusion, written by leaders without followers, and dissolved as soon as the contrasting social bases of the two movements became evident. The origins of the alliance are to be found in the continuing mixture of generous and progressive ideas which probably reached its most intense period with the revolution of 1848, but which was still strong, even in the aftermath of the Commune. The grievances of the oppressed must have a common base, it was thought. They had a common enemy in the monarchy and in the restricted property suffrage (later in the Empire with its facade of democracy) and they had a common aim: to install the republic.

Women and workers were the two most obvious classes of the oppressed. It seemed inevitable that their struggles were closely linked if indeed they were not one and the same. This feeling could be traced back at least to Flora Tristan, the spiritual progenitor of socialist feminism or feminist socialism (as well as of trade unionism!), who called for one big union of the oppressed — women and workers — long before the 1848 revolution. This sentiment underlay the action of socialist women through most of the nineteenth century. Rouzade, for example, had no clear idea why workers and women should march together beyond the fact that they were both oppressed. Toward the end of the century, these sentiments gave way to clearer views of the nature of oppression. On the one hand, feminists such as Auclert perceived that men, even working-class men, were at least in part

184

oppressors of women. On the other hand, working-class women and their leaders, such as Valette and especially Saumoneau, perceived that emancipation meant more than formal equality with men. They admitted in theory that formal equality was necessary, although they sometimes neglected it in practice. Above all, however, they emphasised the need to transform society and its economic base from capitalism to socialism and they argued that most feminists, whether consciously or not, had vested interests in the continuation of the capitalist regime.

Only at Marseilles in 1879 did the sentimental confusion which joined feminism and socialism in most minds give way to a formal treaty of alliance, drawn up by one feminist, Hubertine Auclert. This was the most generous as well as the clearest form the alliance ever took, for the same reason that it was stillborn at Marseilles: it was written by leaders without followers, leaders acting in a vacuum and not coping with social reality. As soon as Auclert had to contend with her followers, few though they were, she broke off the alliance. For was this not the significance of the decision of her group to stay with the mutualists at Le Havre in 1880, despite their anti-feminism? As soon as the socialists began to attract followers, the feminists saw that the ordinary working man was not an ally. As soon as the feminist rank and file became involved, the socialists saw that the feminists were bourgeois women. Auclert's main contribution, ironically, was to help along the sorting out process by which different progressive ideas and ideologies began to stand on their own by the 1890s. After Marseilles, feminism and socialism tore up the alliance projected there and drifted apart.

Nevertheless, there was a long road to walk from the drifting apart after Marseilles to the violent break between the GFS and the feminists in 1900, which symbolised the real, profound break between the two movements just as Marseilles had symbolised their attempted union. Aline Valette, of course, distinguished herself from the feminists as she came to place all her hopes in the party and in this respect is most representative of the evolution of the movement, of socialist men as well as women. But it was Louise Saumoneau who articulated the break between feminism and socialism and who built the lessons she learned from the 1900 congress into the socialist women's movement of the twentieth century.

This break reflected a social reality. The clients of the feminists were very different women from those of the socialist women. The feminists were generally of the bourgeoisie, their leaders often of the upper bourgeoisie. The socialists tended to come from other strata. In theory they drew from the working classes, and in fact their leaders sincerely thought of the workers as their clients, but an increasing number of the socialist rank and file were of the *petite bourgeoisie*, as was virtually all the leadership (with the possible exceptions of Valette and Saumoneau): women who had the time and the leisure to dream of a better world and who were close enough to the working classes to empathise with them, but who themselves had not known the life of the wage earners they sought to represent. Thus our study has teemed with schoolteachers and the wives of petty bureaucrats, from Rouzade to Buisson, and we have encountered piles of utopian novels and household guides. The socialist women, if they were not so much of the working classes as they claimed, were nonetheless from class backgrounds very different from those of the feminists, whose wealth, elegance, and servants they could not, and thought they preferred not, to imitate.

Yet it is not the separation of the two movements which is so important for the twentieth century as the consequences Saumoneau drew from the break and imposed upon the socialist women's movement. Saumoneau not only broke with the feminist movement, but also prevented the socialist women's movement from putting any emphasis on the struggle for equality between the sexes and even from taking into account the problems of women in recruiting them to the party. Women would come into the social-ist party as citizens, like the men, or they would not come at all.

This leads us to the second question: the ideals and ideologies which governed the socialists' conduct toward feminism and toward women. At the heart of this problem is the theoretical weakness of the French socialists. Jules Guesde's economism was certainly more realistic than Proudhon's nostalgia for the France of the peasant and artisan, but it was not Marxism. The leader of the party which purported to introduce German 'scientific' socialism into France could not read German, had read little of Marx, and took only the most rigid elements of what he did read. Thus he initiated the conflict between feminism and socialism with his unfortunate resolution (defeated at the 1880 UFC congress) which denied the value of the suffrage for women. Marxism, instead of enlightening him on this problem, gave him, as he thought, authority for a simplistic argument denying the value to women of the rights men already enjoyed.

Guesde was not without positive sentiments toward women's emanci-pation. He had expressed them strongly in the 1876 articles to which we have often referred. But these articles were the product of the anarchist influence he underwent before becoming acquainted with Marxism through German exiles in the cafés of the Latin Quarter. His swing to what he took for Marxism marked a new rigidity in which emancipation became a simple thing, an idea with one component (as Jaurès once remarked): emancipation from class exploitation. Any other form of emancipation seemed a diversion. The struggle for women's rights appeared almost counter-revolutionary.

Lafargue, Ghesquière, Vérecque, not to mention Aline Valette — indeed all the other theorists of French Marxism — were even more confused theoretically. Their ideas on women's emancipation were closer to those of Proudhon than to those of Marx, for their veneration of maternity could be translated as 'woman's place is in the home' and probably was so translated

186

among the rank and file. For Lafargue as for Valette, the socialist revolution would enable women to return to home and hearth and raise children. This vision was generous, humane, and understandable in terms of the horrors of wage labour and factory conditions of the nineteenth century, but it was narrow and anachronistic compared with the vision of Marx and Engels.

Engels had resolved these problems with his customary incisiveness in *The Origin of the Family, Private Property and the State*. He argued that, wretched as it was, wage labour was giving women the economic foundations for their future independence. For Marx and Engels the path lay not back from the factory to the home but onward through the factory to independence, so that the family, unleashed from economic pressures, could be built on love alone, and so that women, freed from dependence on the male head of household for their daily bread, could develop as human beings in their own right by earning their keep.

This vision assumed that women would gain formal equality with men in bourgeois society, before the socialist revolution. Engels had also resolved the problem of the relation between women's rights and the social movement in *Origin of the Family*. Women's rights in general and the suffrage in particular (Engels like Auclert saw that it was the key to all the others) were just some of the fields on which the battles against bourgeois society would be fought. Women, just as much as men, should participate in these battles. They had a right, indeed a duty to struggle for the same rights as men. Once they had done so, they would be on the same footing as men and men and women together could get on with the task of building a decent society for everyone, fulfilling the empty formal rights by giving them social content.

These ideas were beyond the reach of the principal theorists of French socialism. It is therefore hardly surprising that the leaders of the socialist women's movement did not grasp them. Understanding them would not in itself have changed the nature of the movement, but would undoubtedly have enabled its leaders to view the feminist movement with greater sympathy, perceiving that it too was performing a useful task, even though its class base was different from and even hostile to that of the socialists. Understanding Engels's ideas might even have enabled the socialist women to be more sympathetic to women's needs, to treat their fellow women as sisters as well as citizens, and thus facilitate their coming to socialism.

We can now turn to the third question, the big one: why did the SFIO never develop a strong women's movement? Before we return to the answers to the first two questions, we must introduce a third factor which also helps answer this question: the late start of the French socialist women's movement. The GFS was unable to survive through the unification of the French socialist parties in 1905. It was destroyed by Saumoneau's reaction to the feminist movement, which broke up her partnership with Renaud and thus altered the balance which had made the group successful. The men of the party did the rest, refusing to accept the remains of the group or to create a new one, largely because of the theoretical failings we have just discussed. Saumoneau herself had such a negative vision of the movement that it is scarcely surprising she was unable to persuade her fellow citizens in the party of its usefulness.

Even Madeleine Pelletier never really undertook to fill the resulting void. There was no French socialist women's movement until 1913. Judging by the German and Austrian movements, however, the time for the take-off of such an organisation was the twenty year period before the First World War. At this time social democracy was still the untarnished embodiment of the hopes of progressive men and women, not yet tainted by collaboration with warring governments nor deprived of its militant cutting edge by the departure of the communists. At this time women were not citizens in any of the major nations represented in the International. They could thus justify special treatment in the party and create special groups which took account of the status they did enjoy as women, as sisters, instead of assuming that which they did not enjoy as citizens.

The GDFS was started at the very end of this period and had only eighteen months' existence before the outbreak of the war stopped in its tracks a movement with some promise, however limited. The schism of Tours broke the momentum of the socialist movement once again, so that only by the 1930s did the socialist and communist parties recover. By this time it was too late for the SFIO to implant a strong woman's movement. The party had lost its character as an organisation radically separate from existing society and had lost much of whatever working-class base it had retained before the war. The PCF was now the party which provided such an organisation and which enjoyed a solid working-class base. After the Second World War, women obtained citizenship and so, on the basis of the principles of equality, separate organisations were out of the question and the socialist women's movement, such as it was, came to an end.

The late start of the movement does not fully explain its failure. Indeed, the late start itself was largely due to the break between feminism and socialism and to the party's theoretical weakness. The SFIO's failure to develop a strong women's movement must be attributed to the limitations imposed on it as a result of Saumoneau's reaction to feminism and of the party's theoretical weakness: (a) the policy of integration; (b) the subordination of women's demands to those of the party; and (c) the functioning of the women's movement as an auxiliary to the party rather than as a movement in its own right.

The policy of integration had two disastrous consequences. In the first place it meant that, since women were treated as if they were equal to men, they had to compete with men without any consideration for the difficulties resulting from their real subordination to men. Thus the very advance of the

188

French socialist movement in accepting theoretical equality for women, the very success of Auclert and Rouzade, created an illusion of equality which prevented perception of the reality of inequality. Women who did succeed as militants in the party tended to believe in this illusory or at best limited equality. The party gave them citizenship, as Madeleine Pelletier noted. They thereby increased their self-esteem for having succeeded in the male world. But they thus became citizens of the party, thinking in the same terms as their male comrades; they ceased to be sisters to the women outside the organisation, who were still trapped in real oppression. And they did not thereby become citizens of the republic.

In the second place, the policy of integration meant that the principal focus of women's militant activity was in the male sections. The women's groups — when and where they existed at all (even under the CNDFS only half a dozen federations had them) — were only secondary to the sections. This situation, which would have been difficult to change in any case, was deliberately maintained by Saumoneau through the statutory provision that women must come to the GDFS or the CNDFS through a male section. She meant thereby to keep out the bourgeois women — and here we find the consequence of her break with the feminists in 1900 — but she probably kept out more working women. Bourgeois women after all were less intimidated by political organisations than working-class women. Indeed the experience of feminist groups accustomed them to organisational life. To come to a male section, to find oneself the only woman in a smoke-filled room where the main topic of discussion was electoral politics from which one was barred, this was an heroic undertaking for a woman in the Third Republic. And how much more comfortable would the average woman feel in a socialist section even today? Yet it was on this footing alone that all recruitment took place in the party and still does in the new PS.

Trying to act as citizens in the party, women lost sight of the fact that they did not yet have the real rights of citizens in the society. They themselves preached a subordination of women's demands to the party's needs, forgetting that the party itself was made up of men who already had the real status of citizens. The GFS congratulated the Belgian socialist women for accepting the party's decision to put women's suffrage in limbo. The CNDFS did nothing when, over thirty years later, the SFIO did the same. The nearer the party came to power, the more it feared the women's suffrage it supported in theory. When it finally came to power, it refused to upset the applecart by using that power for women's rights (though it is important to note that the Radical Party, whose participation made the Popular Front possible, would not have supported women's suffrage). At the 1935 congress a quarter of the mandates were cast against women's suffrage. In 1936, in power, the party passed over the issue, with the tacit accord of the CNDFS.

This was defensible, to be sure. The Popular Front's conquests and the fight against fascism could well seem more important than the vote. Yet the pattern of thought seems to have been simplistic, owing more to Guesde than to Marx. It was assumed that women's rights posed a threat to socialism. Yet to introduce women's suffrage in 1936 could hardly threaten the Blum government, for it was already in power and by the next election the social-ists' achievements ought to have drawn women away from the priests. In any case, for the women's organisation to defend women's rights within the party could hardly have threatened the government. Not to do so, as Auclert liked to say, was to give them up. The CNDFS did not thereby render itself more attractive to working-class women. It only confirmed its subordination to the party.

The functioning of the women's movement as an auxiliary to the party was in itself another limitation which rendered the movement less attractive. The women's movement was, strictly speaking, not a movement at all, but an 'internal commission', as Buisson called the CNDFS. It had no life of its own. It did not pretend, it did not seek to offer women the chance to participate in or decide issues for themselves. It could not give them the sense of having a say in their own destiny, but only the illusion of citizenship. The tendency during the twentieth century was more and more in this direction. The GFS had been autonomous, the GDFS somewhat so, but the CNDFS felt it beyond its role even to negotiate on the part socialist women might play in the anti-fascist movement. It consulted the CAP. Why should a woman bother with such a movement? If she were tough enough to enter the party on her own, such a limited role would seem absurd. If she were not in the party, there was nothing in such a group to attract her.

The logical culmination of such an evolution was to renounce all efforts to create a mass organisation of women linked to the party. Was this not what Saumoneau meant when she said at the 1930 congress that she would rather have no women's organisation at all than one which enjoyed any independence? Or what Suzanne Buisson meant when she said (as reported by Collette at the same congress) that it was 'not necessary to be many to do good work'?

Within these limitations, the party continued to turn in a vicious circle. The party was a male organisation, devoted to what was essentially a male preoccupation — electoral politics. So long as women did not have the vote, they did not really interest the party nor did the party interest them. The party thus did not recruit them and therefore it had no clientele of women to satisfy. The women's organisation was only an 'internal commission'. When women became citizens of the republic they had the vote and they interested the party, but now they were faced with the opposite problem. Since women had the vote, they were citizens, and since they were citizens they were indistinguishable from men and needed no organisation at all.

Conclusion

The wheel had revolved back to its starting point, but women were not and still are not members in equal numbers to men.

The architect of the women's organisation of the SFIO, one might almost say the architect of the policy of not really having any women's organisation at all, was Louise Saumoneau. This is not to say that she was the cause of the difficulties we have described. She was essentially the voice of the forces which imposed the limitations discussed above, though she was a very power-ful voice and worked hard and successfully to impose these limitations on the successive women's organisations of the party. Thus in 1914, joined by Lacore and Buisson (then under the name Gibault), she drove out not only the feminists such as Maria Vérone and Hélène Brion, but also those who strove for a synthesis of women's demands with the party's, Elisabeth Renaud above all. The prestige Saumoneau derived from her conduct during the First World War and her consequent position in the party during the 1920s enabled her to maintain the GDFS within these limitations and to stamp them on the CNDFS when it was founded, indeed to stamp them so powerfully that the party still bore her mark when it set up the Commission Nationale Féminine.

Yet, ironically, Saumoneau had also been, with Renaud, architect of the one women's organisation which transcended these limitations (though not by design): the GFS. And it is in the GFS that we see sketched an answer to our fourth question: would separate groups and more autonomous organis-ations have helped the party recruit women? We must conclude that they would have done so, though to what extent we cannot know.

In the minds of socialist women, class oppression was felt more keenly than sex oppression. This is understandable and certainly corresponds to the reality of what they experienced *vis-à-vis* the feminists. Sisterhood between women of different classes was never a reality. Marguerite Durand and Louise Saumoneau had virtually nothing in common. Whatever oppression they may have shared as women paled into insignificance beside the econ-omic oppression felt by working-class women like Saumoneau and even the generalised sense of injustice experienced by lower middle-class women from Rouzade to Buisson. Women like Durand and Pognon were not only wealthy, they were also contented with the basic structure of the society in which they lived. Thus the women who opted for socialism felt they shared much more with their fellow socialists than with the feminists.

Within the party, however, the functional bond was not that of common class oppression so much as the common engagement to seek to remedy the ills of society through political action, in a word, citizenship. This bond is what made the party work for men. For it to work for women, on the other hand, required an intellectual leap of which few women were capable, since women had neither the formal status of citizenship nor the real experience

191

of political concern in their daily lives, because their traditional roles excluded politics.

Citizenship simply did not work for women in the party. It did not provide a common bond for them. Not only did the party remain unattractive to ordinary women, but also the experience of women in the party seems to have been difficult. Even women of Saumoneau's anti-feminist persuasion commented on their difficulty in competing with men in the party, as did Lacore at the 1931 congress. Moreover, there was a high toll of personality difficulties and even personal tragedy among women in the party, of which Pelletier, Renaud, and Saumoneau were only examples. It seems reasonable to suggest that being a woman in the party was so difficult that one had to have an unusually tough personality or suffer from the tensions of trying to compete with men. Those women who escaped these difficulties seem for the most part to have accepted traditional women's roles with gusto. Indeed, women like Alice Jouenne or Suzanne Buisson come across as annoyingly well adjusted.

The only functional bond upon which women could have been brought into the party and drawn together within the party was that of their common situation as women, in a word, sisterhood. The option of the German socialist women was to emphasise sisterhood (though not by name) within the parameters of the common engagement to socialism. The effect of the class hostility which Saumoneau translated into the structures of the French socialist women's movement was to exclude this bond entirely, even though it was the only real justification for having a women's group in the party. If women had really been in the same situation as socialist men, no group would have been needed at all, except perhaps for the negative consideration which played a part in Saumoneau's actions: preventing socialist women from moving toward feminism.

What we are suggesting is that class oppression was indeed experienced as primary, sex oppression as secondary, just as the socialists thought, but that class oppression did not hold people together within the party. Instead it was their common involvement in politics that made the party interesting and attractive to men. Women generally did not have a basis for action in the party, since they had no political rights. Therefore the only bond which would have given them a meaningful basis for action in the party was that of their experience as women. In that sense, separate groups with a feminist perspective, within the limits of socialism, would have been the only viable option for organising socialist women. Madeleine Pelletier was right.

The GFS was successful enough to bear out this argument. It had three qualities which seem to have been responsible for its relative success and which mirror in reverse the limitations imposed on the later groups: it was an organisation of working-class *women*; it was autonomous from the party, with a life of its own; and it defended the demands of women as well as workers. Of course these factors were the result of circumstances which unification of the SFIO brought to an end (and which Saumoneau made certain would never be repeated). But they do suggest the outlines of a more successful socialist women's organisation than the SFIO ever developed.

First, the GFS offered an atmosphere congenial to women. It operated, however unconsciously, on a principle of sisterhood as well as citizenship. It was made up of women and was less intimidating than a male section. Women within it did not have to compete with men to play a game from which they had hitherto been excluded. This did not weaken its commitment to socialism. On the contrary, the GFS was probably more self-consciously working class and more aggressively socialist than any subsequent group. But it was a women's group. The common bond among its members was not only their common experience as proletarians, or at least their common commitment to end the exploitation of workers through socialism, but also their experience as women. Their bond as women was circumscribed by and subordinate to their situation as workers or at least as socialists, but it was nonetheless essential in the functioning of the group.

Second, the GFS was autonomous from the parties. It had a life of its own. It functioned parallel to the male sections and like them took decisions on problems which concerned its members. This was the 'autonomy and freedom of movement' which Clara Zetkin had deemed so essential to the success of the socialist women's movement in Germany. It gave women the chance to play a part, however small, in the politics which governed their lives. By taking into account the reality of their oppression instead of the fiction of their equality, by treating them as sisters instead of as citizens, the GFS gave them something which might be called a taste of real citizenship.

Third, at least while Renaud was involved in the GFS, it fought for women's demands, both within the party and within the society. It thus showed its members that they had demands of their own and an identity of their own as women as well as socialists. By contrast, the end result of the policy of integration was to ask women to give up their demands as women for what men deemed important, precisely as Auclert had feared. Women thus enjoyed a subordinate position in the party in the name of equality. Only the GFS, and it only for a brief period, gave women real citizenship within the party by ceasing to pretend that they already had it in the republic. Subsequently, Saumoneau's experience of the break with feminism, the theoretical weakness of the party, and the needs and perceptions of its leaders, both male and female, contributed to limit the socialist women's movement so severely that it could never really develop as a mass organisation, even in the party's best periods. These limitations persisted through the life of the SFIO and go a long way towards explaining why the party never developed a vital women's movement.

As for the new PS, only time will tell. But the opposition to anything

smacking of a women's group among some of the women leaders and virtually all of the male leaders suggests that the ghost of Louise Saumoneau still
hovers over the party, unbalanced by that of Elisabeth Renaud. Yvette
Roudy and Véronique Neiertz may dream of groups which would render
access to the party easier and more attractive for women, but to implement
them they would have to contend not only with many of their colleagues
but also with the shades of their predecessors.

Appendix 1 The Second International and the woman question 1889 – 1904[1]

The Second International was slow to organise itself and remained extremely loose even in its prime, in the decade before the First World War. Before 1900 it was more a convention than a high command. Its decisions carried a certain moral weight, especially with the POF, the party most committed to internationalism, but were at best no more than statements of the sense of international socialist opinion. Moreover, before unity in 1905, application of the International's resolutions in France was further hampered by the division of French socialism. The quarrels of the French even compromised the birth of the Second International. Two founding congresses were held simultaneously in Paris, July 1889: one Possibilist, organised by the FTSF, the other Marxist, organised by the POF. The Possibilists numbered two French women among their delegates: Astié de Valsayre and Mme Vincent.[2] The Marxists had Aline Valette.[3] Neither congress discussed women's rights as such, but both passed resolutions on labour legislation which included some aspects of the woman question. The Possibilists called for the abolition of night work for women and children, the Marxists for the prohibition of women from all sectors of industry 'which affect more particularly the feminine organism'. Both called for equal pay for equal work. The Marxists declared 'furthermore that it is the duty of workers to admit women into their ranks, on an equal footing'.[4]

The rights of women were brought up at the following congress of the International, at Brussels in 1891 (which, thanks to the Belgian PO, was unified). The topic was not on the agenda, but was submitted during the congress by a group of women, which did not include either of the two French women delegates, Aline Valette and one Eugénie Collot from the Paris Bourse du Travail. It was a German initiative.

The resolution submitted by the women delegates 'invites the socialist and working-class parties of all countries to affirm energetically in their programmes the complete equality of the two sexes and to seek first of all the following: "Abrogation of all the laws which place women outside of common and public law" '. (Interestingly, this is one of the resolutions Aline Valette cited to demonstrate the socialists' commitment to women's rights – cf. chapter 2; but she added two clauses which are not to be found in the official version: 'the same civil and political rights as men; . . . Equal pay for

195

equal work'.) The resolution as passed was no more than what both the Guesdists and the Broussists had already done by 1885. Nevertheless it was not accepted without question. The Belgian socialist leader Vandervelde stated that he was a 'partisan of the equality of the sexes, but believed that women should remain at home and should not be forced to do the same jobs as men. There were protests in the hall that this was not socialist.' The resolution was passed 'unanimously less three votes and vigorous applause burst forth'. The very brevity of the debate indicated the Platonic nature of the resolution. Vandervelde's was the only intervention. No question of real importance was ever decided so quickly at congresses of the International.[5]

The question of the suffrage was conspicuous by its absence. To be sure, it was included in 'complete equality' and in the 'abrogation of all the laws which place women outside of common and public law', but this was a roundabout way of putting it, rather as if the delegates wished to avoid mentioning the suffrage by name. The International did not specifically demand women's political rights until 1900 when, at the Paris congress, it passed a lengthy resolution on 'the struggle for universal suffrage and direct legislation by the people', which included the following: 'Considering that, on the basis of socialist policy, men and women have equal rights, the congress proclaims the necessity of universal suffrage for both sexes'. This position was confirmed by another, specifically devoted to 'universal suffrage for women', at the 1904 congress of Amsterdam.[6]

The International took a position on the question of women's work at the congress of Zurich in 1893. The resolution passed there settled one of the basic questions which separated feminists and socialists. The feminists refused to accept regulation of women's work except to the extent that men were regulated equally. Many feminists, for instance, supported the eight-hour day, but only on condition that it applied equally to men as well as to women. It was not only bourgeois feminists who took this position. So, for instance, did the Communard Nathalie Lemel, a leading woman syndicalist. When, at a meeting in 1886, Gustave Rouanet proposed a gamut of protective laws for women not unlike those demanded by the International in 1893, Lemel replied by denying 'any right to men to make protective laws for women assimilating them to children'. 'Women', she stated, 'do not wish to be protected'; 'women are the only judges of the work and the nature of work that they can do'. Even Aline Valette opposed regulation of women's work except for the period of maternity. Her *Cahier des doléances féminines* was careful to mention regulation only for children.[7]

Valette was not present at the 1893 congress of Zurich at which the International came down hard against this position: 'Considering that certain bourgeois feminist movements refuse all protective legislation in favour of working women, as reducing women's liberty and their equal rights vis-à-vis men', the congress argued that the feminists' stance 'leaves out . . . the character of our present society, which is based on the exploitation of the working class, of the woman as well as the man by the capitalist class'.

Insofar as the International was arguing against the freedom to sleep under a bridge or to starve, it was on solid ground. But insofar as it failed to use the most obvious argument in favour of protective legislation for women — that they were more exploited than men — and insofar as it ignored the fact that the feminists often supported regulation if both sexes were treated equally, it could be accused of perceiving woman's role primarily in terms of motherhood, as did Valette and Lafargue. There are certainly passages of the resolution which support this interpretation. The congress accused the feminists of misunderstanding 'the role assigned to women in the differentiation of the sexes, and of their role as mothers, so important for the future of the society'. Did this not suggest that women were to be reproducers rather than producers, as Valette argued? Specifically, the resolution called for:

1   The eight-hour day for women (six hours for girls under eighteen);
2   Thirty-six consecutive hours of rest each week for women;
3   No night work for women;
4   Prohibition of women from working 'in all the industries harmful to health';
5   Prohibition of women from working two weeks before and four weeks after giving birth;
6   Female inspectors in all sectors of industry employing women;
7   Application of these measures to all working women, including domestics.[8]

The International was subject to the same ambiguity we have discovered within French socialism: a commitment to equality on the one hand — undoubtedly sincere but abstract; and a commitment to traditional social roles on the other — a commitment justified by the exploitation of women in capitalism, but which nevertheless clouded the vision of women's liberation which Engels and Marx had bequeathed to international socialism.

Appendix 2   French socialist women in figures

How many women members were there in the French socialist movement of the Third Republic? I believe that women constituted roughly 2 to 3 per cent of the total membership, perhaps somewhat more in Paris. This figure is suggested by the rare objective data. Applied to the total party membership, it gives results which are borne out by witnesses and supported by my own impressions from the contemporary press.

Three objective data apply. First, Claude Willard, in his monumental study *Les Guesdistes*, was able to obtain nominal lists for a sample of one-sixth of the membership of the POF. In this sample, he counted twenty women in the period 1891–3 (which corresponded to 3 per cent of the sample) and fifty-three in the period 1894–9 (which corresponded to 2 per cent, but 'this proportion probably understates the reality'). In both cases approximately half the women members were wives or daughters of male militants. Willard believes that his sample was representative and therefore that it is reasonable to suppose that the proportion would hold true for the POF as a whole. Second, the number of women delegates at SFIO congresses before the First World War ranged from a high of ten (out of 225 at Limoges, 1906) to a low of one (out of 215 at Amiens, 1914), for an average of 5.27 women delegates per congress, or roughly 2.25 per cent. In nearly every congress where several women attended, half to two-thirds of them were the wives of male delegates. Often, the only single women at congresses were Madeleine Pelletier and Angèle Roussel, the party's token women (if I may be excused the anachronism). Third, the most important, according to a census of women members taken as of 15 March 1933, there were 2995 women in the SFIO, which corresponded to 2.17 per cent of the total membership — the lowest of all European socialist parties at the time! A year later there were 3376 women, or 2.57 per cent — little better.[1]

What results does the 2 to 3 per cent figure give us? A reasonable guess at membership in the socialist parties around 1900 would be 25,000, 2 per cent of which is 500, which may be slightly optimistic for the nation as a whole. There are no figures for the Paris membership, but assuming the relationship between Paris and the nation remained constant 1900–5, we can assume there were some 5000 socialists in the Seine federation. (It is important to remember that this corresponded to the old Department of the Seine, that is the Paris region, and not just Paris proper.) Two to three per cent of this gives us 100—150 women. Upon unification in 1905 there are precise official figures (generally borne out by police estimates): 34,688 members across the nation, 7378 in the Seine. Two to three per cent of this gives us 700—1000 women members in the nation, 150—220 in the Seine. The elections of 1914 provided the SFIO with a great leap forward in membership: from 72,765 in January to 90,725 in July 1914. This leap was, however, unlikely to include women precisely because of their depoliticisation. It therefore seems more reasonable to use the January figures, which give us 1450—2000 women. The Seine federation had reached 11,020 members by 1914, 2 to 3 per cent of which is 220—330.[2]

These figures are borne out by the recollections of women militants. Hélène Brion recalled that there were probably some 500 women in the party on the eve of the First World War; Marianne Rauze added that women had been 'isolated militants'. In 1913, Rauze had lamented that women in the party numbered 'barely a few hundred'.[3]

The penury of women in the party was a constant complaint in the contemporary socialist press. *L'Humanité* gave fairly important coverage to the progress of feminists in Anglo-Saxon countries, usually making the point that France was retrograde in comparison. Longuet lamented in 1910 that 'the organisation of the millions of proletarian women of our country . . . on the political terrain leaves unfortunately a great deal to be desired . . . only just barely do our socialist groups . . . count some hundreds of members'.

Le Socialiste ran occasional articles on the problem of drawing women into the party. In 1912, 'a young socialist woman' complained that there were no young socialist women in the provinces and so few in Paris that one would be ashamed to cite their number. Later in the same year, another militant wrote that the number of women in the party was 'infinitesimal'.[4]

On the basis of such comments, I would be inclined to round down slightly the national totals before the First World War and to maintain those suggested for the Seine. The result nationally would be less than 500 women socialists in 1900, no more than 1500 in 1914, and of course 2995 counted in 1933; for the Seine, 100—150 in 1900 and some 300 in 1914. (To estimate women membership for the Seine in 1933 would be still more difficult, because while the reconstructed SFIO more than recovered its 1922 membership — and *a fortiori* that of 1914 — reaching 130,000 members by 1932, the Seine never did so: its membership in 1930—2 varied between 7000 and 7500.)[5]

For precise figures for the 1930s, see below, table 1, which gives the results of the census of women by the Comité National des Femmes Socialistes taken each spring, generally as of the 15th March, from 1932 through 1939. In table 1 these figures are listed under and compared with the total number of membership cards taken out by 31 December of the previous

Table 1. *Women in the SFIO 1932–9*

	1932	1933	1934	1935	1936	1937	1938	1939
Number of women registered with the Seine federation as of 15 March	350	588	600	666	722	1328	2228	1200[a]
Number of women registered with the party (nationally) as of 15 March[b]	1571[c]	2995	3376	3576	4012	6648	9568	8394
Number of women registering to vote in elections for CNDFS	1002	900[d]	?	?	684	1100[d]	1500[d]	900[d]
Total party membership (membership cards taken out as of the *preceding* 31 December)[b]	130864	137684	131044	110000	120083	202000	286604	275373
Women registered as a percentage of total membership	1.2[e]	2.17[f]	2.57[f]	3.25[g]	3.34[g]	3.29[g]	3.34[g]	3.05[f]

a Membership in the Seine federation dropped by half as a result of a schism.
b Algeria and Morocco included.
c Incomplete census.
d Approximate figures based on the votes obtained by the leading candidates.
e Percentage based on incomplete census of women; the true percentage would certainly be similar to 1933.
f Percentages slightly below the likely reality because the census of women took place three months after the count of cards taken out in a period of overall membership decline.
g Percentages slightly above the likely reality because the census of women took place three months after the count of cards taken out in a period of overall membership increase.

Sources: Parti Socialiste (SFIO), *XIXe congrès national 29–30–31 mai–1er juin 1932 Paris: Rapports* (Paris, 1932), p. 111;
XXXIe congrès national 20–21–22–34 mai 1934 Toulouse: Rapports (Paris, 1934), pp. 117–19;
XXXIIe congrès national 9–10–11–12 juin 1935 Mulhouse: Rapports (Paris, 1935), pp. 157–9;
XXXIVe congrès national 15, 16, 17 et 18 mai 1937 Marseille: Rapports (Paris, 1937), pp. 223–5;
XXXVIe congrès national 27, 28, 29 et 30 mai 1939 Nantes: Rapports (Paris, 1939), pp. 146, 198–200.

year. Given the three months' delay between the count of cards and the census of women, and since the party membership was rising during most of the 1930s, the percentages of women as calculated in table 1 above are somewhat optimistic for the period 1934–7. They are especially optimistic in view of the inability of the CNDFS to mobilise women, as demonstrated by the relatively low number of women who bothered to register to vote for the elections to the CNDFS: only once, in 1938, did it climb substantially above a thousand. In terms of percentages, the best turnout was in 1933, when some 900 women voted out of 2995 counted in the census, which is still less than a third. Still more troublesome for the CNDFS, the relative number of women bothering to vote (as opposed to the total counted) was in constant decline from 1933 to the war. All this bears out our contention that the number of women hardly rose above 3 per cent, even after the constitution of the CNDFS.

Appendix 3   Elisabeth Renaud and the Cambier affair

Renaud's decision to resign from the SFIO in January 1914 was the result of the Cambier affair, known at the time as the 'Affaire du Grand Air'. This was a dispute between Achille and Gabrielle Cambier on the one hand, and the party hierarchy on the other, about the status of a party summer camp called the 'Grand Air'. The camp was founded in 1909. For tax reasons, it was put in the name of an independent board with the understanding that it really belonged to the party. Gabrielle Cambier was director of the camp. At the end of 1911, she was removed as director after numerous disputes with the board. In turn she claimed that certain members of the board, among them a number of leading socialists, were trying to run the camp for their own profit. They then accused her of having ruined the finances of the camp. She brought suit for defamation.[1]

The dispute had political ramifications. The Cambiers were militants on the non-Hervéist extreme left of the party. In May 1913, they began publishing a weekly, *La Lutte de classe*, to defend themselves and to continue their battle against the SFIO's electoralism and collaboration with bourgeois parties. Renaud and Jean Allemane were among its collaborators from the beginning. The national council of the party, at its plenary meeting in July, passed a resolution asking militants not to collaborate with the Cambiers' journal because they were using 'disloyal' tactics. The resolution was based both on the Cambiers' decision to take the 'Affaire du Grand Air' to trial and on their harsh criticisms of party policies. Although they withdrew their suit, they were expelled from the party in December 1913. Renaud resigned in solidarity a few weeks later.[2]

Renaud's involvement with the Cambiers led her (and Toussaint-Kassky) not only to quit the SFIO but to join them and Allemane in the founding of a new Parti Ouvrier (PO). In the spring of 1914, at the age of sixty-eight, she embarked anew as a militant, giving all she had in a hopeless cause. In the mirror of this last effort we see her at her best before the winds of war and time carried her off the stage of social struggle.

It will be the task of the historian of the Allemanists to judge the merits of the Cambiers' case. Even the SFIO in its heroic years undoubtedly had a seamy underside. The police noted in 1913 the development of a mass of party bureaucrats 'sheltered behind their position, well paid, [who] are sometimes rather highhanded with the mass of party members'. It is certain that there was an ascendance of professionals in the unified party and that it included an increasing number of *petit bourgeois* in its electoral base. Moreover, it was a party which was ready at least to support certain kinds of Radical ministries. The congress of Amiens, in January 1914, agreed that socialist candidates could withdraw in favour of Radicals whose positions met certain standards. This stand was taken unanimously: even Hervé (taking the second step in his swing to the right) announced that he was now in favour of an alliance ('bloc') with the Radicals. The police linked Allemane's departure to this decision.[3]

The Allemane–Cambier–Renaud faction was an isolated minority seeking a return to the working-class base and the principles of an earlier period, when the socialist groups had been not national parties competing for votes but crusades educating the workers. Renaud's moral sense fitted her well for this faction. In return, it made far more use of her talents than the SFIO had ever thought of doing. A frequent contributor to *La Lutte de classe*, she was a member from the start of the committee set up to organise the new Parti Ouvrier. Adèle Toussaint-Kassky joined the committee a week after Renaud, in early February. For her too this was to be a last crusade. The Parti Ouvrier held a founding congress in early March: Renaud was elected to the party's Conseil Central and Toussaint-Kassky was named a substitute.[4]

On 18 March, the party brought out a new (daily) edition of *Le Cri du peuple*, to which Allemane had the rights. Renaud was a member of the editorial committee. She wrote an article every two or three days, while continuing to write for *La Lutte de classe* and fulfilling a round of speaking engagements. In her propaganda, she covered four main themes which summed up her career as a militant: to build a truly moral socialist party, to protect working women, to obtain the suffrage for women, and to combat militarism.

'It is with a soul filled with disgust that I leave your pork barrel socialism [*socialisme de l'assiette au beurre*]', she wrote. Now that 'the horizon is clearing . . . the movement is growing . . . the moment has come for the *petits bourgeois* to accept the new doctrine, to circumvent it, and, little by little, to slow down the revolutionary movement of socialism.' Socialism, she continued, must be aimed at 'the conquest of all the means of production and of exchange', at creating 'a collectivist or communist society'. The *petits bourgeois*, she complained, were turning it into 'a vulgar movement of lures, that is of reforms, as vain as they are illusory'. In the face of these tendencies, she preached a return to Marx. The task of the party, virtually the only task, was to educate the proletariat to understand the necessary evolution of society which Marx had discovered, completing the work of Darwin. There could never be, as bourgeois feminists always asked (did she recall Mme Pognon at the 1900 feminist congress?), peace between classes; the only way out was the abolition of classes. This was the only way to end the woes of working women, about which she wrote at length.[5]

On a different level, she renewed her battle for the suffrage. She even permitted herself the reproaches to the SFIO which she had always avoided. On 15 April 1914, *Le Cri du peuple* carried a long and fulsome obituary for Hubertine Auclert, written by Renaud. If in the past the socialists had put women's rights in their election programme, as did the new PO, Auclert, she said, would have come to socialism. Renaud was now prepared to do battle for the vote alongside the feminists, 'ready' she added (in the phrase of Séverine, who was undertaking the same battle) 'after the victory, to resume their places in the ranks for their class interests'. Not only did Renaud support and participate in *Le Journal*'s campaign for women's suffrage (alongside women of every possible political opinion, except the GDFS), but she also participated in and wrote about the feminist lectures being given in *Le Journal*'s assembly hall. And while the new PO lived, from April through June 1914, in both *La Lutte de classe* and *Le Cri du peuple*, she maintained a steady stream of articles on the subject. Nor was she alone. Her friend Jeanne Boyer wrote articles for women's rights (usually the suffrage) nearly every week in *La Lutte de classe*. *Le Cri du peuple* also carried frequent articles on women's suffrage. Both papers also co-operated with the feminist campaigns for the suffrage. When, in June, Séverine managed to form a federation of the feminist groups to co-ordinate the battle for the suffrage, *Le Cri du peuple* gave the event enthusiastic support.

For Renaud, the struggle against militarism was even more important than that for the vote and to it she gave all the passion of her last crusade. From the first issue of *La Lutte de classe* in May 1913, to the last numbers of *Le Cri du peuple* in June 1914, she wrote incessantly for peace: militias, arbitration, opposition to the three-year law, every path that led away from war was good in her eyes. During the summer of 1913, the Balkan war preoccupied her.[6]

But it was only under the pressure of her intense collaboration with the two newspapers in the spring of 1914 that she tried to work out a programme. Its confusion was exemplary. Hitherto she had always relied on the usual call to women to oppose the horrors of war. In her articles for *Le Cri du peuple* she went further. She recognised that those who had nothing in a society had no fatherland; for them, war was just another means by which the capitalists kept them subjugated. But like so many of the French socialists, she was first and foremost a republican. The origins of the Third Republic in the massacre of the Commune never affected her thinking. Thus she asserted, three months before the war broke out, that if despite all their efforts, France should be the victim of aggression (she envisaged no other possibility of war) the socialists would have to defend their country if only to defend the institution through which they would build socialism. In the resolution on militarism passed by the PO (and of which she was the principal author), this was resolved by pushing the question into a socialist future: the resolution called for the arming of the people instead of standing armies; this would be 'the best mode of organisation of national defence, which can and must, at a given moment in the future, become one with the defence of the social Republic itself, if France, for example, were to precede other nations in the installation of a new order'.[7]

But France did *not* precede other nations in building socialism. And through the gap in the thinking of nearly all socialists (even Engels) came the war which destroyed all hope of building socialism. Renaud supported it, like the others. In 1917, when Saumoneau was moving to the forefront of the anti-war struggle, Renaud wrote to Jules Guesde, who was now a minister without portfolio in the wartime government but also the father of her daughter's husband, that 'war to the bitter end' was 'the good cause'.[8]

But the PO died even before the war broke out. In April, the police credited it with only a hundred or so members. *Le Cri du peuple*, which had become weekly instead of daily in May, ceased publication with the 10 June issue. A week later *La Lutte de classe* published its last edition. It ended on a sad note, its columns filled with the expulsion of a group of 'traitors'.[9]

Renaud never returned to the party. Occupied with earning her living during the war, she abandoned politics completely. In 1925 she was converted to Seventh Day Adventism. She died peacefully, reading the Bible in the King James Version, on 15 October 1932. She was eighty-seven. Adèle Toussaint-Kassky had died a month before.[10]

Notes

Where appropriate I have included the name of the author of an article in a newspaper. Where no such name appears, the reader may assume that the reference is to an editorial comment, a regular column, or an anonymous report in the periodical or newspaper cited. Where only the date of the publication is given, the reader may assume that the newspaper is a small one (usually four pages) in which it will be easy to find the relevant passage.

Introduction

1 *Le Monde*, 27 Jan. 1978, p. 2.
2 Stewart Edwards, *The Paris Commune 1871* (London, 1971), pp. 346–8; J[ean]-P[aul] Azéma and M[ichel] Winock, *Les Communards* (Paris, 1964), pp. 162–9; Stewart Edwards (ed.), *The Communards of Paris, 1871* (London, 1973), p. 25.
3 Richard J. Evans, *The Feminists: Women's Emancipation Movements in Europe, America and Australasia 1840–1920* (London, 1977), pp. 18–21, 28–30.
4 *Ibid.*
5 Jacques Chastenet, *Histoire de la Troisième République*, III (Paris, 1955), 204.
6 République française, Ministère du travail et de la prévoyance sociale, Direction du travail, *Statistique générale de la France, Résultats statistiques du recensement général de la population effectué le 4 mars 1906*, I, part II, *Population présente totale, population active* (Paris, 1910); *Statistique ... effectué le 6 mars 1921*, I, part III, *Population active* (Paris, 1927); Madeleine Guilbert, *Les Femmes et l'organisation syndicale avant 1914: Présentation et commentaires de documents pour une étude du syndicalisme féminin* (Paris, 1966), pp. 11–17; Henri Nolleau, 'Les Femmes dans la population active de 1856 à 1954', *Economie et politique* (Oct. 1960), 2–21.
7 'Programme', *Le Droit des femmes* (Nov. 1882); Ligue Française pour le Droit des Femmes, *1870–1920: cinquante ans de féminisme* (Paris, 1921), pp. 89–94.
8 *Ibid.*
9 Patrick Kay Bidelman, 'Maria Deraismes, Léon Richer, and the founding of the French feminist movement, 1866–1878', *Third Republic/Troisième République* [*TR/TR*], 3/4 (1977), 23–31, 40–3. Cf. Patrick Kay Bidelman, 'The feminist movement in France: the formative years 1858–1889' (Ph.D., Michigan, 1975).
10 Bidelman, *TR/TR*, 3/4 (1977), 29–30, 55–6. Cf. Evans, pp. 126–7.
11 Bidelman, *TR/TR*, 3/4 (1977), 50–6; Evans, 126–7.
12 Charles Sowerwine, 'The organisation of French socialist women, 1880–1914: a European perspective for women's movements', *Historical Reflections/Réflexions Historiques* (*HR/RH*), III, 2 (1976), 3–24, esp. 22–3. Steven C. Hause and Anne R. Kenney, 'Legalism and violence in the French women's suffrage movement, 1901–1914' (University of Missouri–St Louis, History Department Colloquium, Mar. 1978).
13 Gordon Wright, *France in Modern Times*, 2nd edn (Chicago, 1974), p. 160. Cf. Tom Kemp, *Economic Forces in French History: An Essay on the Development of the French Economy, 1760–1914* (London, 1971), pp. 155–204.

14 Louise A. Tilly and Joan W. Scott, *Women, Work, and Family* (New York, 1978), pp. 61–77, 123–5.
15 Joan W. Scott and Louise A. Tilly, 'Women's work and the family in nineteenth-century Europe', *Comparative Studies in Society and History*, XVII (1975), 50–61.
16 République française, *Statistique . . . effectué le 4 mars 1906*, vol. I, part II, *Population présente totale, population active*; République française, *Statistique . . . effectué le 6 mars 1921*, vol. I, part III, *Population active*; Guilbert, pp. 11–17; Nolleau, *Economie et politique* (Oct. 1960), pp. 2–21.
17 Tilly and Scott, *Women, Work, and Family*, p. 77.
18 République française, Ministère du commerce, de l'industrie, des postes et des télégraphes, Office du travail, *Salaires et durée du travail dans l'industrie française*, IV, *Résultats généraux* (Paris, 1897), 252.
19 Claude Weyl, *La Réglementation du travail des femmes dans l'industrie (loi du 2 novembre 1892)* (Paris, 1898), pp. 23–5; République française . . . Office du travail, *Salaires et durée du travail*, IV, 262–87.
20 Charles Benoist, *Les Ouvrières de l'aiguille à Paris: Notes pour l'étude de la question sociale* (Paris, 1895), p. 21.
21 Jules Simon, *L'Ouvrière*, 7th edn (Paris, 1871), pp. 286–300. For an analogous model budget for the end of the century, see [Gabriel Paul Othenin de Cléron] Comte d'Haussonville, *Salaires et misères de femmes* (Paris, 1900), pp. 4–10.
22 Weyl, pp. 23–5; République française . . . Office du travail, *Salaires et durée du travail*, IV, 265–87.
23 Bernard H. Moss, *The Origins of the French Labor Movement 1830–1914: The Socialism of Skilled Workers* (Berkeley, California, 1976), pp. 37, 51.
24 Pierre-Joseph Proudhon, *La Pornocratie ou les femmes dans les temps modernes (oeuvres posthumes de P.-J. Proudhon)* (Paris, 1875), p. 262. He went on: 'Rather [than] see woman emancipated, as some desire, I would prefer to put her in seclusion.' Cf. Evelyne Sullerot, *Histoire et sociologie du travail féminin* (Paris, 1968), p. 86. Courbet's portrait is reproduced on the cover of Stewart Edwards (ed.), *Selected Writings of Pierre-Joseph Proudhon* (London, 1970).
25 Moss, p. 51; Pierre-Joseph Proudhon, *De la capacité politique des classes ouvrières* (Paris, 1865).
26 Claude Willard, *Les Guesdistes: Le mouvement socialiste en France (1893–1905)* (Paris, 1959), p. 13.
27 *L'Egalité: Journal républicain socialiste* (18 Nov. 1877); Moss, p. 103.
28 Maurice Dommanget, *L'Introduction du Marxisme en France* (Lausanne, 1969), pp. 153–60; Willard, *Les Guesdistes*, pp. 159–68; Alexandre Zévaès, *Jules Guesde (1845–1922)* (Paris, 1928), pp. 36–8. For a full discussion of Guesde's thinking on the woman question, see chapter 2, below.
29 Karl Marx, 'Economic and philosophical manuscripts' in Erich Fromm, *Marx's Concept of Man* (New York, 1961), p. 125; Karl Marx and Frederick Engels, 'Manifesto of the Communist Party', in David Fernbach (ed.), *Karl Marx, The Revolutions of 1848*, The Pelican Marx Library, I (Harmondsworth, Middlesex, 1973), pp. 83–4.
30 Karl Marx, *Capital: A Critique of Political Economy*, tr. by Ben Fowkes, I (Harmondsworth, Middlesex, 1976), pp. 620–1.
31 Werner Thönnessen, *The Emancipation of Women: The Rise and Decline of the Women's Movement in German Social Democracy 1863– 1933*, tr. by Joris de Brès ([London], 1973), p. 36; Lewis A. Coser, Introduction to August Bebel, *Woman Under Socialism*, tr. by Daniel de Léon, (re-impression, New York, 1971), p. vii.
32 Bebel, pp. 39, 80, 119, 140, 182, 187, 188, 216ff, 224ff.
33 Quoted by Jean H. Quataert, 'Unequal partners in an uneasy alliance: women and the working class in Imperial Germany', in Marilyn J. Boxer and Jean H. Quataert (eds.), *Socialist Women: European Socialist Feminism in the Nineteenth and early Twentieth Centuries* (New York, 1978), p. 120.
34 Bebel, pp. 5, 121.

35 Frederick Engels, *The Origin of the Family, Private Property, and the State*, tr. by Alec West (New York, 1972), pp. 137–8.
36 *Ibid.*
37 Thönnessen, pp. 46, 48; Jean H. Quartaert [Quataert], 'Feminist tactics in German social democracy: a dilemma', *Internationale wissenschaftliche Korrespondenz zur Geschichte der deutschen Arbeiterbewegung*, 13 (Mar. 1977), 51.
38 Karen Honeycutt, 'Clara Zetkin: a socialist approach to the problem of women's oppression' *Feminist Studies*, III, 3/4 (1976), 137, 140; Karen Honeycutt, 'Socialism and feminism in Imperial Germany', *Signs*, V, 1 (1979), 30–55.
39 Thönnessen, pp. 44–5, 49; Honeycutt, *Feminist Studies*, III, 3/4 (1976), 116, 131.
40 Quataert, p. 52; Thönnessen, p. 116.

1. Women and the beginnings of the socialist movement 1876—82

1 *Séances du congrès ouvrier de France, session de 1876, tenue à Paris du 2 au 10 octobre* (Paris, 1877), pp. 85–7. For the origins of the congress, see Daniel Ligou, *Histoire du socialisme en France (1871–1961)* (Paris, 1963), p. 18, and Georges Lefranc, *Le Mouvement socialiste sous la Troisième République* (Paris, 1963), pp. 27–8.
2 *Congrès ouvrier Paris 1876*, pp. 69, 67–107.
3 *Ibid.*, pp. 510, 512–13. The committee which drafted the resolution included two women.
4 *Séances du congrès ouvrier de France, deuxième session, tenue à Lyon du 28 janvier au 8 février 1878* (Lyons, 1878), pp. 34, 45–6, 48, 63. A typical male delegate argued, 'Let her be given the work which best suits her sex; let her leave the interior of her home as rarely as possible; let her, finally, as equal and companion of man, receive for her work the same recompense' (*ibid.*, p. 48).
5 *Ibid.*, pp. 52, 53, 65, 592; Proudhon, *La Pornocratie*.
6 From L'Association du Droit des Femmes to La Société pour l'Amélioration du Sort de la Femme; their newspaper, *Le Droit des femmes*, became *L'Avenir des femmes*.
7 *L'Avenir des femmes*, Jan. 1876; Ligue Française, *1870–1920*, pp. 3–4; *Congrès international du droit des femmes, ouvert à Paris, le 25 juillet 1878, clos le 9 août suitant: Actes, compte rendu des séances plénières* (Paris, n.d.), pp. 1n, 1–4. For the congress, see Bidelman, *TR/TR*, 3/4 (1977), pp. 65–73.
8 *Le Droit politique des femmes, question qui n'est pas traitée au congrès international des femmes* (Paris, 1878), p. 4. For Auclert's life, see the introduction (by her sister, Marie Chaumont) to her *Les Femmes au gouvernail* (Paris, 1923), esp. p. 6; dossier Auclert, BMD; and Auclert's preface to Draigu [Léon Giraud], *Le Roman de la femme chrétienne: étude historique* (Paris, 1880), p. 3.
9 Michelle Perrot, 'Le Premier journal marxiste français, "L'Egalité" de Jules Guesde, 1877–1883', *Actualité de l'histoire*, 28 (1959), 1–26; *Le Prolétaire*, 28 Dec. 1878– 29 Jan. 1879.
10 *Séances du congrès ouvrier socialiste de France, troisième session, tenue à Marseille du 20 au 31 octobre 1879* (Marseilles, 1879), pp. 148–51, 153.
11 *Ibid.*, pp. 163, 169, 222–3. One delegate, Lombard, protested against this denial of freedom of speech by refusing to read his own report (p. 223). Lombard was Guesde's personal representative at the congress (Willard, *Les Guesdistes*, pp. 15– 16). Should we conclude from this that the Guesdists were already hostile to women's rights as at the 1880 UFS congress (cf. below, pp. 32–3)?
12 Nine delegates, including four women, read reports in favour of complete equality for women; five, all of them men, expressed some reservations; and one, a man, was hostile to it (*Congrès ouvrier Marseille 1879*, pp. 148–223). This does not include Lombard (see previous note).
13 *Ibid.*; Auclert, *Les Femmes au gouvernail*, p. 10.

14 *Congrès ouvrier Marseille 1879*, pp. 802—3.
15 *Ibid.*, pp. 154—5, 802—3.
16 *Le Prolétaire*, 24 Jan. (p. 6), 27 Mar. (p. 8), 3 Apr. (p. 4), 18 Dec. 1880.
17 Jean Maitron (ed.), *Dictionnaire biographique du Mouvement Ouvrier français* ([*DMO*], 15 vols. to date, Paris, 1962—   ), VII, 369—70, XIV, 106—7; Edith Thomas, *The Women Incendiaries*, tr. by J. and S. Atkinson (New York, 1966), pp. 28, 116, 205; Gustave Lefrançais, *Souvenirs d'un révolutionnaire* (Paris, 1972), p. 260; *Les Mouches et l'araignée* (Paris), 17, 24 Dec. 1869; *La Revue socialiste* (1891, I), 341; Paule Mink, *Le Travail des Femmes: discours prononcé par Mme Paul [sic] Mink à la réunion publique du Vauxhall le 13 juillet 1868* (Paris, n.d.).
18 *Le Petit Havre*, 15, 16 Nov. 1880 (dossier, MS); Léon de Seilhac, *Les Congrès ouvriers en France de 1876 à 1897* (Paris, 1899), pp. 61ff.
19 *Le Petit Havre*, 19, 23 Nov. 1880.
20 *Le Ve congrès national ouvrier socialiste tenu à Paris du 27 novembre au 5 décembre 1881* (ms account, MS); *Le VIe congrès national ouvrier de Bordeaux, septembre 1882* (ms account, MS); *Le Prolétaire*, 11 Dec. 1880; Auclert, *Les Femmes au gouvernail*, pp. 6, 359; *Le Cri du peuple*, 15 Apr. 1914. Richer took back the name *Le Droit des Femmes* in 1882, when he founded the Ligue Française pour le Droit des Femmes.
21 'Biographies', *L'Equité*, 1 May 1914; 'Biographie', *La Femme affranchie*, 23—4 (Aug.—Sept. 1906), 12—13; 'Voix voilées', *La Citoyenne*, Oct. 1885; Jehan des Etrivières [Astié de Valsayre], *Les Amazones du siècle (les gueulardes de Gambetta)* (Paris, 1882), p. 11.
22 Léonie Rouzade, *Connais-toi toi-même* (Paris, 1871); *Ci et ça, ça et là* (Paris, 1872).
23 Léonie Rouzade, *Le Monde renversé* (Paris, 1872); *Voyage de Théodose à l'île d'Utopie* (Paris, 1872); *Le Roi Johanne* (Paris, 1872).
24 *Congrès du droit des femmes Paris 1878*, p. 10; des Etrivières, pp. 10—14; *Le Prolétaire*, 29 Jan., 16 Aug. (p. 8), 13 Sept. (p. 7), 22 Nov. (p. 7) 1879; 10 Jan. (p. 7), 7 Feb. (p. 5), 6 Mar. (p. 6), 27 Mar. (p. 2), 17 Apr. (p. 6) 1880.
25 Bidelman, *TR/TR*, 3/4 (1977), 65—6; *Le Prolétaire*, 28 Feb. 1880 (p. 5); AN, BB24 852, No 732, S. 79; Thomas, *The Women Incendiaries*, pp. 10—15, 66—87, 116—17, 216; Jules Paty [Marguerite Tinayre], *La Marguerite* (Paris, 1864, according to Thomas, p. 11 — I have not located a copy) and *Un Rêve de femme* (2 vols., Paris, 1865).
26 Léonie Rouzade, *Développement du programme de la société 'l'Union des Femmes'* (Paris, 1880), pp. 10—11, 13, 23.
27 *Les Droits de l'homme*, 16, 18 Oct. 1876.
28 *L'Egalité*, 28 July 1880.
29 *Le Prolétaire*, 31 July 1880. Kéva was listed as *passementière* (lace and trim maker), Pierre and Tinayre as teachers.
30 *Ibid.*; *L'Egalité*, 28 July 1880.
31 *Le Petit Havre*, 17, 21, 23 Nov. 1880. Cf. *Le Prolétaire*, 4 Sept. 1880 (p. 2).
32 [Mink], *Le Travail des femmes*; *DMO*, XIV, 106; Thomas, *The Women Incendiaries*, p. 28.
33 *Le Petit Havre*, 21, 23 Nov. 1880.
34 *Ibid.* Cf. 'Résolutions du 4e congrès national ouvrier socialiste tenu au Havre', Parti Ouvrier Socialiste Français (POSF), *Compte rendu du 5e congrès national tenu à Reims du 30 octobre au 6 novembre 1881* (Paris, 1882), p. 85; Willard, *Les Guesdistes*, p. 19.
35 *Ibid.*; 'Programme', *L'Egalité*, 21 Jan. 1880, 30 June 1880; Willard, *Les Guesdistes*, pp. 94—6. The London and Le Havre versions of the programme must be distinguished from the version as amended at Roanne in 1882 (see below, p. 45), which became definitive. Lefranc (pp. 395—6) and Claude Willard (ed., *Jules Guesde: textes choisis [1867—1882]* [Paris, 1959], pp. 117—19) both give the Roanne version, Lefranc calling it the Le Havre version, Willard calling it the London version.
36 We have hardly any information for Roger and Legall. A man named Legal[l?],

'employé [white collar worker]', was a delegate at the 1880 UFC congress of the Cercle d'Etudes Sociales du 12e Arrondissement (*Le Prolétaire*, 31 July 1880), which supported Rouzade's candidature (see below, p. 37); was he the husband of Ismène?

37 *Le Prolétaire*, 27 Nov. 1880, 1 Jan., 19 Feb., 16 Apr. 1880. The Union probably participated in the second congress of the UFC, where a resolution in favour of 'free love' was passed (*ibid.*, 11 June 1881), but there is no record of the delegates at the congress.

38 *Ibid.*, 2 Apr., 7, 21 May, 2, 9, 23 July, 17 Sept., 1, 8 Oct., 26 Nov., 2 Dec. 1881; Adéodat Compère-Morel, *Jules Guesde, le socialisme fait homme, 1845—1922* (Paris, 1937), p. 198.

39 POSF, *Congrès Reims 1881*, pp. 12, 13, 110; *Le Prolétaire*, 1 Oct., 26 Nov., 2 Dec. 1881.

40 The feminist pioneer Jeanne Deroin stood for the Chamber in 1849, but this was an isolated, personal effort, without the backing of any regular political organisation (Alexander Zévaès, 'Une candidature féministe en 1849', *Révolution de 1848*, 28 [1931—2], 127—34; Thomas, *The Women Incendiaries*, p. 140).

41 *Le Petit Havre*, 21 Nov. 1880; *Le Havre*, 21, 22 Nov. 1880 (see file on the congress, AN F7 12.489).

42 *Le Prolétaire*, 1 Jan. 1881 (p. 4); Willard, *Les Guesdistes*, p. 12n; *Le Citoyen de Paris*, 22 Dec. 1880.

43 *Le Prolétaire*, 13 Aug. 1881; *La Citoyenne*, 19 Dec. 1881; APP B/a 549, 20 Nov. 1881.

44 As was customary, the voter registration card was required at the entrance (APP B/a 549, 7 Dec. 1881). This obviously prevented women from attending, as they had no cards. How did Rouzade get in?

45 *Ibid.* There was a second official election meeting, but Rouzade did not go; Roblet spoke for her (APP B/a 549, 10 Dec. 1881).

46 APP B/a 549, 9 Dec. 1881; *La Citoyenne*, 12, 19 Dec. 1881; *Le Citoyen*, 11 Dec. 1881.

47 'Biographies', *L'Equité*, May 1914; *Le Prolétaire*, 10 Dec. 1881 (p. 3); APP B/a 549 for the manifesto, which was signed by Angélique Salve, Marie Pie, Ismène Legall, Léopol [sic] Florentine Bigot, Marie Bruchu, and Elise Roger.

48 *Le Prolétaire*, 10 Dec. (pp. 1, 3), 24 Dec. 1881.

49 *Ibid.*, 11, 17, 24 Dec. 1881; *La Citoyenne*, 18 Dec. 1881; APP B/a 549, 11 Dec. 1881; *Le Figaro*, 12 Dec. 1881; *Le Temps*, *Le Rappel*, *Le National*, 13 Dec. 1881.

50 *Le Prolétaire*, 24 Dec. 1881; *Le Citoyen*, 22 Dec. 1881 (AR, Versailles annex).

51 POSF, *Congrès Reims 1881*, *passim*; Ligou, pp. 45—6; *L'Egalité*, 11 Dec. 1881; *Le Prolétaire*, 7 Jan. 1882.

52 She played an important role at Reims as member of the organising commission and delegate of the Comité Fédéral de la Région de l'Est (POSF, *Congrès Reims 1881*, pp. 6, 65).

53 Parti Ouvrier Socialiste Révolutionnaire Français (POSRF), *Compte rendu du sixième congrès tenu à St-Etienne du 25 au 31 [sic] septembre 1882* (Paris, 1882), p. 164; *Sixième congrès national du Parti ouvrier tenu à Roanne du mardi 26 septembre au dimanche 1er octobre 1882* (Paris, 1882), p. 26. Three women remained at Saint-Etienne with the Broussists: Gillier; Louise Joanny; and Paule Mink, who stayed only to show the reformists the error of their ways (POSRF, *Congrès St-Etienne 1882*, p. 108). In 1884, Mink was a delegate to the Guesdist congress (*Septième congrès national du Parti ouvrier tenu à Roubaix du 29 mars au 7 avril 1884* [Paris, n.d.]).

54 Two women went with the Guesdists to Roanne: Roche and Laurent (POSRF, *Congrès St-Etienne 1882*, pp. 9—15; *L'Egalité*, 1 Oct. 1882).

55 *Le Prolétaire*, 24 Feb., 4, 11, 25 Mar., 1 Apr., 6, 20 May, 19 Aug. 1882; Benoît Malon, *Oeuvres complètes: Le nouveau parti*, II: *Le Parti ouvrier et sa politique* (Paris, 1882), 115—19.

56 Rouzade, 'Le Socialisme', *La Revue socialiste* (1885, I), 97–8; 'Les Femmes devant la démocratie', *ibid.* (1887, I), 519–34; *La Femme et le peuple, organisation sociale de demain* (Meudon, 1896, 1905); *Petit catéchisme de morale laïque et socialiste* (Meudon, 1895, 1903, 1904, 1906). Rouzade was buried on 27 October 1916 (dossier Rouzade, BMD).

57 Jean Guétré [Marguerite Tinayre] and Louise Michel, *Les Méprisées* (Paris, n.d.), *La Misère* (Paris, n.d.); Edith Thomas, *Louise Michel ou la velléda de l'anarchie* (Paris, 1971), p. 298; Thomas, *The Women Incendiaries*, pp. 116–17.

58 The classic statement of this argument is Georges Duveau's *1848: The Making of a Revolution*, tr. by Anne Carter (New York, 1967). It was of course inspired by Marx's brilliant pamphlets, *The Class Struggles in France: 1848–1850* and *The Eighteenth Brumaire of Louis Bonaparte*. Roger Price led the attacks on this tradition with *The French Second Republic: A Social History* (London, 1972), but moved closer to it subsequently in his excellent introduction to Roger Price (ed.), *1848 in France* (London, 1975).

59 *Le Prolétaire*, 13, 20 May, 17 June, 9 Sept., 11, 19 Nov., 9 Dec. 1882; Fédération des Travailleurs Socialistes de France, *Compte rendu du 7e congrès national tenu à Paris du 30 septembre au 7 octobre 1883* (Paris, 1883). The delegates of the Union to the 1883 UFC congress were Pie, Dupré, and Pignon (*Le Prolétaire*, 19 May 1883); to the 1884 congress, Marie Dupré and Isménie [*sic*] Legall (*ibid.*, 12, 19, 26 Apr., 3 May 1884).

60 *Le Prolétaire*, 6, 13, 20 Sept. 1884.

61 *L'Egalité*, 8 Oct. 1882; AN F7 12.489 ('congrès 1882').

62 *Ibid.*, 23 May 1885; POSRF, *Congrès St-Etienne 1882*, pp. 165n. 166ff.; FTSF, POSR, *Compte rendu du XIe congrès national tenu à Charleville du 2 au 8 octobre 1887* (Paris, 1888), p. 55.

63 Benoît Malon, *Le Socialisme intégral* (2 vols., Paris, 1890–1), I, 358–61; Malon, *Le Parti ouvrier*, pp. 115–19.

64 *Le Prolétaire*, 26 Mar., 24 Dec. 1881, 7 June 1882, 7 Jan. 1883.

2. Socialist parties in search of women 1882–99

1 These developments are sketched clearly in James Joll, *The Second International 1889–1914*, 2nd ed. (London, 1974), pp. 14–17, and discussed in more detail and with excellent bibliographical indications in R.D. Anderson, *France 1870–1914: Politics and Society* (London, 1977), chapter 8. A particularly enjoyable account is Harvey Goldberg, *The Life of Jean Jaurès* (Madison, 1962). The best analyses are Madeleine Rebérioux, 'Le Socialisme français de 1871 à 1914', in Jacques Droz (ed.), *Histoire générale du socialisme*, II, *De 1875 à 1918* (Paris, 1974), 155–71, and Moss, pp. 121–35.

2 Cf. Anderson, chapter 1; D.W. Brogan's classic, *The Development of Modern France*, 2nd ed. (London, 1967), pp. 183–8; and, for an excellent analysis of the socialists and Boulanger, Goldberg, pp. 46–56.

3 Willard, *Les Guesdistes*, p. 59.

4 Cf. Maurice Dommanget, *Edouard Vaillant: Un grand socialiste (1840–1915)* (Paris, 1956), p. 24 and *passim*; Jolyon Howorth, 'The Myth of Blanquism under the Third Republic (1871–1900)', *The Journal of Modern History*, XLVIII, 3 (1976), IJ-00010. I am indebted to Jolyon Howorth for corrections to this section.

5 Malon, *Le Socialisme intégral*, I, 329–43; 'Le Socialisme dans les corps élus', *La Revue socialiste*, Jan. 1888, p. 88. Cf. Charles Letourneau, *L'Evolution du mariage et de la famille* (Paris, 1888). For Lafargue's work, see below, pp. 56–9.

6 Cf. Michel Winock, 'Naissance du parti "allemaniste" ', *Le Mouvement social*, 75 (Apr. 1971), 31–63.

7 *DMO*, X, 332; *Revue encyclopédique Larousse*, 28 Nov. 1896; dossier Bonnevial, BMD; Ligue Française, *1870–1920*; *Le Congrès ouvrier international socialiste*

devant la Xe Chambre [Paris, 1879], pp. 119—24; *Le Prolétaire*, 19 June—17 July 1886. Bonnevial was born on 28 June 1841 at Rive-de-Gier and died on 4 December 1918 at Paris.

8 Hélène Brion, 'Squelette ébauche de la grande encyclopédie féministe' (ms, 6 vols., BMD), I, 50; Jean Misère [Astié de Valsayre], *Le Retour de l'exilé* (Paris, 1887); Astié de Valsayre, *Mémoire sur l'utilité de l'enseignement de la grammaire dans l'instruction de la femme* (Paris, 1883). Brion states that Astié was born at Paris in 1846.

9 *Le Prolétariat*, 13, 20 Aug. 1887; *La Citoyenne*, Sept. 1887.

10 *Le Prolétariat*, 23, 30 June 1888; FTSF, *Compte rendu du IXe congrès régional de l'Union fédérative du centre, tenu à Paris du 17 au 26 Juin 1888* (Paris, 1888), pp. 26, 79, 126; *La Citoyenne*, Aug. 1888 (where Astié claimed to have also obtained the insertion, in the resolution on education, of a phrase calling for 'similar education for both sexes').

11 *Le Prolétariat*, 1 July 1888; *La Citoyenne*, Aug., Dec. 1888.

12 FTSF, *Compte rendu du congrès international ouvrier socialiste tenu à Paris du 15 au 20 juillet 1889* (Paris, 1891), p. 42; *Bulletin de l'Union universelle des femmes*, Apr. 1891; FTSF, *Compte rendu du Xe congrès régional de l'Union fédérative du centre, tenu à Paris, les 1er, 2, 3 et 5 octobre 1890 et les 12—17 mai 1891* (Paris, 1891), p. 47. The congress had two 'sessions', the first on 'discipline', the second (after the schism) on issues. The League was represented only at the second. The other two delegates were Brou and Charrière.

13 *La Citoyenne*, Nov. 1890. The Patronage did have a feminist side: it had a delegate in the Fédération Française des Sociétés Féministes (see below, pp. 60, 62—3, 68—9).

14 La mère Marthe [Astié de Valsayre], *L'Aisance par l'économie* (Epinal, 1892); POSR, *Compte rendu du Xe congrès national tenu à Paris du 12 au 19 juin 1891* (Paris, 1892), p. 24. There were two other delegates of the League: Charrière and Marette. The League chugged along until 1895 (APP, B/a 1651, *passim*).

15 Dossier Vincent, BMD (includes an ms autobiography); dossier Egalité, BMD; *Bulletin de l'Union française pour le suffrage*, Jan.—Mar. 1914; *Le Droit des femmes*, 15 Mar. 1914, p. 53; *La Citoyenne*, Aug. 1889; *Congrès français et international du droit des femmes, 1889 [Paris, 15—19 juin]* (Paris, 1889), p. 128. Born near Dreux in 1841, Mme Vincent died at her home at Asnières on 20 February 1914. In 1866, she joined André Léo and Maria Deraismes in founding the Société pour la Revendication des Droits de la Femme (Bidelman, *TR/TR*, 3/4 [1977], 28—9).

16 FTSF, *Congrès international Paris, 1889*, p. 42; 'Le Palais des femmes', *La Question sociale*, 1 Aug. 1892, pp. 277—8; 'La Solidarité des femmes', *Le Journal des femmes*, Sept. 1892; POSR, Fédération du Centre, *Compte rendu du XIe congrès régional de l'Union fédérative du centre, tenu à Paris du 21 août au 11 septembre 1892* (Paris, 1892), p. 36; Charles Sowerwine, *Les Femmes et le socialisme: un siècle d'histoire* (Paris, 1978), p. 48 and n.

17 POSR, *Compte rendu du XIe congrès national tenu à Saint-Quentin du 2 au 9 octobre 1892* (Paris, 1893), pp. 54—5 (Art. 4, 13); Jean Allemane, *Notre programme développé et commenté, suivi d'un projet de règlement de groupe* (Paris, 1895), p. 32; *Programme municipal adopté par l'Union fédérative du centre, commenté* (Paris, n.d.), pp. 10—47.

18 POSR, *Compte rendu du XIIe congrès national tenu à Dijon du 14 au 22 juillet 1894* (Dijon, 1895), pp. 45—6; AN F7 12.490 (report on same congress). Cf. Eugénie Potonié-Pierre, 'La Campagne électorale féminine', *La Question sociale*, 15 Nov. 1892, p. 386.

19 POSR, *Compte rendu du XIVe congrès national tenu à Paris [24—25 septembre 1896]* (Paris, 1897); POSR, *Compte rendu du XVe congrès national tenu à Paris [26—28 septembre, 1, 3, 5 octobre 1897]* (Paris, 1898).

20 Willard, *Les Guesdistes*, pp. 77, 159; Emile Bottigelli (ed.), *Friedrich Engels, Paul et Laura Lafargue: correspondance* (3 vols., Paris, 1956—9), I, 149, 301, 332.

21   Lefranc, p. 43; Maurice Dommanget, *L'Introduction du marxisme en France* (Paris, 1969), pp. 67ff.
22   Willard, *Les Guesdistes*, pp. 160—1.
23   *L'Egalité*, 22, 24 Oct.—6 Nov. 1882; Bottigelli (ed.), *Engels—Lafargue: Correspondance*, I, 327, 330—3.
24   *Le Cri du peuple*, 12 June 1884.
25   Jules Guesde and Paul Lafargue, *Le Programme du Parti ouvrier: son histoire, ses considérants, ses articles* (Paris, 1883), pp. 59, 96—8.
26   *Ibid.*
27   Engels, pp. 137ff, 221. Cf. David McLellan, *Karl Marx, His Life and Works* (London, 1973), p. 424.
28   Bebel, p. 31; Engels, pp. 76—7; Paul Lafargue, 'Le Matriarcat: Etude sur les origines de la famille', *Le Socialiste*, 4 Sept.—16 Oct. 1886; 'Le Matriarcat', *La Nouvelle Revue*, Mar. 1886, pp. 301—36. Bottigelli (ed.), *Engels—Lafargue: Correspondance*, I, 203, 239, 300, 347; III, 281.
29   *Ibid.*, III, 62; August Bebel, *La Femme dans le passé, le présent et l'avenir*, tr. by H. Ravé, (Paris, 1891) — this was the title of the first German edition.
30   P. Argyriadès, *La Femme et le socialisme: Traduction analytique de l'ouvrage de Bebel* (Paris, n.d.). Member of the Commission Administrative of the CRC from 1890 until his death in 1901 (note from J. Howorth), Argyriadès edited *La Question sociale*, which was sympathetic to feminism: Chéliga, Potonié-Pierre and Mink collaborated in it and Mink was editorial secretary from September 1894 until its demise in 1897.
31   Bottigelli (ed.), *Engels—Lafargue: Correspondance*, III, 283, 326; Charles Vérecque, 'A toutes les femmes', *Le Travailleur picard* (Amiens), 5—9 Aug. 1893, reprinted in Charles Vérecque, *Histoire de la famille des temps sauvages à nos jours* (Paris, 1914), pp. 254—8. Vérecque's book depended entirely on Lafargue; chapter 13 was virtually plagiarised from 'Le Matriarcat'.
32   Paul Lafargue, *La Question de la femme* (Paris, 1904); 'La Femme', *L'Humanité*, 14 Aug. 1906.
33   H. Ghesquière, *La Femme et le socialisme* (Lille, 1893).
34   Bebel, p. 343; Engels, pp. 139—46.
35   Marie Bonnevial, 'Aline Valette', *La Fronde*, 23 Mar. 1899; Adéodat Compère-Morel, *Grand dictionnaire socialiste du mouvement politique et économique national et international* (Paris, [1924]); Charles Vérecque, 'Aline Valette', *La Femme socialiste* (*FS*), Dec. 1932; Willard, *Les Guesdistes*, p. 648; Marilyn J. Boxer, 'Socialism faces feminism: the failure of synthesis in France, 1879—1913', in Boxer and Quataert, *Socialist Women*, p. 87; Mme [Aline] Valette, *La Journée de la petite ménagère* (Paris, 1883): 34th édition advertised in *L'Harmonie sociale*, 24 June 1893; Marilyn Boxer tells us that it was adopted for use by the Paris schools. Valette was born Goudeman at Lille on 4 October 1850 (*DMO*, XV, 274).
36   *L'Harmonie sociale*, 22 Oct. 1892; *Oeuvre des libérées de Saint-Lazare* (Alençon, 1889 — Valette identified as author in preface).
37   Aline Valette, 'Le Rôle de la femme et de l'enfant dans l'industrie', *La Revue socialiste* (1891, I), pp. 241—3; Valette, 'Une Journée historique', *ibid.* (1890, II), pp. 129—55, 433—48; *Congrès ouvrier international socialiste de Paris (du 14 juillet au 20 juillet 1889): Appel, Liste des délégués, Résolutions* (Paris, 1889), p. 16; *Congrès international ouvrier socialiste tenu à Bruxelles du 16 au 23 août 1891: Rapport publié par le secrétariat belge* (Brussels, 1893), p. 247. Cf. Maurice Dommanget, *Histoire du premier Mai* (Paris, 1972), pp. 103—45.
38   *Le Journal des femmes*, Dec. 1891, Jan., Mar., June, July 1892; APP B/a 1651; Eugénie Potonié-Pierre, 'Un Jalon', *La Question sociale*, 1892, p. 233; Sowerwine, *Les Femmes*, p. 55n. for Federation.
39   Marya Chéliga-Loevy, 'Sans issue', *L'Harmonie sociale*, 15 Oct. 1892ff. Chéliga was the only child of a family of Polish nobles whom she scandalised by marrying a Jew

('Ma Première Révolte', *Almanach de la Question sociale*, 1896, pp. 21—3). Author of numerous plays and stories, she founded L'Union Universelle des Femmes (which was a member of Potonié-Pierre's Federation and which published a *Bulletin* 1890—1) and published the *Almanach féministe*, 1899.

40 *L'Harmonie sociale*, 15 Oct. 1892. For the International on the woman question, see Appendix 1.

41 Engels, pp. 137—8; Bebel, p. 182.

42 *L'Harmonie sociale*, 15 Oct. 1892, 7 Jan. 1893.

43 Boxer in Boxer and Quataert, p. 88; Marilyn J. Boxer, 'French socialism, feminism, and the family', *TR/TR*, 3/4 (1977), 139. Boxer argues that Bonnier 'allowed credit for his ideas to be attributed to [Valette] ', but in fact Valette developed these ideas independently; Bonnier supplied the scientific veneer (cf. Bonnier's articles, signed 'Dr Z.', *Le Socialiste*, 1895—7, *passim*).

44 *L'Harmonie sociale*, 15 Nov. 1892, 29 Apr. 1893; [Aline Valette and Pierre Bonnier], *Socialisme et sexualisme: Programme du Parti socialiste féminin* (Paris, 1893), pp. 11—13.

45 Eugénie Potonié-Pierre, 'La Solidarité des femmes', *La Question sociale* (1893, II), p. 77; 'Le Sexualisme et . . . [sic] l'humanisme', *Le Journal des femmes*, Nov. 1894. Cf. Bebel, pp. 183—7.

46 [Valette and Bonnier], *Socialisme et sexualisme*, p. 83 (the appendix also included the POF programme); Paule Mink, 'Le Premier Mai', *La Question sociale*, 15 May 1893, p. 107.

47 *L'Harmonie sociale*, 25 May 1893; APP B/a 1651, 20 June 1895; *Le Radical*, 23 June 1895; Sowerwine, *Les Femmes*, p. 58n.

48 'Communications', *L'Harmonie sociale*, 14 Jan. 1893; Willard, *Les Guesdistes*, pp. 119—23, 361—2, 362n. These estimates are based on Willard's sample, which included a sixth of the total membership; he has told me that he feels the sample is representative of the total population of women. For Ghesquière's pamphlet, see above, pp. 58—9.

49 Letter, Vérecque to Guesde, 22 June 1892, cited in Vérecque, *FS*, Dec. 1932; *Neuvième congrès national du Parti ouvrier tenu à Lyon du 26 au 28 novembre 1891* (Lille, 1891), pp. 12—13.

50 Willard, *Les Guesdistes*, pp. 119—23; *L'Harmonie sociale*, 23 Apr. 1893; Vérecque, *FS*, Dec. 1932; *Onzième congrès national du Parti ouvrier tenu à Paris du 7 au 9 octobre 1893* (Lille, n.d.), p. 20.

51 *Le Socialiste*, 26 May, 9, 23 June, 14, 21, 28 July, 18 Aug., 13 Oct., 17, 24 Nov., 22 Dec. 1895, 5 Jan. 1896. These articles formed the basis of her report on women's working conditions to the 1895 POF congress, where she presented a resolution calling for the organisation of women with other workers, which was adopted (*Les Débats*, 12 Sept. 1895).

52 *Le Socialiste*, 26 May 1895. Valette does not seem to have read Marx's *Capital* until long after her election to the national council of the POF. In 1898 she wrote an article for *La Fronde* which reflects apparently recent discovery of the theory of surplus value (ms, dossier Valette, BMD — *La Fronde* did not print it).

53 Charles Bonnier, *La Question de la femme* (Paris, 1897); Aline Valette, 'Féminisme et socialisme', *La Petite République*, 9 Dec. 1896; *Le Socialiste*, 31 Jan. 1897, p. 4; AN F7 13.071, 'Congrès POF 1897'; *Quinzième congrès national du Parti ouvrier tenu à Paris du 10 au 13 juillet 1897* (Lille, 1897), p. 34; Willard, *Les Guesdistes*, pp. 132, 606.

54 'Le Congrès de Montluçon', *La Revue socialiste* (1898, II), p. 504; AN F7 13.071, 'Congrès POF 1898'; *XVIe congrès national du Parti ouvrier français tenu à Montluçon du 17 au 20 septembre 1898* (Paris, 1898).

55 'Aline Valette', *La Revue socialiste* (1899, I), pp. 491—4; letter, Valette to Marguerite Durand, 28 May 1898, dossier Valette, BMD.

56 Aline Valette, 'Le Travail des femmes: évolution pacifique?', *La Fronde*, 3 July 1898. For an annotated list of her articles in *La Fronde*, see Guilbert, pp. 287—8.
57 Letter, Valette to Marguerite Durand, 16 Apr. 1898, dossier Valette, BMD. Cf. [Valette and Bonnier] , *Socialisme et sexualisme*, pp. 63—9.

3. Feminists in search of a mass base: the rise and fall of social feminism 1889—1900

1 'Salaires et misères de femmes', *La Fronde*, 17 Jan. 1900.
2 *Exposition universelle internationale de 1889: Actes du congrès international des oeuvres et institutions féminines (Paris, 12—18 juillet 1889)* (Paris, 1890), p. i; *Congrès du droit des femmes 1889*, pp. 212—21.
3 *La Citoyenne*, Nov. 1889; Brion, 'Squelette' (BMD), I, 50.
4 Maria Martin took over *La Citoyenne* in 1888, when Auclert went to Algeria. Following disagreements Martin began *Le Journal des femmes*, which she published from 1891 until her death in December 1910 (*Le Journal des femmes*, Jan. 1911).
5 *La Citoyenne*, 1 July, 1 Aug., 15 Sept. 1891; *Le Journal des femmes*, June 1892; *L'Equité*, 1 Apr. 1914; Thomas, *The Women Incendiaries*, pp. 207—9, 217—19; *DMO*, VII ('Lemel'). Cf. Caroline Kauffmann, *Questionnaire sur les sujets suivants: revendications féministes, éducation, mariage, prostitution, charité, politique* (Paris, 1900), p. 3.
6 *La Citoyenne*, 15 Sept., 1 Nov. 1891; 'Premier congrès de la Fédération Française des Sociétés Féministes jointe à l'Union Universelle des Femmes', dossier APP B/a 1651 and dossier BMD; *Le Journal des femmes*, Apr.—July 1892.
7 Willard, *Les Guesdistes*, pp. 619—20; Jean Maitron, 'Le Groupe des étudiants socialistes révolutionnaires internationalistes de Paris (1892—1902)', *Le Mouvement social*, 46 (1964), 6—7, 15; *Le Journal des femmes*, July 1892. 'Outstretched hand' referred to the resolution of the 1891 international socialist congress at Brussels (see Appendix 1).
8 Eugénie Potonié-Pierre, 'Un Jalon', *La Question sociale*, 1892, p. 233; Potonié-Pierre, *Un peu plus tard* (Paris, 1893), p. 74. Edmond and Eugénie Potonié-Pierre were the joint authors: they always signed their joint work by their hyphenated last name (*Le Journal des femmes*, Dec. 1893).
9 Potonié-Pierre, *Un peu plus tard*, p. 7. The structure and the mechanical gadgetry of this novel recall Edward Bellamy's *Looking Backward*, published in the US in 1888, but I have no evidence that the Potonié-Pierres knew this work.
10 Eugénie Potonié-Pierre: 'Une Eclaircie', *La Question sociale*, 1893, pp. 438—9; 'Les Allumettiers', *ibid.*, 1895, p. 203; 'Faut-il un budget de la maternité?', *ibid.*, 1896, pp. 414—15; 'Dans la banlieue', *Almanach de la Question sociale*, 1895, p. 147. Cf. her 'Les Foins coupés', *ibid.*, 1896, pp. 65—7; 'Un entre mille', *ibid.*, 1897, pp. 84—6.
11 *Le Journal des femmes*, Feb. 1892.
12 *Ibid.*, Sept. 1892, Nov. 1893; *Congrès PO Paris 1893*.
13 *La Question sociale*, 1892, pp. 386—7; *ibid.*, 1893, p. 7; letter, Eugénie Potonié-Pierre to Jules Guesde, 13 Oct. 1892 (Am IISG, Guesde Archives 219/92); *Le Journal des femmes*, Jan., Feb. 1893.
14 APP B/a 1651, 20 Apr. 1884; letter, Paule Mink 'Aux citoyens du congrès international ouvrier collectiviste de Paris', 17 July 1889 (Am IISG, Guesde Archives 607/18); Paule Mink, 'L'Emancipation de la femme et le socialisme', *La Question sociale*, 1891, pp. 6—7, 30—2. Cf. *La Citoyenne*, Sept. 1885. Mink was conscious of problems specific to women, but until 1893 she subordinated them to problems of class. Thus, for example, she regarded abortion as an 'appalling massacre', but justified so long as capitalism made life so difficult for women and children ('Le Droit à l'avortement', *Almanach de la Question sociale*, 1893, pp. 63—9).
15 [Potonié-Pierre] , 'Rapport sur la Fédération', *Le Journal des femmes*, June 1892; cf. 'Un Terrain de conciliation', *La Question sociale*, 1892, p. 158.

16 Willard, *Les Guesdistes*, pp. 187, 195; *Congrès St.-Etienne 1882*, p. 108; *La Question sociale*, 1892, pp. 333, 348; *Almanach de la Question sociale*, 1892, pp. 140–2. Mink also maintained anarchist tendencies: cf. her 'Mortalité ouvrière', *Almanach de la Question sociale*, 1894, pp. 164–5, and 'La Mère de Cyvoct', *La Question sociale*, 1896, p. 330.

17 *La Question sociale*, 1893, p. 106; Willard, *Les Guesdistes*, p. 635; *Le Journal des femmes*, Sept. 1893; letter, Paule Mink to La Solidarité des Femmes [*c.* Feb. 1893] (Am IISG, Guesde Archives 564/12).

18 *Le Journal des femmes*, July, Sept. 1893; Maitron, *Le Mouvement social*, 46 (1964), 12–13; *La Question sociale*, 1893, p. 107.

19 Paule Mink: 'Pierre Lerin', *La Question sociale, supplément littéraire*, 1893, pp. 41–2; 'Croquis à la vapeur: patronne et servante', *ibid.*, p. 57; 'Pauvre vieux', *La Revue socialiste*, 1894, pp. 562–7; 'Bras cassé', *ibid.*, 1895, pp. 570–4. Cf. 'Pour la vie', *Almanach de la Question sociale*, 1894, pp. 121–6.

20 *Le Journal des femmes*, Apr., June 1895; *Congrès international de la condition et des droits des femmes tenu les 5, 6, 7 et 8 septembre 1900* (Paris, 1900), p. 12; *Voeux adoptés par le congrès féministe international, tenu à Paris en 1896, pendant les journées du 8 au 12 avril* (Paris, n.d.), p. 4; Eugénie Potonié-Pierre, 'Le Congrès féministe international', *La Question sociale*, 1896, pp. 378–9; *Le Figaro*, 9 Apr. 1896.

21 Eugénie Potonié-Pierre, 'Le Congrès féministe de Bruxelles', *La Question sociale*, 1897, pp. 637–8; Paule Mink, 'Le Congrès féministe de Bruxelles', *La Revue socialiste*, 1897, p. 345; letter, Paule Mink to Marguerite Durand, 8 Sept. 1897, dossier Mink, BMD.

22 *Almanach féministe*, 1899, p. 86; *La Fronde*, 13 June 1898; *XIXe siècle*, 16 June 1898; APP B/a 1651, 23 June 1898; *Le Journal des femmes*, Sept.–Oct. 1898. For Kauffmann, see *Le Féminisme intégral*, Mar. 1913.

23 International Council of Women, *Importance de l'éducation physique scientifique ... congrès féministe de Londres; rapport au conseil municipal par Mme Caroline Kauffmann, secrétaire, et Paule Mink, déléguées du Groupe de la solidarité des femmes* (Paris, 1899); *Congrès général des organisations socialistes françaises tenu à Paris du 3 au 8 décembre 1899, compte rendu sténographique officiel* (Paris, 1900); *Le Journal des femmes*, Dec. 1899, Jan., Feb. 1900; *L'Aurore*, 6, 25 Oct. 1899; *La Lanterne*, 26 Oct., 22 Dec. 1899, 13 Sept. 1900; *Deuxième congrès général des organisations socialistes françaises tenu à Paris du 28 au 30 septembre 1900, compte rendu sténographique officiel* (Paris, 1901). Cf. below, p. 219, n. 37.

24 Marilyn Boxer, 'Socialism Faces Feminism in France: 1879–1913' (Ph.D., University of California–Riverside, 1975), pp. 175–6; *DMO*, XIV, 106; *La Fronde*, 29 Apr. 1901.

25 *L'Aurore*, 25 Apr., 2, 9, 15, 23 May, 13, 27 June 1901 (for Groupe); for La Solidarité, see *Le Journal des femmes*, 1898–1905, and above, pp. 68–70.

26 *Congrès des droits des femmes 1900*, p. 13; dossier Durand, BMD; Chastenet, III, 204.

27 'Après le congrès', *La Fronde*, 14 Sept. 1900; *ibid.*, 16 Mar. 1899, 13 Jan., 9 Mar. 1900; dossier Syndicats, BMD; APP B/a 1651, 'Foureur', 22 Dec. 1900.

28 *Congrès des droits des femmes 1900*, p. vii; *La Petite République*, 14 Sept. 1900.

29 Marie Bonnevial, 'Le Congrès de la condition et des droits des femmes', *Le Mouvement socialiste*, 15 Oct., 1 Nov. 1900, pp. 504, 512, 547; *Congrès des droits des femmes 1900*, pp. 42, 44, 66, 73.

30 Bonnevial, *Le Mouvement socialiste*, 15 Oct. 1900, p. 504; *Congrès des droits des femmes 1900*, pp. 12–13.

31 Letters, Louise Saumoneau to Marguerite Durand, 23 Apr., 9 May 1900, dossier Saumoneau, BMD; *La Fronde*, 2 Jan. 1900.

32 *Congrès des droits des femmes 1900*, pp. 42, 44, 66, 73.

33 Vice-president of Féresses-Deraismes' Société, a founding member of a mixed

Masonic lodge (Le Droit Humain), of a *patronage* (Les Amis de l'Adolescence), and, in 1901, of the Conseil National des Femmes Françaises. Her husband was mayor of the eighteenth arrondissement. She was present at all the feminist congresses from 1878 until her death on 21 December 1903 (*Le Journal des femmes*, Jan. 1904).

34   *Congrès des droits des femmes 1900*, pp. 75–9. Even feminists of the left preferred to keep their domestics at home rather than let them run the risks of being alone in the streets. E.g. Séverine: 'To overcome the problems mentioned in regard to, I won't say the laziness, but the isolation of a child in Paris', it would be better not to give young domestics an entire day off (*ibid.*, p. 76).

35   *Ibid.*, pp. 73, 95–6.

36   *Ibid.*, p. 113.

37   *Ibid.*, pp. 44, 86–92, 296.

38   *Ibid.*, pp. 290–1; *La Fronde*, 12 Sept. 1900; *La Petite République* 14, 18 Sept. 1900. In 1904, after the death of her husband and the bankruptcy of her hotel, Pognon went to Noumea to live with her son (dossier Pognon, BMD; *Le Journal des femmes*, Nov. 1904). Marie Bonnevial succeeded her at the head of the League.

39   *La Petite République*, 14, 18 Sept. 1900; 'Vieux papiers', *La Femme socialiste* (*FS*), Feb.–Mar. 1932; *La Lanterne*, 15 Oct. 1900.

40   *Le Journal des Femmes*, Mar. Apr. 1901; Karen M. Offen, 'The woman question as a social issue in republican France, 1870–1914' (Woodside, California, privately circulated ms, 1973), p. 55.

41   APP B/a 1651, 'Foureur', 27 Dec. 1900.

42   *La Fronde*, 29 Dec. 1900, 28 Mar. 1901, 24, 27 Mar.–1 Apr. 1902; *Le Journal des femmes*, Feb. 1907; Guilbert, pp. 228–30, 298–9, 400; *La Typographie française*, 16 Aug. (p. 3), 1 Dec. (pp. 1, 3) 1900; 1 Dec. (pp. 2–3) 1901; 16 Jan. (p. 4) 1902.

4. The Groupe Féministe Socialiste 1899–1905

1   Louise Saumoneau, 'Pour les femmes du prolétariat', *L'Internationale*, 10 May 1919.

2   Interview with Mme Fernande Fourton (Saumoneau's niece), 7 Dec. 1972; interview with Mme Suzanne Benoist-Guesde (Elisabeth Renaud's granddaughter), 14 Oct. 1972; letter, Mme Fourton to the author, 10 Oct. 1972; APP B/a 1545, 22 May 1915; 'Dernière minute', *FS*, June 1901.

3   Interview with Mme Jeanne Alexandre (née Halbwachs), 19 Dec. 1971. She went on, 'but obviously we were students and we hardly had any contact with the workers of the [party] section'.

4   Interview with Mme Benoist-Guesde; 'Elisabeth Renaud', *Le Populaire*, 17 Oct. 1932 (obituary).

5   Elisabeth Renaud, 'La Femme au XXe siècle', *L'Humanité nouvelle*, Mar.–Apr. 1898, p. 338.

6   'Groupe des Etudiants Collectivistes', APP B/a 1527, 11 May 1897, 31 Dec. 1898, 12 Feb. 1899, 9, 22 Dec. 1900. Cf. Maitron, *Le Mouvement social*, 46 (1964), 16–18.

7   *Ibid.*; 'Groupe de Paris', *L'Equité*, 15 Apr. 1913; AN F7 12.490, 'Congrès POSR 1897'; POSR, *Congrès Paris [1897]*, pp. 32–3; *Congrès PO Paris 1897*, p. 26; AN F7 13.071, 'Congrès POF 1897'.

8   Goldberg, *passim*; interview with Mme Alexandre.

9   Elisabeth Renaud, *Pourquoi les américains sont allés à Cuba* (Paris, 1898); *La Femme au XXe siècle: Conférence faite à l'Hôtel des Sociétés Savantes le 28 octobre 1897* (Paris, 1897: also published in *L'Humanité nouvelle*, Mar.–Apr. 1898); APP B/a 1651, 'Boudin', 7 July 1898.

10   'Appel', *L'Aurore*, 2 July 1899; *La Petite République*, 3 July 1899.

11   *Ibid.*; 'Statuts', *FS*, Mar. 1901 (cf. Louise Saumoneau, *Principes et action féministes socialistes* [Paris, n.d.] , p. 3); Louise Saumoneau, 'Les Buts', *Principes*, p. 12; Renaud, *L'Humanité nouvelle*, Mar. 1898, p. 338.

12   Louise Saumoneau, 'Le Mouvement féministe socialiste', *Etudes et critiques* (Paris, n.d.); letter, Elisabeth Renaud to Marguerite Durand, 1 Dec. 1899, dossier Renaud, BMD.
13   'Statuts', *FS*, Mar. 1901: 'L'Action féministe socialiste depuis 1899', *FS*, 15 Apr. 1912.
14   Cf. Goldberg, pp. 250–6; Anderson, pp. 18–24.
15   *La Lanterne*, 18 Sept., 7 Oct. 1899; *L'Aurore*, 6 Oct. 1899.
16   Letter, Renaud to Durand, 1 Dec. 1899; *Congrès général Paris 1899*, p. 453.
17   Hall at 23, rue de Pontoise (APP B/a 1527, 'Arthur', 2 Dec. 1899). Longuet was still secretary of the Groupe des Etudiants Collectivistes and Renaud was still an active member: in January 1900 the group elected her its delegate to the Fédération des Républicains Socialistes Indépendants (*La Petite République*, 11 Jan. 1900).
18   *L'Aurore*, 31 Dec. 1899, 4 Feb., 12 Mar. 1900; AN F7 12.494, 'Indépendants', Mar. 1900; *La Lanterne*, 1 Jan. 1900. *L'Aurore* subsequently announced meetings for 7, 14, 21, 28 Jan., 4, 25 Feb., 4 Mar., 1, 15, 22, 29 Apr., 6, 13 May, 3 June 1900. The absence of an announcement in the press does not indicate there was no meeting. Some typical titles of the lectures: 'Military convict prisons' (Renaud, 31 Dec. 1899); 'Of the necessity for feminine action in the social struggle' (Saumoneau, 7 Jan. 1900); 'What is socialism?' (Renaud, 14 Jan. 1900); 'The Communist Manifesto' (Renaud, 4 Feb. 1900); 'The fatherland of the capitalists and the fatherland of the socialists' (Renaud, 25 Feb. 1900).
19   *L'Aurore*, 21 Jan. 1900; 'L'Action', *FS*, May 1914. Cf. Fernand and Maurice Pelloutier, 'La Femme dans l'industrie', *L'Ouvrier des deux mondes*, Sept.–Oct. 1897, pp. 113, 129, 165; see *Congrès général Paris 1900*, p. 76; Jaurès in *La Petite République*, 23, 26 Dec. 1899; Lafargue in *Le Socialiste*, 28 Jan., 4 Feb. 1900. For the International's resolutions, see Appendix 1.
20   'Les Grèves', *La Petite République*, 18, 25 June 1900; 'L'Action', *FS*, July 1914.
21   *Ibid.*; *L'Aurore*, 12 Mar. 1900.
22   In addition to Renaud and Saumoneau, the group elected 'citizens Allemane [Jean's wife?] and S. Baduel [Renaud's daughter] ' as delegates (*La Lanterne*, 21 Aug. 1900), but they did not speak, if they went at all – there is no list of delegates.
23   'Tribune féminine', *Le Petit Sou*, 19 Oct. 1900; Saumoneau, *Principes et action*, p. 12; 'Vieux papiers: les réformes ouvrières au congrès féministe', *FS*, Feb.–Mar. 1932; *La Petite République*, 14 Sept. 1900.
24   *FS*, Aug. 1902; *Le Journal des femmes*, Mar. 1902.
25   'Le Mouvement féministe socialiste', *FS*, Oct. 1901; 'Vieux papiers: les réformes', *FS*, Feb.–Mar. 1932.
26   *La Petite République*, 14 Sept. 1900; *Le Petit Sou*, 19 Oct. 1900. GFS meetings were regularly announced in *La Lanterne*, *L'Aurore*, and *Le Petit Sou*.
27   Saumoneau, *Principes et action*, p. 4; 'Vieux papiers: les réformes', *FS*, Feb.–Mar. 1932; 'Dernière heure', *FS*, June 1901; 'Tribune féminine', *Le Petit Sou*, 18, 23 Nov. 1900; 'Mouvement social', *La Lanterne*, 22 Nov. 1900.
28   'Tribune féminine', *Le Petit Sou*, 14 Mar. 1901; *Le Libertaire*, 16 Mar. 1901; *La Voix du peuple*, 17, 24 Feb., 17 Mar. 1901; 'Résolutions', *FS*, Mar. 1901. Cf. *Le Petit Sou*, 10, 13, 14 Feb. 1901.
29   *La Fronde*, 13 Feb., 12, 18 Mar. 1901.
30   'Les Grèves', *FS*, Mar. 1901; 'Communications', *FS*, Apr. 1901; 'Organisation', *FS*, June 1901.
31   'Communications', *FS*, Apr. 1901; *FS*, Oct. 1901, July 1902; 'Tribune féminine', *Le Petit Sou*, 6 May 1901; AN 13.266, 'Louise Saumoneau', Oct. 1915.
32   'Tribune féminine', *Le Petit Sou*, 15 Dec. 1900; *FS*, Mar.–Dec. 1901; *L'Aurore*, 28 May 1901.
33   *FS*, Mar.–Dec. 1901; APP B/a 1651, 'Foureur', 2 Apr. 1902.
34   'Tribune féminine', *Le Petit Sou*, 21 Dec. 1900; 'Nos militantes: Adèle Kassky', *La Lutte féministe*, 20 Oct. 1921.

35 *Ibid.* Neither Thomas (*The Women Incendiaries*) nor the *DMO* mention Duvignaud, who Kassky claimed (*ibid.*) had been deported to New Caledonia after the Commune. For LeRoy, see *DMO*, VII, 135.
36 *La Lanterne*, 13 Nov. 1902; *La Petite République*, 15 Dec. 1901.
37 Two other groups appear to have been created in their image: (1) Le Groupe des Femmes Socialistes Révolutionnaires du 16e PSR founded by Paule Mink and Mme Argyriadès in January 1901 (*Le Petit Sou*, 1 Jan. 1901) — is this the Groupe Socialiste Révolutionnaire des Citoyennes de Paris (PSR, AC) which delegated Mink to the 1900 socialist congress? (2) L'Union des Femmes Socialistes de Saint-Ouen (PSR) founded by Thérèse Roques in April 1901 (*L'Aurore*, 28, 29 Apr., 12 May 1901). Thérèse and Jules Roques were founders, with Astié de Valsayre and Eugénie Potonié-Pierre, of the Ligue Socialiste des Femmes, still-born in 1889.
38 *Le Petit Sou*, 12 Feb. 1901; *FS*, Mar., May, June 1901.
39 Suzanne Péchin [Elisabeth Renaud] , 'Femmes du prolétariat', *FS*, Jan. 1902. Cf. Goldberg, pp. 250—338.
40 *FS*, Apr., Dec. 1901, Aug. 1902; *La Petite République*, 31 July 1902.
41 *FS*, Sept., Oct. 1901, Feb., Mar. 1902. Cf. Gaston Dubois-Dessaule, *Camisards, peaux de lapins et cocos: Corps disciplinaires de l'armée française* (Paris, 1901), pp. 43—8.
42 *FS*, July 1902. Saumoneau took no part in Renaud's anti-militarist campaign. There was no indication at this time that Saumoneau would be at the head of the anti-war campaign in 1915 or that Renaud would support the war, except that her anti-militarism was never anti-nationalist and never anti-colonialist, though she did oppose harsh repression in the colonies: 'We think that one can colonise in most excellent fashion by other means than missionaries, guns, opium and brandy' (*FS*, Mar. 1901). Renaud wrote against the Franco-Russian alliance with great prescience (*FS*, Oct. 1901).
43 *FS*, June 1901, July 1902.
44 *FS*, June 1901, Oct.—Nov. 1914; 'Tribune féminine', *Le Petit Sou*, 23 Jan. 1902.
45 *FS*, Mar. 1901.
46 *FS*, Nov. 1901, Mar. 1902.
47 *FS*, Sept. 1901. Emile Pasquier was a stained-glass maker (*DMO*, XIV, 212) and a socialist well enough known to be chosen chairman of the tumultuous first session of the *Congrès général Paris 1900* (p. 13). Julie Pasquier was a friend of Eugénie Potonié-Pierre and treasurer of the 1892 feminist congress (APP B/a 1651, 13 May 1892). The other two representatives were Mme Vernhert and M. Beaufumé.
48 *FS*, Nov., Dec. 1901.
49 *FS*, Sept. 1901.
50 *FS*, Aug., Dec. 1901, Feb. 1902. Cf. Chastenet, III, 233.
51 *FS*, Feb., Mar., July 1902; *La Petite République*, 30 Mar., 14 Apr., 25 July, 8, 27 Sept. 1902; *L'Aurore*, 13, 23, 26 Sept., 25 Oct., 29 Nov. 1902; *La Lanterne*, 4, 17 Sept., 26, 29 Oct., 30 Nov. 1902.
52 See Appendix 2.
53 *FS*, Sept., Oct. 1901.
54 *L'Aurore*, 4 Feb. 1900; AN F7 12.494, 'Indépendants', Mar. 1900; AN F7 13.071, 'Congrès des Indépendants', Aug. 1900; 'Vieux papiers', *FS*, Nov. 1926; *Congrès général Paris 1900*, 'liste des groupes représentés'.
55 *FS*, May 1901; *Congrès général Lyon 1901*, pp. 18—37.
56 *L'Aurore*, 15 Apr. 1901; *Congrès général Lyon 1901*, 'liste des groupes représentés'; *FS*, Nov. 1901.
57 *Congrès général Lyon 1901*, pp. 455—6.
58 *Ibid.*, pp. 414—29.
59 *La Petite République*, 4 July, 15 Nov., 8 Dec. 1901, 7 Feb. 1902, 30 Apr. 1903; AN F7 12.496, 'Comité général'.
60 *Quatrième congrès général du Parti socialiste français tenu à Tours du 2 au 4 mai 1902: Compte rendu sténographique officiel* (Paris, 1902), pp. vii—xii.

61 *Ibid.*, pp. 190—4; AN F7 12.522, 'Congrès de Tours 1902'; *Congrès général Lyon 1901*, p. 513.
62 *Congrès PSF Tours 1902*, pp. 356—8, 368, 372, 375—86.
63 *La Petite République*, 27 Feb. 1902.
64 *Ibid.*, 9 Mar., 16 Apr., 18, 21 Sept., 30 Oct., 4 Dec. 1902, 25 Jan., 5 Feb. 1903; *Le Petit Sou*, 16, 20 Apr. 1902; *L'Aurore*, 11 Sept., 29 Oct. 1902; *La Lanterne*, 18, 22 Sept., 4 Dec. 1902, 2 Feb. 1903; *L'Humanité*, 26 Sept. 1904 *et seq.*, *passim*. Kassky's development paralleled that of Edmond Toussaint, former Allemanist deputy whom she married in 1905 (*La Lutte féministe*, 20 Oct. 1921): he joined the PSDF in February 1902 and became its treasurer in September (*La Petite République*, 27 Feb. 1902; *L'Aurore*, 11 Sept. 1902).
65 *La Petite République*, 28 June 1902; *FS*, Sept. 1902.
66 *Propagande et documentation*, 3, 1930, p. 18n. Renaud had moved her *pension* to the rue des Feuillantines, where she had a room seating fifty. She remained on the Comité Interfédéral (successor to the Comité Général) and participated in feminist and Allemanist meetings as well — ideological divisions were still fuzzy (*L'Aurore*, 7 Nov., 23 Dec. 1902; *La Lanterne*, 2 July 1903). In August 1902 she was named to the propaganda commission, which sent her to speak at many provincial meetings. An interesting account of one such meeting may be found in *L'Yonne*, 1 Oct. 1902 (450 persons attended). In January 1903 she was named to the Comité de Règlement Intérieur, whose report she read at the 1903 congress at Bordeaux (*La Petite République*, 22 Jan., 16 Apr. 1903).
67 'Le Mouvement', *FS*, Oct. 1902; 'L'Action', *FS*, Nov.—Dec. 1925; *Propagande et documentation*, 4, 1930, p. 13.
68 *L'Aurore*, 7 Dec. 1902; *La Petite République*, 5 Jan., 2 Feb., 19 Mar., 6 Apr., 4 May, 8 June, 7 Sept., 5 Oct., 7 Dec. 1903; 8 May 1904; *L'Humanité*, 19 Aug. 1904; 'Vieux papiers', *FS*, Jan. 1932.
69 *La Petite République*, 4, 19, 31 Mar., 4 May 1903; *L'Humanité*, 7 July, 14 Sept., 17 Nov. 1904, 14 Apr., 27 June 1905.
70 See Appendix 3.
71 'Rapport de la délégation française', *FS*, Jan. 1924; 'Fédération de la Seine', *L'Humanité*, 19, 27 June, 5, 28 July, 6 Aug., 5 Oct., 22 Dec. 1905; 'Conseil national', *L'Humanité*, 22 Feb. 1906.
72 'Convocations', *L'Humanité*, 22 Feb. 1906.
73 Madeleine Pelletier, 'Organisons les femmes', *Le Socialiste*, 4 Oct. 1908.
74 Thönnessen, p. 116.
75 Honeycutt, *Feminist Studies* III, 3/4 (1976), 131—44.

5. Women and the SFIO 1905—14

1 Paul Louis, *Histoire du socialisme en France: Les faits, les idées, les partis ouvriers, de la révolution à nos jours*, 5th edn (Paris, 1950), pp. 290—3; Lefranc, p. 187. Cf. Appendix 2.
2 Sowerwine, *Les Femmes*, pp. 257—61.
3 *L'Humanité*, 6 Sept. 1907; Barodet, *Professions de foi et programmes électoraux des députés élus, 9e législature* (Paris, 1906), pp. 266—9; 'La Proportionnelle et le vote des femmes', *Le Droit des femmes*, Dec. 1913.
4 *L'Humanité*, 22 Dec. 1906, 17 Jan. 1907; *Le Socialiste*, 1 Apr. 1907; Madeleine Pelletier, 'Le Féminisme et les partis politiques en France', *La Suffragiste*, Feb. 1912.
5 The Radicals finally permitted women in the 'Jeunesses Républicaines', but not in the party (Madeleine Pelletier, 'La Tactique féministe', *La Revue socialiste*, Apr. 1908, p. 320).
6 'Le Suffrage des femmes', *Le Journal*, 15 Mar. 1914. Sembat often presided at the banquets of the Ligue Française pour le Droit des Femmes (see, e.g., *Ligue française pour le droit des femmes*, Apr. 1910; *L'Humanité*, 10 Mar. 1913, 8, 13 Mar. 1914

[in which year, Sembat and the future communist leader Marcel Cachin were seated at the head table with Avril de Sainte-Croix and Mme Jules Siegfried!]). Tarbouriech was a founder of the Ligue des Droits de l'Homme and a vice-president of the Ligue Française pour le Droit des Femmes (*Ligue française pour le droit des femmes*, Jan. 1911).

7 Chambre des députés: septième législature, session de 1901, n° 2529, *Annexe au procès-verbal de la 1re séance du 1er juillet 1901*; neuvième législature, session de 1906, n° 253, *Annexe . . . 10 juillet 1906*; *Journal Officiel, séance du 29 octobre 1909*; *ibid., séance du 13 juin 1910*; *Le Journal des femmes*, June 1908; *Ligue française pour le droit des femmes*, Oct. 1911; Ferdinand Buisson, *Le Vote des femmes* (Paris, 1911), p. 326. Even the very advanced Fédération Féministe Universitaire (FFU) resolved in 1913 to support the bill (*L'Equité*, 15 Sept. 1913).

8 *L'Humanité*, 26 Jan., 2 Mar., 6 Nov., 21 Dec. 1912; *Le Droit des femmes*, Mar. 1912, p. 12.

9 *L'Action féministe*, Nov. 1913, June, July 1914; Chambre des députés, *Journal Officiel, séance du 4 février 1914*. Cf. Steven C. Hause, 'The rejection of women's suffrage by the French Senate in November, 1922: a statistical analysis', *TR/TR*, 3/4 (1977), 205—37.

10 '23 novembre 1939, Asile de Vaucluse' (ms in Brion's hand, dossier Pelletier, BMD). Cf. Madeleine Pelletier, *La Femme vierge: roman* [autobiographical] (Paris, 1933). Steven Hause has found a letter (Pelletier to Arria Ly, 22 Aug. 1911, BHVP) in which she states explicitly that she was a virgin.

11 Madeleine Pelletier, 'Les Demi-émancipées', *La Suffragiste*, Jan. 1912; Pelletier, 'Les Femmes et le féminisme', *La Revue socialiste*, Jan. 1906, pp. 39—40, 42—4; Pelletier, 'Les Facteurs sociologiques de la psychologie féminine', *La Revue socialiste*, Jan. 1907, p. 517; Pelletier, 'La Tactique féministe', *La Revue socialiste*, Apr. 1908, p. 323; Parti Socialiste (SFIO), *4e congrès national tenu à Nancy les 11, 12, 13 et 14 août 1907: Compte rendu sténographique* (Paris, n.d.), p. 528; 'Mme Pelletier', *L'Eclair*, 9 Apr. 1910; interviews with Mme Benoist-Guesde and Mme Alexandre. Cf. photograph of Pelletier, Hélène Brion, 'Squelette ébauche' (BMD), I, 650; and portrait of Marguerite Durand, BMD.

12 'Féminisme', *La Fronde*, 30 June 1899; Madeleine Pelletier, 'Nos aînées: Caroline Kauffmann', *La Fronde*, 17 Aug. 1926; *Le Journal des femmes*, Feb. 1906; Madeleine Pelletier, 'Les Femmes dans la Maçonerie [*sic*]', *L'Acacia*, June 1906, p. 442.

13 'Maria Deraismes', *L'Eclair*, 8 Feb. 1894; Madeleine Pelletier, 'Admission des femmes dans la Franc-maçonnerie' (Paris, extrait de *L'Acacia*, May 1905); Pelletier, 'Les Femmes dans la Maçonerie [*sic*]', *L'Acacia*, June 1906, pp. 441—2 (cf. commentary by O. Pontet, *L'Acacia*, June 1906, pp. 444—5); Pelletier, *La Revue socialiste*, Apr. 1908, p. 321. Cf. Jean Bossu, 'La Femme et la libre pensée', *L'Idée libre*, May 1957, pp. 212—13; Léo Campion, *Les Anarchistes dans la franc-maçonnerie, ou les maillons libertaires de la chaîne d'union* (Marseilles, 1969).

14 *Le Journal des femmes*, Nov., Dec. 1900, *et seq*. For the Conseil, cf. above, pp. 79—80.

15 Kauffmann, *Questionnaire*, p. 3; *Le Journal des femmes*, Dec. 1904, Jan. 1905. She was acquitted. Auclert and Mme Vincent also tried to demonstrate by burning a copy of the Code in the Place Vendôme, but the police prevented them (Offen, 'The woman question', pp. 63—4). Steven Hause has found a letter (Caroline Kauffmann to Arria Ly, 28 May 1913, BHVP) with her recollections of the demonstration and police reports on both efforts (APP B/a 1651 and APP B/a 885).

16 Pelletier, *La Fronde*, 8 Aug. 1926. Cf. *Le Petit Almanach féministe illustré*, 1907 (Am IAV), p. 31.

17 *Le Journal des femmes*, May 1906; *Le Gaulois*, 19 May 1906; Baron Marc de Villiers [du Terrage], *Histoire des clubs de femmes et des légions d'Amazones 1793—1848—1871* (Paris, 1910), p. 416; *L'Eclair*, 4, 11 May 1908; Steven C. Hause, 'Hubertine Auclert's second suffragist career, 1893—1914: to an unchanging goal with con-

stantly changing tactics' (paper presented to Fourth Berkshire Conference, Mount Holyoke College, 24 Aug. 1978), p. 9.

18 Madeleine Pelletier, 'La Question du vote des femmes', *La Revue socialiste*, Oct. 1908, pp. 329—30; Pelletier, *La Revue socialiste*, Apr. 1908, pp. 318—25.

19 Madeleine Pelletier, 'Comment préparer la révolution?', *La Guerre sociale*, 14 Aug. 1907; Pelletier, 'Ma Candidature à la députation', *Les Documents du progrès*, July 1910, p. 12; *L'Humanité*, 27 June, 8 Aug. 1906; Parti Socialiste (SFIO), *3e congrès national tenu à Limoges les 1er, 2, 3 et 4 novembre 1906: Compte rendu analytique* (Paris, n.d.), p. 151. A typical lecture was billed as follows: 'La Recherche, société de libre pensée, . . . "Le génie est-il une névrose?" par Mme la doctoresse Pelletier' (*L'Humanité*, 12 Feb. 1905).

20 SFIO, *Congrès Limoges 1906*, pp. 146—51.

21 *L'Humanité*, 22, 23 Dec. 1906.

22 She was not the only one. Even Avril de Sainte-Croix, who was far from being a socialist, praised the party for these acts: 'L'Indépendance économique de la femme', in *L'Humanité* itself (under her pen name, Savioz: 17 Jan. 1907). Once again the men of the party were ready to collaborate with bourgeois feminists.

23 *Le Socialiste*, 1 Apr. 1907; Odette Laguerre and M. Carlier, *Pour la paix: Lectures historiques, à l'usage de l'enseignement élémentaire* (Paris, 1905). Laguerre's husband Max was a Radical deputy.

24 Barodet, 1903, p. 808; 1906, pp. 887, 914; 1910, p. 984; *Le Socialiste*, 21 July 1907. No report of the socialist group before the war ever mentioned women's suffrage, although proportional representation took much space (*ibid.*, 20 Sept. 1908, 4 Apr. 1909, 9 Jan. 1910, 10 Mar. 1912).

25 *Le Socialiste*, 5 May 1907.

26 *Ibid.*, 28 July 1907; SFIO, *Congrès Nancy 1907*, pp. 525—33. Cf. Madeleine Vernet, 'Une Question à Mme Madeleine Pelletier', *Le Libertaire*, 26 July 1908.

27 Citizen Sorgue was the *nom de guerre* of Antoinette Cauvin, who is variously reported as having joined the POSR in the Aveyron in 1896 (Andrée Marty-Capgras, 'Pionnières', *Almanach populaire*, 1939, pp. 151—5) and the PSR in 1900 (Willard, *Les Guesdistes*, p. 718). She died in London in February 1924 (*DMO*, XV, 175). Cf. her brochures: *Socialisme ministériel*, 3rd edn (Paris, 1900) and *L'Unité révolutionnaire* (Paris, 1901); interviews with anarchists in *La Guerre sociale* (Emma Goldmann, 11 Sept. 1907; Errico Malatesta, 2 Oct. 1907). At the congress, she recalled having made lecture tours with Hervé in the spring of 1907 (SFIO, *Congrès Nancy 1907*, pp. 244—5). She was also a delegate to the international congress of Stuttgart and the conference of socialist women (she did not speak — cf. below, pp. 117—18), to the *Congrès général des organisations socialistes 1899*, and to the SFIO, *Congrès Paris 1905*. But she generally confined herself to syndical activity.

28 SFIO, *Congrès Nancy 1907*, pp. 532—6.

29 *Ibid.*, p. 581; 'Conseil National', *L'Humanité*, 16 Sept. 1905 *et seq.*; 'Fédération de la Seine', *ibid.*, 21 June 1907; 'Comité National', *Le Socialiste*, 10 Nov. 1907. Roussel was invariably delegated by the Isère federation. We have no biographical information for her (*DMO*, XV, 103).

30 Honeycutt, *Signs*, V, 1 (1979), 3—55; Honeycutt, *Feminist Studies*, III, 3/4 (1976), 139.

31 Of all the SFIO congresses between 1905 and 1920, only Limoges (1906) had more than eight women delegates: it had ten.

32 *Le Socialiste*, 18 Aug. 1907; *Septième congrès socialiste international tenu à Stuttgart du 16 au 24 août 1907: Compte rendu analytique publié par le secrétariat du bureau socialiste international* (Brussels, 1908), pp. 61—2; 'Anhang: Erste internationale Konferenz sozialisticher Frauen', *Internationaler Sozialistenkongress zu Stuttgart, 18. bis 24. August 1907* (Berlin, 1907), p. 154. Gauthiot's name appears only in 'Anhang'; was she delegated to the conference but not the congress?

Pelletier's name appears as a party delegate except in 'Anhang', where she is listed (p. 154) as the delegate of a 'Société des femmes': La Solidarité?

33 'Anhang', p. 126 (tr. by P. Howorth). Later, Pelletier expressed her disagreement openly: '[The German socialist women] rejected what they call bourgeois feminism with an ostentation truly lacking in dignity' (*La Revue socialiste*, Oct. 1908, pp. 329–30).

34 'Anhang', p. 128; *Congrès international Stuttgart 1907*, pp. 258–9. Miss Murby (England) raised the same objections as Pelletier (*ibid.*, p. 343).

35 *Congrès international Stuttgart 1907*, pp. 258–60, 262, 343, 347; 'Anhang', pp. 131, 141; *Le Socialiste*, 18 Aug. 1907. Cf. SFIO, *Congrès Limoges 1906*, p. 150; SFIO, *Congrès Nancy 1907*, pp. 532–3.

36 *L'Humanité*, 30 Aug. 1907. We have no biographical information for Chaboseau. She wrote 'Allemagne: L'organisation des femmes socialistes', *Le Mouvement socialiste*, 15 Dec. 1904.

37 'Convocations, 13e section', *L'Humanité*, 17 Apr., 15 June 1907; *Le Socialiste*, 28 Apr. 1907; Madeleine Pelletier, 'Organisons les femmes', *Le Socialiste*, 4 Oct. 1908.

38 Jean-Claude Peyronnet estimates its press run at 60,000 to 70,000 copies ('Un Exemple de journal militant: La "Guerre sociale" de Gustave Hervé (1906–1914)' [DES, Univ. of Paris, n.d.; CHS], p. 78); cf. *L'Humanité*'s press run of 85,000 to 90,000, probably corresponding to an average sale of 65,000 (Claude Bellanger *et al.*, *Histoire générale de la presse française*, III [Paris, 1972], 376).

39 *Le Socialiste*, 28 July 1907; Pelletier, *La Revue socialiste*, Apr. 1908, p. 326; Pelletier, *La Guerre sociale*, 14 Aug. 1907; 'Guesdisme ou syndicalisme?', *ibid.*, 25 Sept. 1907. Cf. Pelletier, 'Par-delà Guesde', *ibid.*, 4 Sept. 1907; 'Après Toulouse: La fin du guesdisme', *ibid.*, 6 Jan. 1909.

40 SFIO, *Congrès Nancy 1907*, pp. 169–70.

41 Madeleine Pelletier, 'Danger du Parlementarisme', *La Guerre sociale*, 16 Sept. 1908; and *ibid.*, 14 Aug. 1907. Cf. Pelletier, 'Défendrons-nous la République?', *ibid.*, 3 Feb. 1909; and 'Sommes-nous des Républicains?', *ibid.*, 11 Aug. 1909.

42 Pelletier: 'L'Inévitable épuration', *La Guerre sociale*, 30 Oct. 1907; 'La Leçon des faits', *ibid.*, 13 May 1908; 'Etre apache', *ibid.*, 9 June 1909; and 'La Tactique de l'attentat', *ibid.*, 14 July 1909. Cf. *La Revue socialiste*, Jan. 1907, pp. 516–17: Pelletier showed herself an excellent psychologist in her analyses of marginal character.

43 *La Guerre sociale*, 30 Jan., 20 Mar. 1907, 24 June, 1 July 1908. The paper shared Pelletier's views on women only in regard to the right not to bear children. Cf. her articles in *Le Malthusien*, 1913–14, *passim*; her *Le Droit à l'avortement* (Paris, 1913); and *La Guerre sociale*, 4 Dec. 1907, 16 Mar. 1910.

44 *La Suffragiste*, June 1910; APP B/a 767, 'Les Insurrectionnels', 27 Feb. 1909.

45 Peyronnet, 'Un Exemple', pp. 131–5; *L'Humanité*, 29 Mar. 1909; Parti Socialiste (SFIO), *6e congrès national tenu à Saint-Etienne les 11, 12, 13 et 14 avril 1909: Compte rendu sténographique* (Paris, n.d.), pp. 351–3, 470–1, 525; AN F7 13.072, 'Congrès Saint-Etienne', 14 Apr. 1909; Pelletier, *Les Documents du progrès*, July 1910, pp. 12–13.

46 *Le Socialiste*, 7 Nov. 1909.

47 *Journal officiel, Chambre des députés, Séance du 29 octobre 1909*; *Séance du 13 juin 1910*; *Le Journal des femmes*, Nov. 1909; *Ligue française pour le droit des femmes*, Nov. 1909; *L'Humanité*, 30 Oct. 1909.

48 *Le Socialiste*, 21 July, 7 Aug. 1910; *L'Humanité*, 3 Aug. 1910; *8e congrès socialiste international tenu à Copenhague du 28 août au 3 septembre 1910: Compte rendu analytique* (Gand, 1911), pp. 26–7, 487–97. Cf. *La Suffragiste*, Sept. 1910.

49 *La Suffragiste*, June 1910; AN F7 13.072, 11 Feb. 1910 (and for Hervé's evolution AN F7 13.071); *Le Socialiste*, 23 Apr. 1911, 4, 18 Feb. 1912. Pelletier's last article in *La Guerre sociale* appeared on 29 Dec. 1910, but she had written rarely during 1910.

50 Pelletier, *Les Documents du progrès*, July 1910, p. 13; *Le Socialiste*, 17 Apr. 1908; poster, dossier Pelletier, BMD.

51 Pelletier, *Les documents du progrès*, July 1910, p. 15; *L'Eclair*, 9 Apr. 1910.

52 *L'Humanité*, 23 Apr. 1910; 'Discours prononcé par Madeleine Pelletier dans le préau de l'école rue de Florence samedi 23 avril 1910' (ms in Brion's hand, dossier Pelletier, BMD). Charles Rappoport of the SFIO and Rodolphe Broda, editor of *Les Documents du progrès*, spoke in favour of Pelletier.

53 Pelletier, *Les Documents du progrès*, July 1910, p. 16; *L'Humanité*, 25 Apr. 1910.

54 *L'Humanité*, 10, 13, 19, 22—6, 30 Apr. 1910; *Le Journal des femmes*, May 1910; *La Suffragiste*, June 1910. There were several other women candidates, notably Marguerite Durand, but lacking the support of any regular party, none were successful (Durand estimated her votes at 34).

55 'Historique de la Fédération Féministe Universitaire', *L'Action féministe*, Aug.—Sept. 1913; *ibid.*, Oct., Dec. 1909. Pellat-Finet played a major role during the Couriau affair (see below, p. 135).

56 *Le Droit des femmes*, Mar. 1913, p. 6.

57 *Le Droit du peuple*, 22, 24 Apr. 1910; *L'Action féministe*, June 1910, pp. 117, 123; *L'Humanité*, 23 Apr. 1910; *Ligue française pour le droit des femmes*, Apr.—July 1910, pp. 9—10.

58 *L'Humanité*, 23, 26, 27 Apr. 1910; *Le Rappel*, 25, 26 Apr. 1910.

59 *L'Humanité*, 27, 28 Apr. 1910. The official *Tableau des élections à la Chambre des députés pendant la 10e législature* gives 2875 nil or irregular ballots and 54 for the man who signed for her (p. 44), which tallies with the party's estimate by its observers at the counting.

60 *L'Humanité*, 25 Apr., 4—7 May 1912.

61 *Ibid.*, 30 Apr., 3, 5 May 1912; *La Suffragiste*, June 1912. On 24 Apr. 1912, Pelletier wrote to Brion that she did not expect a party nomination (dossier Pelletier, BMD, which also contains the estimate of 306 votes; *L'Humanité*, 6 May 1912, gave her 250). Pelletier was nonetheless a delegate to the Parti Socialiste (SFIO), *9e congrès national tenu à Lyon les 18, 19, 20 et 21 février 1912 (compte rendu sténographique)* (Paris, n.d.), but she did not intervene.

62 Pelletier: *L'Acacia*, May 1905, p. 2; *Les Documents du progrès*, July 1910, p. 11; 'La Classe ouvrière et le féminisme', *La Suffragiste*, July 1912; and 'Le Féminisme et ses militants', *Les Documents du progrès*, July 1909, p. 19. She used the expression 'nous, les déclassés' at SFIO, *Congrès Saint-Etienne 1909*, p. 471.

63 Pelletier: *La Revue socialiste*, Oct. 1908, pp. 325—30; *La Suffragiste*, July 1912. Cf. 'Les Institutrices et le mouvement féministe', *Les Documents du progrès*, May 1910, pp. 437—8; and *La Suffragiste*, Feb. 1912.

64 *Le Socialiste*, 23, 30 July 1911; SFIO, *Congrès Nancy 1907*, p. 528.

65 Madeleine Pelletier, 'Un Traître', *Trois contes* (Paris, n.d.), p. 6.

66 [Madeleine Pelletier] : 'Qu'est-ce que le bolchevisme?', *La Suffragiste*, Dec. 1919—Jan. 1920; *Mon voyage aventureux en Russie communiste* (Paris, 1922); and *Capitalisme et communisme* (Nice, 1926); *L'Œuvre*, 26 Apr., 6 June 1939; dossier Pelletier, BMD. Mme Benoist-Guesde stated that Pelletier was known as an abortionist (interview).

6. The Groupe des Femmes Socialistes 1913—14

1 AN F7 13.266, 'La Campagne féministe en faveur de la paix', Oct. 1915; letters, Madeleine Pelletier [to Hélène Brion], 27 Dec. 1912, 7, 9 Jan. 1913, dossier Pelletier, BMD; letters to the author from Odette Nagler, 26 Feb. 1973, and from Germaine Degrond, 21 Jan. 1973; *La Vague*, 14 Aug. 1919; Marianne Rauze, 'Nelly Roussel', *La Voix des femmes*, 4 Jan. 1923; BHVP, Fonds Bouglé, carton 'Rauze'.

2 AN F7 13.266, 'La Campagne féministe'; 'Aux Femmes socialistes', *L'Humanité*, 10 Jan. 1913, p. 3; *Le Socialiste*, 19 Jan. 1913, p. 3; *FS*, 15 Feb. 1913.

3 Letters, Pelletier [to Brion], 27 Dec. 1912, 7, 9 Jan. 1913; interview with Mme Benoist-Guesde.
4 APP B/a 1545, '1915 (2230—10) 22 mai'; AN F7 13.266, 'La Campagne féministe'; interviews with Mmes Fourton and Benoist-Guesde.
5 *L'Humanité*, 10, 23, 30 Jan. 1913; *FS*, 15 Feb. 1913; *Le Socialiste*, 9 Feb. 1913.
6 *Ibid.*
7 Maria Vérone (1874—1938), wife of G. Lhermitte, began her career as a primary-school teacher and militant in the co-operative movement. She completed a law degree and was admitted to the bar at Paris, in 1907, and became the first active woman lawyer (note from Steven Hause; *DMO*, XV, 305).
8 Brion was born at Clermont-Ferrand, 27 Jan. 1882; and died at Ennery (Seine-et-Oise), 31 Aug. 1962, the daughter of an army career officer. Raised in the Ardennes by her grandmother, she became a primary-school teacher in the Paris suburbs in 1905, assistant secretary of the Syndicat des Instituteurs, 1914—18; and member of the editorial board of *L'Action féministe*, organ of the FFU (Henri Dubief, 'Hélène Brion', *Le Mouvement social*, 44 [1963], 94—5; *L'Action féministe*, Aug. 1913; *DMO*, XI, 60—1).
9 Marguerite Martin was a member of the central committee of the Union Française pour le Suffrage des Femmes (AN F7 13.375, 14 Apr. 1915).
10 Couteaudier was Saumoneau's closest ally during the war (see chapter 7). Gibault remarried after the war; as Suzanne Buisson she succeeded Saumoneau in 1931 (see chapter 8). Jouenne took Saumoneau's place as secretary of the GDFS during the war (see chapter 7). Grumbach's husband, Salomon, was Paris correspondent of the German SPD newspaper.
11 *Ligue française pour le droit des femmes* (Apr.—July 1910), p. 9; *FS*, 1 Apr. 1913; *L'Equité*, 15 Mar. 1913.
12 *L'Equité*, 15 Apr. 1913; *L'Humanité*, 25 May 1913. The same decision was taken in regard to the demonstration against the three-year law (*ibid.*, 13 July 1913), while the Comité Féminin contre la Loi Millerand-Berry held its own meeting the night before the demonstration. The featured speaker was Madeleine Pelletier (*ibid.*, 13 July 1913 [p. 6]; AN F7 13.331, 'M/8079', 11 July 1913; *La Bataille syndicaliste*, 12 July 1913). The Comité was syndicalist, if not anarchist in its orientation, but Renaud, Sorgue, and even Maria Vérone spoke for it on occasion (AN F7 13.331, 31 July 1913).
13 Fanny Clar, 'Notre coin', *La Guerre sociale*, 19 Mar. 1913; *L'Humanité*, 24 Mar., 3 Apr., 8 May, 5 June, 29 July, 7 Sept. 1913; *La Bataille syndicaliste*, 14, 20 May 1913; *FS*, 20 July, 1 Sept., 1 Oct. 1913; *L'Equité*, 15 June 1913.
14 *L'Equité*, 15 Mar. 1913. Rauze coupled such rhetoric with standard feminist and suffragist ideas, supporting women's right to vote because it would enable women 'to combat effectively the scourges: war, alcohol, misery, which the government of men has not been able or has not wished to stop' (*ibid.* 15 Feb. 1913).
15 Lacore was born on 30 May 1875 at Glandier (Corrèze) and became a primary-school teacher at Ajat (Dordogne) in 1903. After a brief flirtation with the anarchist ideas of Sébastien Faure, she joined the SFIO in 1906. Léon Blum named her sous-secrétaire d'état à la protection de l'enfance in 1936 (*DMO*, XIII, 163—4; Hubert-Rouger, *Les Fédérations socialistes* [vol. II of *Encyclopédie socialiste* (3 vols., Paris, 1912—21)], p. 236; *Les Hommes du jour*, 23 Apr. 1937). Her ideas had not changed (cf. her *Femmes socialistes* [Paris, 1932]).
16 *L'Equité*, 15 June 1913.
17 *Ibid.*, 15 Oct. 1913.
18 *Ibid.*, 15 Feb., 15 Apr., 15 May 1914; Lacore, preface to Marianne Rauze, *Féminisme économique* ([Paris, 1915]).
19 *FS*, 1 Oct. 1913; Compère-Morel, 'Féminisme et socialisme', *L'Humanité*, 8 Nov. 1913; *Le Socialiste*, 23 Feb. 1913.
20 *L'Equité*, 15 Aug., 15 Nov. 1913. Cf. Brion, 'Billet féministe', *Le Populaire*, 25—31

Dec. 1916, and *La Voie féministe, les partis d'avant-garde et le féminisme* (Epône, [1918]).

21 *L'Equité*, 15 Sept., 15 Dec. 1913, 1 Apr. 1914. Cf. Marguerite Martin, *Les Droits de la femme* (Paris, 1912); *Féminisme et coopération* (Paris, 1914); Suzanne Gibault, 'L'Evolution de la femme', *L'Equité*, 15 July 1913.

22 *L'Equité*, 15 Nov. 1913; Rauze, *Féminisme économique*, p. 16.

23 *FS*, 1 Sept. 1913 (cf. *L'Humanité*, 7 July 1913), 1 Oct. 1913–June 1914.

24 *La Bataille syndicaliste*, 21, 23 Aug., 14 Sept. 1913; *L'Equité*, 15 July, 15 Aug. 1913; *La Vie ouvrière*, 5 July 1913 (p. 54), 5 Aug. 1913 (p. 190); *La Typographie française*, 16 Aug. 1913 (p. 4).

25 'Statuts', *La Typographie française*, 16 Sept. 1881 (p. 1); Fédération Française des Travailleurs du Livre, *Dixième congrès national tenu à Bordeaux du 18 au 23 juillet 1910* (Paris, n.d.), pp. 463–85; *Neuvième congrès national tenu à Lyon du 5 au 10 juin 1905* (Paris, 1905), p. 96; L.-M. Compain, *La Femme dans les organisations ouvrières* (Paris, 1910), p. 24; Paul Chauvet, *Les Ouvriers du livre en France*, II (Paris, 1956), 261–75, and III (Paris, 1971), 27–8, 35–6.

26 *La Typographie française*, 16 Aug. 1913 (p. 4); *La Bataille syndicaliste*, 21 Aug. 1913 (p. 1), 14 Sept. 1913 (p. 2); *La Lutte de classe*, 27 Dec. 1913. Even the Ligue des Droits de l'Homme took up the affair (*Bulletin officiel de la Ligue*, 15 Nov. 1913 [p. 1252]).

27 *La Bataille syndicaliste*, 24–6, 28, 29, 31 Aug., 2, 5, 7, 9, 28 Sept. 1913. Rosmer had no hesitation in citing the English suffragist women as examples of revolutionary courage from which French men and women could profit. The anarchists had similar reactions: cf. Emile Pouget in *La Guerre sociale*, 13 Aug. 1913 (p. 2), 27 Aug. 1913 (p. 2), 27 May 1914 (p. 2); Georges Allombre [Yvetôt] in *La Voix du peuple*, 21 Dec. 1913 (p. 2); *Le Libertaire*, 6 Sept. 1913 (p. 3), 29 Nov. 1913 (p. 2).

28 *La Bataille syndicaliste*, 12 Aug. 1913 (p. 2); *Le Réveil typographique*, June 1913; *La Typographie française*, 16 Aug., 16 Sept., 16 Oct., 1, 16 Nov. 1913, 1 Feb. 1914; Louis Couriau, 'Action syndicale féminine', *La Voix du peuple*, 6 Apr. 1914. Cf. Charles Sowerwine, 'Socialists, syndicalists and women: the Couriau affair', paper delivered 29 Dec. 1977 at the Annual Meeting of the American Historical Association, Dallas, Texas.

29 'Communications', *L'Humanité*, 1 Oct. 1913; Brion, *Grande encyclopédie féministe* (ms, 60 vols., IFHS), XII, 17; letter, Brion to Durand, 21 Oct. 1913, BMD, dossier Brion.

30 'Convocations', *L'Humanité*, 6 Nov. 1913; *ibid.*, 17, 22 Nov. 1913. The meeting was a great success, with at least a thousand persons present (AN F7 13.266, 'Paris 1913–28', 16 Dec. 1913; *L'Equité*, 15 Dec. 1913, 15 Jan. 1914).

31 *La Lutte de classe*, 25 May, 20, 27 July, 5 Oct., 1, 15 Nov. 1913, and esp. 31 Jan. 1914 (p. 2); *Le Socialiste*, 20 July, Nov. 1913; see Appendix 3.

32 *FS*, 15 Nov. 1913; *L'Humanité*, 14, 16 Dec. 1913.

33 See Appendix 3.

34 AN F7 13.074, 'Congrès de la Fédération de la Seine', 20 Dec. 1913, 19 Jan. 1914; *La Lutte de classe*, 27 Dec. 1913, 31 Jan., 7 Feb. 1914; *L'Humanité*, 2, 13, 29 Jan. 1914; *FS*, 1 Apr. 1914. Bouvard was elected as substitute (*suppléante*) for Toussaint-Kassky and took her place upon her resignation (*L'Humanité*, 8 Apr. 1914).

35 *FS*, 1 Apr. 1914; *L'Equité*, 15 Feb. 1914.

36 *FS*, June 1914; *L'Equité*, 15 May 1914; *L'Humanité*, 14, 19, 29 May, 9, 12 June, 8, 9 July 1914.

37 Cf. Fanny Clar, 'Notre coin', *La Guerre sociale*, 19 Mar. 1913.

38 'Convocations', *L'Humanité*, 21, 28 Jan., 5, 9, 16, 20, 25 Feb., 5, 9–11, 18, 25 Mar., 2, 8, 15, 22 Apr., 7, 10, 13, 14, 19, 20, 29 May, 4, 9, 10, 12, 13, 17, 24, 26, 30 June, 1, 2, 7–9, 12, 22, 24, 29 July 1914.

39 *Ibid.*, 28 Jan., 9, 16, 20, 25 Feb. 1914; 8, 9 Mar. 1914, pp. 1, 6; *L'Equité*, 15 Mar., 1 Apr. 1914; *FS*, 1 Apr. 1914.
40 The feminists ran a vast campaign in the major daily *Le Journal*, which published articles by leading feminists every day from 9 Mar. through 5 May 1914 and organised a parallel 'election' for women: over 500,000 deposed bulletins marked 'I desire to vote' in its urns.
41 *FS*, 1 May, June 1914; *L'Equité*, 1 May 1914; 'Manifestation pacifiste à Berlin', *L'Humanité*, 23 Apr., 4 May 1914. Chats were given by Désormonts (*ibid.*, 29 May 1914), Despeuch (10 June, 7 July), Gibault, Jouenne (26 June), and Saumoneau (30 June), who published her chat under the title *Luttes et souffrances de la femme* (Paris, n.d.).
42 Marie Laignier, 'A la besogne', *L'Equité*, 15 Jan. 1914; *L'Humanité*, 17, 22 Nov. 1914.
43 *L'Equité*, 15 July 1913; *L'Humanité*, 15 Mar., 24 Nov. 1913; *Le Socialiste*, 23 Feb. 1913; *FS*, 15 Apr., 20 July 1913.
44 *L'Equité*, 15 June 1913.

7. The First World War and socialist women 1914—20

1 Joll, pp. 163—4. Cf. Georges Haupt, *Socialism and the Great War: The Collapse of the Second International* (Oxford, 1972), pp. 183—94.
2 'Convocations, Parti socialiste', *L'Humanité*, 22, 24, 29 July 1914; *FS*, July 1914.
3 Goldberg, pp. 458—74; Louise Saumoneau, *Les Femmes socialistes contre la guerre*, III ([Paris, 1923]), 2—3.
4 Sowerwine, *Les Femmes*, pp. 267—8; Saumoneau, *Les Femmes*, III, 4—5; *FS*, Dec. 1914.
5 Saumoneau, *Les Femmes*, III, 5; APP B/a 1545, '2230—10', 22 May 1915. Ludmila (or Ludimila) Stigliss (or Stiglus, according to the police) was born Elma Anna Zaslawsky-Golikoff on 2 Mar. 1879 at Ever, Russia (AN F7 13.374, 'Louise Saumoneau', 22 May 1915). Cf. Jean Rocher, *Lénine et le mouvement zimmerwaldien en France* (Paris, 1934), pp. 21—3; Annie Kriegel, *Aux origines du communisme français, 1914—1920: Contribution à l'histoire du mouvement ouvrier français* [2 vols., Paris, 1964], p. 82n.
6 Saumoneau, *Les Femmes*, III, 6; *FS*, Dec. 1914. Cf. Haupt, p. 21.
7 Louise Saumoneau, *Les Femmes socialistes contre la guerre*, I ([Paris], n.d.), 7; *FS*, Dec. 1914.
8 *FS*, Feb. 1915. Saumoneau remained on the 'commission de contrôle'.
9 Sima Debora Gopner, sometimes called Véra, was born in Kerson, near Odessa, on 26 March 1880; her father was a 'notable intellectuel israélite' (AN F7 13.374, 'Louise Saumoneau', 22 May 1915). A close collaborator of Lenin since 1907, she had fled from Odessa in 1907 after 'a wave of arrests which annihilated our network' (S[ima] Gopner in *Souvenirs sur Lénine* [Paris, 1956], pp. 248—53). At Paris, she was 'one of the most active propagandists of Bolshevik ideas' (Rocher, p. 8). The police listed her as the 'former student' with whom Saumoneau was most in contact (APP B/a 1545, '2230—10', 22 May 1915).
10 Rocher, p. 13; Louise Saumoneau, *Les Femmes socialistes contre la guerre*, I, 2—6, II (Paris, n.d.), 1, III, 7; *FS*, Feb., Mar. 1915, Supplément, 1917—18; AN F7 13.374, 'Louise Saumoneau', 22 Jan. 1915. Cf. Nicod, AN F7 13.374, 'Manifeste', 28 Jan. 1915.
11 *L'Equité*, 15 Mar. 1913; *FS*, Mar. 1915. Cf. Saumoneau, *Les Femmes*, II, 2—3. Alice Stein: born at Champagne (Vosges), 14 August 1873; died at Paris, 10 January 1954; married Jouenne, a militant of the co-operative movement, in 1904; became *chef de cabinet* for Suzanne Lacore when the latter was named 'sous-secrétaire d'état à la protection de l'enfance' in 1936 (*DMO*, XIII, 121—2; dossier Jouenne, BMD; *Le Mouvement féministe* [Geneva], 12 Dec. 1936).

12 *L'Equité*, 15 Feb. 1915; *FS*, Mar. 1915; Saumoneau, *Les Femmes*, II, 4–5; AN F7
   13.266, 'La Campagne féministe en faveur de la paix', Oct. 1915, p. 6. The women
   of *L'Equité* and a number of prominent feminists confirmed this position in
   February. In response to the visit to Paris of an anti-war Englishwoman, they published a statement written by Hélène Brion (who would herself be tried for pacifist
   propaganda in 1918): 'We do not believe that the time has come to disarm' (*L'Action
   féministe*, Feb. 1915; *L'Equité*, 15 Apr. 1915).
13 APP B/a 1545, '2230–10', 22 May 1915. The police mentioned Bouvard, Couteaudier, Variot, and Gauvin as supporters who avoided direct involvement in the
   CAFSPC (AN F7 13.266, 'La Campagne féministe'). Saumoneau later credited them
   with being the 'first nucleus which later became the CAFSPC' (*Les Femmes*, I, 7–8).
14 *FS*, Apr. 1915; APP B/a 1537, '7', 2 Mar. 1915. The resolution was published in the
   Berner Tagwacht; a copy in Saumoneau's hand, addressed to 'Le Social Democraten,
   Copenhague', was intercepted (AN F7 13.374; cf. APP B/a 1545, 22 May 1915, p. 4).
15 AN F7 13.266, 'La Campagne féministe'; AN F7 13.374, 'Louise Saumoneau', 22
   Mar. 1915.
16 AN F7 13.374, 'Louise Saumoneau', 24 Apr. 1915; Olga Hess Gankin and H.H.
   Fisher, *The Bolsheviks and the World War: The Origins of the Third International*
   (Stanford, 1940), p. 286. Marguerite Thévenet (later Rosmer's wife) was in Switzerland on 9 March and expressed a desire to attend the conference, but nothing came
   of it (Christian Gras, *Alfred Rosmer et le mouvement révolutionnaire international*
   [Paris, 1971], p. 154).
17 *FS*, Apr. 1915; O[lga] Ravich, 'Mezhdunarodnaia zhenskaia sotsialisticheskaia
   kontferenciia 1915 g.', tr. in Gankin and Fisher, pp. 291ff; Rocher, pp. 16–17.
18 *FS*, May 1915; a copy typed by Saumoneau is in IFHS 14 AS 183 (4)d, dossier
   'divers mouvements féminins'.
19 *Sotsial Demokrat*, 42 (21 May 1915), tr. in Gankin and Fisher, p. 300. Cf. N. Lenine
   and G. Zinoviev, *Contre le courant (1914–1917)*, tr. by V. Serge and Parijanine (2
   vols., Paris, 1927), I, 113–15.
20 APP B/a 1545, '2230–10', 10, 22 May 1915; AN F7 13.374 'Louise Saumoneau',
   20 Aug. 1915, for the tract.
21 *L'Humanité*, 6 Apr. 1915 (but cf. *La Bataille syndicaliste*, 16 Apr. 1915; *Berner
   Tagwacht*, 3 Apr. 1915); APP B/a 1535, '7', 4 May 1914; AN F7 13.074, 'Les
   Révolutionnaires russes et la guerre'. The police mention an earlier incident: the
   Russians once finding themselves in a majority at the fifth section had named
   Saumoneau their delegate to the federal Commission Exécutive (CE), where it was
   regarded as just another display of Russian bad taste. Jean Longuet, though soon to
   emerge as a leader of the internationalist minority, supported the CE's measures
   against Saumoneau.
22 APP B/a 1545, '2230–10', 22 May 1915; *FS*, June 1915; IFHS, 14 AS 183(4)d.
23 APP B/a 1545, '2230–10', 10, 22 May 1915 *et passim*; AN F7 13.374, 'Louise
   Saumoneau', 20, 31 Aug. 1915; AN F7 13.266, 'La Campagne féministe'; *FS*, July
   1915. For the Haute-Vienne resolution, see Alfred Rosmer, *Le Mouvement ouvrier
   pendant la guerre*, I (Paris, 1936), 292–6, and Sowerwine, *Les Femmes*, pp. 269–70.
24 AN F7 13.374, 'Louise Saumoneau', 27 May, 3 June 1915; APP B/a 1545, '2230–
   10', 2 July 1915.
25 *La Bataille syndicaliste*, 26 June 1915; AN F7 13.266, 'La Campagne féministe'; AN
   F7 13.374, 'Louise Saumoneau', 7 June 1915; letters, Louise Saumoneau to Robert
   Grimm, 15 June and 24 July 1915, Am IISG, Grimm Archives (unclassified); *FS*,
   Sept.–Oct. 1915.
26 Printed tract, beginning 'Alors que, confinées dans votre foyer': APP B/a 1545,
   '2230–10', n.d., and IFHS 14 AS 183(4)d, dossier 'divers mouvements féminins'
   (cf. *FS*, Aug. 1915); typed tract, beginning 'Laisserez-vous la classe capitaliste': AN
   F7 13.374, 'Louise Saumoneau', 7, 10 Jan. 1916 (cf. *FS*, Sept.–Oct. 1915).
27 APP B/a 1558, 'CRRI Rapport', 9 Sept. 1915. Alfred Rosmer observed that, instead

of distributing her tracts 'haphazardly, in the Metro, under doors, anywhere at all', Saumoneau would do better to cover the socialists more systematically (letter to Pierre Monatte, 23 Nov. 1915, in Gras, p. 145).

28 Title of chapter 4, section 1, Kriegel.

29 Letter, Louise Saumoneau to Robert Grimm, 1 Sept. 1915, Am IISG, Archives Grimm S2B 139 (and in Horst Lademacher, ed., *Die Zimmerwalder Bewegung: Protokolle und Korrespondenz* [2 vols., The Hague, 1967], II, 99); letter, Jean Longuet to Louise Saumoneau, 7 Sept. 1915 (AN F7 13.374, 'Louise Saumoneau', 7 Sept. 1915); APP B/a 1545, '2230—10', 27 Sept. 1915; AN F7 13.069, dossier 'Zimmerwald', report of meeting 7 Nov. 1915; AN F7 13.374, 'Louise Saumoneau', 19 Oct. 1915; *FS*, Jan. 1916.

30 Hubert Bourgin, *Le Parti contre la patrie* (Paris, 1924), pp. 41—2 (an eyewitness — cf. Rosmer, I, 269); AN F7 12.891(4), 13, 21 Oct. 1915; APP B/a 1535, '7', 9 Nov. 1915; *FS*, Nov.—Dec. 1915, and Sowerwine, *Les Femmes*, pp. 269—70, for the Haute-Vienne resolution, on which Alfred Rosmer commented as follows: 'They have voted a very good resolution for Saumoneau, and *Le Populaire* has published it. She's a brave woman, Saumoneau, she has her flaws, but she keeps going, lost though she is' (letter to Pierre Monatte, 20 Oct. 1915, in Jean Maitron and Colette Chambelland [eds.], *Syndicalisme révolutionnaire et communisme: Les archives de Pierre Monatte, 1914—1924* [Paris, 1968], p. 195).

31 APP B/a 1535, '7', 9 Nov. 1915.

32 See Kriegel, pp. 109—12; Rosmer, I, 554ff, II (Paris, 1959), 21ff; Ligou, pp. 262—4. Documents in Lademacher, and in Gankin and Fisher, pp. 309—70.

33 Bourderon was a member of the twelfth section, where he knew Berthe Saumoneau; he and Louise had worked together to support the Haute-Vienne resolution (APP B/a 1535, '79', 10 July 1915). The other delegate was Alphonse Merrheim, secretary of the metal-workers' federation. He also knew Saumoneau, who had given him Liebknecht's manifesto, which she had obtained at Berne from Zetkin (Kriegel, p. 103n). She also served as an intermediary for letters to Merrheim for the arrangement of Zimmerwald (AN F7 13.374, 'Louise Saumoneau' for disguised letter to Merrheim from the Swiss syndicalist F. Brupbacher, dated 12 Aug. 1915, confirming holding of conference). But Marcel Martinet wrote to Pierre Monatte that Merrheim had little confidence in Saumoneau (letter, 23 [Aug. 1915], Maitron and Chambelland, p. 153).

34 AN F7 12.891(4), 23 Oct. 1915.

35 *Ibid.*, 10 Nov. 1915; AN F7 13.069, dossier 'Zimmerwald'; APP B/a 1558, 'CRRI', 7 Nov. 1915. Cf. Marcel Martinet's account: 'Bouvard, the *conseillère prud'homme*, comes to speak of what women have done, of Saumoneau . . . Merr[heim], R[osmer] too warned me against her. But today in any case, extremely moved, her words were moving and right and made a good impression' (letter to Pierre Monatte, 8 Nov. 1915, Maitron and Chambelland, p. 197).

36 Kriegel, p. 118n, for growth of movement. Merrheim had it on good authority that Briand had decided upon her release against the wishes of Guesde and Sembat (the two socialist ministers! — AN F7 12.891[4], 25 Nov. 1915).

37 Interview Mme Fourton; typed tracts: (1) beginning 'Lorsqu'il y a 16 mois', and (2) beginning 'Jusqu'où ira votre résignation': AN F7 13.374, 'Louise Saumoneau', 7, 10 Jan. 1916 (cf. *FS*, Jan. 1916). Saumoneau also wrote an account of her stay in prison, found with the tracts, in *FS*, Jan. 1916, and in *Socialist Review*, Jan.—Mar. 1916, p. 76.

38 After 1919, the Women's International League for Peace and Freedom. Dr Aletta Jacobs, one of the founders, had sought a French delegate for the founding congress at The Hague in April 1915, but had ruled out Saumoneau and all the GDFS, wishing 'to go beyond party lines' (see Charles Sowerwine, 'Women against the war: a feminine basis for internationalism and pacifism?' *WSFH*. VI [1978], 361—70). The secretary of the French section (founded in June) was Jeanne Halbwachs; she and

her fiancé (Michel Alexandre), both students of Alain, prepared 'Section Française des Femmes pour une paix permanente', *Un Devoir urgent pour les femmes* (Paris, 1915 — IFHS, 14 AS 183[4] e), which they rightly termed 'a wish ... that the government listen to any peace proposals' (AN F7 12.891[4], 25 Nov. 1915). *Le Journal* of 2 Dec. 1915 denounced it as German propaganda. The police search followed that afternoon (Rosmer, II, 40—3).

39   *FS*, Jan. 1916; APP B/a 1535, '7', 11 Dec. 1915, '79', 6 Dec. 1915; AN F7 13.073, 'Congrès', 19 Dec. 1915. The police informer reported that 'Mme Roussel' had interrupted a speech, shouting 'Russia is leading a war of conquest' (AN F7 12.891[4], 'Congrès du PS, 2e jour'). This was beyond Angèle Roussel (cf. *Le Populaire*, 12 Feb. 1917). Could it have been Rauze?

40   APP B/a 1558, Comité pour la Reprise des Relations Internationales (CRRI), 22 Nov., 20 Dec., 1915.

41   AN F7 13.374, 'Louise Couteaudier', 20 Jan., 4 Feb. 1916; *La Lutte de classe*, 24 Aug. 1913, 17 Jan. 1914; *L'Equité*, 15 May 1913, 1 May 1914.

42   *FS*, Feb., Mar. 1916.

43   *La Vague*, 14 Aug. 1919; *L'Equité*, 30 Nov. 1915.

44   *L'Equité*, 31 Dec. 1915, 31 Jan., Mar., June 1916; 'Groupe des Femmes Socialistes', *L'Humanité*, 3, 11 Jan., 1 Feb. 1916; *FS*, Jan.—Mar., Sept. 1916.

45   *FS*, Apr.—May 1916; AN F7 13.374, 'Louise Saumoneau', 19 May 1916. Cf. Gustave Téry in *L'Oeuvre*, 15 Sept. 1916; *Ce qu'il faut dire*, 30 Sept. 1916; 'A M. Gustave Téry', in Louise Saumoneau, *Etudes et critiques, 2e opuscule* (Paris, [1924]).

46   AN F7 13.374, 'Louise Couteaudier', 18 Jan. 1916.

47   *FS*, Aug., Oct., Nov.—Dec. 1916, Jan.—Mar. 1917.

48   *Ibid.*, Sept. 1916. The other officers were Pautet, treasurer; Frioux, assistant treasurer; Hubert, librarian-archivist. Cf. AN F7 13.374, 'Louise Couteaudier', 4 Feb. 1916.

49   *FS*, Nov.—Dec. 1916.

50   Tract beginning, 'Depuis plus de deux ans et demi', IFHS, 14 AS 183[4] d.

51   *FS*, Apr. 1917; AN F7 12.911, 'Rapport mensuel', Mar. 1917. The result of this success was a search of the homes of Saumoneau, her mother, and Couteaudier; the police found 300 copies of the tract (AN F7 13.375, 10 May 1917).

52   *FS*, June—Aug. 1917.

53   *Le Populaire*, 27 Nov. 1916 (Rauze's first article), 25 Sept. 1917 (p. 2); *Circulaire de la minorité du Parti socialiste: Aux fédérations* (N.p., [Nov. 1916]), p. 32; APP B/a 1558, 'CRRI', 23 Jan. 1917; *Ulysse Leriche contre Jean Longuet et ses acolytes* (Paris, 1917 — AN F7 13.072, pièce 411). Rauze later claimed that she had opposed the war from the start and had been so effective in mobilising anti-war feeling among the socialists of Chartres that the government 'let it be known to the officer [Captain Comignan] that it was incumbent on him to "control" his wife'. Having refused he was sent to join 'the mountain light infantry, whence there is no return' ('Portrait', *La Vague*, 14 Aug. 1919). She also claimed that she had written an anti-war manifesto in November 1914 (when she was in fact organising a pro-war response to the Dutch socialist women). A manifesto by Rauze was published in *Demain*, May 1917, pp. 8—10, with the indication that it was 'revised' in November 1916.

54   *Le Populaire*, 21 July, 11, 25 Aug., 15, 22 Sept. 1917; *FS*, Sept.—Dec. 1917. Cf. Kriegel, pp. 146—50, 167—8. The organisers actually announced abandonment of their plans on 15 September, but news travelled slowly.

55   *FS*, June—August, Sept.—Dec. 1917. The journal served mainly to hide the tracts of the CRRI; for this reason the director of the mails sought unsuccessfully to have it prohibited (AN F7 13.375, 'Femme socialiste', 12 Dec. 1917 *et passim*).

56   First CRRI tract, APP B/a 1558, 'CRRI'; AN F7 13.086, '2', 4 June 1916; APP B/a 1558, 'CRRI', 4 Aug. 1916 (last report mentioning Couteaudier).

57   Kriegel, pp. 127—8, 127n.

58   Letter, Alfred Rosmer to Pierre Monatte, 16 Jan. [1916], IFHS, 14 AS 246(c), letter

9; APP B/a 1558, 'CRRI', 7, 11 Apr., 9 May, 6 June, 4 July, 1, 4, 11, 15, 29 Aug., 15 Sept. 1916: AN F7 13.349, 'Réunions pacifistes', 2, 9 May 1916; *FS*, Aug. 1916; *Journal officiel, Chambre*, 25 June 1916; Kriegel, p. 153n.

59 APP B/a 1558, 'CRRI', 21, 23, 24 Nov. 1916, 5 Jan. 1917; Rosmer, II, 210—11; CRRI, section socialiste, *Aux militants du parti socialiste* (AN F7 13.375, dossier 'Femme socialiste', Apr. 1917); *L'Humanité*, 19 Dec. 1916; Louis, p. 343; Ligou, p. 290; AN F7 13.071, 'congrès', 25 Dec. 1916; *La Vague*, 14 Aug. 1919; interview with M. et Mme Gilbert Nowina, 24 Jan. 1973; interview with Mme Alexandre.

60 APP B/a 1558, 'CRRI', 9, 19 Jan., 2, 16, 17 Feb., 2 Mar., 8 June, 19 Oct. 1917; *FS*, Supplément No 1, 1916—17, Sept.—Dec. 1917; *Demain*, May 1917, p. 41; Brion, *La Voie féministe*, p. 21; interview with M. Nowina.

61 AN F7 13.072, 'congrès socialiste', pièce 451; *ibid.*, 8, 10 Oct. 1917; CRRI, *Aux militants* (AN F7 13.375, dossier 'Femme socialiste').

62 Kriegel, pp. 171—2, 193.

63 AN F7 13.072, 'Congrès national SFIO', 8, 12 Oct. 1918; Louis, p. 351. Kauffmann and Saumoneau were representatives of the CRRI on the resolutions committee, Rauze of the minority.

64 Saumoneau, 'Pour l'internationale communiste', Saumoneau, *Etudes et critiques, 2e opuscule*; *FS*, Apr. 1919.

65 *L'Humanité*, 21—3 Apr. 1919; Louis, pp. 357, 359; Kriegel, pp. 251—3; *FS*, 10 June 1919.

66 Saumoneau wrote in *L'Internationale*, organ of Péricat's abortive communist party, from its founding in February 1919 through the 5 July issue on her old theme that proletarian women must join the party: 'Feminism is to the emancipation of the sexes as pacifism is to our conception of peace . . . that is an error which would be fatal to the proletariat if we let ourselves be fooled' (8 Mar. 1919). She wrote in the revolutionary syndicalist weekly, *La Vie ouvrière*, every week through October 1919, then every month through March 1920.

67 *La Vie ouvrière*, 13 Aug. 1919; letter, Louise Saumoneau to Jean-Richard Bloch, 31 July 1919, BN mss, n.a.f. 15900, 11.48; *FS*, 15 Aug., 10 Nov. 1919; *La Vie ouvrière*, 20 Aug., 24 Sept., 1 Oct. 1919; *L'Humanité*, 15 Sept. 1919.

68 Parti Socialiste (SFIO), *17e congrès national tenu à Strasbourg les 25, 26, 27, 28 et 29 février 1920: Compte rendu sténographique* (Paris, n.d.), pp. 386—7, 472—6; *L'Humanité*, 28 Feb. 1920; Louis, p. 362; *La Vie ouvrière*, 19 Mar. 1920.

69 SFIO, *Congrès Strasbourg 1920*, pp. 17—18, 560; *L'Humanité*, 12 Oct. 1918, 3 May 1920; Brion, *Grande encyclopédie féministe* (IFHS), X, 65.

70 Charles Rappoport, 'Autobiographie' [typewritten], Am IISG, p. 54, n. 113 (communicated by H. Goldberg); APP 'archives non versées' (*DMO*, XV, 138).

71 SFIO, *Congrès Strasbourg 1920*, pp. 472—6. Cf. Loriot, *ibid.*, p. 469.

72 *FS*, 1 Aug. 1920; Louis, p. 364; letters, Louise Saumoneau to Paul Faure, 13 Nov. 1920, 3 Jan. 1920 (Saumoneau, *Etudes et critiques, 5e opuscule*); interview with Mme Fourton.

73 Parti Socialiste (SFIO), *18e congrès national tenu à Tours les 25, 26, 27, 28, 29 et 30 décembre 1920: Compte rendu sténographique* (Paris, 1921).

74 Madeleine Pelletier, *Journal* (ms, dos. Pelletier, BMD).

75 Marianne Rauze, *La Propagande socialiste révolutionnaire* (Paris, 1919), p. 23; AN F7 12.967, 'Rapport mensuel', Aug. 1920; Marianne Rauze, *La Femme du communisme primitif au communisme futur: Conférence faite à l'Ecole communiste marxiste* (Asnières, n.d., cf. *Cahiers de l'école communiste marxiste*, 10 [1922?]). By 1923, Rauze decided that the Red Army was becoming a professional army instead of dissolving itself after the Allied invasion had been repulsed. She turned to a pacifism so absolute that Romain Rolland warned her that her doctrine was 'too exclusively (nearly exclusively) anti, that is negative'. She formed a 'union against death', a nearly mystical pacifist group, whose cause she preached on the fringes between anarchism, mysticism, and Esperanto. See Marianne Rauze, *L'Anti-guerre:*

essai d'une doctrine et d'une philosophie de l'anti-militarisme en 1923, postface by Romain Rolland, prefaces by W. Wellock and by Dr Stoecker (Niort, 1923), pp. 47, 187, 194—6; and Marianne Rauze, preface to Cheng-Tcheng, *La Chine pacifique: Conférence faite au groupe ouvrier espérantiste de Cette* (Lyons, 1926), where she indicated that she published a pacifist newspaper at Lyons.

8. Reconstruction, decline, and rebirth 1921—79

1 Kriegel, pp. 791—862, esp. 837. Cf. Tony Judt, *La Reconstruction du Parti socialiste 1921—1926* (Paris, 1976).

2 Parti Socialiste (SFIO), *XXIVe congrès national tenu à Lyon les 17, 18, 19 et 20 avril 1927: Compte rendu sténographique* (Paris, n.d.), p. 344; *XXVIIe congrès national tenu à Bordeaux les 8, 9, 10 et 11 juin 1930: Compte rendu sténographique* (Paris, n.d.), p. 398.

3 *FS*, 1 Feb., 1 June, 15 July, 15 Aug. 1922.

4 *Ibid.*, May, July 1923; Parti Socialiste (SFIO), *XXIe congrès national 30—31 janvier— 1er—2—3 février 1924, Marseille: Rapports* (Paris, 1923), p. 49.

5 *FS*, Apr.—May 1924.

6 SFIO, *Congrès Bordeaux 1930: Compte rendu*, pp. 173—4; Parti Socialiste (SFIO), *XXVIIIe congrès national tenu à Tours les 24, 25, 26 et 27 mai 1931: Compte rendu sténographique* (Paris, n.d.), pp. 206, 211; *XXXVIe congrès national 27, 28, 29 et 30 mai 1939, Nantes:.Rapports* (Paris, 1939), p. 146.

7 SFIO, *Congrès Bordeaux 1930: Compte rendu*, pp. 180, 197.

8 Parti Socialiste (SFIO), *XXXVIe congrès national tenu à Nancy les 9, 10, 11 et 12 juin 1929: Compte rendu sténographique* (Paris, n.d.), p. 386.

9 SFIO, *Congrès Bordeaux 1930: Compte rendu*, p. 169; *Le Populaire*, 18 Apr. 1930.

10 SFIO, *Congrès Bordeaux 1930: Compte rendu*, pp. 163, 165, 169—70, 178—9, 202—4, 208—9.

11 *Ibid.*, p. 398; Parti Socialiste (SFIO), *XXVIIe congrès national 8, 9, 10 et 11 juin 1930 Bordeaux: Rapports* (Paris, 1930), p. 43; *FS*, July, Dec. 1930, Jan., Feb., Mar. 1931.

12 Daniel Mayer, *Pour une histoire de la gauche* (Paris, 1969), pp. 273—4, 280; letter, Germaine Degrond to the author, 21 Jan. 1973; interview with Berthe Fouchère, 15 Dec. 1971.

13 SFIO, *Congrès Tours 1931: Compte rendu*, pp. 194—207.

14 *Ibid.*, pp. 209—30, 237.

15 *Ibid.*, pp. 372—4; Parti Socialiste (SFIO), *XXIXe congrès national 29—30—31 mai— 1er juin 1932, Paris: Rapports* (Paris, 1932), p. 107.

16 Parti Socialiste (SFIO), *XXXIXe congrès national tenu à Paris les 29, 30, 31 mai et 1er juin 1932: Compte rendu sténographique* (Paris, n.d.), p. 268; interviews, Fouchère, Fourton.

17 For membership figures, see Appendix 2.

18 Parti Socialiste (SFIO), *XXXIIe congrès national 9, 10, 11, 12 juin 1935, Mulhouse: Rapports* (Paris, 1935), pp. 163—4.

19 SFIO, *Congrès Tours 1931: Compte rendu*, p. 202; see Appendix 2.

20 Parti Socialiste (SFIO), *XXXIe congrès national tenu à Toulouse les 20, 21, 22 et 23 mai 1934: Compte rendu sténographique* (Paris, n.d.), p. 27.

21 SFIO: *Congrès 1935 Mulhouse: Rapports*, p. 198; Parti Socialiste (SFIO), *XXXIIe congrès national tenu à Mulhouse les 9, 10, 11 et 12 juin 1935: Compte rendu sténographique* (Paris, n.d.), pp. 520—5.

22 Cf. Jean Lacouture, *Léon Blum* (Paris, 1977), p. 302.

23 *FS*, Oct. 1937, Feb., Mar. 1940.

24 *Propagande et Documentation*, 2 (1947), p. 6, 2 (1948), p. 4n.; 'Commission nationale féminine', IFHS, Fonds Vassart, 14 AS 206(d), dossier XVI—D annexe

nº 3; interview, Fouchère; letter, Odette Nagler to the author, 26 Feb. 1973; *FS,*
Nov. 1932; *Le Populaire,* 14 Oct. 1932.
25 Daniel Mayer, *Les Socialistes dans la Résistance: Souvenirs et documents* (Paris,
1968), pp. 109, 136—9.
26 Interview, Fouchère; 'Commission', IFHS, Fonds Vassart.
27 *Ibid.; DMO,* Part IV (ms: 'Fouchère').
28 Interview with Janette Brutelle, 14 Dec. 1971; letter, Janette Brutelle to the author,
28 Jan. 1978.
29 *Ibid.;* Thierry Pfister, *Les Socialistes: Les secrets de famille, les rites, le code et les
hommes du premier parti de France* (Paris, 1977), p. 23.
30 Pfister, p. 130; interview with Yvette Roudy, 15 Nov. 1977; telephone conversation
with Colette Audry, 22 Nov. 1977.
31 Pfister, p. 101; interview, Brutelle; J.R. Frears, *Political Parties and Elections in the
French Fifth Republic* (London, 1977), p. 117.
32 Interview, Roudy.
33 *Ibid.;* press release and other documents from Secrétariat National à l'Action
Féminine, PS.
34 Interview, Roudy; Pfister, pp. 196—7; conversation, Audry.
35 'Le projet socialiste', *Le Poing et la rose,* 85 (Nov.—Dec. 1979), 14—15.
36 Véronique Neiertz, letter to the author, 4 Jan. 1980; Parti socialiste, *Femmes en
lutte: femmes et socialisme* (Paris, 1979); *Le Monde,* 11, 28 Nov., 8 Dec. 1979.
37 *Unité,* 14 Dec. 1979.

Appendix 1. The Second International and the woman question 1889—1904

1 For the period 1904—14, see chapter 5. Cf. Madeleine Rebérioux, 'La Question
féminine dans les débats de la Deuxième Internationale', in *Actes du colloque con-
sacré à Anna Kulischoff* (Milan, 1978).
2 Fédération des Travailleurs Socialistes de France (FTSF), *Compte rendu du congrès
international ouvrier socialiste tenu à Paris du 15 au 20 juillet 1889* (Paris, 1891),
p. 42.
3 *Congrès international ouvrier socialiste de Paris (du 14 juillet au 21 juillet 1889):
Appel de la Commission d'organisation, liste des délégués et partis socialistes
représentés, télégrammes et lettres d'adhésion, résolutions* (Paris, 1889), p. 16.
4 FTSF, *Congrès international Paris, 1889,* p. 67; *Congrès international Paris, 1889:
Appel,* p. 19.
5 *Congrès international ouvrier socialiste tenu à Bruxelles du 16 au 31 août 1891:
Rapport publié par le secrétariat belge* (Brussels, 1893), pp. 84—5, 246—7; cf. Aline
Valette, 'La Femme et le socialisme', *L'Harmonie sociale,* 15 Oct. 1892.
6 *Cinquième congrès international tenu à Paris du 23 au 27 septembre 1900: Compte
rendu analytique* (Paris, 1901), p. 112; *Sixième congrès socialiste international tenu
à Amsterdam du 14 au 20 août 1904: Compte rendu analytique publié par le secrétariat international* (Brussels, 1904), p. 125.
7 'Société républicaine d'économie sociale', *La Revue socialiste* (1886, I), 345, 368.
Cf. [Valette and Bonnier], *Socialisme et sexualisme,* pp. 91—2.
8 *Les Congrès socialistes internationaux: Ordres du jour et résolutions (publié par le
Bureau socialiste international de Bruxelles)* (Gand, 1902), p. 71.

Appendix 2. French socialist women in figures

1 Willard, *Les Guesdistes,* p. 362n.; interview with Claude Willard, 4 Nov. 1977;
Marthe Louis-Lévy, *L'Emancipation politique des femmes: Rapport présenté à la
première conférence nationale des femmes socialistes (4—5 juin 1933)* (Paris, 1934),
p. 29. Cf. table 1 below, p. 200.

2 Louis, pp. 290–1, 382–7; AN F7 13.071, 'PS, Fédération de la Seine'; Jolyon Howorth, 'Socialists and syndicalists in France (1884–1900): the symbiosis of struggle', paper presented at the meeting of the American Historical Association, Dallas, Texas, 29 Dec. 1977, p. 1; Willard, *Les Guesdistes*, p. 316.

3 Heinzely, pp. 155–6; 'Vers une fédération nationale des femmes socialistes', *L'Equité*, 15 Feb. 1913.

4 *L'Humanité*, 31 July 1910; *Le Socialiste*, 16 June, 28 July 1912. Cf. *L'Humanité*, 22 Feb. 1906, 29 Apr. 1907, 9, 19 Jan. 1912; *Le Socialiste*, 17 Oct. 1909, 30 Jan. 1910, 19 Jan. 1913. The feminists remained just as weak. The police estimated in 1904 that Auclert had collected 125 names in twenty years of militant activity, and that this included even the most tepid sympathisers (APP B/a 1651, 22 July 1904). At a meeting of La Solidarité at the same period, Louise Réville, a prominent feminist, stated without fear of contradiction that there were hardly 500 feminists in all Paris (*Le Libertaire*, 30 Jan. 1904).

5 These figures hide the brutal changes in membership following the war, the schism, reconstruction, etc. The party reached 130,000 members at the end of 1920, of which only a quarter left it to join the reconstruction of the SFIO (Louis, p. 382; Judt, p. 17). The SFIO regained this membership (i.e. 130,000) by 1932, when the first census of women was undertaken (Louis, pp. 386–7; Louis-Lévy, p. 29). The Seine federation, however, did not regain its pre-schism membership: 11,020 members in 1914, 21,200 in 1920, 2605 in 1923, 7000–7500 in 1930–2 (Judt, Annexe VI; Parti Socialiste [SFIO], *XXIXe congrès national, 29, 30, 31 mai, 1er juin 1932, Paris* [Paris, 1932], p. 87). We may suppose that these changes did not affect women to the extent that they reflected political changes to which women, less politicised than men, were less subject.

Appendix 3. Elisabeth Renaud and the Cambier affair

1 *La Lutte de classe*, 31 Jan. 1914.

2 *Ibid.*, 25 May, 20 July, 27 Dec. 1913, 31 Jan. 1914; *Le Socialiste*, 20 July 1913; AN F7 13.074, 20 Dec. 1913, 19 Jan. 1914.

3 AN F7 13.072, 26 Mar. 1913, 26, 27 Jan. 1914; AN F7 13.074. 'Mouvement socialiste', Jan. 1914; Lefranc, p. 189; Louis, p. 310; *L'Humanité*, 27 Jan. 1914.

4 *La Lutte de classe*, 31 Jan., 7 Feb., 7 Mar. 1914.

5 *Le Cri du peuple*, 22, 26, 29 Mar., 3, 17, 19 Apr., 1, 3, 16 May 1914; *La Lutte de classe*, 21 Feb. 1914.

6 *La Lutte de classe*, 25 May, 14, 21 June, 10 Aug. 1913.

7 *Ibid.*, 7 June, 17 Aug. 1913, 7 Mar., 25 Apr. 1914; *Le Cri du peuple*, 5, 13 Apr., 3 June 1914.

8 Letter, Elisabeth Renaud to Jules Guesde, 27 Mar. 1914 (Am IISG, Guesde Archives, 482/19).

9 AN F7 13.074, 'Mouvement socialiste', Apr. 1914; *La Lutte de classe*, 20 June 1914.

10 Interview with Mme Benoist-Guesde; *Le Populaire*, 17 Oct. 1932; *FS*, Nov. 1932.

Bibliography

The following bibliography, while reasonably thorough, is not exhaustive. It is meant to serve three purposes: first, to provide complete references for works cited a second time in the notes under shortened titles or simply author; second, to give an indication of the sources used in this study; and, third, to make possible the pursuit of topics raised in this book in research libraries of the English-speaking world, at least in the secondary literature and ideally in some of the printed sources as well (for which purpose reference must also be made to the notes, especially for periodicals and works cited only once, as these are not listed in this bibliography, except for some particularly interesting works). Those who require an exhaustive bibliography as a research tool are referred to Sowerwine, *Les Femmes et le socialisme*. The bibliography there gives complete publication information (including all title variations and dates for periodicals), locations and call numbers for all works and includes cross-referenced lists of all publications of militants, articles and pamphlets as well as books.

    I. Archival sources
   II. Interviews and conversations
 III. Printed works of French women militants: books, brochures, articles
 IV. Printed works of critics, friends, militants, theorists, and witnesses
   V. Printed works of organisations
 VI. Congresses
VII. Secondary sources:
    (a) Books and theses
    (b) Articles

I. Archival sources

(a) Archives Nationales (AN)

I used the Commune prosecution files in the BB24 series and the reports of left-wing activity in the F7 series, the latter extensively.

(b) Archives de la Préfecture de Police (APP)

The following were especially useful: B/a 549 (1881 elections); B/a 612–13 (1885 elections); B/a 767 (Hervéists); B/a 1527 ('Etudiants collectivistes'); B/a 1535, 1537, 1545, 1558 (anti-war movement); B/a 1651 ('Mouvement féministe').

(c) Bibliothèque Historique de la Ville de Paris (BHVP)

The BHVP has Auclert's diary for 1883–5 and over 100 yards of uncatalogued materials from the Bouglé collection, which Maïté Albistur and Daniel Armogathe are presently cataloguing.

Bibliography

(d) Bibliothèque Marguerite Durand (BMD)

I used 'dossiers' on the following, nearly all of which contain significant correspondence: Auclert, Bonnevial, Brion, Chéliga, Durand, L'Egalité, Femmes socialistes, Groupe la Solidarité des Femmes, Kauffmann, Laguerre, Mink, Nelly Roussel, Pelletier, Gabrielle Petit, Potonié-Pierre, Rauze, Renaud, Rouzade, Saumoneau, Starkoff, Vincent. Also Hélène Brion, 'Squelette ébauche de la grande encyclopédie féministe' (6 vols., ms.).

(e) Bibliothèque Nationale, Cabinet des manuscrits (BN, mss.)

Saumoneau, letters and lecture notes (BN, mss, n.a.f. 15900, 11.48–50).

(f) Institut Français d'Histoire Sociale (IFHS)

14 AS 183(1) a–f: Hélène Brion, 'Grande encyclopédie féministe' (60 vols., ms.).
14 AS 183(4) d–e: tracts.
14 AS 206(d): Fonds Vassart, reports on women in SFIO and PCF, 1930–60.
(I have given to the IFHS all the materials I collected in the course of this study, including a complete collection of *La Femme socialiste* and of Saumoneau's other printed works.)

(g) International Instituut voor Sociale Geschiedenis (Am IISG)

The Guesde Archives contain letters of Bonnevial, Mink, Potonié-Pierre, and Renaud; the Grimm Archives contain four letters of Saumoneau.

II. Interviews and conversations

Mme Jeanne Alexandre (née Halbwachs), Colette Audry, Suzanne Benoist-Guesde, Janette Brutelle, Berthe Fouchère, Fernande Fourton, Jules-Marie Guesde, M. and Mme Gilbert Nowina, and Yvette Roudy all gave me interviews and most have continued correspondence as well. I have also corresponded with Olga Choquet, Germaine Degrond, Guy Mollet, Odette Nagler, and Véronique Neiertz.

III. Printed works of French women militants: books, brochures, articles

In most cases, locations are given after publication information. For abbreviations, see p. xx above.

[Astié de Valsayre] Etrivières, Jehan des. *Les Amazones du siècle (les gueulardes de Gambetta).* 3rd edn. Paris, 1882. BMD.
Auclert, Hubertine. *Le Droit politique des femmes, question qui n'est pas traitée au congrès international des femmes.* Paris, 1878. BN.
　Les Femmes au gouvernail. Paris, 1923. BN.
　Le Vote des femmes. Paris, 1908. MS.
Brion, Hélène. *La Voie féministe: Les partis d'avant-garde et le féminisme.* Epône [1917].
Deraismes, Maria. *Oeuvres complètes.* 3 vols. Paris, 1895–6. BHVP.
Etrivières, Jehan des. *See* Astié de Valsayre.
Lacore, Suzanne. *Femmes socialistes.* Paris, 1932, IFHS.
Louis-Lévy, Marthe. *L'Emancipation politique des femmes: Rapport présenté à la première conférence nationale des femmes socialistes (4–5 juin 1933).* Paris, 1934. BN.
Mink, Paule. See her articles and stories in *La Question sociale* and *Almanach de 'La Question sociale'*, 1891–6.
Pelletier, Dr Madeleine [Anne]. *L'Education féministe des filles.* Paris, 1914. BHVP.
　L'Emancipation sexuelle de la femme. Paris, 1911. BN/MS.

La Femme en lutte pour ses droits. Paris, 1908. BN. [Earlier version: *La Revue féministe* (1908, I), 318—31].

La Femme vierge: Roman. Paris, 1933. BN.

'La Question du vote des femmes'. *La Revue socialiste* (1908, II), 193—207, 329—42.

Potonié-Pierre, Eugénie. See her articles and stories in *La Question sociale* and *Almanach de 'La Question sociale'*, 1891—7.

Potonié-Pierre, [Edmond and Eugénie]. *Un peu plus tard.* Paris, 1893. BN

Rauze, Marianne. *L'Anti-guerre: essai d'une doctrine et d'une philosophie de l'anti-militarisme.* Niort, 1923. BN.

Féminisme économique. Preface by Suzanne Lacore. Paris, 1915. IFHS.

Féminisme intégral. Paris, 1919. BHVP.

La Femme, du communisme primitif au communisme futur. Conférence. Asnières [1921].

Renaud, Elisabeth. *La Femme au XXe siècle.* Paris, 1898. APP B/a 1651 [also *L'Humanité nouvelle* (1898), 337—44, 454—64].

Pourquoi les américains sont allés à Cuba. Paris, 1898. Am IISG.

Roudy, Yvette. *La Femme en marge.* Paris, 1975.

Rouzade, Léonie. *Développement du programme de la Société 'l'Union des Femmes'.* Paris, 1880. BN.

La Femme et le peuple. Organisation sociale de demain. Meudon, 1896. BN.

Le Monde renversé. Paris, 1872. BN.

Petit catéchisme de morale laïque et socialiste. Meudon, 1895. BN.

Le Roi Johanne. Paris, 1872. BN.

Voyage de Théodose à l'île d'Utopie. Paris, 1872. BN.

Saumoneau, Louise. *Etudes et critiques.* 5 opuscules. Paris, 1924. BN.

Les Femmes socialistes contre la guerre: I. *Appel de Clara Zetkin: Son introduction en France.* Paris, n.d.; II. *Autour du manifeste de Clara Zetkin.* Paris, n.d.; III. *Avant l'appel de Clara Zetkin.* Paris, 1923.

Luttes et souffrances de la femme: I. *La Femme dans son intérieur.* Paris, n.d. BHVP.

Principes et action féministes socialistes. Paris, n.d. Am IISG.

Sorgue. *Socialisme ministériel.* Paris, n.d. IFHS.

L'Unité révolutionnaire. Paris, 1901. BN.

Starkoff, Vera. *Le Bolchevisme.* Preface by Han Ryner. Paris, 1922. BHVP.

Valette, Aline. 'Féminisme et socialisme'. *La Petite République*, 9 Dec. 1896.

La Journée de la petite ménagère. Paris, 1883. BN.

'Une Journée historique: le premier mai en France', *La Revue socialiste* (1890, II), 129—55, 433—48.

[Valette, Aline]. *Oeuvre des libérées de Saint-Lazare, fondée en 1870, reconnue d'utilité publique par décret du 26 janvier 1885.* Alençon, 1889. BN.

[Valette, Aline and Bonnier, Pierre]. *Socialisme et sexualisme: Programme du Parti socialiste féminin.* Paris, 1893. BN.

IV. Printed works of critics, friends, militants, theorists, and witnesses

Allemane, Jean. *Notre programme développé et commenté, suivi d'un projet de règlement de groupe.* Paris, 1895. IFHS.

Programme municipal adopté par l'Union fédérative du centre, commenté. Paris, n.d. MS.

Argyriadès, P. *La Femme et le socialisme: Traduction analytique de l'ouvrage de Bebel.* Paris, n.d. MS [also *Almanach de 'la Question sociale'*, 1893, 131—52].

Bebel, August Ferdinand. *La Femme dans le passé, le présent et l'avenir.* Tr. by Henri Ravé. Preface by Paul Lafargue. Paris, 1891. MS.

Woman Under Socialism. Tr. by Daniel de Léon. New York, 1904; repr. 1971.

Benoist, Charles. *Les Ouvrières de l'aiguille à Paris: Notes pour l'étude de la question sociale.* Paris, 1895. MS.

Bibliography

Bonnier, Charles. *La Question de la femme*. Paris, 1897. BN.

Bourgin, Hubert. *Le Parti contre la patrie*. Paris, 1924. IFHS.

Compain, L.-M. *La Femme dans les organisations ouvrières*. Paris, 1910. MS.

Engels, Friedrich. *The Origin of the Family, Private Property and the State, In the Light of the Researches of Lewis H. Morgan*. Tr. by Alec West. New York, 1972.

    L'Origine de la famille, de la propriété privée et de l'Etat (pour faire suite aux travaux de Lewis H. Morgan). Tr. by Henri Ravé. Paris, 1893. MS.

Ghesquière, Henri. *La Femme et le socialisme*. Lille, 1893. BN.

[Guesde, Jules]. *Le Collectivisme devant la 10e Chambre (affaire du congrès ouvrier international socialiste). Défense collective présentée par le prévenu, J. Guesde.* Paris, 1878. MS.

    Textes choisis, 1867–1882. Ed. by Claude Willard. Paris, 1959.

Guesde, Jules and Lafargue, Paul. *Le Programme du Parti ouvrier: Son histoire, ses considérants, ses articles*. Paris, 1883. BN.

Haussonville, [Gabriel Paul Othenin de Cléron,] Comte d'. *Salaires et misères de femmes*. Paris, 1900. BN.

Lafargue, Paul. 'Le Matriarcat: Etude sur les origines de la famille'. *La Nouvelle Revue*, Mar. 1886, pp. 301–36; *Le Socialiste*, 4 Sept.–6 Oct. 1886.

    La Question de la femme. Paris, 1904. BN.

    Textes choisis. Ed. by Jacques Girault. Paris, 1970.

Malon, Benoît. *Le Parti ouvrier et sa politique*. Vol. II of *Oeuvres complètes de Benoît Malon: Le nouveau parti*. 2nd edn. Paris, 1882. BN.

    Le Socialisme intégral. 2 vols. Paris, 1890–1. BN.

Milhaud, Caroline. *L'Ouvrière en France: Sa condition présente, les réformes nécessaires*. Paris, 1907. MS.

Pelloutier, Fernand. 'La Monogamie et l'union libre'. *La Revue socialiste* (1894, I), 535–59.

    'La Femme dans la société moderne'. *La Revue socialiste* (1894, II), 285–311.

Pelloutier, Fernand and Maurice. 'La Femme dans l'industrie'. *L'Ouvrier des deux mondes*, Sept.–Dec. 1897, pp. 113ff, 129ff, 165ff.

Simon, Jules. *L'Ouvrière*. Paris, 1861. 7th edn. Paris, 1871. BN.

Stackelberg, F[réderic]. *La Femme et la révolution*. Paris, 1883. MS.

Vérecque, Charles. *Histoire de la famille des temps sauvages à nos jours*. Paris, 1914. BN.

Weyl, Claude. *La Réglementation du travail des femmes dans l'industrie (loi du 2 novembre 1892)*. Paris, 1898. MS.

V. Printed works of organisations

Fédération Française des Sociétés Féministes. *Cahier des doléances féminines*. Paris, 1893. APP B/a 1651.

Ligue Française pour le Droit des Femmes. *1870–1920: Cinquante ans de féminisme*. Paris, 1921. MS.

VI. Congresses

Feminist, socialist, and international socialist congresses have been a major source. Feminist congresses were consulted at the BMD, socialist congresses at the IFHS and the MS, and international socialist congresses at the BDIC and the Am IISG. A complete list of all congresses consulted may be found in Sowerwine, *Les Femmes*. For socialist congresses, it includes locations of official, police and journalists' accounts, indications of resolutions concerning women, women who spoke, and women delegates, cross-referenced with a complete index of all women delegates.

Bibliography

VII. Secondary sources

(a) Books and theses

Anderson, R.D. *France 1870–1914: Politics and Society*. London, 1977.

Bidelman, Patrick. 'The feminist movement in France: the formative years 1858–1889'. Ph.D., Michigan, 1975.

Boxer, Marilyn J. 'Socialism faces feminism in France: 1879–1913'. Ph.D., California-Riverside, 1975.

Boxer, Marilyn J. and Quataert, Jean H. (eds.). *Socialist Women: European Socialist Feminism in the Nineteenth and Early Twentieth Centuries*. New York, 1978.

Chastenet, Jacques. *Histoire de la Troisième République*. III. *La République triomphante*. Paris, 1955.

Chauvet, Paul. *Les Ouvriers du livre en France*: II. *De 1789 à la constitution de la Fédération française des travailleurs du livre*. Paris, 1956; III. *La Fédération française des travailleurs du livre*. Paris, 1971.

Dommanget, Maurice. *L'Introduction du marxisme en France*. Lausanne, 1969.

Droz, Jacques (ed.). *Histoire générale du socialisme*. 3 vols. Paris, 1974.

Evans, Richard J. *The Feminists: Women's Emancipation Movements in Europe, America and Australasia 1840–1920*. London, 1977.

Gankin, Olga Hess, and Fisher, H.H. *The Bolsheviks and the World War: The Origins of the Third International*. Stanford, California, 1940.

Goldberg, Harvey. *The Life of Jean Jaurès*. Madison, Wisconsin, 1962.

Gras, Christian. *Alfred Rosmer et le mouvement révolutionnaire international*. Paris, 1971.

Guilbert, Madeleine. *Les Femmes et l'organisation syndicale avant 1914*. Paris, 1966.

Haupt, Georges. *Socialism and the Great War: The Collapse of the Second International*. Oxford, 1972.

Heinzely, Hélène. 'Le Mouvement socialiste devant les problèmes du féminisme (1879–1914)'. Mémoire (DES), Paris, 1957. CHS.

Joll, James. *The Second International 1889–1914*. 2nd edn, London, 1974.

Judt, Tony. *La Reconstruction du Parti socialiste 1921–1926*. Paris, 1976.

Kriegel, Annie. *Aux origines du communisme français, 1914–1920: Contribution à l'histoire du mouvement ouvrier français*. 2 vols. Paris, 1964.

Lacouture, Jean. *Léon Blum*. Paris, 1977.

Lademacher, Horst, ed. *Die Zimmerwalder Bewegung: Protokolle und Korrespondenz*. 2 vols. The Hague, 1967.

Lefranc, Georges. *Le Mouvement socialiste sous la Troisième République (1875–1940)*. Paris, 1963.

Ligou, Daniel. *Histoire du socialisme en France (1871–1961)*. Paris, 1962.

Louis, Paul. *Histoire du socialisme en France: Les faits, les idées, les partis ouvriers de la Révolution à nos jours*. 5th edn. Paris, 1950.

McMillan, James F. 'The effects of the First World War on the social condition of women in France'. D.Phil., Oxford, 1976.

Maitron, Jean, (ed.). *Dictionnaire biographique du Mouvement Ouvrier français [DMO]*. 15 vols. to date. Paris, 1962–77.

Maitron, Jean and Chambelland, Colette (eds.). *Syndicalisme révolutionnaire et communisme: Les archives de Pierre Monatte, 1914–1924*. Paris, 1968.

Mayer, Daniel. *Pour une histoire de la gauche*. Paris, 1969.

Les Socialistes dans la Résistance: Souvenirs et documents. Paris, 1968.

Moss, Bernard. *The Origins of the French Labor Movement 1830–1914: The Socialism of Skilled Workers*. Berkeley, California, 1976.

Offen, Karen M. 'The woman question as a social issue in republican France, 1870–1914'. Privately circulated ms., Woodside, California, 1973.

Bibliography

Peyronnet, Jean-Claude. 'Un Exemple de journal militant: La "Guerre sociale" de Gustave Hervé (1906–1914)'. DES, Paris, n.d. CHS.

Pfister, Thierry. *Les Socialistes: Les secrets de famille, les rites, le code et les hommes du premier parti de France.* Paris, 1977.

Rocher, J. *Lénine et le mouvement zimmerwaldien en France.* Paris, 1934.

Rosmer, Alfred. *Le Mouvement ouvrier pendant la première guerre mondiale: I. De l'Union sacrée à Zimmerwald.* Paris, 1936; II. *De Zimmerwald à la révolution russe.* Paris and The Hague, 1959.

Schulkind, Eugene. 'Les Clubs et réunions populaires pendant la Commune de 1871'. Question annexe, doctorat, Paris, 1951.

Sowerwine, Charles. *Les Femmes et le socialisme: Un siècle d'histoire.* Paris, 1978.

Sullerot, Evelyne. *Histoire et sociologie du travail féminin.* Paris, 1968.

Thomas, Edith. *Louise Michel ou la Velléda de l'anarchie.* Paris, 1971.

 The Women Incendiaries. Tr. by J. and S. Atkinson. New York, 1966 (*Les 'Pétroleuses'.* Paris, 1963).

Thönnessen, Werner. *The Emancipation of Women: The Rise and Decline of the Women's Movement in German Social Democracy.* Tr. by Joris de Brès. London, 1973.

Tilly, Louise, and Scott, Joan. *Women, Work, and Family.* New York, 1978.

Willard, Claude. *Les Guesdistes: Le Mouvement socialiste en France (1893–1905).* Paris, 1959.

Willard, Claude (ed.). *Jules Guesde: Textes choisis. See* Guesde, under IV, above.

(b) **Articles** (for abbreviations employed, see p. xx, above)

Bidelman, Patrick. 'Maria Deraismes, Léon Richer, and the founding of the French feminist movement, 1866–1878'. *TR/TR*, 3/4 (1977), 20–73.

Boxer, Marilyn J. 'Foyer or factory: working-class women in nineteenth-century France'. *WSFH*, II (1975), 192–203.

Hause, Steven C. 'The rejection of women's suffrage by the French Senate in November, 1922: a statistical analysis'. *TR/TR*, 3/4 (1977), 205–37.

 'Women who rallied to the tricolor: the effects of World War I on the French women's suffrage movement'. *WSFH*, VI (1978), 371–8.

Hause, Steven C. and Kenney, Anne R. 'Legalism and violence in the French women's suffrage movement, 1901–1914'. Paper, St Louis, March 1978.

Honeycutt, Karen. 'Clara Zetkin: a socialist approach to the problem of women's oppression'. *Feminist Studies*, III, 3/4 (1976), 131–44.

 'Socialism and feminism in Imperial Germany'. *Signs*, V, 1 (1979), 30–55.

Maitron, Jean. 'Le Groupe des étudiants socialistes révolutionnaires internationalistes de Paris (1892–1902)'. *Le Mouvement social*, 46 (Jan.–Mar. 1964), 3–26.

Quartaert [Quataert], Jean H. 'Feminist tactics in German Social Democracy: a dilemma'. *Internationale wissenschaftliche Korrespondenz zur Geschichte der deutschen Arbeiterbewegung*, 13 (Mar. 1977), 48–65.

Rebérioux, Madeleine, Dufrancatel, Christiane and Slama, Béatrice. 'Hubertine Auclert et la question des femmes à "l'immortel congrès" (1879)'. *Romantisme, Revue du dix-neuvième siècle*, 13/14 (1976).

Schulkind, Eugene. 'Le Rôle des femmes dans la Commune de 1871'. *1848: Revue des révolutions contemporaines*, Feb. 1950, pp. 15–29.

Scott, Joan W. and Tilly, Louise. 'Women's work and the family in nineteenth-century Europe'. *Comparative Studies in Society and History*, XVII (1975), 36–64.

Sowerwine, Charles. 'Le Groupe féministe socialiste (1899–1905)'. *MS*, 90 (Jan. 1975), 87–120.

 'The organisation of French socialist women, 1880–1914: a European perspective for women's movements'. *HR/RH*, III, 2 (Winter 1976), 3–24.

 'Socialists, syndicalists and women: the Couriau affair'. Paper, AHA, Dallas, Texas, 29 Dec. 1977.

Bibliography

'Women against the war: a feminine basis for internationalism and pacifism?' *WSFH*, VI (1978), 361—70.

'Women and the origins of the French Socialist Party: a neglected contribution'. *TR/TR*, 3/4 (1977), 104—27.

Index

This index is in two parts: an alphabetical index and a chronological index of congresses.

A. Alphabetical index

This index includes all proper names except those to which only passing reference is made. Organisations whose abbreviations are listed on pp. xv–xix are listed under those abbreviations. In addition, synthetic entries will be found as follows: abortion, anti-clericalism, candidatures, feminism, mutualism, schisms, socialism (-ist), strikes, *syndicats*, and women('s).

abortion, 126–8, 182–3, 215 n. 14
Addams, Jane, xv, 152
Alexandre, Jeanne (Halbwachs, Jeanne), xv, 83, 229 n. 38
Allemane, Jean (Allemanists), xvii, xviii, 14, 129; and Cambier affair, 137–8, 202–3; and feminists, 50–4; and GFS, 83–4, 86, 87, 93, 95, 218 n. 22; and POSR, 48, 50
Ankersmit, Heleen, 146–7, 157
anti-clericalism, 7, 30, 40, 43, 44, 49–50, 92–4, 96–7, 112, 114
Argyriadès, P., 58, 68, 72–4, 213 n. 30, 219 n. 37
Armand, Inessa, 139, 145, 158
Association pour le Droit des Femmes, 7, 208 n. 6, 209 n. 20
Astié de Valsayre, Marie-Rose, 51–4, 67–8, 195, 212 nn. 8, 10, 13, 219 n. 37
Auclert, Hubertine: and *La Citoyenne*, 28, 39, 44, 51, 52, 68, 215 n. 4; on feminism and socialism, 24, 184–5; life and death of, 23, 28, 204; and socialism, 24–8, 43, 204; and women's suffrage, 28, 110, 113; *see also* Droit (Le) des Femmes
Audry, Colette, 181
Avant-Garde (L') Féministe, 97

Baader, Ottilie, 16, 19
Beauquier, Charles, 77–8, 109
Bebel, August, 15–17, 57–9, 61
Bellay, M du, 53, 70
Berne, international conference of socialist women at, xv, 146–8
Blanqui, Auguste, xvi, 30, 49
Blum, Léon, 170, 175–6, 190
Bolsheviks: opposition to war of, 144, 146–9; and Saumoneau, 158–9; and schism, 147–8, 151, 155, 160, 163–4
Bonnevial, Marie: feminist activity of, 52, 68,

72–3, 75–6, 131, 217 n. 35; and GDFS, 131, 138; and *L'Harmonie sociale*, 61; life and death of, 51, 211–12 n. 7; Saumoneau on, 89; and socialism, 51–2, 100–1
Bonnier, Charles, 61, 64
Bonnier, Pierre ('Dr Z'), 61–2
Bourderon, Albert, 151–2, 159, 229 n. 33
Bouvard, Stéphanie: anti-war action of, 151–3, 158, 228 n. 13, 229 n. 35; and feminists, 75, 77–8, 136; and GDFS, 136, 138, 154, 167, 226 n. 34
Bracke (Bracke-Desrousseaux), 109, 139, 170, 174–5
Brion, Hélène, 225 n. 8; anti-war action of, 159, 228 n. 12; and GDFS, 131, 136, 138, 191; and Pelletier, 111, 123–4, 127–8; on women, 132–5, 171
Brousse, Paul, 13–14, 41, 50; *see also* FTSF
Brutelle, Janette, 179, 180
Buisson, Ferdinand, 109, 110
Buisson, Suzanne (Gibault, Suzanne, *q.v.*), 167–72, 177, 191, 192

Cabet, Etienne, 21, 29
Cacheux, Denise, 180–1
CAFSPC, xv, 146–58 *passim*, 228 n. 13
Cahier des doléances féminines, 60, 62–3, 72, 196
Cambier, Achille and Gabrielle (affair), 103, 137–8, 202–5
candidatures, women's: Deroin, 210 n. 40; Kauffmann, 124; Mink, 70–2; Pelletier, 123–4, 126, 224 n. 52; Renaud, xvi, 124–6; Rouzade, 36–41, 210 nn. 44–5
Chabert, 36, 37, 52
Chaboseau, Louise Napias, 119, 127
CGT, xv, 120, 171, 176

242

Index

243

Index

schisms (*cont.*)
    1920: 161–6
seamstresses, 11, 89–91
Sembat, Marcel, 109, 110, 115, 220–1 n. 6,
    229 n. 36
Séverine (Rémy, Caroline), 70, 204, 217 n. 34
sexualism (Valette's theory), 61–2, 64–5
SFIO, xix; and Cambier affair, 137–8, 202–4;
    and Third International, 161–3; during
    Fourth and Fifth Republics, 178–80;
    schism and reconstruction of, 163–70;
    unification of, 81–2, 103, 108, 114; and
    women's suffrage, 108–10, 113–16,
    122–6, 174–5; and First World War,
    143–4, 147–50, 159–61, 204–5; and
    Second World War, 175–7; *see also*
    socialist women's movement, French
social feminism, *see* feminism
socialism: 1871–79: *see* Guesdists (1); social
    movement; UFC; 1879–82: *see* Guesdists
    (1); FTSF; UFC; 1882–1905: *see* CRC;
    FTSF; POF; POSR; socialists, indepen-
    dent; UFC; 1905–71: *see* Guesdists (3);
    SFIO; after 1971: PS, 180–3
socialists, independent, 13, 48, 74, 82–7,
    97–103, 218 n. 17
socialist women's movement, Dutch, 146–7,
    155, 157
socialist women's movement, French, 1–3,
    187–92; before 1905: *see* GFS; POF;
    Union (L') des Femmes; 1905–13:
    104–7, 110, 119, 127, 128; 1913–31:
    see GDFS; 1931–44: xv, 166, 168–75,
    189, 190, 198–201; 1944–71: 177–80,
    190–1; 1971–79: 180–3; membership
    of, 82, 97, 104, 106, 174, 198–201
socialist women's movement, German, 18–19,
    106; characteristics of, 18–19, 106, 192,
    193; GFS compared with, 81, 82, 92, 98,
    104, 106; international women's day of,
    132, 139, 155; Pelletier on, 118,
    223 n. 33
socialist women's movement, international, 19,
    117–19, 122–3, 145–52, 156, 167
social movement (early socialism), 12–14, 21–2,
    24–8; *see also* FTSF; Guesdists (1); UFC
Société pour l'Amélioration du Sort de la Femme,
    7, 208 n. 6
Société pour la Revendication des Droits de la
    Femme, 7, 212 n. 15, 216 n. 33
Solidarité (La) des Femmes: action of, 70,
    112–13, 115–16, 123; development of,
    68–70, 72–5 *passim*; and socialism, 53,
    70, 74, 115, 123, 222–3 n. 32; and soc.
    women's mvt., 82, 89, 132
Sorgue, Citizen (Cauvin, Antoinette), 116–17,
    122, 222 n. 27, 225 n. 12
SPD, xix: and French socialism, 54, 106; and
    soc. women's mvt., 16, 18–19, 106, 117;
    and war, 144, 145
Stigliss, Ludmila, 144–9 *passim*, 154, 227 n. 5

Stockholm, international socialist conference at
    (projected), 156–7, 230 n. 54
strike, general, 71, 84
strikes, 8, 88, 90, 93, 132
Suffrage (Le) des Femmes, 28, 51–2; *see also*
    Droit (Le) des Femmes
suffrage, women's: *see* women's suffrage
Syndicat de Femmes de Lettres et d'Artistes, 80
Syndicat des Dames, 52
Syndicat des Femmes Typographes, 80
Syndicat des Fleuristes Plumassières, 75, 77
Syndicat des Membres de l'Enseignement, 51, 59,
    75
syndicats, 8, 22, 51, 59, 120, 124; Durand and,
    75, 80, 90; GFS and, 88–92; and women,
    22, 52, 135–6

Tarbouriech, Ernest, 109, 220–1 n. 6
Tarbouriech, Mme Ernest, 117
Tinayre, Marguerite, 30, 33, 34, 42–4, 51
Toussaint, Edouard, 129, 220 n. 64
Toussaint-Kassky, Adèle, *see* Kassky, Adèle
trade unions, *see syndicats*; *chambres syndicales*
Trotsky, 158, 159
typographers (printers), 27–8, 80, 135–6

UFC, xix; feminists and, 26–8, 51–3; pro-
    gramme of, 45–6; schisms of, 27–8,
    40–1, 50; and soc. women's mvt., 33,
    36–7, 39–41, 44–7
Union (L') des Femmes: development and
    decline of, 29–31, 41–7; and Rouzade's
    candidature, 36–40; and schism 1882,
    40–1; and socialism, 33, 36–7, 39–41,
    44–7
Union Féministe Socialiste, 95–7, 101–2
Union Universelle des Femmes, 63, 214–15 n. 39

Vaillant, Edouard (Vaillantists), 91, 116, 122;
    and CRC, xv–xvi, xviii, 13, 48; and
    feminism, 68, 72, 74; and women, 49–50;
    and war, 144
Valette, Aline (Goudeman, Aline), 59–66; and
    feminism, 60–3, 68; life and death of, 59,
    65, 185; and socialism, 60, 63–4, 70, 195;
    on women's role ('sexualism'), 59–62,
    64–5, 186, 214 n. 43; on women's work,
    60–1, 195–7, 214 nn. 51–2
Variot, 144, 145, 228 n. 13
Vérecque, Charles, 58, 63, 186, 213 n. 31
Vérone, Maria, 131, 132, 137, 138, 191, 225
    nn. 7, 12
Vincent, Eliska: and feminism, 61, 63, 68, 75,
    112; life and death of, 53, 212 n. 15; and
    socialism, 53–4, 63, 70, 195
Viviani, René, 75, 101

Waldeck-Rousseau, René, xviii, 86, 93
Wiggishoff, 77, 216–17 n. 33
women, socialist, social origins of, 2, 43–4, 122,
    138–40, 185–6

B. Chronological index of feminist and socialist congresses

Congresses are indexed chronologically in groups according to the sponsoring organisation. Only congresses discussed in the text are listed, while the dates in brackets refer to the period of activity of the organisation. A complete index to socialist and feminist congresses may be found in Sowerwine, *Les Femmes.*